An Essay on Rights

Hillel Steiner

BLACKWELL
Oxford UK & Cambridge USA

Copyright © Hillel Steiner 1994

The right of Hillel Steiner to be identified as author of this work has been asserted
in accordance with the Copyright, Designs and Patents Act 1988.

First published 1994

Blackwell Publishers
108 Cowley Road
Oxford, OX4 1JF
UK

238 Main Street,
Cambridge, Massachusetts 02142
USA

British Library Cataloguing in Publication Data

A CIP catalogue record for this book is available from the British Library.

Library of Congress Cataloging-in-Publication Data

ISBN 0-631-13165-5   ISBN 0-631-19027-9 (pbk.)

Typeset in 11.5 on 13.5 pt Sabon
by Photo·graphics, Honiton, Devon
Printed in Great Britain by T.J. Press Ltd, Padstow, Cornwall

This book is printed on acid-free paper

for
Ruth Lillian Steiner
and
Harry Steiner

sceptics, dreamers

Contents

Acknowledgements

In the grand scheme of things, a quarter of a century is probably not a long time to be writing a book. But it's a painfully long time to be accumulating debts. Mine are many and various.

This enterprise was initially funded by a University of Manchester Research Assistantship and then by a Canada Council Doctoral Fellowship. In subsequent years, additional time for writing and reflection has been purchased with a British Academy Research Award and a Social Science Research Council Personal Research Grant. I'm grateful to all these institutions for their generous support.

Over this period, my work has greatly benefited from conversations and correspondence with many persons whose help it is a pleasure, indeed a relief, finally to be able properly to acknowledge. The length of this list is a pretty good measure of my aggregate indebtedness and no indication at all of how much is owed to each of them. They include: Wallace Arthur, Pranab Bardhan, Brian Barry, David Beetham, Samuel Bowles, David Braybrooke, Robert Brenner, Alan Carling, Ian Carter, James Child, Alan Coddington, John Cunliffe, Martin Currie, Patrick Day, Keith Dowding, Alistair Edwards, Diane Elson, Jon Elster, Michael Evans, R. G. Frey, Norman Geras, Sydney Goldenberg, Robert Goodin, Barbara Goodwin, David Gordon, John Gray, Tim Gray, Stuart Hampshire, R. M. Hare, John Harris, H. L. A. Hart, Martin Hollis, David Howell, Attracta Ingram, Lawrence Jablecki, Alison Jaggar, Timothy Kenyon, Percy Lehning, Harry Lesser, William Lucy, Eric Mack, John Mackie, Douglas MacLean, Barbara MacLennan, C. B. Macpherson, David Miller, Fred Miller, Christopher Morris, Peter Morriss, Robert Nozick, Onora O'Neill, Felix Oppenheim, Derek Parfit, Geraint Parry, Jeffrey Paul, Lansing Pollock, Adam Przeworski, D. D. Raphael, Joseph Raz, Andrew Reeve, John Roemer, David-Hillel Ruben, Alan

Ryan, Amartya Sen, Nigel Simmonds, Joseph Steiner, Miriam Steiner, Robert Sugden, Michael Taylor, Nicolaus Tideman, Robert Van der Veen, Philippe Van Parijs, Ursula Vogel, Jeremy Waldron, Albert Weale, Andrew Williams, Robert Wokler, Erik Wright.

A special debt of thanks is owed to Jerry Cohen, Raymond Plant and Ian Steedman for providing a constant supply of encouragement, painstaking criticism and just plain indulgence.

The patience of Job also lives on in the person of John Davey of Blackwell Publishers. This book's imminent publication was first advertised over ten years ago, and it's been footnoted as "Blackwell, forthcoming" for even longer than that. John's lenient promptings and unflagging support, in the face of my repeatedly postponed submissions, have been more than any author could justifiably expect. I've been additionally fortunate to have the help of Clare Braithwaite and Henry Maas, whose skill and consideration greatly eased the trauma of passing into print.

Others' advice and encouragement notwithstanding, those engaged in it will know what a solitary business doing philosophy can be. And their partners know it too. In that regard, Caroline Steiner has contributed to this work in more ways than can readily be described. A shared absorption in its arguments, acute commentary, stubborn optimism and gentle reminders of the vanity of trying to write in stone are only a few of the ones that can. And Joshua Steiner has borne the burden of a preoccupied father with a fortitude that is further testimony, if any were needed, to the fact that justice is very far from being the only virtue.

It's no mere effusion of filial piety to say that my greatest debt remains that owed to my parents. For, looking back beyond their steadfast support over these writing years, I find it quite difficult to identify many core ideas in this book that weren't first inspired by our countless, sometimes relentless, dinner-table discussions of long ago. And I'd like to think that their rather pronounced aversion to several familiar forms of fudging also receives some reasonably faithful reflection in this work. So, for these and many other reasons, it's entirely appropriate that it be dedicated to them.

That I am solely responsible for the errors and failings of this book hardly needs saying. After such a protracted gestation, who else could be?

H.I.S.

I
Introduction

Two questions. What is justice? And what is it for? A principal theme of this book is that, insofar as the first question has an answer, the second does not. Perhaps this will strike you as a somewhat affected way of signifying the intrinsic and non-derivative value of justice, its existence as an independent citizen in the republic of values. But it's more than that.

"The whole creation," Francis Edgeworth once observed, "groans and yearns, desiderating a principle of arbitration, an end of strifes."[1] To be sure, a world free of groaning is no mean aspiration. And any principle promising to secure it ought therefore to command our respectful attention on that ground alone. Nonetheless, human nature being what it probably is, not least in my neighbourhood, we should be unduly sanguine to reckon on the efficacy of justice (or any other principle) as a sure-fire prophylactic against groaning.

Nor indeed would a just and even groanless world – a world devoid of strifes – be a best world, though I think it would be a better one. Not best, because there are other values whose realization our best worlds would still await. Our problem is that these other values are not the same for each of us, but the world in which we pursue them is.[2]

These several pursuits can and do obstruct one another. We unavoidably restrict one another's freedom. And justice is about how those restrictions ought to be arranged. What it's *not* about are the ends which

---

[1] Edgeworth, *Mathematical Psychics*, 51. However, he continues, "the star of justice affords no certain guidance ... unless it reflect the rays of a superior luminary – utilitarianism," 52.

[2] This interpersonal diversity of values is certainly true of our non-moral ends and may or may not be true of our moral ends.

might be achieved by that arrangement. Questions of justice arise precisely where the moral permissibility of one person's restricting another's freedom is not determined by the comparative merits of the ends to which they are respectively committed.

Delineating a desirable arrangement of restrictions, without reference to any purpose which might be advanced by that arrangement, is evidently a tricky business. And it's thus not surprising that we currently find ourselves confronted with a plethora of competing theories of justice, some of which have made quite singular contributions to our understanding of the interpersonal impartiality suggested in the previous paragraph. Yet however much these theories may be seen as engaged in a common enterprise and even as sharing many basic premisses, they are different.[3] Societies deemed just by some of them must be condemned as unjust by the rest. Worse still, in the apparent view of some critics, there is not one of these theories that allows all of our cherished intuitions about justice to emerge unscathed. So how are we to choose?

A sensible strategy, it seems to me, is to begin at the elementary particle level since all big things are made from small ones. The elementary particles of justice are *rights*. Rights are the items which are created and parcelled out by justice principles. We learn something about justice by examining the formal or characteristic features of rights. These features constrain the possible content of justice principles in much the same sense as architectural precepts must be informed by the properties of the construction materials they orchestrate.

And we learn something more about justice when we discover how there can be two (or more) of these elementary particles. That is, the linch-pin of this essay's argument is that the mutual consistency – or *compossibility* – of all the rights in a proposed set of rights is at least a necessary condition of that set being a possible one.[4] A set of rights being

---

[3] Sen, *Inequality Reexamined*, ch. 1, characterizes this common enterprise as one of advancing arguments for interpersonal equality, with the differences consisting in the choice of space for equality, i.e. of what is to be equalized. Interpersonal differences of values and capacities pretty much guarantee that equality in one space sustains or produces inequality in others.

[4] The notion of "compossibility" is due to Leibniz. For him, some things (objects, events, concepts) which are each independently possible may not be jointly possible, that is, elements of one and the same possible world. Mates, *The Philosophy of Leibniz: Metaphysics and Language*, 43–4, explains: "Now some things that in themselves are possible are not compossible. There could be a world in which there was no sin, and there can be (indeed, is) a world in which there is forgiveness of sin, but there cannot be a world with both of these features; likewise, there could be a world in which there was no poverty, but such a world would exclude the exercise of charity, which in itself is possible (and also desirable)."

a possible set is, I take it, itself a necessary condition of the plausibility of whatever principle of justice generates that set. Any justice principle that delivers a set of rights yielding contradictory judgements about the permissibility of a particular action either is unrealizable or (what comes to the same thing) must be modified to be realizable. Particular applications of such a principle would too frequently drive us to say, "Leave it to the judge/the legislator/heaven to sort this one out." And they, after all, seem sufficiently busy already.

Quite a lot of mileage can be got out of this compossibility test, which does exemplary service in filtering out many candidate conceptions of justice. A few more can be dismissed by reference to certain formal features of rights, apart from those bearing on compossibility. Our aspiration, obviously, is to pass through the eye of this needle with at least one theory of justice still intact. But it would be unduly optimistic to imagine that all our intuitions could similarly survive such a journey.

The reason for this, familiar enough, is that our moral intuitions tend to be uncomplex. In particular, they don't respond well to problems where what is wanted is *not* some missing piece from a best world jigsaw puzzle, but rather some way of distinguishing the pieces of second-best worlds from those of third-best ones. Demarcating this elusive boundary is quintessentially a task of justice theories.

Now for a few disarming apologies. The experience of presenting bits of this argument in articles and papers suggests that many persons deeply exercised by the evils of oppression, exploitation, discrimination and poverty will doubtless find much of it exceedingly intricate and overly preoccupied with abstract niceties so remote from the substance of these problems as to be utterly frivolous. A measured apology is offered to such readers. An apology, because these matters are indeed urgent. Much is morally at stake in discussion of them. And it is, to say the least, unbecoming to fiddle while others burn. But a *measured* apology, because of the unwelcome fact that these issues cannot be effectively engaged without an armoury of abstract niceties. Unedifying gallops, from fragmentary moral convictions to full-blown institutional and policy prescriptions, can be avoided only through preliminary conceptual analysis. Only with the distinctions supplied by such analysis can one make informed consumer choices from among the multiplicity of justice theories presently on offer.

For contrary to what some have suggested, it's simply untrue that exploring the meanings of words can furnish little assistance in assessing these competing theories, and that we must perforce consult our moral intuitions and assorted unreflective beliefs about the propriety of various activities in order to reach any practical conclusion. Indeed, there's a certain oddity in the related claim that analyses of the meanings of moral concepts are, ineluctably, a form of moral advocacy. It's true that moral commitments frequently influence the choice of concepts to be analysed. There is, for instance, an obvious sense in which much philosophical work done over the past five decades on the subject of justice has been haunted by the Holocaust and has participated in the struggle to grasp its significance. But there's simply no necessary connection between the factors motivating the choice of an analysandum and the content of its analysis. A misanthrope is perfectly capable of delivering a philosophically respectable account of benevolence, a coward of courage, and so forth. And it's difficult to see why the case of justice should be any different in this respect.

Which brings me to a second and less measured apology. Large parts of this exposition are presented in the form of some pretty limp dialogue, ranging from the slightly stilted to the downright didactic. What this dialogue lacks in animation it more than makes up for in pedantry. The jointly sufficient explanations for this are my own sheer dramaturgical incompetence and my desire to exhibit certain technical points – in moral philosophy, jurisprudence and economic theory – as informally as possible. Theories of justice are inseparable from the concerns of these several disciplines and need, I think, to be worked out in generally accessible terms.

But clarity is an expensive virtue. And the cost of trying to practise it here has been that ideas which are commonplace in one or another of these fields sometimes receive rather laboured elucidation at the hands of my unscintillating protagonists. Chief among the latter are two persons, Blue (female) and Red (male), whose differing genders ought to make for less ambiguous adjectival and pronominal reference. They're assisted by a host of other colourful colleagues, as well as various specialized functionaries, who will be trotted out when the need arises.

The argument of the book works like this. Getting a grip on what makes two rights incompossible requires an understanding of what makes two actions incompossible: that is, incapable of jointly occurring. In the next chapter, on liberty, I develop an account of unfreedom as action-incompossibility and try to display the conditions under which it makes sense to say that someone is free or unfree to do a particular action. The third chapter supplies an analysis of the concept of "a right" along the lines of the Will or Choice Theory of rights, a theory which it defends and extends. Utilizing the preceding argument about freedom, it then sets out requirements for all the rights in any proposed set of rights to be compossible.

Rights and liberty are then put temporarily aside in order to inspect some features of consistent moral reasoning, in chapter 4. Here my aim is to identify the structural properties of those moral codes into which a set of rights can be embedded. I do this by looking at several ways of understanding and dealing with moral dilemmas. Chapter 5 tours the axiomatic foundations of economic reasoning. Since interpersonal exchange is a principal form of exercising rights, and since such activity is often held to be exploitative and hence subversive of just distributions, it seems germane to consider whether the nature of economic reasoning itself presupposes conduct that is incompatible with the kind of moral code examined in the previous chapter.

All of these analyses get fed into the discussion of justice, in chapter 6. Taking justice as a rule for rights, it isolates the sort of adversarial circumstance in which rights are characteristically and non-redundantly invoked. Principled resolutions of such conflicts are shown to derive only from a rule allocating spheres of personal freedom. Moreover the content of this rule, as well as its ordered location within moral codes containing it, are seen to be strictly constrained by the requirements of rights-compossibility. And the upshot of this argument is that justice is a lexically-prime rule which distributes freedom equally through a set of foundational and derivative rights. The seventh chapter, on original rights, explores the general content and incidence of these foundational rights. And the final chapter interprets their application to persons who are generationally differentiated and who inhabit a limited natural environment: that is, who are real people.

What emerges is an historical entitlement conception of justice with some reasonably strong redistributive implications. My hope, of course, is that this will succeed in capturing a fair proportion of your intuitions. But my own chastening experience suggests that, if it captures all of them, something has gone badly wrong.

2
Liberty

BLUE: But surely you aren't denying that he was free to do it.
RED: I most certainly am.
BLUE: But . . . but . . . we both know that he actually did it!
RED: What's that got to do with it?

That's one conversation. Here's another:

BLUE: Look, it says here in the newspaper that they're going to stop us
doing that from now on. We're going to be less free than before.
RED: I don't see why we are. No rational, prudent or decent person
would ever do that anyway.
BLUE: What's that got to do with it?

And yet another:

BLUE: Look, it says here in the newspaper that they're going to stop us
doing that from now on. We're going to be less free than before.
RED: I don't see why we are. They're perfectly entitled to stop us from
doing that.
BLUE: What's that got to do with it?

Not everyone, it must be admitted, shares Blue's linguistic intuitions
here. For that is what they are: linguistic intuitions. A good deal of
philosophical debate consists, among other things, in duelling with
linguistic intuitions. And you don't need to have spent long years toiling
in the fields of political philosophy – nor even, indeed, in the cosier

confines of common parlance – to know that our uses of the word "free" and other cognate terms rest upon diverse and often opposed intuitions.

Blue's intuition is that there is something more than a little odd about conceptions of liberty that logically commit us heroically to denying that you were free to do what you, in fact, did. And she is similarly troubled by the idea that someone's stopping you from doing things doesn't curtail your freedom. Put this way, perhaps Blue's intuitions are shared by all of us.[1] Unfortunately, not all of us are entitled to share them.

A point of order is called for. It's assuredly not the job of philosophers to legislate on which linguistic (much less, moral) intuitions we may hold nor, therefore, on what conception of liberty we may employ. They utterly lack the authority to do so. Rather, their brief is the more modest one of indicating which set of intuitions can be held *consistently*. Intuitions have implications. Conceptions carry logical commitments. And the job of philosophers is to tell us when our several uses of a word like "free" are inconsistent – inconsistent inasmuch as the conceptions respectively underpinning them deliver mutually contradictory judgements in particular cases.

When such inconsistencies occur, the court of first appeal must unquestionably be ordinary language. We need to ask ourselves which of the opposed judgements more closely reflects the way in which normal speakers of that language employ that word. The trouble is that, in the case of "free" and its cognates, this court frequently refuses to pronounce on such appeals. Ordinary usage's treatment of freedom is not univocal and it stubbornly persists in licensing such inconsistencies. In effect, it leaves the litigants to settle their differences in the time-honoured fashion of duelling with their intuitions.

How do we duel with these intuitions? The non-univocality of ordinary usage suggests that, very often, it's *we* who are amongst our most determined opponents. That is, we each use the word "free" inconsistently ourselves, as well as in ways that are inconsistent with other persons' uses. What's worrying is that these several uses, however mutually inconsistent, probably each reflect some entrenched intuition we have about a kind of circumstance in which a person is describable as free.

To achieve consistency, we have to expel some of these reflections from our usage, to silence the intuitions they express. This is never an easy thing to do. It means having to face an uncomfortable linguistic

---

[1] Assuming, as she is, that the liberty under consideration here is not liberty in the normative sense of that word (signifying the absence of a duty to refrain from, and the consequent permissibility of, doing something): a subject to be discussed in the next chapter.

future in which we're bound to find some of our own uses of "free," as well as our appraisals of others' uses, distinctly counter-intuitive. Accordingly, in picking and choosing among our intuitions, we should take some care to silence only those whose absence from our usage promises to cause us less discomfort than would the absence of those it continues to reflect. And, of course, that usage can continue to reflect any set whose absence is not a requirement of consistency. For although consistency is surely worth its price in counter-intuitiveness, we don't want to pay over the odds for it.

What, then, is the price of Blue's intuitions? What conception of freedom is she invoking in the previous conversations? What are its more salient attributes and implications? And which uses, ordinary or otherwise, of the words "free" and "unfree" does it deny us? Like Blue, I find it especially difficult to let go of the idea that persons are free to do what they actually do. They're also free to do many of the things they don't do and would never consider doing. Simply stated, the rest of this chapter is devoted to looking at some implications of an unswerving commitment to those ideas.

Broadly speaking, it suggests that a person is unfree to do an action if, and only if, his doing that action is rendered impossible by the action of another person. We ordinarily regard an action as rendered impossible by another action if the latter either (i) does occur, or (ii) would occur if the former were attempted, and the latter's occurrence implies the impossibility of the former's occurrence. When these two actions are the respective actions of two different persons, one of them makes the other unfree inasmuch as one prevents the other from acting.[2] Thus I'm ordinarily unfree to leave my prison cell if the guard has locked my door, or even if he hasn't done so but would do so were I to attempt to leave.

Traditionally, arguments about the nature of liberty have taken the form of disputes over the relative merits of various positive and negative conceptions of liberty. Salient aspects of these disputes are best understood as rival attempts to address two questions. The first asks whether one person's rendering another's action *ineligible* – as distinct from

---

[2] This also covers "compelling." See von Wright, *Norm and Action*, 54–5: "There are two types of act which ... relate to one agent's ability to interfere with the ability of another to perform a certain act. These are the types of act which we call *hindering* or *preventing* and *compelling* or *forcing*. These two types of act are obviously interdefinable. Therefore we can here limit discussion to one of them. To compel an agent to do something is the same as to prevent him from forbearing this thing. And to hinder an agent from doing something is the same as to force him to forbear it."

impossible – makes the latter unfree to do it. And the second asks whether one person's prevention of another's action implies the latter's unfreedom to do it, only if that prevented action possesses eligibility or the preventing action lacks it. In both questions "eligibility" is meant to cover diverse moral or motivational conditions which proponents of rival conceptions variously impose on ascriptions of freedom and unfreedom. Somewhat surprisingly, in my view, the affirmative replies standardly offered by positive libertarians to these two questions have been repeated rather than rejected by many negative libertarian accounts.

In exploring the implications of Blue's intuition, the present account firmly rejects these affirmative replies. Blue's conception of liberty is thus a particular type of negative conception – one famously associated with Hobbes but probably more consistently employed by Bentham. In recent years it has been carefully distinguished and appropriately labelled by Michael Taylor as "pure negative liberty" and, less approvingly, by Charles Taylor as "crude negative liberty."[3]

This pure negative conception is uncontroversially an empirical or descriptive one. That is, statements using it to describe a person as free or unfree to do a particular action presuppose nothing about the significance or permissibility either of that action or of any action preventing it. Nor, for that matter, do they presuppose anything about whether someone believes either of those actions to be significant or permissible. However disparagingly, Charles Taylor is not mistaken in identifying this conception as the one which is also at work when scientists and engineers refer to the "freedom of some physical object, say a lever."[4]

There can be little doubt that our ordinary language does contain such a purely descriptive conception. And even if it cannot claim a monopoly on the use of the words "liberty," "freedom" and their cognates, we should be loath simply to abandon it – not least, because we typically want to retain the linguistic capacity to express intelligible and non-redundant judgements about the freedoms which people do and do not want or should and should not have. As we'll presently see, other conceptions of liberty rather oppressively consign such judgements to either redundancy or nonsense.

---

[3] Cf. Michael Taylor, *Community, Anarchy and Liberty*, 142; Charles Taylor, "What's Wrong with Negative Liberty." An earlier attempt at analysing this conception is to be found in my "Individual Liberty." Gorr, *Coercion, Freedom and Exploitation*, ch. 2, provides an excellent recent account, most of which I agree with.

[4] Taylor, "What's Wrong with Negative Liberty," 183.

(A) ACTIONS AND ELIGIBILITY

Current philosophical discussion of the concept of liberty often takes, as its starting point, Sir Isaiah Berlin's inaugural lecture "Two Concepts of Liberty." In his introduction to the revised version of that seminal work, Berlin undertakes to correct what he considers to be a serious error in the negative libertarian argument of the original version.[5] That earlier version had claimed that liberty, properly understood, consists in not being prevented by other persons from doing whatever one *desires* to do and, thus, that one is free to the extent that one is not prevented by another from doing what one desires to do. "If I am prevented by others from doing what I want I am to that degree unfree."[6] Berlin now acknowledges that this formulation of the negative conception paradoxically licenses the positive libertarian inference that my unfreedom can be reduced by the suppression of my desires, i.e. those which others prevent me from satisfying. And conversely, it implies that my unfreedom can increase merely by virtue of an increase in my desires and without any increase in the restrictive treatment meted out to me by those others. In short, this formulation suggests that ultimately one's oppressor is oneself.

In a similar vein, J. P. Day has pointedly remarked that ridding oneself of the desire to do an action which is prevented by another does not make one free to do that action.[7] He suggests that to treat an action's being desired as a necessary condition of the actor's being free or unfree to do it is to confuse the condition of *being free* with that of *feeling free*. Thus Blue, Day and the later Berlin concur that, if there are persons who would make it impossible for me to import heroin into this country, then I'm unfree to do so. And I'm unfree to do so irrespective of whether I want to do so, am indifferent to doing so or want not to do so. Being imprisoned makes me unfree to go to the theatre regardless of whether I want to go to the theatre or not.

Obviously, the extent to which such prevention engenders a feeling of frustration in me, the extent to which I experience it as an obstacle to my satisfaction or contrary to my interests, *does* depend on what I actu-

---

[5] Berlin, *Four Essays on Liberty*, xxxviii–xl.
[6] Berlin, *Two Concepts of Liberty*, 7.
[7] Day, "On Liberty and the Real Will," 191.

ally desire to do. Perhaps the only freedom that really matters to me is the freedom to do what I desire to do. But it doesn't follow from this that I can be free or unfree to do only those actions which I want to do. We have no problem understanding the statement "I am free to go to the theatre, i.e. am not prevented from doing so, though I have no desire to do so." And it's equally intelligible to say, "I am unfree to go to the theatre and don't want to do so." Since ordinary usage evidently embraces such claims without strain, it really is incumbent on those who suggest that desires cannot be excluded from any analysis of the meaning of liberty to account for these perfectly common pieces of counter-evidence.[8]

Much the same would seem to be true of actions whose relation to their agents is specified in various evaluative terms. When we ask whether a person is free to do a particular action, we typically don't imagine ourselves to be asking an evaluative question. Rather we're asking a factual question, the (affirmative) answer to which is presupposed by any evaluative question about his doing that action, since "is prevented" implies "cannot" whereas "ought" implies "can." How, after all, could persons ever do actions which they ought not to do unless they're unprevented from doing them?

Banal as it is, one cannot point out too often that *such actions do happen*. And Blue's intuition is that their doers must *ipso facto* have been free to do them. She thus emphatically rejects the claim that "our conception of freedom is bounded by our notions of what might be worthwhile doing."[9] Such claims embrace the evaluative counterpart of the failure to distinguish "being free" from "feeling free." They neglect the difference, noted by John Rawls, between liberty and the worth of liberty.[10]

These considerations suggest that statements to the effect that "Blue is free to do B" do not imply or presuppose statements to the effect either that "Blue wants to do B" or that "It is contrary to Blue's interests or duties to refrain from doing B." Nor therefore do they imply or presuppose statements about what Blue really wants or what it is in her real interests to do. Judgements about whether an agent is free to do an action are logically independent of any judgement concerning the eligibility of that action.

What about preventions? Does *their* eligibility affect our judgement

[8] Cf. Flathman, *The Philosophy and Politics of Freedom*, 32.
[9] Benn and Weinstein, "Being Free to Act and Being a Free Man," 195.
[10] Rawls, *A Theory of Justice*, 204. This is not to say that Rawls's way of drawing that distinction corresponds to my own.

about whether they are making Blue unfree to do B? If Red's doing A prevents Blue's doing B, does our judgement that "Blue is unfree to do B" further depend on A being an ineligible action? The answer offered to these questions by the pure negative conception of liberty is an unequivocal "no": Red's A makes Blue unfree to do B if A prevents Blue from doing B. However, many otherwise negative libertarian accounts apparently disagree.

Thus Thomas Scanlon and G. A. Cohen correctly detect a "moralised definition" of freedom at work in part of Robert Nozick's account of distributive justice.[11] This account famously asserts that "taxation of earnings from labour is on a par with forced labour." But what makes the paying of such taxes "forced," according to Nozick, is *not* the fact that the tax authorities would employ force to prevent the labourer's withholding funds. Contrary to what one might infer from the interdefinability of forcing and preventing,[12] it's not that the former prevent the latter from forbearing to pay the tax. It is, rather, that such a forcibly imposed tax violates what Nozick sees as the moral rights of the labourer. Hence this kind of prevention of some of his action-possibilities is to be distinguished from preventions in "other cases of limited choices which are not forcings."[13] "Other people's actions place limits on one's available opportunities. Whether this makes one's resulting action non-voluntary depends upon whether these others had the right to act as they did."[14] On this view not all preventions, not all actions placing limits on one's opportunities, count as forcings. My action is non-voluntary – I am describably unfree to forbear it – only if others' actions which prevent me from forbearing it are ones which are impermissible for them to do. In Nozick's account, only such ineligible preventions are instances of unfreedom.

Another way in which freedom judgements are thought to be predicated on the eligibility of preventions is illustrated in the following set of examples adapted from an argument offered by David Miller.[15] Suppose that I'm the unfortunate occupant of a room whose door can be opened only from the outside, and consider the following ways in which I might become trapped in the room.

---

[11] Cf. Scanlon, "Nozick on Rights, Liberty and Property," 13–14; Cohen, *History, Labour and Freedom*, 252, 256, 295.

[12] See n. 2 above.

[13] Nozick, *Anarchy, State and Utopia*, 169.

[14] Nozick, *Anarchy, State and Utopia*, 262.

[15] Miller, "Constraints on Freedom," 70–5.

1 I'm working in my room. Knowing that I'm inside and wishing to confine me, you shut the door.

2 You walk along the corridor and, without checking to see whether anybody is inside, shut my door.

3 You shut my door because there's a pack of wild animals roaming the corridors and posing a considerable danger to the building's occupants.

4 You, whose job it is to check rooms, come to my room and look round it. I've concealed myself in a cupboard and you shut the door without having seen me.

Miller's claim is that, although your causal role in preventing me from leaving my room is exactly similar in all four cases, you can be said to have made me unfree to do so in only the first three. The first three are respectively characterized as instances of deliberate, negligent and justified prevention. More precisely, and following Miller's contention that "when we describe a person as unfree to do something we imply that an obstacle exists which stands in need of justification,"[16] we can array these instances as follows: (i) deliberate and unjustified, (ii) non-deliberate and unjustified, and (iii) deliberate and justified. What's said to unite all these instances and qualify them as constraints on freedom is that you are "morally responsible" for the preventions they involve.

However, according to Miller, you are *not* morally responsible for the prevention in the fourth case. This prevention can be characterized as (iv) non-deliberate and justified. Just why this conjunction of characteristics, which are each disjunctively possessed by the second and third preventions for which you *are* morally responsible, negates your moral responsibility for the fourth prevention is unclear. At any rate, Miller's view too is that only ineligible preventions – here, ones which lack the joint quality of being both non-deliberate and justified – count as instances of unfreedom.

Yet another attempt to distinguish eligible from ineligible preventions, and to deem only the latter as restrictive of liberty, is to be found in a recent argument of Jan Narveson:

A might be drunk, for instance, or acting thoughtlessly, or contrary to what A has previously represented to be A's own best interests. Does the right to liberty . . . permit or forbid interference in such cases? . . . If I try to prevent A from doing x, where x is what A

---

[16] Miller, "Constraints on Freedom," 72.

currently seems to want to do but is contrary to what A has clearly
insisted are A's own deeper desires or best interests, I am still
respecting A's liberty . . . [17]

Here the eligibility of the prevention, implying that it's not an instance
of unfreedom, is due to the ineligibility of the action it prevents. On this
understanding of what it is to be free or unfree, John Stuart Mill's famous proscription – of paternalistic curtailments of the liberty to do self-
harming acts – would not be mistaken: it would be simply unintelligible.

What we've been looking at, then, is a collection of proposals that
emanate from various avowedly negative accounts of liberty and that
impose far greater restrictions, than does the pure negative conception,
on the sorts of preventing occasion that warrant describing someone as
"unfree." For these "impure negative" conceptions, the preventing of an
action is not an instance of unfreedom if either the prevented act lacks
eligibility or the preventing act doesn't or both. In this regard, it's worth
noting Charles Taylor's cogent arguments for the untenability of such
"hybrid or middle positions": that is, ones lying between pure negative
liberty and characteristic formulations of positive liberty.[18] Be this as it
may, what possible motivations might lie behind these proposed restrictions?

Well one, of course, is the ever equivocal guidance of our ordinary
usage of freedom. We just don't feel comfortable saying, as in the familiar caricature of the negative conception, that "Rich and poor alike are
free to sleep under the bridges of London" (assuming that no one prevents them from doing so). Affirming the intelligibility and possible truth
of this claim is part of the price which Blue has to pay for her intuitions.
Is it too high a price?

Acknowledging the undesirability of sleeping under the bridges of
London and deploring the sort of society in which the poor have no
better place to sleep, don't we still want to be able to distinguish between
that situation and one in which the police actually do prevent people
from sleeping under the bridges? And doesn't part of that distinction
consist in saying that people are unfree in the latter situation, but not
in the former, to sleep under the bridges of London? Conversely and
responding to Nozick's argument, do we really think that the fact that
the police would be acting permissibly and exercising the public's right
to have its property thus cleared of vagrants is a reason for denying that
they thereby make them unfree?

---

[17] Narveson, *The Libertarian Idea*, 17.
[18] Taylor, "What's Wrong with Negative Liberty," 187ff.

If discomfort in uttering things like the previous irony is one motivation of those wishing to modify the pure negative conception, it's
closely related to another more general motivation recorded by Miller:
namely "a presumption that humans should not obstruct one another's
activity."[19] No doubt we do entertain such a presumption – allowing it
to be overridden, as Miller suggests, only when we don't hold the
obstructer morally responsible for his obstruction. But it's one thing to
entertain this moral presumption, along with that caveat, and quite
another to insist that suitably qualified obstructions are not restrictions
of freedom at all.

Trivially, ascriptions of moral responsibility, being predicated on
judgements about justifiability, presuppose particular moral values. Persons and cultures often entertain different sets of moral values and,
hence, differ over what obstructions people may be held morally responsible for. For example, from some moral standpoints you, as Miller's
case (4) room-checker, might be held not to have fulfilled your duty in
merely glancing round my room before shutting the door. In which
event, you *would* be morally responsible for locking me in, as in case
(2), and you *would* be deemed to have made me unfree.

The cost of letting Miller's moral presumption inform our judgements
of *whether* persons are free or unfree is that we would be linguistically
disabled from urging our moral opponents to allow people to have certain freedoms. This disability would not be due, as one might normally
suppose, to our opponents' obduracy in clinging to their moral values.
Rather, it would be due precisely to their acceptance of Miller's proposed modification and their consequent sheer incomprehension of our
belief that their obstructive practices actually are sources of unfreedom,
much less ones which they should discontinue. Such disablement does
seem a high price to pay for modifying the pure negative conception of
liberty. And it's evidently a purchase which many ordinary language
users are as yet unwilling to make.

A third factor motivating resistance amongst negative libertarians to
the pure negative conception arises from the indisputable difficulties surrounding the quantification of liberty.[20] Both in everyday conversation
and in technical political philosophy, we regularly register claims that
imply the measurability of freedom. We casually judge some persons to
be more free than others, we urgently demand that persons be allowed

---

[19] Miller, "Constraints on Freedom," 69; cf. Flathman, *The Philosophy and Politics of
Freedom*, 149–50.
[20] Cf. Arneson, "Freedom and Desire"; Gray, "On Negative and Positive Liberty," esp.
p. 515. See also Taylor, "What's Wrong with Negative Liberty," 182–4.

equal freedom, we develop theories to show that freedom should be
maximized or maximinned or leximinned, and so forth. What do we
mean when we say these things? What *could* we be meaning? Freedoms,
others object, are not exactly like apples. So counting or measuring them
is not the most transparent sort of computational exercise. We'll be looking at this problem in greater depth later in this chapter. For the moment
it will suffice to note that some of the aforesaid resistance stems from
the conviction that these metrication difficulties can be surmounted only
by taking into computational account the eligibility of actions, since
variations in eligibility are – at least in principle – presumed to be more
amenable to measurement. And since the pure negative conception is
avowedly uninformed by considerations of eligibility, it is thought by
some to be incapable of being the conception at work in statements
about more, less and equal freedom.

A final indictment which is sometimes brought against the pure negative conception is that it is "behaviourist." John Gray complains that
"in leaving us no way of characterising freedoms except in the physicalist
language of unimpeded behaviours, this approach ignores the vital truth
that the subject matter of freedom is action rather than behaviour."[21]
And Richard Flathman, while duly acknowledging the service of the pure
negative conception in picking out "paradigm cases of unfreedom,"
avoiding the "philosophical quagmire that is the theory of desires and
other motives to and reasons for action" and consistently sustaining the
"undeniably important distinction between feeling free and being free,"
nonetheless echoes and amplifies Gray's charge against it:

> Pure Negative Freedom ... makes unimpeded *movement* a suf-
> ficient condition of human freedom. But the subject matter of the
> theory and practice of human freedom is not movement, it is action
> ... Pure Negative Freedom is a behaviorist theory in the generic
> sense that it does not concern itself (*qua* theory of freedom) with
> *why* self-moving agents move or attempt to move. Given observ-
> able self-movement or an observable tendency to self-movement,
> questions about freedom are answered exclusively in terms of the
> further observable fact that impediments or obstacles do or do not
> prevent the movements. By contrast, theorists of ordinary or
> "impure" negative freedom and theorists of positive freedom are
> antibehaviorist.[22]

[21] Gray, "On Negative and Positive Liberty," 515.
[22] Flathman, *The Philosophy and Politics of Freedom*, 31, 32. Flathman's reference
exclusively to movement needs amplification. Pure negative freedom is equally concerned

What is the basis of this charge? Flathman himself recognizes that "Of course movements of the bodies of human actors are components in most human actions. This is why obstacles to such movements are typically obstacles to human freedom."[23] Thus the behaviourism charge, levelled by these proponents of the impure negative conception, *appears* to rest on the unquestionably correct claim that actions are only a subset of behaviours. The usual distinction between behaviours which are also actions and those which are not is that only the former satisfy some motivational condition. Gray is representative in suggesting that this condition consists in the actor's being weakly rational, in the sense that some "goal or end may be imputed to him which renders intelligible what he does. . . . The conception of rational choice that is appropriate there is a minimalist and meagre one, stipulating only that an agent *have a reason* for what he does."[24] Proponents of pure negative liberty are said to be guilty of a category mistake, in the manner of someone who speaks about fruit in general when he is purportedly talking only about apples.

The charge is, however, unjustified and its real basis lies elsewhere. Pure negative libertarians don't deny the validity of the action–behaviour distinction but only its relevance to the matter of freedom judgements. That distinction *would* be relevant if the proper subject matter of such judgements was limited, as Gray suggests, to only those behaviours in which persons *actually do* have a reason to engage. This was the limitation which was implicitly assumed in the original 1958 version of Berlin's lecture and which, as he later came to appreciate, generates the paradox that our unfreedoms are due to ourselves. But even aside from that consideration, what's also true is that there are simply no philosophical or ordinary usage grounds for such a limitation. Recall that, imprisoned, I am negatively unfree to go to the theatre whether or not I actually happen to have a reason to do so.

For our freedom judgements are equally concerned (as in Berlin's revised version) with those behaviours in which persons actually do not, but *could*, have a reason to engage. I could, though I don't, have a reason to go to the theatre. Yet I am perfectly describable as "free" or, if prevented, "unfree" to do so. Our freedom judgements are concerned, that is, with *conceivable* actions and not just their subset of actual

---

with impediments to, or preventions of, a person remaining or being stationary. When you force me to walk, you make me purely negatively unfree to stand still.

[23] Flathman, *The Philosophy and Politics of Freedom*, 31.

[24] Gray, "On Negative and Positive Liberty," 520; cf. Flathman, *The Philosophy and Politics of Freedom*, ch. 7.

ones.[25] And since any piece of behaviour is one in which someone could conceivably have a reason to engage – one which is a conceivable action – the pure negative conception construes the prevention or non-prevention of any behaviour as an instance of unfreedom or freedom: that is, the freedom or unfreedom to do whichever actions that behaviour could be. The "physicalism" of this conception is not, then, due to any failure to discriminate between behaviour and action. Rather it's entirely due to its refusal to restrict freedom judgements to the subset of actions associated with only actually held reasons, and to its insistence on extending such judgements to the full set of actions associated with possibly held ones.

That it is indeed this latter non-discrimination, and not the former one, that underlies the behaviourism charge against the pure negative conception is starkly revealed in Flathman's contention that the actions comprising the subject matter of freedom judgements are restricted to only those informed by "the ends and purposes that human beings are known to adopt and pursue."[26] Freedom judgements, on this impure negative view, are exclusively reserved for actions associated with only those aims which people actually happen to have. Other actions don't count and, consequently, their being prevented doesn't amount to unfreedom.

As a report on ordinary usage, this is plainly false. So what are the consequences of embracing the restriction it proposes? Some of these were indicated earlier, including in this chapter's opening "conversations." Perhaps a reasonably simple example will help to display them more vividly.

Suppose I am back in my room with the door that opens only from the outside. Just as I sit down to read my newspaper, you shut the door, thereby locking me in. What is my situation, as far as freedom and unfreedom are concerned? The pure negative conception implies simply that I am unfree to leave my room but free to remain in it. That I am describable as free to remain in it follows from the fact that remaining in it is a piece of behaviour in which I could conceivably have a reason to engage: it's an action which I would be prevented from doing, unfree to do, if I were to be forcibly ejected from my room. Moreover, since I am patently free to do any number of actions while locked in that room – sit at my desk, read my newspaper, use my telephone – it would be

[25] Cf. Feinberg, *Social Philosophy*, 5–7.
[26] Flathman, *The Philosophy and Politics of Freedom*, 202.

peculiar to suggest that an action which is a necessary condition of my doing those actions (namely, my remaining in my room) is one which I am *un*free to do.[27]

What the impure negative conception implies of this situation is more problematic. If I actually have no reason to leave my room then, presumably, my leaving my room (even if I could do it) would fail to satisfy the requisite motivational condition for being an action. Not being an action, it's not the proper subject matter of freedom judgements and, hence, I cannot be described as unfree to leave my room, in impure negative liberty terms. On the other hand, since I do have a reason to remain in my room – namely, to read my newspaper – my remaining in my room *is* an action and, being one which I'm unprevented from doing, it's one which I'm properly describable (as with the pure conception) as free to do.

Why the deliverances of the impure conception are problematic can be seen in the following way. Suppose I *do* have a reason to leave my room. Suppose I've undertaken to deliver a lecture in another room, for a colleague who has fallen ill. And suppose, therefore, that my sitting down to read the newspaper is nothing less than a work-avoiding piece of moral delinquency: I just don't feel like doing the lecture, not even if (as seems likely) this delinquency adversely affects my longer-term interests. So what I have, under these suppositions, are reasons both to leave my room and to remain in it.

Readers already acquainted with philosophical debates about the concept of liberty will immediately recognize this rival-reasons landscape as the native habitat of positive liberty. Significantly, impure negative liberty has sought to occupy this same terrain. Is there any plausible distinction between them? On the one hand, we have Charles Taylor's previously cited claim as to the untenability of the impure conception's "hybrid" position. Perhaps this claim is too sweeping, given the diverse forms which both impure negative and positive conceptions can take.[28] Still, we also have Flathman's acknowledgement that his own "[impure] version of the negative view of freedom substantially reduces the conceptual distance between negative and positive conceptions of it."[29] So what

---

[27] See below, pp. 37–8, for a discussion of the freedom to do an action of which the *prerequisite* actions have been prevented.

[28] A diversity helpfully itemized by Flathman, *The Philosophy and Politics of Freedom*, 322.

[29] Flathman, *The Philosophy and Politics of Freedom*, 2.

is it about the rival-reasons landscape that offers at least some common ground to these ostensibly distinct and opposed conceptions? What are their affinities?

Their basic affinity consists in the relevance (to freedom judgements) they both attribute to the *eligibility differential* between the rival reasons and, hence, the behaviours respectively associated with them. Here am I, locked in my room and actually having both reasons to remain there (not feeling like doing the lecture, wanting to read my newspaper) and reasons to leave the room (my moral duty to lecture, the adverse effects on my own interests of not doing so). If these reasons can be said to differ in weight – to be different either in denumerable magnitudes or in rank-ordering – then this will have implications for the action status of those two behaviours.

A characteristic positive view would be that my wanting to remain in my room constitutes my falling prey to my impulses and is not the course I would choose if I were to reflect in a fully moral and rational way upon the matter. Were I so to reflect, I would wish to leave the room and deliver the lecture. Different positive accounts offer different criteria for what is involved in moral and rational reflection. And they often invoke different psychological and metaphysical theories to explain the occurrent variations in my behavioural responses to such reflection. These details need not detain us here. The point is that, on a positive account, my delivering the lecture and, consequently, my leaving the room would be the proper subject matter of freedom judgements whereas my remaining in the room would not. My door being locked, I am thus positively unfree to leave the room. But I am positively neither free nor unfree to remain in my room (even if the door were not locked) since my reasons for doing so are ineligible to render that behaviour an action.

Impure negative conceptions work in much the same way, though generally with less demanding eligibility standards for reasons. As we've seen, they do demand that the reasons be ones which persons actually have rather than, more inclusively, ones which they could have. But they are more prone than positive conceptions to allow for the possibility that, in some situations, eligibility differentials may be absent. My reasons for leaving the room may be no relevantly better than my reasons for remaining in it. In which case and with the door locked, I am (as with the pure conception) unfree to do the former and free to do the latter. Some impure negative conceptions further impose veracity requirements on the (presuppositions of) reasons for behaviours. If my reason for leaving the room is that I want to lead my troops in battle against the Duke of Wellington at Waterloo, then my leaving the room is not an action and the door's being locked doesn't make me unfree.[30] Some impure negative conceptions go further still in the positive libertarian direction, requiring that the reasons for a behaviour should not be inferior, on some value scale, to the reasons for another person's behaviour that interferes with it.[31]

Disqualifying some actions from the subject matter of freedom judgements, proponents of the impure negative conception thereby commit themselves to the view that "judgements about freedom are inescapably evaluative."[32] Whether this view is fatally impaired by the paradoxes which notoriously beset it – such as denying the unfreedom of the contented slave or underwriting the notion of one's desirous self as one's oppressor – is not our present concern. The earlier remarked promiscuity of ordinary usage guarantees some refuge to each rival conception of liberty. All that has been attempted thus far is to demarcate and distinguish the pure negative conception of liberty from its rivals, to defend its coherence as a conception of liberty and to demonstrate its entrenchment in many of the distinctions and descriptions we characteristically advance when talking about persons and their freedom.

We *do* possess and frequently use a purely descriptive, culturally neutral, non-evaluative conception of freedom. We *do* often want to make – and to be understood to be making – judgements about whether a delirious person should have his freedom curtailed, whether someone should be deprived of the freedom to do a possibly but not actually desired action and whether freedom to do a less desirable action should be denied when it conflicts with a more desirable one. And even if our verdicts in such cases were to prove invariably affirmative (which they don't), we should still want them to be our *verdicts*. That is, we don't want to have these questions pre-emptively removed from our agenda by conceptions of liberty that consign them to the dustbin of unintelligibility. Blue's pure negative conception rescues them from that dustbin.

---

[30] Cf. Gray, "On Negative and Positive Liberty," 520, where those who are delirious, incorrigibly delusional, phobia-ridden or hypnotized are disqualified from having a reason for their behaviour.

[31] Cf. Flathman, *The Philosophy and Politics of Freedom*, 204.

[32] Gray, "On Negative and Positive Liberty," 515–16. For a lucid discussion of these types of evaluative commitment and of the consequently blurred distinction from positive liberty, see Plant, *Modern Political Thought*, 222–33.

Deeply embedded in our thinking about liberty is the idea that we are unfree to do an action when we are threatened by others with a penalty – or at least a serious penalty – for doing it. While preventing (making impossible) a person's action is commonly acknowledged to be the paradigm form of unfreedom, most accounts have no hesitation in speaking of prevention *and* penalizability in the same breath as if there were no relevant distinction between them so far as unfreedom is concerned.

The object of this section is to show that for Blue's pure negative conception of liberty, and perhaps for others too, there is indeed such a distinction. And inattention or indifference to it generates a good deal of descriptive imprecision in our thinking about freedom. Specifically, I shall argue that although penalization does indeed curtail our freedom, the penalizability of an action does not make us unfree to do it.

Suppose that I'm offered a teaching post at a university other than the one that currently employs me. Suppose, further, that the duties and privileges attached to the offered post are quite similar to those of my present post except that the offered salary is considerably greater than my present one. And suppose, finally, that I'm not averse to receiving a higher salary and would positively welcome it. Is there some significant sense in which this offer makes it *impossible* for me to remain in my present post?

Alternatively, suppose that I have no offer of a teaching post other than the one I currently occupy. Suppose, further, that the university authorities have informed me that unless I substantially increase the amount of teaching I am to do in the next academic session, my contract of employment will be terminated. And suppose, finally, that I'm utterly loath to surrender still more of my time to teaching as I much prefer to spend it reading and writing. Is there some significant sense in which this threat makes it *impossible* for me to reject the extra teaching?

Offers and threats are interventions by others in persons' practical deliberations. They are intended by their authors to influence how their recipients act, by altering the extent to which they actually desire to do a particular action: that is, by altering that action's eligibility. If the interveners are correct in their assessment of the recipients' desires and if they have designed their interventions accordingly, they necessarily succeed in bringing about the intended alteration in those desires.[33] However, despite this shared characteristic of interventions which are offers and interventions which are threats, few negative libertarians regard the making of an offer as curtailing the liberty of its recipient, whereas many of them do so regard threats. (Positive libertarians allow that both offers and threats, as heteronomous influences, may curtail personal liberty.) Four questions thereby suggest themselves:

1   What, if any, are the grounds for distinguishing offers from threats?
2   If such a distinction can be established, does it imply a difference between the ways in which offers and threats affect the practical deliberations of their recipients?
3   If such a difference exists, does it supply a reason for claiming that threats, but not offers, reduce personal liberty?
4   And if no such difference exists, can we nevertheless claim (as positive libertarians do) that both threats and offers may reduce personal liberty?

Cinema-goers will recall that in the popular Hollywood film *The God-father* the *padrone*, when periodically confronted with an uncooperative business associate, orders his subordinates to make the recalcitrant "an offer he can't refuse." That the wonderful irony of this phrase has been so widely appreciated might readily be taken as evidence that we are all perfectly able to distinguish an offer from a threat, because we can distinguish a gain from a loss. But if a distinction of this kind can be drawn, it cannot be done simply upon such grounds as these. For what's true of both offers and threats is that acceding to them promises to make their recipients better off than not doing so. So the differences that must exist if a distinction is to be drawn between offers and threats are those (i) between the gains of acceding to an offer and a threat respectively and, correspondingly, (ii) between the losses of not acceding to an offer and a threat respectively.

It's unnecessary to rehearse the accounts supplied by the literature on this subject to appreciate that the existence of such differences presupposes a conception of *normalcy* into which the threatening or offering action is taken to be an extraneous intrusion. The need for such a

---

[33] If they are *not* correct in their assessments of those desires – if they underestimate their recipients' attachment to the non-compliant alternative – and/or fail to design their interventions appropriately, they *a fortiori* cannot succeed in altering that action's eligibility. Cf. Gorr, *Coercion, Freedom and Exploitation*, 69–70.

presupposition is evident from the casual distinction commonly drawn between offering and threatening interventions: that acceding to the former promises to increase wellbeing whereas not acceding to the latter promises to decrease it. This distinction tends to obscure the fact that not acceding to offers promises a relative decrease in wellbeing, while acceding to threats promises a relative increase in wellbeing.

To establish the distinction between offers and threats it's therefore necessary to suppose that the accession-consequences of the former, and the non-accession-consequences of the latter, respectively promise not merely relative increments and decrements of wellbeing but absolute ones. And this entails a baseline or norm from which such consequences are deemed to be departures. In the literature, the conception of this norm is the description of the normal and predictable course of events: that is, the course of events (and associated level of wellbeing) that would confront the recipient of the intervention were that intervention not to occur.

Given this conception of the norm, we can derive a simple configuration of the alternative consequences posed by various types of intervention. For an offer – "You may use my car whenever you wish" – the accession-consequence promises a situation which is more desired than the norm, while the non-accession consequence is on the norm, no more or less desired than it because identical to it. For a threat – "Your money or your life" – the accession-consequence (no money) is less desired than the norm, but the non-accession-consequence (no life) is still less desired. We can additionally identify a third kind of intervention which I'll call a *throffer*: "Kill this man and you'll receive £1000; fail to kill him and I'll kill you." Here the accession-consequence may be more desired than the norm, while the non-accession-consequence is definitely less desired than the norm.

This configuration can be displayed diagrammatically (figure 2.1). The vertically aligned pairs of points represent the alternative consequences promised by offers (1, 2), threats (3, 4) and throffers (5, 6); and the odd-numbered points represent accession-consequences, with the even-numbered points representing non-accession-consequences. (It need not be assumed that levels of wellbeing are cardinally measurable.) Hence it appears that the answer to the first of our four questions is an affirmation that we *can* distinguish offers from threats and that the grounds for doing so consist in the fact that the alternative consequences posed by the former occupy different positions relative to the norm than do those posed by the latter.

Let's consider our answer to the second question in the light of this distinction. Does this difference between offers and threats imply any

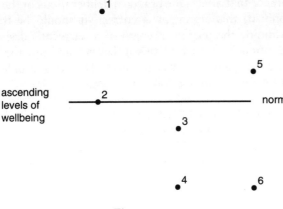

Figure 2.1.

difference between the ways in which each respectively affects the practical deliberations of their recipients? The short answer is "no." For the way in which both offers and threats affect their recipients consists in the *reversal* of the relative preferability of doing an action with that of not doing it. Whereas in the normal and predictable course of events – in the absence of an intervention – Blue's desire to do B (use my car, surrender her money, kill this man) is less than her desire not to do it, in the presence of an intervention her desire to do B is greater than her desire not to do it.

What is salient for Blue's deliberations is not whether the alternatives confronting her are above, on, or below the norm. Rather, it is the fact, true of both offers and threats, that acceding promises to leave her in a more desired position than does not acceding. The *modus operandi* of an intervention – its method of promoting an acceding response – consists in promising a non-zero difference when the wellbeing associated with not acceding is deducted from that associated with acceding. This is true irrespective of where the two alternative consequences lie in relation to the norm: that is, irrespective of whether the intervention is an offer or a threat.

And while it's certainly true that acceding to an offer is more desired than acceding to a threat, it's very far from being true that the promised non-zero difference in wellbeing is always greater in the case of threats than in the case of offers. This simply means, as we already know from common experience, that offers are not invariably more resistible or less impelling than threats. With respect to any intervention, it's the existence of this difference that affects the practical deliberations of the recipient.[34]

If (and only if) this argument is correct, it should be true that the factor determining the relative strength of a recipient's desire to accede to an intervention is the size of this difference and not the distance of either of its consequences from the norm. That this is indeed the case can be seen by comparing the following threats:

1   Give me £100 or I'll kill you.
2   Give me £1000 or I'll kill you.
3   Give me £1000 or I'll kill you and your brother.
4   Give me £100 or I'll kill you and your brother.

Making the usual assumptions about persons' relative preferences concerning money, personal survival and fraternal welfare (i.e. that the latter two are preferred to the former), we can readily see that Blue's desire to accede would be greatest in the case of (4) and least in the case of (2). What this indicates is that the strength of a threat is not a function of how much less its accession-consequence is desired than the norm: (2) is weaker than both (1) and (4). Nor is its strength a function of how much less its non-accession-consequence is desired than the norm: (3) is weaker than (4), and (2) is weaker than (1). Differences in wellbeing between consequences and the norm are utterly irrelevant in assessing the strength of a threat. All that's relevant is the extent of the difference between acceding and not acceding.

In that respect, it's not strictly mistaken (as it is in the case of threats) to regard the strength of an offer as a function of the promised difference between its accession-consequence and the norm. But this provides no reason to suppose that the strength of offers is determined by considerations different from those pertaining to threats. For it's simply an analytic fact, true by definition, that the non-accession-consequence of an offer lies on the norm. The strength of an offer, like that of any sort of intervention, is purely a function of the promised difference between its alternative consequences. That this is true of all interventions is further borne out by a comparison of the following throffers:

[34] A plausible suggestion is that persons *resent* receiving threats whereas this is not the case with offers. But, though true, this does not imply a recipient's greater willingness to accede to offers than to threats since the (thereby augmented) undesirability of acceding to the latter simply reduces the wellbeing differential between doing and not doing so. It can't be presumed to make it less than the corresponding differential for any offer, much less, to eliminate it.

1 Do B and I'll give you £100; fail and I'll kill you.
2 Do B and I'll give you £1000; fail and I'll kill you.
3 Do B and I'll give you £100; fail and I'll kill you and your brother.
4 Do B and I'll give you £1000; fail and I'll kill you and your brother.

Again, on the same relative preference assumptions, it's clear that the greatest desire to accede arises in (4) and the least in (1). This ordering, in terms of capacity to affect the desire to accede, exactly corresponds to the ordering of these throffers in terms of the promised difference between their alternative consequences. It doesn't correspond to their ordering in terms of the difference between acceding and the norm, nor of the difference between not acceding and the norm.

A further point should be made in this connection. Thus far I've been talking about how offers and threats affect their recipients' *desires*, that is, about the relative *preferability* of acceding and not acceding. But it's equally possible to formulate a parallel discussion in terms of how such interventions affect their recipients' *duties*, that is, in terms of the *morality* of acceding and not acceding. So whereas in the normal course of events Blue may have no duty to refrain from doing B, in the presence of an offer or a threat she may have this duty. The only difference between the descriptive account and the prescriptive one is that, in the latter case, the relative positioning of the two alternatives is not necessarily a matter of the difference between them being a positive quasi-numerical one. Interventions, in the prescriptive account, do not make the recipient better off by acceding than by not acceding. Rather, acceding becomes obligatory and not acceding becomes prohibited. The difference in the prescriptive account is, so to speak, one of quality rather than quantity. This, however, doesn't alter the point that whether interventions affect desires or duties, the ways in which these are affected are of the same form: namely, the creation of a difference between the value of acceding and that of not acceding.

Briefly then, both the *modus operandi* of an intervention and its strength are determined without reference to the norm. What the normal course of events would have been simply has no bearing on the impact an intervention has on its recipient. Since it's with reference to the norm that we define offers and threats and distinguish between them, we may conclude – in answer to our second question – that there is no difference between the ways in which offers and threats respectively affect their recipients' practical deliberations.

And this provides us with the answer to the third question as well. Since no such difference exists, it cannot constitute a reason for claiming that threats, but not offers, reduce personal liberty. Which brings us to the fourth question. This asks whether, in the absence of such a difference, it is nevertheless possible to claim – as do positive libertarians – that both threats and offers may reduce liberty.

We've already seen, in the previous section, that "Blue is free to do B" implies or presupposes neither that "Blue wants to do B" nor that "Blue has no duty to refrain from doing B." Whereas in the normal course of events it might be the case that "Blue wants to do B" or that "Blue has no duty to refrain from doing B," the occurrence of Red's threat or offer to Blue may cause it to be the case that "Blue wants to refrain from doing B" or that "Blue has a duty to refrain from doing B." But neither of these latter two statements, nor the fact that they are true because of another's action, implies that "Blue is unfree to do B." They do not imply that the event "Blue doing B" is impossible. Of course, the truth of the first of these statements rules out the possibility of "Blue doing B eagerly" and the truth of the second rules out "Blue doing B justifiably." But that is another matter.

Hence neither the making of threats nor the making of offers reduces liberty. When an aspiring Casanova reports that "The look she gave me *stopped* me in my tracks," we know that he's speaking metaphorically regardless of whether the look was an offer or a threat. Interventions don't count as preventions.

The claim to the contrary would be that Red's intervening action A, in behalf of "Blue refraining from doing B," *does* render "Blue doing B" impossible. For this claim to be true it must be the case that making accession (not doing B) preferable or morally superior to non-accession (doing B), implies rendering the latter impossible and the former therefore necessary. And this in turn implies that only that one, which is the preferred or morally superior of the two alternative courses of action, can be done. Clearly however, this is just false with respect to any *morally superior* alternative since its being a moral alternative implies that it's possible not to do it.

Is it nonetheless true of *preferred* alternatives? If it were, then we should have to say that Red's intervening action A must be preferred by him to not doing A. And this would imply, on this account, that "Red not doing A" is impossible and thus that "Red doing A" is necessary. But observe that if this were so, then "Red doing A" – as a necessary event – must itself be a constituent part of the normal and predictable course of events, since it's analytically true that all necessary events are predictable events. In which case, however, "Red doing A" cannot be construed as an intervention, that is, as an extraneous intrusion into the normal and predictable course of events.

So the view that intervention is prevention is self-contradictory because anyone entertaining it is committed both to affirming and denying that an intervening action is part of the normal and predictable course of events. This contradiction seems to me to be implicit in the writings of many of those who embrace positive conceptions of liberty. And it's therefore all the more surprising to discover it in the opposing arguments of some negative libertarians.

Taking exception to the general argument just advanced, J. P. Day has proposed a different account of why threats do, but offers don't, reduce negative liberty.[35] Day agrees that one is to be described as unfree to do an action only if others render one's doing of that action impossible. But he contends that threats, unlike offers, make their recipients unfree because they render impossible their doing a *complex* (conjunctive) action. The highwayman's threat to the traveller – "Your money or your life" – is said to render impossible the traveller's doing the complex action of keeping his money *and* keeping his life.[36]

I suggest, however, that we need to consider carefully whether this alleged impossibility can be the effect of the highwayman's threat. If Red's threat against "Blue keeping money" renders impossible the complex action of "Blue keeping money and keeping life," what can be the effect of Red's *execution* of his threat? On Day's argument, it's hard to see how Red's act of executing the threat can add anything further to Blue's unfreedom than has already been achieved by Red's act of issuing the threat. If Blue withholds her money and Red executes his threat, is Blue thereby released from her unfreedom to do that complex action?

Suppose that Blue does withhold her money and the execution is nonetheless not forthcoming. This entails that Blue keeps her money and her life. Day concedes that it is "illogical" to describe a person as unfree to do an action (simple or complex) which she in fact does. Hence, anticipating this rejoinder, he suggests that threats are generally executed. But this empirical generalization, even if true, is insufficient to imply what is in any case patently false: namely, that it is the threat and not its execution that is doing whatever prevention occurs in such circumstances. Neither threats nor warnings nor, for that matter, friendly advice about the malign intentions of third parties serve to render

---

[35] Day, "Threats, Offers, Law, Opinion and Liberty."

[36] Similarly, Spector, *Autonomy and Rights*, 18, claims that a threat causes its recipient to lose freedom by restricting his menu of options, i.e. by removing this conjunctive option from it.

impossible any action (simple or complex) of their recipients. Intervention, we must conclude, is simply not the same as prevention.[37]

Sometimes it's suggested that *rules* restrict our liberty. Thus I might decline a dinner invitation, explaining that I'm unfree to accept because I've promised to mark examination scripts that evening. This explanation implicitly invokes the moral rule prohibiting promise-breaking as a limitation on my freedom. But as T. H. Green himself remarked, this use of the term "freedom" is purely metaphoric.[38] For there's no suggestion here that my declining the invitation is the result of another's action, nor that accepting it is impossible. It's true that accepting the invitation is impermissible. And we might wish to describe actions which are impermissible in this sense as *morally impossible*. But moral rules, though they might thus imply that certain actions are morally impossible, do not imply that they are literally impossible, i.e. incapable of occurring. Otherwise, wrong actions could not occur.

While it's therefore acknowledged, at least by negative libertarians, that moral rules don't curtail liberty, it's commonly contended that *legal* rules do. What are the grounds for this contention? The reason why legal rules are considered to curtail liberty is that, unlike moral rules, they are enforced. (We can set aside those legal rules which are unenforceable because they are non-prescriptive and are merely ancillary to enforceable rules, inasmuch as they simply define or describe a particular condition which is regulated by various enforceable rules, e.g. the legal rules defining marital status.)

Enforcedness is indeed one of the essential marks distinguishing legal rules from moral ones. Since "enforcing" means "imposing by force" and since "imposing" is what some philosophers have called an *achievement word*,[39] it would seem to follow that if Blue is indeed subject to an enforced rule prohibiting the doing of B, she is unfree to do B. That is, her doing of B would be rendered impossible by the enforcers of that rule. Let's assume that legal rules are invariably enforced. Does this entitle us to say that Blue's being subject to a law prohibiting the doing of B makes her unfree to do it? Many writers who subscribe to the negative conception of liberty would return an unequivocal "yes" to this question.

But they would be mistaken. For when we say that a particular rule

---

[37] A more closely argued refutation of Day is offered in Gorr, *Coercion, Freedom and Exploitation*, 71–6.

[38] Green, *The Works of Thomas Hill Green*, vol. II, 309. See also n. 1, above.

[39] Cf. Ryle, *The Concept of Mind*, ch. V; and Hare, *Essays on the Moral Concepts*, 2–6. Thus "convincing" is an achievement word whereas "arguing" is not.

is enforced, we can mean either or both of two quite different things. We may mean that conduct in contravention of the rule is actually prevented by the legal authorities: that such conduct would be rendered literally impossible by them. Or we may mean that contravening conduct, once it actually occurs, is followed by the authorities' forcible imposition on the perpetrator of certain constraints on the range of actions subsequently open to her: in short, punishment.

A legal rule in the first case, a preventatively enforced rule, does indeed imply Blue's unfreedom to do the B it prohibits. But a legal rule in the second case, a punitively enforced one, does not. Certainly it's true that the existence of a punitively enforced rule does imply that the perpetrator has her freedom reduced. So the common view is correct in that respect. Being imprisoned or fined or, as in earlier times, maimed, renders impossible the doing of a range of actions which she would otherwise have been free to do, *including many unprohibited actions*. But such a rule does not imply that persons are unfree to act in ways that contravene its prohibition. If anything, it implies the reverse. With regard to prohibited conduct, a punitive legal rule is an intervention and not a prevention.

In fact, of course, some sorts of legally prohibited conduct are the objects of both kinds of enforcement. Persons are legally prohibited from importing cocaine into the United Kingdom. This rule is often enforced in a manner such that, when I enter the country through an official port of entry, any cocaine found by customs officials to be in my possession will be taken from me. But were the authorities to fail to prevent me from entering the country with cocaine in my possession – either through their failure to detect it as I passed through the customs point or because I entered the country elsewhere – it is not true that I would thereby have escaped the enforcement of that legal prohibition. That rule is, after all, one prohibiting any cocaine importation, and not merely one prohibiting the importation of cocaine detected at customs points. Thus the law also provides for the punishment of persons subsequently found to have been successful in importing cocaine. Indeed, it's difficult to imagine that any kind of legally prohibited conduct which is the object of prevention is not also the object of punishment.

But the reverse is not true. For the enforcement of much the greater proportion of legal prohibitions is confined solely to punishment. Doubtless this is in part due to the fact that, unlike some cocaine importation, much legally prohibited conduct is extremely difficult to identify as such instantaneously. This is not to deny that there are some forms of such conduct which could also be subjected to preventive measures. It's possible to imagine arrangements aimed at rendering them impossible, however unacceptable such measures might be on other grounds. One can conceive, for example, of an unbreachable shell constructed around the entire land mass of a country, such that entry to it is blocked except through points where electronic devices which screen persons for possession of cocaine also operate the otherwise immovable barriers. Less fancifully, we can think of some arrangements which prevent unauthorized persons from entering areas where strategic materials are located or which have been placed under medical quarantine.

Nevertheless, and for whatever reasons, there are many legal prohibitions the enforcement of which consists solely in punishment. And thus it would be incorrect to say that persons are thereby unfree to act in contravention of those rules. Hence the existence of an invariably enforced legal rule prohibiting the doing of B does not imply that persons subject to it are unfree to do B. And if they *are* unfree to do B this unfreedom is due not to the existence of that rule but to acts of prevention. Thus Hobbes correctly depicts legal rules as "artificial chains" which are "fastened at one end, to the lips . . . of the sovereign power; and at the other end to [the subjects'] ears."[40] It's not only ear-wigglers who will appreciate how much latitude this still leaves them.

[40] Hobbes, *Leviathan*, 138.

(C) PREVENTION AND POSSESSION

In the preceding two sections I've advanced and defended a pure negative conception of liberty according to which (i) a person is unfree to do – is prevented from doing – an action if and only if the action of another person would render his doing it impossible, and (ii) an intervening action by one person, in behalf of another's not doing an action, does not make the latter unfree to do that action. Intervention is not prevention. And this is so irrespective of whether an intervention is a single threat (or offer) or is an instance of an enforced system of rule-governed punishments (or rewards). We have now to consider what *does* count as prevention. How does one person's action make another's impossible?

Prevention is a relation between the respective actions of two persons such that the occurrence of one of them rules out, or implies the impossibility of, the occurrence of the other. If both such actions can occur – if they are *compossible* – then neither prevents the other. So the first thing we want to know is the kind of circumstance under which either of two persons' actions can occur, but not both: the kind of circumstance under which they are incompossible.

All actions are events. Some events are inherently, i.e. logically, incapable of occurring. For instance, it's logically impossible for a planet and one of its moons to move in orbits around each other simultaneously. Similarly, my (or anyone else's) drawing a square circle is an event the occurrence of which is impossible. More precisely, my drawing a square circle is a kind of action or *act-type* of which no instances or *act-tokens* can occur. Nor could this impossibility be due to someone's preventing me from drawing square circles. It's due simply to the fact that we don't know what it would mean to draw a square circle, any more than we know what it would mean to multiply a radish by a preposition. (Presumably bad maths, bad semantics and bad salad.)

On the other hand, we have no such problem with the action of my attending a performance of Shakespeare's *Richard III*. Here is an act-type which we can understand and tokens of which can conceivably occur. What, then, would be meant by claiming that it is impossible for me to do the action of attending a performance of *Richard III*?

This is where the notorious ambiguity of our ordinary use of the word "action" comes into play. Does this claim mean that no event fitting the description "my attending a performance of *Richard III*" can occur? Or does it mean that what can't occur is only my attending a particular performance of *Richard III*, say, one due to be held tonight in the auditorium of my son's high school? While the first impossibility certainly implies the second, the reverse is obviously not true. My inability to attend that particular performance, the impossibility of my doing that act-token, in no way precludes my going to see *Richard III* at the auditorium tomorrow night, or at the Globe Theatre tonight or at the cinema sometime next week.

For it to be impossible for me to do the act-type of attending a performance of *Richard III*, it has to be impossible for me to do each of these (and many other) act-tokens. Indeed strictly speaking, the only things we do when we act are act-tokens. Or alternatively, we do act-types only by virtue of doing act-tokens. Of course, we don't bother to speak so strictly in everyday conversation and it would be intolerably tedious and pedantic if we did. Still, I would commonly be regarded as exaggerating my plight were I to complain of the impossibility of my attending tonight's auditorium performance as if it were tantamount to the impossibility of my attending any performance of *Richard III*. A person whose complaint that he can't secure employment is based solely on his failure to get a particular job is not generally taken seriously.

So one thing we need in order to assess the truth of a claim that a person's doing an action is impossible is some criterion or test for distinguishing act-types from act-tokens. We want to know whether the impossible action referred to is one particular event or several of them. And the obvious candidate for such a test is whether there is more than one event that fits the proffered description of what is claimed to be impossible. If there is and if all of them are incapable of occurring, then the claim is true. It's also true if there is only one such event and if it is incapable of occurring. But the claim is false if there is more than one and if it's possible for at least one of them to occur.

Actions are impossible if all their tokens are impossible. So what we also need to know to assess an action-impossibility claim are the conditions under which its act-tokens cannot occur. Suppose I've spent the day in London and it's now too late for me to get back to Manchester in time for this evening's auditorium performance of *Richard III*. As we've seen, this impossibility in no way implies the impossibility of my attending a performance of *Richard III*.

Does it at least imply the impossibility of my doing so tonight in Manchester? Well, no, because there are other, later performances of *Richard III* going on tonight in Manchester: it's playing at a theatre and in a cinema or perhaps I can watch a video recording of it on my television. So even if we add somewhat more specificity to the action claimed to be impossible – my attending a performance of *Richard III* tonight in Manchester - we find that it's still an act-type and not an act-token. That is, there is still more than one conceivable instance of it, more than one event fitting its (now more specific) description, some of which are not incapable of occurring despite my late departure from London. My doing an action (act-type) is possible if my doing at least one of its tokens is possible. That's why the veracity of an action-impossibility claim requires the veracity of the impossibility of each of its tokens. Or, what amounts to the same thing, we need sufficiently to specify the action in question so that it has only one token and then to verify that token's impossibility. What does such sufficient specification amount to?

Again, all actions are events. As such, they consist in the occupation of a set of contiguous temporal locations and (sometimes) a set of contiguous spatial locations by a set of physical objects. These physical objects will include the actor's body and may include anything from tables and chairs to electromagnetic waves and the bodies of other actors. My standing and waiting for a bus consists in my body occupying a spatial location and a set of contiguous temporal locations. My running to catch a bus consists in my body occupying a set of contiguous spatial locations and a set of contiguous temporal locations. My throwing a ball consists in my body and the ball occupying a temporal and a spatial location and in the ball's occupying sets of temporal and spatial locations respectively contiguous to one another and to the initial temporal and spatial locations. And so forth.

Let's call these locations and objects the *physical components* of an action. What I want to suggest is that the only sort of specification of an action sufficient to ensure that it has only one token is one identifying all its physical components. Without an indication of precisely where, when and which things are involved, "my attending a performance of *Richard III*" remains an action description to which quite a few events may answer.

Of course, and as was noted previously, ordinary conversation typically requires no such precise identification since this is often contextually apparent. It's only in response to requests for explanation or expressions of doubt concerning the impossibility of my attending *Richard III* that I would feel called upon to volunteer more detail along these lines, and then only to the extent required by my questioner's persistence.[41]

---

[41] Or to the extent required to make me think that my claim is mistaken, i.e. that some instances of the proffered action description are, after all, not impossible.

An act-token is fully identified, then, by an *extensional* description of
the action in question: a description indicating the physical components
of that action.[42] There cannot be more than one act-token (of a particular act-type) answering to the same extensional description, i.e. having
the same set of physical components. Purely *intensional* descriptions of
actions, by contrast, do cover more than one act-token. Such descriptions are couched in terms of the purpose or meaning attached by the
actor (or others) to what he does: my attending *Richard III*, my running
for a bus, my throwing a ball and so on. It's true of each of these descriptions that there are many events that would answer to it.

The impossibility of an action entails the impossibility of all its tokens.
What makes an act-token impossible? Stated generally, it's the actor's
lack of access to or control over at least one of that token's physical
components. My late departure from London implies tonight's inaccessi-
bility to me of the Manchester high school auditorium and its assorted
personnel and paraphernalia engaged in performing *Richard III*. A high
wall blocks my path in running and denies me access to the spatio-
temporal locations I need to occupy if I am to catch this afternoon's two
o'clock bus at the West Didsbury stop on Palatine Road. A paralysis in
my right arm denies me the control of it that I require to throw the
baseball to home plate at a certain point in the fifth inning. But for such
deficiencies of access and control, those act-tokens would be capable
of occurring.

This analysis enables us to see more clearly the conditions under which
two actions are incompossible, that is, are incapable of joint occurrence.
As a first approximation, we can say that such conditions exist if the
extensional descriptions of the two actions respectively identify sets of
physical components that each contain some, but not all, components in
common. My attending tonight's auditorium performance and my taking tonight's seven o'clock London–Manchester train have, as common
physical components, myself and all temporal locations between seven-
thirty and nine-forty-five this evening. (That is, the three-hour

---

[42] *Complete* extensional descriptions of actions (i.e. act-tokens) don't generally figure in
ordinary conversation, due to the normal superfluity and tedium of their detailed specificity. They have, however, long been employed in certain fields of activity – notably ath-
letics, industrial work processes and, latterly, certain areas of medicine – where fine-
grained analyses of actions (often assisted by decelerated films and computerized charting
of the movements involved) can facilitate improved performance; cf. Marey, *Movement*,
and Shaw, *The Purpose and Practice of Motion Study*, esp. chs. 4–7. Modern motion study
techniques were pioneered by Frank and Lillian Gilbreth, nicely portrayed in the 1950
Hollywood film *Cheaper by the Dozen*. On the underlying biomechanical analysis and
metrication, see Fung, *Biomechanics*, ch. 1, and Pennycuick, *Newton Rules Biology*.

performance begins at seven-thirty and the train gets in at nine-forty-five.) What they rather crucially don't have in common are their respective spatial locations, as well as other things. And they are thus incompossible.

We're all familiar with the exasperated expression "I can't be in two places at once." This is inconveniently true. What is conversely true is that I *can* be in one place at two times, in two places at two times and that I must necessarily be in one place at one time. The same, of course, goes for you. Though what is also true is that the two of us can't be in (literally) one place at one time. From all of which it follows that if two actions are such that their joint occurrence requires either (i) the same object being in different places at the same time, or (ii) different objects being in the same place at the same time, then they are incompossible. They are incompossible by virtue of the *partial coincidence* between their extensional descriptions:[43] object-temporal coincidence in the first case and spatio-temporal coincidence in the second. (Object-spatial coincidence, however, is a form of partial coincidence that does *not* imply incompossibility.)

Another pertinent feature of many actions is that their occurrence requires (is impossible without) the prior occurrence of other actions. My driving my car to Edinburgh requires someone's repairing or replacing its flat tyre. The non-occurrence of the latter action implies the impossibility of the former. Let's say that the latter is a *prerequisite* of the former. This relation of prerequisiteness is evidently a transitive one. Repairing or replacing the flat tyre requires the lifting of the car's weight off that wheel. The non-occurrence of the latter thereby implies the impossibility of my driving my car to Edinburgh. So the lifting, too, is properly described as as prerequisite of the driving.

These considerations furnish us with the basis for a general statement of the conditions of action-incompossibility:

> *Two actions, A and B, are incompossible if there is partial (either object-temporal or spatio-temporal) coincidence between the extensional description of A and either (i) B's extensional description, or (ii) C's extensional description if C is a prerequisite of B.*

The presence of such coincidence implies that A and B are incapable of

---

[43] By "partial coincidence" I mean what is referred to in set theory as *intersection*. Some, but not all, components in the set of components indicated in the extensional description of action A are identical with some, but not all, components in the set of components indicated in the extensional description of action B.

jointly occurring. This incapacity is due to one of them involving a different disposition, of the same object or spatial location at the same time, than does the other or one of that other's prerequisites. These actions suffer, we may say, from *extensional overlap*. Their respective sets of components intersect.

So how does one person (you) prevent another (me) from doing an action? Consider again my attending tonight's auditorium performance of *Richard III*. This event cannot occur because of my late departure from London. If (and only if) I had taken the four o'clock instead of the seven o'clock London–Manchester train, it could have occurred. What made the occurrence of my attending tonight's auditorium performance impossible was my not taking that earlier train. And that was due, let's suppose, to the fact that my taking the four o'clock train was impossible.

Where do you come into this? Well, it was you who caused that impossibility. You detained me in London by keeping the door of the room where we were meeting locked until after four o'clock. Your action is incompossible with my leaving the room before four o'clock and hence with my taking the four o'clock train and hence with my attending tonight's auditorium performance. That is, since your detaining me stopped various prerequisites of that attendance from occurring, that detaining action is incompossible with that attending action. These two actions cannot both occur. And since one of them actually did occur, the other's occurrence is impossible. You prevented me from attending tonight's performance and, thus, made me unfree to do so.

Now this tale of woe, as it happens, is not quite as unfortunate as it may sound. For if the truth be told, I actually had no desire to attend that performance and indeed no intention of doing so. In fact, I was thoroughly enjoying our meeting and fully intended to remain in that room and to continue participating in it. None of that, however, has any bearing at all on the freedom judgement of the last paragraph since we previously saw that, when imprisoned, I am unfree to go to the theatre whether I wish to or not. Nor would that freedom judgement need revising even if you hadn't actually locked me in the room, so long as it's (subjunctively) true that – had I attempted to leave before four o'clock – you would have locked me in. Nor, again, would that judgement be subject to revision even if you had no intention of causing me to miss tonight's performance or even if you were impeccably entitled to detain me. In all these cases, the simple fact that my attending that performance was or would have been made impossible by you is sufficient reason for claiming that you made me unfree to attend it.

I'm unfree to do an action, then, if control of at least one of its physical components is actually or subjunctively denied to me by another person. Conversely, I'm free to do it if I actually or subjunctively have control of all its components. My unfreedom implies my actual or subjunctive exclusion from at least one of those things by another person. And it thus implies that person's actual or subjunctive *possession* of at least one of those things. So my freedom to do that action implies my actual or subjunctive possession of all those components. In general, possession is a triadic relation between a person, a thing and all other persons. And statements about the freedom or unfreedom of a person to do a particular action are thus construable as affirmative or negative claims about that person's (actual or subjunctive) possession of that action's physical components. *Freedom is the possession of things.*[44]

This identification of freedom with possession helps to illuminate and ultimately to explain some paradoxes and ironies we standardly encounter when we speak of increasing, decreasing or maximizing freedom and, more generally, when we assess the achievements of great historical liberation movements. How it helps in this way is something we'll look at in the next section. Before that, we can explore and further clarify this identification by considering Michael Taylor's well-aimed objection levelled against the earlier version of it: a version which erroneously neglected the subjunctive aspect of this conception of liberty.[45]

Agreeing that "to be free to do A entails that all of the physical components of doing A are (simultaneously) unoccupied and/or undisposed of by another," Taylor nonetheless claims that "Steiner's further inference, that freedom is the personal possession of physical objects, is incorrect." His argument for this claim runs as follows:

> It is true that while one individual has possession – enjoys exclusive physical control – of an object, possession during that time is denied to all others. But it does not follow that an individual possesses an object *if* nobody else does. Steiner's error was to assume

---

[44] Most dictionary definitions of "possession" refer to either or both "control" and "exclusion of others." But it's clear that, where the former is used, it is intended to be synonymous with the latter. That is to say, one *controls* (in the sense of *possesses*) a thing inasmuch as what happens to that thing – allowing for the operation of physical laws – is determined by no person other than oneself. One's own lack of dexterity or skill in using that thing, though describable as a lack of control, is not a lack of control in the possessory sense: it doesn't imply a lack of possession. I certainly possess the three eggs I'm holding, even though the chances of my successfully making an omelette with them are practically nil.

[45] The earlier version is to be found in Steiner, "Individual Liberty." Taylor's objection is set out in *Community, Anarchy and Liberty*, 153–4.

tacitly that at any moment every object is in *somebody's* possession. An individual (on Steiner's own account) has pure negative freedom with respect to an action just as long as nobody else has possession of the physical components of that action; pure negative freedom does not require that *he* possesses these components.

Taylor is right. I was mistaken to suggest that everything must always be in the possession of one person or another. For although our doing actions (which we are *ipso facto* free to do) entails our possessing their components, we can also be free to do actions which we don't do. And thus the components of those unperformed actions may well be things unpossessed by ourselves, as well as being necessarily unpossessed by others. There can, as Taylor insists, be unpossessed things.

So there's no correlation between the set of things actually possessed by me and the set of actions I'm free to do. Nor, indeed, is there any correlation between the things possessed by others and the actions I'm unfree to do, since it's possible that others would acquire possession of some unpossessed things only if I were to attempt actions involving those components – attempts which I may not make. Hence I'm also unfree to do those actions, even though their components remain actually unpossessed.

But Taylor parlays his correct point into error when he continues:

I am free at this moment, and at most times, to perform a variety of acts on the open fields I can see from my window, because neither their legal owner nor any other person has at this moment exclusive physical control of them (of the ground, of the air space directly above them, of the cabbages and corn and other objects on and in them). Of course, if I exercised this freedom – if I actually performed one of the acts I am free to do – then I would be in possession of certain physical objects, so would *then* restrict the pure negative freedom of all other persons. But until I do so, they too have the relevant freedoms.

Can this be true? Can other persons as well as Taylor be said to have those freedoms? One such freedom, let's suppose, is Taylor's freedom to throw a particular cabbage fifty feet into the air above the spot where it's growing in two minutes' time. Can it be true as he suggests that, until he actually does this, everyone else is free to do actions involving that same cabbage or space at that same time?

I think not. Taylor's insistence on divorcing freedom from possession rests on the recognition that we can and typically do describe a person as being "at this moment" free to do a *later* action. We don't say that Taylor is unfree to throw that cabbage in two minutes' time if we believe that he won't be prevented from throwing it then. That's why we can be described as free to do actions whose components are actually unpossessed by us, given (as he says) that they will be possessed by us when we do those actions. But if Taylor is indeed free to do that action in two minutes' time, his neighbour cannot be similarly described as free to do any action then which requires (any of) those same physical components. Her being free to do such an action implies that, were she to attempt it, it would be she who would possess those things at that time. But if that were true, then it cannot be true that Taylor is free to do his throwing action since that implies that those things would be unpossessed by her at that time. Were she, in the event, successfully to attempt to use those components then, we should be bound to regard our earlier judgement – that Taylor is free – as mistaken.

Like actual possession, subjunctive possession cannot be ascribed to more than one person for any one time. Although it's true that both Becker and McEnroe were free to compete in the 1990 Wimbledon Men's Singles Tennis Championship, it cannot be true that they were both free to win it. Of course, it's often difficult to predict which one of many possible worlds will become actual.[46] But there's no possible world in which two (or more) such attempters can both be unprevented.

What remains true is that not everything is actually possessed. But what's also true is that everything is a physical component of some conceivable action or other. Hence, for any given time, everything which is not actually possessed is subjunctively possessed. For since any conceivable action is one which Taylor is either free or unfree to do – one which, were he to attempt it, would be either unprevented or prevented – it follows that every actually unpossessed component of that action would be possessed either by Taylor or by others.

So there *is* a correlation between the set of things actually *and* subjunctively possessed by Taylor and the set of actions he's free to do. And conversely, the same correlation holds between the things so possessed by others and the actions he's unfree to do. Freedom, then, is the actual and subjunctive possession of physical things. And a person actually or subjunctively possesses a thing if nobody else does. For any moment, everything is in someone's actual or subjunctive possession.

---

[46] Or to retrodict which one of many possible past worlds would have become actual, if the actual past world had not.

(D) LIBERTY AND COMPUTATION

If there's one thing that Blue especially enjoys, it's break-dancing in cinema lobbies. "What I really like," she told a recent interviewer, "is to
get out there on a Saturday evening and whirl around the floor on my
shoulder-blades with my cassette player blasting away." Unfortunately,
as she complained, she'd been unable to develop this talent to its full
extent because she couldn't put in the amount of practice required to do
so. Apparently, there has been a rigorously enforced law prohibiting
such activity, so she would hardly get started before the police would
arrive and stop her. "I have to wait for my annual holiday, when I can go
abroad to places with cinemas where I can get on with it undisturbed."

Even more recently, however, that law was repealed. So, following an
early Saturday evening party to celebrate this liberation, Blue and a
group of her friends duly trooped off to the local cinema to exercise
their new-found freedom. But she had barely begun to get into her stride
when the cinema's owner emerged from his office and ordered her to
stop, threatening to call the police if she wouldn't. Her protest, that
break-dancing in cinema lobbies was no longer illegal, was met with the
owner's irrefutable rejoinder that it *is* illegal in his cinema unless he
agrees to permit it, which he doesn't. Blue's similar attempts at other
cinemas encountered the same response. And her friends' concerted
efforts, to purchase a cinema and even to purchase the land, labour and
materials to construct a cinema, proved equally unavailing. The latest
instalment in this saga of disappointment is that one cinema owner has
slightly relented and is willing to let Blue do her thing for fifteen minutes
on the first Wednesday evening of every month.

What counts as an increase in a person's liberty, and how much of an
increase it amounts to, are questions fraught with conceptual problems.
Still less clear is the basis on which we compare the extent of different
persons' liberty and, hence, of the aggregate personal liberty enjoyed in
different societies.[47] That such extent-of-freedom judgements are
commonplace features of our history books and everyday political

---

[47] A not very satisfying attempt to address some of these problems is to be found in
Steiner, "How Free? Computing Personal Liberty." My subsequent thinking on this subject
has benefited from many probing conversations with Ian Carter whose research on measuring freedom promises greatly to illuminate the philosophical issues involved.

debates serves only to make even more perplexing the complete elus-
iveness of the sort of metric they implicitly invoke.

Alas, I'm not competent to remedy this deficiency. What I think I can
do, however, is to show that some such judgements presuppose metrics
which are paradoxical or incoherent. This can be done by considering a
number of commonsensical properties which we might expect any plausible metric to possess and by then demonstrating the denial of one or
another of these properties by various types of extent-of-freedom judgement. The point of this exercise is that it yields conclusions that, even
in the absence of a metric, shed interesting light on our understanding
of policies and larger-scale historical changes which are commonly credited with increasing or decreasing aggregate personal liberty. These conclusions will, in turn, yield significant inferences (in chapter 6) about the
content of principles of justice.

One thing we want of a freedom-metric is to be such that the total
amount of personal liberty attributed to any group of persons be the
sum of the amounts of personal liberty it severally attributes to each and
every member of that group. I take this to be sufficiently uncontroversial
as to require no defence. But how do we conceive the extent of one
person's liberty? To this question I have, as I said, no full answer. But
part of any such answer is commonsense's second suggestion: that we
take into account not only what he is free to do but also what he is
unfree to do. If Red and Blue are equally free, and if both then acquire
equal increments of freedom but Red alone also acquires an increment
of unfreedom, we want our metric to be such that Red is then deemed
by it to be less free than Blue.

This elementary requirement is violated by a widely held view that
members of technologically advanced societies are *ipso facto* more free
than their counterparts in more primitive societies. That is, because technological development and increased production have enlarged our repertoire of actions, we are held to be more free than persons lacking these
possibilities. Even an inmate of a modern prison, it's been suggested,
may be able unobstructedly to do many more actions than the most free
member of a less advanced society.

This view can be seen to rest on a failure to integrate unfreedoms into
the metric implied by its extent-of-freedom judgements. Part of that failure rests, in turn, on the previously discussed equivocation of the term
"action," as between act-types and act-tokens. Residents of classical
Athens could not perform the action (act-type) of going to the refrigerator to fetch a can of beer. Are we more free than they were? Possibly,
but not for that reason. For as we've already seen, whether I'm free to
do this act-type entirely depends upon whether I'm free to do at least

one of its tokens. Suppose I am. Does this imply that I'm more free than the classical Athenian? No, because there are many of these tokens which I'm unfree to do. My cranky neighbour, for instance, would no more allow me to fetch a beer from his refrigerator than he would give me the time of day. Our technologically enhanced repertoire of act-types also increases our inventories of act-tokens which we're prevented by others from doing. No classical Athenian was ever prevented from fetching a beer from the refrigerator of even his crankiest neighbour.

Freedom is a social relation, not a technological one. It's a relation between persons and persons, not between persons and nature. A modern solitary Robinson Crusoe equipped with a fair share of current scientific and technical knowledge would not thereby be more free than Defoe's eighteenth-century hero, whatever other advantages he might enjoy. It is not to physicists, doctors, and engineers that we turn to find out how free we are, even though they can provide expert advice on the contents of our act-type repertoires. So any freedom-metric that reflects these considerations cannot rule out *a priori* the possibility that a less technologically advanced person might be more free than a more technologically advanced one. And it must, therefore, integrate unfreedoms into its computations.

Another commonsensical requirement of any freedom-metric is that it implies that my total liberty increases whenever, *ceteris paribus*, I become free to do an act-token which I was previously unfree to do. And conversely for decreases. If I add an apple to those already in a barrel and none are taken out, it seems reasonable to demand of any apple-metric that, however it measures the quantity in the barrel (whether by weight, volume or simply enumeration), that total should be greater than it was before I added the extra apple. Yet some proposals for judging the extent of a person's liberty implicitly fail to satisfy even this rather meagre demand. Why?

The problem here is the one of how we are to count actions. Berlin suggests an expansive approach to any such computation:

> The extent of my freedom seems to depend on (a) how many possibilities are open to me (although the method of counting these can never be more than impressionistic. Possibilities of action are not discrete entities like apples, which can be exhaustively enumerated); (b) how easy or difficult each of these possibilities is to actualize; (c) how important in my plan of life, given my character and circumstances, these possibilities are when compared with each other; (d) how far they are closed and opened by deliberate human acts; (e) what value not merely the agent, but the general

sentiment of the society in which he lives, puts on the various possibilities. All these magnitudes must be "integrated", and a conclusion, necessarily never precise, or indisputable, drawn from
this process.[48]

But this is too expansive. Magnitude (b) encompasses both technological
capacities and what were earlier referred to as actions *prerequisite* to
other actions. The former are irrelevant to the measurement of liberty,
for the reasons just discussed. And the latter must be subsumed under
magnitude (a) if the computation is not to be impaired by double-
counting.[49] And since others can curtail our liberty non-deliberately,
magnitude (d) is also irrelevant.[50] The proposals I wish to criticize focus
on magnitudes (c) and (e) which I'll conjunctively label "valuational
magnitudes." Can these figure in our assessment of the extent of a
person's liberty?

Evidently our first reactions strongly incline us to the view that the
significance of the actions which we are or are not free to do must enter
into our estimations of how free we are and not just how valuable the
freedom we have is. Joel Feinberg argues that

> When two or more properties or "respects" are subject to precise
> mathematical comparison, they will always have some quantitative
> element in common. The difficulty in striking resultant totals of
> "on balance freedom" derives from the fact that the relation
> among the various "areas" in which people are said to be free is
> not so much like the relation between the height, breadth and
> depth of a physical object as it is like the relation between the
> gasoline economy, styling, and comfort of an automobile . . . What
> we more likely mean when we say that one subject is freer on
> balance than another is that his freedom is greater in the more
> valuable, important or significant dimensions, where the "value"
> of a dimension is determined by some independent standard.[51]

Can it be seriously maintained that an action of twiddling one's thumbs
and an action of casting a ballot in an unrigged election should *not* be

---

[48] Berlin, *Four Essays on Liberty*, 130.
[49] Cf. Steiner, "How Free? Computing Personal Liberty," 76–9, for an argument suggesting the reducibility of the cost or difficulty of doing an action to the extent of the
actions prerequisite to it.
[50] Cf. the discussion of Miller's examples above, pp. 12–13, 15.
[51] Feinberg, *Social Philosophy*, 18–19.

accorded different weights in measuring the extent, and not just the worth, of an individual's liberty?

Charles Taylor attacks the "crude" and "tough-minded" (i.e. pure) negative conception of liberty underlying this suggestion, on the grounds that "it has no place for the notion of significance" and "will allow only for purely quantitative judgments." This conception is said to license the "diabolical defence of [communist] Albania" against the charge of being a less free society than Britain, since the presence of severe restraints on religious practice in the former – and their absence in the latter – could thereby be forensically countered by invoking the considerably fewer traffic restrictions in Albania than in Britain.[52] Surely, he insists, the value or significance of the actions we are free (and unfree) to do must enter into our calculations of how free we are.

Can this be so? For the moment, at least, we may leave aside questions like whether the harassed London commuter, diabolical or not, would necessarily be disposed to accept this judgement of relative significance. Taylor is certainly correct to attribute the view, that significance doesn't count, to the pure negative conception. We've seen that, on that conception, an action's significance or eligibility has no bearing on *whether* a person is free to do it. So it cannot have any bearing on *how much* freedom he has if he is free to do it. For it makes no sense to say that my being prevented from doing it is an instance of unfreedom but, because it lacks significance, that prevention cannot be counted in estimating the extent to which I'm unfree. Instances, as was suggested, necessarily count in the computation of whatever they instantiate.

Clearly the significance of various actions does vary. And whatever may be the basis for assigning numerical values to these variations, such assignability is certainly a necessary condition of comparing the relative amounts of valuationally-weighted liberty enjoyed by any two persons – like an Albanian and a Briton – who are free or unfree to do different sets of actions. Taylor's complaint against the quantitativeness of the pure negative conception is thus somewhat overstated, since even a conception of liberty that *does* allow the metric relevance of action-significance must obviously permit its quantification if it is to enable its users to make the sort of comparative judgement he proposes. That said, however, it's also true that computing a person's liberty in this valuationally-weighted way is not without its logical difficulties nor is it devoid of paradoxical consequences.

Proposals that valuational magnitudes be integrated into the measure-

---

[52] Taylor, "What's Wrong with Negative Liberty," 183.

ment of personal liberty are typically underspecified. For it's evident not only that the actions which we're free or unfree to do vary in their significance, but also that these variations must be negative as well as positive. Wealth measurements include debts and felicific calculi integrate pains. Thus if saving a person's life is a highly significant act, it's necessary to regard an act of taking a person's life not as lacking significance but rather (infelicitously) as *anti*-significant. That is, proposals to integrate values need to assign negative as well as positive numbers to actions to represent valuations of their significance. Otherwise, a sufficiently large number of life-takings would, absurdly, have the same value as a life-saving.

Observe now how this leads to very peculiar results. Suppose that Blue is free to do acts A and B, the significance of each of which is respectively valued as +10 and +8, and that she is unfree to do C which is valued as −9. On whatever formula these figures are combined to yield the extent of her total freedom with respect to these three actions, the implication of removing the restraint against her doing C – and thereby making her free to do it – is a *reduction* in that total. Blue's acquisition of the added freedom to do C would entail a *decrease* in her overall freedom!

To avoid such contradictions, while still integrating valuational magnitudes into computations of personal liberty, it would therefore be necessary to exclude the use of negative numbers from valuational assessments of actions. But how can this be done? The answer is that it can't, at least not within the framework of a negative conception of liberty. To do it, one has to make a move which is indeed commonplace in most accounts of the *positive* conception of liberty. That move is, simply and boldly, to delete all negatively valued actions from the set of actions which persons are describable as free or unfree to do. (Often these disqualified actions are denied the status of actions altogether and/or their performance is said to be an exercise of "licence," not liberty.) For Blue, act C, being negatively valued, would thus be one which she cannot be said to be either free or unfree to do. The fact that she is prevented from doing it, or that that restraint gets lifted, would not affect her total liberty.

It's this move that underlies and explains the familiar difference between negative and positive libertarian appraisals of the extent of freedom enjoyed by average members of societies where negatively valued actions are commonly prevented. And it's for this same reason that Taylor is correct in claiming that "more discriminating" negative conceptions, i.e. impure ones, cannot easily sustain the distance between themselves and positive conceptions. For their insistence on an action's "eligibility" – that is, its not being negatively valued – as a condition of its being the subject matter of freedom judgements, implies that preventing an ineligible action is not an instance of unfreedom and, hence, that the introduction of such a prevention constitutes no decrease in a person's aggregate freedom.

Since the integration of valuational magnitudes into computations of a person's freedom violates the requirement that a person's total liberty vary directly with each increment (and inversely with each decrement) of liberty, such magnitudes cannot figure coherently in extent-of-freedom judgements. We must and do distinguish between whether we have a freedom and what that freedom is worth. Aggregating our freedoms does not eliminate this distinction. Valuation integration does. What's more, it does so at the cost of metrical incoherence. Since eliminated distinctions are not philosophically desirable commodities, whereas coherence is, valuation integration seems a doubly bad bargain.[53]

Does this mean that, in aggregating a person's freedom, we should simply count up all the act-tokens he is free (and unfree) to do, treating them each as one unit? This, I must acknowledge, used to be what I believed.[54] Now I am doubtful. What's the problem here? Part of it, I suppose, stems from the same underlying concerns that motivate valuation integration proposals: namely, the perception that act-tokens are very heterogeneous, along with the vague sense that some are larger or contain *more* than others. But more *what*? We cannot, for purposes of freedom measurement, say "more value" – for the reasons we've just seen. When we ask how free someone is or, more commonly, whether he is more free than another person, what are the units employed by the freedom-metric we have (very loosely!) in mind?

Selling ears of corn at a roadside stand, we might express our total sales for the day in terms either of the aggregate number of ears sold or the aggregate weight of corn sold or, of course, our aggregate money receipts. Elevators in tall office buildings sometimes state their maximum load capacity in terms of kilograms and sometimes in terms of numbers of passengers. Passengers, like ears of corn, vary in weight. We know that what matters to those who set elevator capacities is weight. What is it that matters to freedom-measurers? Do they want to know how *many* freedoms we have or how *much* freedom? Does "How free?"

---

[53] It may be worth remarking that the valuations in valuation integration proposals can range over moral values or real interests, as in Taylor's account; over desires, as explored in the sceptical argument of Arneson, "Freedom and Desire"; or over preferences, as suggested in Sen, "Welfare, Freedom and Social Choice: A Reply," 470.

[54] Cf. Steiner, "How Free? Computing Personal Liberty," 82–3.

ask how many actions we're free (and unfree) to do, or how much action?

One worrying aspect of the "how many actions" approach to the question of "how free" is an apparent danger of *double-counting*. This is a consideration alluded to earlier, in the rejection of Berlin's magnitude (b). For it is certainly a further commonsensical requirement of any decent metric that, whatever kind of unit it operates with, it does not count the same instance as if it were two different instances, in reaching a figure expressing the total number of instances. So how might simply counting unprevented and prevented act-tokens, as units of freedom and unfreedom, threaten double-counting?

One way it might be thought to do so arises from the multiplicity of act-descriptions applicable to one and the same behavioural event. My attending tonight's auditorium performance of *Richard III* at my son's high school could be an act of my going to see a play, or an act of making amends for missing the last dramatic production he was in, or an act of getting in out of the rain, or an act of avoiding some domestic chore, and so forth. Since each of these intensional descriptions could be one that actually fits, and since the actions we're free or unfree to do include all those behaviours we could have reasons to do as well as the ones we actually do have reasons to do, it seems that my being unprevented from attending tonight implies that I'm free to do all these actions. Each one of these tokens must be counted in computing my total liberty.

Is this double-counting? I'm inclined to think that, if it is, it's not of a sort that is metric-distorting. Since my freedom to do one of these act-tokens implies my freedom to do all of them, were I to be prevented from doing one of them, the total amount of unfreedom engendered by this prevention would simply be the product of the same multiple as is used to calculate my total freedom in the absence of that prevention. That is, if my attending the play actually amounts to four possible act-tokens – an exercise of four freedoms – your stopping my doing so imposes four unfreedoms on me. As long as we count freedoms and unfreedoms symmetrically, the multiplicity of intensional act-token descriptions poses no danger of deforming our resultant calculation. Increments and decrements still receive their due deserts.

But although intensional multiplicity itself presents no serious double-counting difficulty for the "how many actions" approach to the "how free" question, it gestures in the direction of more formidable obstacles. One of these is that "multiplicity" may well be an understatement. For it seems that, in principle, my attending the auditorium performance could be not merely four different intensionally described act-tokens, nor even forty or four hundred, but rather an infinite number of them. Any of an indefinitely large number of reasons could be a reason for my attending. In which case, and keeping the example as simple as possible, how can token-counting yield the following comparative judgement which we know to be true: namely, that my friend who is free to attend both tonight and tomorrow is *more free* than I who am free to attend only tonight?[55] If we're each thereby free to do a virtually infinite number of act-tokens, how can sense be made of the true claim that he is more free than I am?[56]

Token-counting raises yet another problem of infinities, and one that threatens double-counting which clearly *is* distortive. An indication of it is to be found in an objection put by Onora O'Neill:

> If liberties are liberties to do certain actions, and actions can be individuated in diverse ways, then liberties can be individuated in diverse ways. If so it would always be possible to show that any given set of liberties was as numerous as any other merely by listing the component liberties more specifically. We can, if we want to, take any liberty . . . and divide it up into however many component liberties we find useful to distinguish – or for that matter into more than we find it useful to distinguish.[57]

Just as any behavioural event can be given an infinite number of intensional act-descriptions, so too (as we know from Zeno's paradoxes) can any action be subdivided into an infinite number of component actions. My attending tonight's play, for example, can be subdivided into my attending Act I, scene i, my attending Act I, scene ii, and so forth, with each of these being further and indefinitely subdivisible. The token-counter, counting each act-token as one unit, is committed to counting my

[55] Thus Lukes and Galnoor, *No Laughing Matter: A Collection of Political Jokes*, 126, report the following (pre-1989) conversation.

DUTCHMAN: Housing problems we Dutch can understand, but what must be so terrible for you is not having freedom of speech to complain about them.
CZECH: But we do have freedom of speech!
DUTCHMAN: What do you mean?
CZECH: We are free to say absolutely anything we like. The only difference is that we don't have freedom *after* speech.

[56] It may be mathematically true that some infinities are greater than others. And thus it might be thought that our comparative judgement in this particular example is based on the fact that my infinity is a subset of his, since we're both free to attend tonight but only he is free to attend tomorrow. But the subset relation promises no general solution to the multiple infinities problem and it may not even be a solution in this case.

[57] O'Neill, "The Most Extensive Liberty," 50.

attending tonight's performance along with its components along with their components and so on *ad infinitum*. That is, he is committed to an eternity of double-counting. Can he cope with this? Can we wait?

Clearly not. The "how many actions" approach must yield to the "how much action" approach to freedom measurement. We know that the infinite number of component actions doesn't *eo ipso* amount to an unperformable quantity of action. Achilles *does* win his race with the tortoise, despite the infinitely many stages at which the tortoise is leading. And we know, from the applicability of the subset relation in this case, that there is the same amount of action (whatever it is) involved in my attending tonight's performance as is involved in the sum of my attending Act I, scene i, my attending Act I, scene ii, etc.

How do we know this? What guarantees the subset relation here? It's simply and solely the fact that the *extensional* elements of each component action are a subset of the extensional elements of my attending tonight's performance. All the physical components – the physical objects and spatio-temporal locations – of each component action are identical to some of the physical components of my attending tonight's performance, and the latter's set of physical components is identical to the set of all component actions' physical components.

So once again, extensional description comes to our rescue. By specifying an action's physical components we can overcome the metrication problems posed by the threatened infinities of both O'Neill's individuation objection and the previously discussed multiplicity of intensional descriptions. Infinite divisibility and multiplicability are reduced to finite variables, the size of which determines how much action an act-token "contains" and hence how much freedom is enjoyed by or denied to a person unprevented or prevented from doing it.

Well then, just how much action is there in the act of my attending tonight's performance? To this question I respond with an embarrassed nod at my earlier disclaimer of the competence to supply a fully developed metric. The principal difficulty here is one of commensuration. How do we measure the sizes of an action's various physical components? Spatio-temporal locations, it's true, present no problem: we simply measure the differences between their co-ordinates. But what of heterogeneous physical objects? And how, in any case, would these two measurements be integrated in a single scale? I have no satisfying answers to these pressing questions. The author of a viable freedom-metric will.[58]

---

[58] And in doing so, will no doubt need to consult the sort of literature indicated in n. 42, above.

Nevertheless, some fairly illuminating inferences can be drawn from the foregoing discussions. Chief among these is what might grandiosely be called the *Law of Conservation of Liberty*, hereafter LCL. Being free to do an action is, we've seen, being in (actual or subjunctive) possession of its physical components. And everything is in someone's such possession. What I am free to do is a function of the things possessed by me, and what I am unfree to do is a function of the things possessed by others. My total liberty, the extent of my freedom, is inversely related to theirs. If I lose possession of something, someone else gains it and thereby gains the amount of freedom (whatever it is) which I've lost.

Accordingly, Berlin is wrong to claim that there can be social circumstances in which "an absolute loss of liberty occurs," and correct to claim that "Freedom for the pike is death for the minnows; the liberty of some must depend on the restraint of others."[59] If I may be indulged with a little bit of self-quotation, LCL captures the truth that "within the universe of agents, that is, within the class of beings who count as authors of actions and who are therefore the subjects of statements concerning freedom and prevention, there can be no such thing as an absolute loss of (or gain in) individual liberty."[60]

Intimations of something like LCL can be found in the works of others. Bentham observes that "As against the coercion applicable by individual to individual, no liberty can be given to one man but in proportion as it is taken away from another."[61] And interestingly, Marx, not commonly identified with the use of the negative conception of liberty, writes: "But does not freedom of the press exist in the land of censorship? . . . True, in the land of censorship the state has no freedom of the press, but one organ of the state has it, viz. the *government* . . . Does not the censor exercise daily an unconditional freedom of the press, if not directly, then indirectly?"[62] Thomas Pogge detects an implicit tendency, in Nozick's *Anarchy, State and Utopia*, "to think of freedom as a constant-sum good."[63]

What does the Law of Conservation of Liberty illuminate? Put quite generally, it helps to explain why projects for widespread emancipation and increasing personal liberty so often fail to deliver. Negative libertarians standardly treat the number of legal prohibitions prevailing in a society as an (inverse) index of the extent of personal liberty it affords.

[59] Berlin, *Four Essays on Liberty*, 125, 124; cf. Tawney, *Equality*, 238.

[60] Steiner, "Individual Liberty," 49–50.

[61] Bentham, "Anarchical Fallacies," 495.

[62] Marx, "Debates on Freedom of the Press, 1842," 155. I'm grateful to Jerry Cohen for drawing this passage to my attention.

[63] Pogge, *Realizing Rawls*, 51.

By "legal prohibitions" is meant activities (i.e. act-types) which are enforceably proscribed. The fewer such prohibitions there are, the more free its members are said to be.[64]

But this view of the matter is quite mistaken. For an oppressive tyrant may quite consistently promulgate only the briefest list of legal prohibitions governing his subjects' conduct – his statute books may be impeccably liberal – so long as he also takes the precaution of assigning to himself the legal possession of most things within his realm.[65] It's true that reference to this brief list would indicate that, to the extent that subjects are free in that society, their actions may be quite *varied*. But it would indicate nothing about the extent to which they are free. Thus it is common, and similarly mistaken, to regard the Hobbesian state of nature as a condition of maximum negative liberty. Mistaken, because although in it no legal officials get in the way of a person's acting, other people do. Act-type availability is no index of act-token availability.

Of course, proponents of this view could say (though they usually don't) that, among legal prohibitions, they would include enforced rules proscribing the use of other persons' legal possessions. The trouble with this reply is that there's no clear sense in which the repeal of such rules, or their modification by other enforced rules permitting persons to make some use of others' possessions, would increase liberty. A rule giving ramblers rights of way over agricultural land increases the freedom of ramblers. But it also reduces the liberty of farmers, by mandating the legal prevention of many actions which they might do involving their use of the land over which ramblers enjoy rights of way.

Similarly, a law abolishing slavery may confer a great deal of liberty on the emancipated slaves, as well as on others who are thereby no longer legally prevented from entering into various kinds of relation with those emancipated. But such a measure also considerably reduces some persons' freedom: namely, that of slave-owners. For prior to emancipation, slave-owners are not legally prevented from forcing their slaves to do anything. After it, they are. Conversely, emancipated slaves – who are thereby given legal possession of their own bodies but, typically,

---

[64] I leave aside, as irrelevant here, the distinction drawn earlier between enforcement by prevention and enforcement by punishment. For simplicity's sake, let's adopt these negative libertarians' tendency to speak of enforcement as preventative. Punitive enforcement *does* curtail liberty, but not the liberty to perform at least one token of the prohibited act-type.

[65] Cf. Steiner, "Liberty and Equality," 556–7, for a (then!) allegorical tale in which the Central Committee of the Communist Party of the Soviet Union, having resolved to liberalize the economy by deregulating and privatizing state industries, assigns all their private titles severally to its members.

little else – have often discovered their new-found liberty to be less extensive than advertised.

Two things, I think, lie behind this mistaken view. One is the already encountered failure to distinguish between act-types and their tokens, leading to a failure to appreciate that being unprevented from doing at least one of the latter is a condition of being free to do the former. Repealing a legal restriction on an act-type does not abolish legal preventions of its tokens. At most, it only redistributes the legal entitlement to initiate such preventions, from legal officials to others, as we saw in the earlier break-dancing example.

The second culprit seems to me to be an admirable but misguided inclination to think that aggregate personal liberty must be greater in those societies where its distribution is less unequal. Thus, to take the example just mentioned, it's a reasonably common view that liberty is greater in a society where slavery is absent than in one where it exists. Persons and political movements committed to its abolition have generally proclaimed themselves as acting to increase personal liberty within their societies. And yet slave-owners remained not only unconvinced of this but were, for the most part, firmly persuaded that they were faced with the prospect of a drastic diminution of their liberty. Was their incredulity misplaced? Was it the product of a simple failure to understand the concept of liberty and the contours of its quantification?

There is, in general, no reason to suppose that the range over which something is distributed implies anything much about its aggregate quantity. Indeed, the drearily familiar historical experience – of struggles for avowedly universal emancipation that succeed only in transferring large concentrations of liberty from one group to another – is more perspicuously described when the constant-sum character of liberty is understood. LCL tells us that aggregate personal liberty is not a variable social magnitude.[66]

Negative liberty is such that it makes no sense to speak of it as being aggregately increased or diminished – much less maximized or minimized – but only as being dispersed or concentrated to some particular extent. A universal quest for greater personal liberty is a zero-sum game. Undue neglect of this fact has resulted in many players having their attention distracted from normative questions about the distribution of liberty.

---

[66] Though the aggregate amount of personal liberty present in a particular society may vary, due to interaction (i.e. the imposition and removal of preventions) between its members and those of other societies. For a very schematic analysis of the interplay between intra- and inter-societal preventions, see Steiner, "How Free? Computing Personal Liberty," 85–9.

3
Rights

Much recent discussion of rights begins by reporting – and deploring – a proliferation of demands for rights of every imaginable sort. The demands are understandable since rights are, on the whole, highly desired items. Not so much in themselves, but rather for the contribution they make to one's doing and getting desired things: things desired either for oneself or in behalf of others. The worry is that these burgeoning shopping-lists of rights are compiled with insufficient regard for the fact that rights also have costs.

Those costs, like the rights they purchase, are almost infinitely varied. But what they all ultimately amount to are restrictions on persons' conduct. Any right entails a prescribed restriction on the activities of persons other than that right's holder or subject. And obviously enough, there can be deep disagreement over whether some rights are worth the restrictions they entail.

The philosopher's role in these circumstances is again a limited one. For there's no philosophically privileged answer to any question of whether some particular right is worth the restriction it entails. Philosophy cannot help to control the proliferation *that* way. But one thing it can do is to look at any item on these swollen shopping-lists and assess its credentials for being regarded as a right in the first place. To be sure, its deficient credentials wouldn't expel an item from some broader list of plausible moral and political values. Rather, such deficiencies would indicate simply that the item in question should be entered in a different section of the shopping-list than the rights section. The philosophical credentials-check can't reduce the overall length of our shopping-lists, but it can help to organize them better so we can know which shelves to go to for what, when we visit the relevant supermarket.

Credentials-checks do, however, presuppose that we're already in possession of a set of credentials. But that supposition is, at the moment anyway, somewhat optimistic. Only somewhat, because there *are* significant points of consensus on some of the features a thing must have to count as a right. Nevertheless optimistic, because not all such features are as yet matters of general agreement. And this suggests the possibility, which is indeed an actuality, that disputes about whether some shopping-list entries really are rights occur between credentials-checkers themselves.

Do these disputes matter? Should we care whether some particular moral or political value really is a right rather than some other type of value? After all, when we go to the supermarket in search of tomatoes, we're not much bothered by the fact that they're typically to be found in the vegetables section even though, strictly speaking, they are a fruit. Should we be any more concerned about the proper classification of different values?

As with most interesting questions, the answer to this one is "yes and no." No, if all we're concerned about is having an exhaustive inventory of our values. But yes, if we think that circumstances may frequently compel us to discriminate amongst our values, to advance some at the expense of others, *and* that a value's classification may have a bearing on such (usually painful) choices. It might matter to me whether a tomato is really a vegetable if my doctor has recommended an increase in my consumption of vegetables or if there is currently some virulent strain of bacteria afflicting fruit crops. Similarly, there may be reasons why rights should be given higher or lower priority than other types of value in situations where choices must be made. (Some of these reasons will be examined in chapter 6.) So a classified inventory of values is not without its uses. And to secure that, we need a set of credentials for rights.

Here are some features which have been attributed to rights or presupposed about them in legal and moral discussion of them. I list these in loosely ascending order of contestability since general agreement on the full characterization of what counts as a right is lacking.

1 Rights are constituted by rules. (The rules constituting *moral* rights are standardly taken to be those of *justice*.)
2 Rights signify a bilateral normative relation between those who hold them (their subjects) and those against whom they are held (their objects).
3 These relations entail the presence or absence of constraints on the conduct (performances and forbearances) of objects.
4 These constraints consist in objects' duties (obligations) or in

their disabilities (lack of capacities to alter subjects' normative relations with objects).

5   Rights are exercisable.

6   This exercisability consists in subjects' capacity to control objects' constraints by either extinguishing them or securing compliance with them.

7   This capacity to control objects' constraints is a capacity to determine whether objects' actions should be prevented.

8   Rights prescribe interpersonal distributions of pure negative liberty.

Most credentials-checkers, most accounts of what rights are, accept features (1) to (4) on this list. But only some accept (5) and (6), and fewer still have included (7) and (8) as features of rights. I believe that all eight items are features of any right: that is, that (6) is a correct interpretation of (5), that (7) and (8) are successively inferable from (6) and that (5) is independently defensible.

Indeed on the face of it, it may seem odd that (5) should require any defence at all. The idea that rights are things which are exercisable deeply permeates both ordinary language and standard legal usage. Next to our minds and our muscles, rights are what we exercise most.

So it may be as well to note, at this early stage of the discussion, that those who deny a place on this list to (5), as well as (6), (7), and (8), are not committed to some valiant defence of the utterly untenable view that *no* rights are exercisable. Some rights, they would readily acknowledge, are indeed exercisable. But in their view exercisability is thus a contingent feature of rights, not a necessary one, and hence not a credential of rights. Part of my argument to the contrary will be an effort to show that the leading proffered examples of non-exercisable rights are defective and fail to support that denial.

These opposed views on exercisability are respectively associated with the *Will* or *Choice Theory* of rights on the one hand and the *Interest* or *Benefit Theory* on the other. Hereafter I'll refer to these simply as the Choice Theory and the Benefit Theory.[1] One way of characterizing the difference between these rival theories is this. According to Choice Theory, a right exists when the necessary and sufficient condition, of

[1] The classic statement of modern Choice Theory is Hart's 1973 essay "Bentham on Legal Rights," republished in his *Essays on Bentham*; see also his "Are There Any Natural Rights?" Some of the more influential recent presentations of the Benefit Theory include: Raz, "On the Nature of Rights," and *The Morality of Freedom*, part III; MacCormick, "Rights in Legislation"; and Lyons, "Rights, Claimants and Beneficiaries." On the early modern origins of this controversy, see Tuck, *Natural Rights Theories*.

imposing or relaxing the constraint on some person's conduct, is another person's choice to that effect. Whereas according to Benefit Theory, such imposition or relaxation must be in conformity with what would generally better serve that other's important interests, i.e. regardless of his or her own choices in the matter.

This way of formulating the distinction enables us to see how Benefit Theory can allow that some rights are exercisable. For there can be many circumstances where subjects' important interests are better served by those persons themselves having controlling choices over the constraints on objects' conduct. But where such circumstances are absent and subjects lack such control, Benefit Theory can nevertheless ascribe rights to them whereas Choice Theory cannot.

It hardly needs saying that for the difference between these theories to be as non-trivial as their respective advocates consider it to be, our criteria for what count as persons' choices and what constitute their important interests must be logically independent of one another. If no choice of mine could be understood to *be* a choice unless it selected the option that better served my important interests or, conversely, if my important interests were to be definitionally construed as consisting in having my choices prevail, much of the analytical and practical difference between these rival theories would evidently evaporate. But since we *are* able to recognize many situations as ones where persons' choices are at variance with what would advance their important interests, the requisite logical independence exists to underwrite the authenticity of the difference between Choice Theory and Benefit Theory.

Disagreement over what count as rights is, however, not confined to the controversy between Choice and Benefit theorists. For differences also exist within each of these two camps. Accordingly, another aim of my argument is to show that several qualifications conceded by some Choice Theorists on the analytical scope of their account are unwarranted, inasmuch as these rest upon Benefit Theory assumptions. By shedding these qualifications and attending closely to how coherent sets of rights assign control to their subjects, we shall see more clearly how rights operate to prescribe distributions of pure negative freedom.

(A) CHOICES AND BENEFITS

The beginning of wisdom in these matters is widely agreed to be the classification of juridical positions developed by Wesley N. Hohfeld.[2] Complaining of the imprecision with which both lawyers and the general public have tended to use the word "rights" when referring to the conduct-constraining implications of legal rules, Hohfeld distinguished no fewer than four quite different positions any one of which might be held by persons commonly and indiscriminately described as right-holders: claims, liberties, powers and immunities. Holders of any one of these positions are placed, by the rules constituting them, in certain bilateral relations to others who thereby hold correlatively entailed positions with regard to the conduct governed by those rules.

Only a brief rehearsal of the basic aspects of the Hohfeldian classification of positions and relations will be needed here. Among the more recent analytical discussions of it, those supplied by Carl Wellman and L. W. Sumner are especially illuminating and repay careful study.[3]

The reason why this classification is important and not restricted in its interest to the technical concerns of lawyers is that only some of these positions (or combinations of them) imply the presence of constraints on others' conduct. Since such constraint is an uncontested feature of rights, it is the holding of only some of these positions, or some combinations of them, that amounts to having rights.

The position most commonly identified with having a right is what Hohfeld calls a *claim*. If Red has a claim that Blue pay him five pounds, that claim correlatively entails that Blue has a *duty* to pay Red five pounds. Claims are regarded by Hohfeld as rights "in the strictest sense." Almost equally common, however, are misleading assertions that one has a right to do things which one has no duty not to do: "I have a right to wear mis-matched socks." What is actually being asserted here

---

[2] Hohfeld, *Fundamental Legal Conceptions*.

[3] Cf. Wellman, *A Theory of Rights*, chs 1, 2; Sumner, *The Moral Foundation of Rights*, ch. 2. Both works propose several critical amendments of Hohfeld's interpretation of his classificatory scheme. Sumner helpfully distinguishes its "pragmatic" from its "semantic" aspects. A considerably more elaborate scheme is presented by Kocourek, *Jural Relations*.

is more precisely denoted as a *liberty*.⁴ Other terms sometimes used to
refer to this absence of a duty include privilege, licence and permission.⁵
If Red has no claim that Blue pay him five pounds, Blue has a liberty
not to pay him five pounds and Red has what is called (for lack of an
idiomatic term) a *no-claim* that Blue pay him five pounds.

These paired relationships between Red and Blue – claim/duty and no-
claim/liberty – hold in respect of some specified act on the part of Blue
(the act of paying Red five pounds) and determine the permissibility of
its performance or forbearance. Red's having a claim and Blue a duty
with respect to this act entail that Blue's not paying is impermissible.
Conversely, Blue's having a liberty and Red a no-claim with respect to
it entail that Blue's not paying is permissible.

Sets of rules constituting these relationships also create positions
which have to do with their alterability. Thus although Blue may have
no duty (may have a liberty not) to pay Red five pounds – and Red thus
have a no-claim that she do so – Red may have the authority, or what
is often called a *power*, to impose such a duty on her. In which case,
she is describable as having a *liability* to be subjected to this duty.⁶
Conversely, if Red lacks this power, Blue enjoys an *immunity* against
being subjected to this duty by Red and he, correspondingly, has a *disability* to subject her to it.⁷

In general, we may regard this latter set of positions and the relationships between them as "second-order" or "procedural" ones. They are
so because they signify rule-constituted capacities and incapacities to

⁴ Liberty, in this *normative* or *evaluative* or *rule-constituted* sense, is to be distinguished
from the *descriptive* or *empirical* concept – absence of prevention – which formed the
subject of the previous chapter and which I shall henceforth refer to as "freedom" where
confusion between the two might otherwise occur. Cf. Feinberg, *Social Philosophy*, 55.

⁵ As various writers have noted, these terms may have slightly different additional con-
notations depending on the other contents of the set of rules implying this absence of duty:
a privilege or a licence is typically an exceptional absence of a duty of a type which is
normally present. Nevertheless all of them refer to an absence of duty.

⁶ A further aspect of any power is that it entails the liberty to exercise it. Thus Red can
be said to have the power to subject Blue to a duty to pay him five pounds only if he has
the liberty to do so and she the correlative no-claim that he not do so. If, on the contrary,
Red lacks this liberty and thus has a duty not to subject Blue to the duty of paying him
five pounds, he would also lack the power to subject her to that payment duty. So powers
and their correlative liabilities respectively entail liberties and their correlative no-claims.

⁷ Following the previous footnote's reasoning, we can see that since Red's disability is
his lack of a power, this entails his lack of a liberty and thus his having a duty which, in
turn, correlatively entails that someone (as the holder of the immunity correlative to Red's
disability), usually Blue, has a claim. On the reducibility of power/liability and
immunity/disability relations to liberty/no-claim and claim/duty relations, see Ross, *Directives and Norms*, 118–20, and Lindahl, *Position and Change*, 212ff.

alter "first-order" (claim/duty, liberty/no-claim) relationships and, indeed, other second-order relationships as well. Second-order positions are of particular significance since it is these that come into play when we consider the vexed question of whether rights are necessarily exercisable. To ask whether a right is exercisable is to ask whether its subject is vested with powers both to waive and to secure its object's compliance with the duty or disability correlatively entailed by it.[8]

Simply stated then, the (unqualified) Choice Theory thesis is that something is a right if it is either a claim or an immunity to which are attached powers of waiver and enforcement over its correlative constraint.[9] Looked at the other way round, the thesis states that anyone who holds those powers over a duty or disability holds a right correlative to it.

Equipped with this Hohfeldian terminology, we can now turn to the substance of what is at issue between the two rival theories of rights. A fact of some immediacy here is that not all of the benefits which our duties require us to bestow on others are ones to which they have rights (claims). I'm quite certain that I have a duty to supply you with directions if you've lost your way in my neighbourhood, to loan you my car if you're a reliable friend, and to be courteous in my dealings with you. But I'm equally certain that you have no right that I do so. So my duties to *benefit* you can outnumber your rights against me.

In another respect, however, your rights against me can outnumber my duties to benefit *you*. For you can have a right, and I the correlative duty, the beneficiary of which is not you at all but rather some third party. Suppose I am a florist. The order you place with me makes you, and not the bride and groom, the holder of the right correlative to my duty to deliver flowers to their wedding. What if you were to cancel your order? Would I still be said to have that duty to deliver? Evidently not.[10]

---

[8] "Compliance with a disability" is, at best, an awkward formulation and not a little opaque in terms of both ordinary and legal usage. What securing compliance with a disability amounts to is securing the nullification of an object's presumed exercise of a power which, having that disability, he or she lacks.

[9] Much ink has been needlessly spilt in disputes over whether all rights entail correlative constraints. The view that some don't trades on the undiscriminating use of the term "rights" noted by Hohfeld. Clearly, neither no-claims nor liabilities are in themselves constraints on the conduct of those who have them: they do not imply, of any act, that it is impermissible. And thus neither liberties nor powers are rights in themselves. Duties and disabilities *are* constraints and only their correlatives (claims, immunities) count as rights.

[10] Of course, I may nonetheless have *a* duty to deliver but this would not be a correlative one. That is, I may have a duty quite independently of your placing the order (and hence, irrespective of your cancelling it) to deliver the flowers: perhaps because not to would greatly disserve the couple's interests, or because they are friends of mine, or because they

It's important to notice, however, that the position is quite otherwise when we consider the matter of loaning my car to you. For your indication that it's not incumbent upon me to do so – your saying "You needn't; I can manage without it" – would not absolve me from my duty to do so. Your having no right to this loan is utterly beside the point, so far as what I ought to do for you is concerned. Only Plato and a few misguided others have ever imagined that the demands of rights or justice encompass all our duties, that all our duties are correlative ones.

Here then is a significant feature of *correlative* duties and one which sharply distinguishes them from other duties we have to confer benefits. It is that their existence is controllable and that our non-compliance with them is rendered permissible – they are extinguished or waived – by virtue of a choice to that effect by the persons who control them but not by the persons whose interests are served by their being performed (where the two are different parties). If your flower order stands, I have a correlative duty to deliver. And if you cancel, I no longer have that duty: not even if my not delivering would seriously disserve the marrying couple's interests. With respect to my delivering the flowers, they are the beneficiaries but they are not the right-holders.

This fact, that the beneficiaries of a claim/duty relation can be rightless third parties, poses a considerable difficulty for Benefit Theory. (Nor, as we shall presently see, are such cases confined to claim/duty relations created by contract, as occurs in the flower delivery example.) For these are cases where right-holders not only lack the essential characteristic required by that theory, but also they possess the essential characteristic required by Choice Theory. It is the controllers of the duty, and not its beneficiaries, who are the right-holders. Your possession of the powers both to demand my performance of the delivery duty and, alternatively, to waive it makes you the holder of the right correlative to it. Contrary to Benefit Theory, there is no one-to-one correspondence between being a right-holder and being the beneficiary of a correlative duty.

What avenues of reply are open to Benefit Theorists? They could argue, unpersuasively I think, that you too are a beneficiary of my duty to deliver the flowers inasmuch as your interests are served by the satisfaction you derive from bestowing this gift on the marrying couple. But apart from posing the previously mentioned danger of trivializing the Benefit Theory thesis, this argument fails to explain why, of these putatively two benefiting parties, it is only you and not also the couple who

---

deserve such a service. But whatever might be the reasons for my having this duty, it entails no corresponding right on their part. That is, this duty (if it exists) is implied by a moral rule other than the rule enjoining respect for rights.

are the right-holder. It fails to explain why, if both parties would benefit from my delivering, my duty to do so can nonetheless be permissibly cancelled by your choice to that effect and, moreover, cancelled only by *your* choice and not theirs as well or instead.

A more effective line of reply might be to argue that you are indeed a benefiting right-holder in this case, not perhaps because of your derived satisfaction, but rather because this is an instance where an important interest of yours is served precisely by your having controlling powers over the disposition of some of your resources: in the present case, the resources needed to enter into that contract with me. The trouble with this reply is that what is doing the explanatory work here is not your interest but your control: the reference to your interest is entirely superfluous. Information about your interests would doubtless furnish some insight into why you exercise your right against me in whichever way you choose to do. It may even go some distance toward justifying your having that right. But it sheds little light on the reasons why what you have can be said to *be* a right. That is, it sheds no light on the conceptual difference between your position in the flower-delivery contract and your position as my friend to whom I ought to loan my car.

A further attempt by Benefit Theorists to meet the challenge of third party beneficiary arguments is to be found in a nice example devised by Neil MacCormick who begins by conceding the difficulty involved:

> If A and B make a contract which has a provision for the benefit of C, it follows that there is a duty under the contract for the benefit of C. Therefore, if the benefit theory is true, C has a right under the contract, but in some (indeed most) legal systems the existence of third-party rights under contract is not recognized, so the benefit theory cannot be true.

This seems to support the Choice Theory thesis. But, says MacCormick,

> Observe that the argument proves too much, for with an obvious modification it applies to the will [choice] theory too. If A and B make a contract containing a provision in favour of C, to be carried out by B if C requests, but not if C does not request, is there a right in favour of C? Not under English law, even though that duty of B's has been set up so that its performance is at C's option. The point in both cases is that under English law (unlike Scots law in either case) A and B retain the power to alter the provisions of their contract without C's consent.[11]

---

[11] MacCormick, "Rights in Legislation," 208–9.

The intended force of this example, if it works, is evidently not to defend Benefit Theory so much as to embarrass Choice Theory. Does it work?

Surely not. Just who has a right here, A or C, turns entirely on whether that contractual provision is *revocable*. What is certain in either case, however, is that only one of them has a right. If it is revocable, as English law maintains, then it gives C no right despite her status as beneficiary. Her request that B perform his duty, or her declining to request it, does not amount to control inasmuch as either can be overridden by the contracting parties. As a term of the contract affecting B's duty, the role of C's option is essentially that of an operative fact and not a set of powers. It has much the same functional status as contractual stipulations regarding variable weather conditions: "If it rains, the game is off; if not, you play unless I decide otherwise." On the other hand, if the contractual provision is irrevocable, as it can be under certain circumstances in Scots law, then C indeed has a right but A hasn't, and his choices cannot override C's with regard to B's performance.[12] The effect of making a contractual provision irrevocable is to transfer control over B's duty from A to C. In short, whether the provision is revocable or irrevocable, the right-holder is whoever controls B's duty. Whether that party is also the beneficiary is of no relevance.

Thus we can see that what the Benefit Theory badly needs, in order to offset the damage inflicted on its thesis by rightless third party beneficiary cases, are some significant cases exemplifying reverse situations. That is, some cases where either (i) right-holders benefit from but do not control others' duties, or (ii) controllers of others' duties are not right-holders. And it purports to find just such cases in many provisions of criminal and constitutional law. Indeed, it is precisely these cases that are acknowledged by many leading Choice Theorists, including H. L. A. Hart, as warranting what was previously referred to as a qualification on the scope of the Choice Theory account of rights. How strong are the grounds for this warrant?

The limiting cases in question are what I shall call the *unwaivables*. Unwaivability, it is argued, is a characteristic feature of the duties imposed by criminal or public – as opposed to civil or private – law. For example, insofar as the criminal law is construed as conferring upon me a right not to be assaulted, the duty of others not to do so is not waivable by me. My expression of a willingness to be assaulted (with the licensed exceptions of things like boxing matches, rugby games, etc.) is insuf-

[12] Cf. Walker, *The Law of Contracts and Related Obligations in Scotland*, ch. 29, "Rights of third parties under contracts," 449–82.

ficient to preclude my assailant's being charged with a breach of duty. These are cases where "consent is no defence." And they are thus contrasted with those of duties to deliver flowers, where the right-holder's consent to non-delivery *does* supply a defence against any breach of duty charge.

The implications of such cases for Choice Theory have been variously interpreted. One conclusion might be that they suggest the greater generality and, hence, superiority of the Benefit Theory account of rights. David Miller remarks:

> May it not be that one reason for depriving a person of the choice whether or not to exercise his right is the overriding importance of that right to him? This hypothesis would fit the circumstances of the criminal law, where the most serious kinds of harm that could be done to a man are prohibited by legal duties over which he has no control. In the sphere of civil law, by comparison, where a person generally has a choice whether or not to press his rights, much less serious forms of injury are involved. Hart wants to establish a basic connection between the having of a right and the exercise of free choice, and no doubt the connection holds in many cases, but it seems equally vital to link rights with the basic security of the person.[13]

An alternative view, advanced by more sympathetic critics of Choice Theory and wholly or partly conceded by many Choice Theorists themselves, is that criminal law duties are simply not correlative ones at all and, hence, entail no rights whatsoever. Richard Flathman points out that

> Jones can be arrested and punished for reckless driving even if no A [member of society] is harmed by or so much as witnesses Jones' violation. Thus on Hart's theory one must say either that Cs (policemen, judges, etc.) have a blanket authorization to exercise the rights of As on their behalf or that the element of "self-administration" [control] that is usually part of having a right is simply not a necessary part of many of the rights one has as a member of political society. It seems preferable to say that Jones has the obligation under the law (as opposed to owing it to other citizens with

---

[13] Miller, *Social Justice*, 63. See also Marshall, "Rights, Options and Entitlements," 234–9, and MacCormick, "Rights in Legislation," 197–8.

a correlative right) and that Cs have both authority and a duty to arrest and punish Jones for his violation.[14]

Is it therefore true that criminal law duties must be understood as entailing either Benefit Theory rights or, indeed, no rights at all? Are criminal law duties uncontrollable? Are they like my duty to loan my car to my friend? What is certainly true is that any Choice Theory rights which might be correlatively entailed by criminal law duties cannot be located in ordinary citizens. Miller and Flathman are quite correct to observe that such citizens lack the requisite control over those duties.

But contrary to the theory's critics, it's not true that Choice Theory rights do not exist in the criminal law. A first step toward seeing why they do exist there is to note the significance of the fact that both of the previous quotations appeal to considerations of the *harm* to be incurred or avoided by those persons whom they presume to be the putative hold-ers of any rights correlative to criminal law duties. That is, they suggest that the Choice Theory of rights is defective because of its inability to account for the fact that it is *ordinary citizens*, as the beneficiaries of those criminal law duties, who cannot control them.

This criticism, however, suffers from severely disabling circularity inasmuch as it simply presupposes the truth of the Benefit Theory thesis. In finding that the criminal law vests no Choice Theory rights in those whose interests it broadly protects (i.e. ordinary citizens), and thence inferring that the criminal law creates no Choice Theory rights at all, it ineluctably relies on the unstated assumption that a necessary condition of being a right-holder is being the beneficiary of a duty. We have al-ready seen that this is not the case. For what such reasoning entirely overlooks is the fact that the juridical position of an ordinary citizen can readily be described as that of a *third party beneficiary* of criminal law duties and that Choice Theory rights, correlative to those duties, can straightforwardly be located in *state officials*.[15]

As noted above, some Choice Theorists have themselves been reluc-tant to extend the application of their analytical model from civil to criminal law. We'll presently examine the grounds for this reluctance. Before doing so, it's worth remarking that writers on the criminal law itself appear not to share this reluctance, insofar as they perceive no

---

[14] Flathman, *The Practice of Rights*, 237–8. See also Hart, *Essays on Bentham*, 181–6, and Kearns, "Rights, Benefits and Normative Systems," 478–9.

[15] It is, of course, a disputed matter as to whether there are *any* beneficiaries of such criminal law duties, past and present, as prohibit attempted suicide, voluntary euthanasia or homosexual activity between consenting adults.

great conceptual divide between civil and criminal law. In his classic text on the subject, C. S. Kenny observes:

> There is indeed no fundamental or inherent difference between a crime and a tort . . . In the first stages of national development there is little or no police organization and the sanctions of crime are freely left to the hands of ordinary citizens . . . Crimes therefore originate in the government policy of the moment.[16]

And G. W. Paton, having suggested that the principal reason for distinguishing between public and private law is to accord due recognition to the "importance of the peculiar character of the State," comments that

> Nevertheless, this distinction has not always been clearly marked. Until the State itself has developed, public law is a mere embryo. Even in the days of feudalism there is much confusion; for no clear line can be drawn between the public and private capacities of the king. Jurisdiction, office and even kingship are looked upon as property – indeed public law might almost be regarded as "a mere appendix" to the law of real property so far as the feudal ideal is realized.[17]

Nor has the underlying conceptual structure of the juridical relations involved in criminal offences changed with the passage of time. P. J. Fitzgerald reports that it's still the case that "in England prosecutions are nearly all in theory private prosecutions. Not only may any private person in general prosecute another, but in most cases the prosecutor, who is normally a police officer, prosecutes by virtue of his right to prosecute as a private citizen."[18] Hence on the face of it, there would seem to be no obstacle to extending the Choice Theory model to cover criminal law duties and saying that, whereas civil law confers Choice Theory rights on ordinary citizens, criminal law vests them in state officials.

Why, then, have Choice Theorists – let alone their critics – been reluctant to make this move? Some of the motivation for this reluctance arises

---

[16] Turner, *Kenny's Outlines of Criminal Law*, 1, 2, 4. See also Goebel, *Felony and Misdemeanor: A Study in the History of Criminal Law*, passim, and Ashworth, *Principles of Criminal Law*, 1–2.

[17] Paton, *A Text-book of Jurisprudence*, 328.

[18] Fitzgerald, *Criminal Law and Punishment*, 2.

from considerations alluded to in the passages just quoted from Kenny and Fitzgerald and concerns the *enforcement* of criminal law duties. Specifically, it has to do with the lack of discretionary control available to state officials over the enforcement of such duties, a discretion which right-holders uncontestedly do possess in respect of civil law duties. Thus Flathman, a critic of some aspects of Choice Theory, was previously quoted as reporting that officials have not only the authority to arrest and punish criminal law violators but also the *duty* to do so.

And Thomas Kearns, himself a Choice Theorist, conceding that the Choice Theory model seems to have the "awkward result" of conferring rights on state officials, seeks to finesse this apparently unwanted implication by arguing as follows:

> It might be supposed, for example, that under the criminal law I have a right not to be robbed. But unlike, say, a promisee, I cannot discharge the intruder of his obligation not to rob me (the crime, we say, is against the State) ... It might appear, then, that my robber offends only an official's rights, but not mine ... Two responses are in order. First, it is by no means clear that I acquire any rights under the criminal law ... Second, the enforcement official does not acquire any rights on my account for he is under an obligation to take the enforcement action and is, therefore, unfree under the legal rules to discharge or in any other way to alter the obligation or forgive its breach.[19]

So the question we need to consider is whether this latter argument successfully resists the view that the criminal law vests rights in state officials.

Kearns's remarks serve to illuminate a particularly important aspect of Choice Theory rights: namely, the connection between the waivability and the enforceability of their correlative duties. These two characteristics and, more generally, the discretionary control they *jointly* confer on a right-holder over another person's duty are uncontestedly present in civil law and have been lucidly described in a well-known passage by Hart:

> In the area of conduct covered by that duty the individual who has the right is a small-scale sovereign to whom the duty is owed. The fullest measure of control comprises three distinguishable elements:

---

[19] Kearns, "Rights, Benefits and Normative Systems," 478. See also Ross, *On Law and Justice*, 163–4, and *Directives and Norms*, 128.

(i) the right holder may waive or extinguish the duty or leave it in existence; (ii) after breach or threatened breach of duty he may leave it "unenforced" or may "enforce" it by suing for compensation or, in certain cases, for an injunction or mandatory order to restrain the continued or further breach of duty; and (iii) he may waive or extinguish the obligation to pay compensation to which the breach gives rise.[20]

These three elements, which are the *powers* associated with a right, are also a set of *liberties*. That is, each of them (including the third) refers to a pair of mutually opposed or alternative procedural actions which it is permissible for the right-holder to do – which he "may" do – and which he therefore has no duty not to do, in respect of the duty owed him. To have a duty to perform a procedural action, i.e. exercise a power, is to lack the liberty to perform its alternative and, hence, it is to lack that power.[21]

The argument that the criminal law vests no Choice Theory rights in officials (much less anyone else) can thus be seen to rest on the contention that state officials are vested with only some, but not all, of these powers. Having duties to exercise some of these powers, they lack the liberties to exercise their opposed alternatives which they therefore do not have. Lacking those latter powers, they lack the discretionary control which Choice Theory attributes to right-holders.

To make this more clear, let's set out the six powers involved:

1   to waive compliance with the duty (i.e. extinguish it);
2   to leave the duty in existence (i.e. demand compliance with it);
3   to waive proceeding for the enforcement of the duty (i.e. for the restraint of, or compensation by, the duty-holder in the face of threatened or actual breach) and thereby forgive its breach;
4   to demand proceeding for the enforcement of the duty;
5   to waive enforcement;
6   to demand enforcement.[22]

---

[20] Hart, *Essays on Bentham*, 183–4.

[21] See nn. 6 and 7, above, on powers as entailing liberties and on absence of liberties (presence of duties) as entailing absence of powers (presence of disabilities).

[22] I add this sixth power to Hart's listed five for the sake of completeness. In non-legal and other non-institutional contexts, there may be no rules enjoining others to provide proceedings or enforcement services. In which case, powers (3) and (4) would not exist and (6) would simply be one to secure enforcement oneself.

Kearns's reasons for denying that the criminal law duty not to rob vests a correlative right in a state official can now be stated more precisely. According to him, while it's true that officials possess (4) and (6), what they lack is (5) and "therefore" (1) and (3).

That is, although officials are empowered and thus at liberty to demand compliance with the duty not to rob and to demand proceedings and enforcement against suspected and convicted robbers, they also have duties to do so. Having duties to do so, they lack the liberties *not* to do so. Lacking the liberties not to do so, they lack the powers not to do so. If state officials *did* have the waiving powers as well as the demanding ones, they would undeniably be Choice Theory right-holders. So we need to inspect more closely the case for supposing officials to lack waiving powers.

Is it true that they lack them? Evidently *some* state officials do. But I suggest that, if these powers were lacking in *all* state officials, we should be very hard put to explain the occurrence of such standard criminal law practices as plea-bargaining and the granting of clemency, pardons, reprieves, paroles and immunities from prosecution. In most modern legal systems, these practices account for the disposition of the vast majority of criminal cases.[23] And what they consist of, *inter alia*, is subordinate officials having their duties to exercise (4) or (6) waived by their superiors. It is of course true that, in so waiving, superior officials also impose duties on their subordinates not to exercise (4) or (6), i.e. they deprive them of (4) or (6).

The withdrawal of these powers is certainly sufficient grounds for denying that rights correlative to criminal law duties are vested in *those* subordinate officials. But it's not sufficient grounds for denying – on the contrary, it confirms – that such rights vest in their superiors.

Superior officials are related to their subordinates as principals to agents.[24] In the standard nominal treatment of criminal law offences, superiors assign (4) and (6) to their subordinates. They thereby mandate them to prosecute and punish offenders. But in many cases, and for a variety of reasons, superior officials withhold (4) or (6) and instead man-

---

[23] Cf. Ashworth, *Principles of Criminal Law*, ch. 1, and Waldron, *The Law*, ch. 6. A colourful depiction of these practices at work is provided in Tom Wolfe's novel, *The Bonfire of the Vanities*. See also Zander, "How Bargains are Struck," and Wertheimer, "Freedom, Morality, Plea-Bargaining and the Supreme Court," 203–34. What the plea-bargaining or immunity-granting official is doing, in forgiving the breach of one duty and securing the enforcement of another – duties whose respective beneficiaries may well be different persons – is clearly acting *as if* both of the correlative rights in question were *his* and not those of the beneficiaries.

[24] Cf. Hohfeld, *Fundamental Legal Conceptions*, 53.

date the exercise of (3) or (5). That is, in the manner of typical civil law right-holders, such superior officials have the breach of a criminal law duty forgiven or its enforcement waived.

Isn't this sufficient to prove that *superior* state officials are indeed vested with Choice Theory rights correlative to criminal law duties? Almost but not quite. For it could nonetheless be objected that, even if they do control powers (3) and (5) as well, they still lack (1). That is, although superior officials are empowered to forgive non-compliance with such duties *ex post*, they still lack the power to waive compliance with them *ex ante*. Their being able to waive (proceeding for) enforcement against a robber does not itself imply their being able to waive his duty not to rob.

What sorts of argument are needed to prove that such state officials lack (1)? To be disempowered in this way, they must lack the liberty, i.e. have duties not, to exercise (1). Such a duty is a Hohfeldian disability. For superior state officials to have this disability, they must lack the power to waive a person's duty not to commit a robbery.

Now there clearly are legal systems where superior state officials do have this power. Having it, they're at liberty to exempt persons from compliance with an otherwise general criminal law duty such as that not to rob: they can confer privileges and immunities upon themselves and others. No doubt this power is exercised sparingly, and for sound reasons. But that is beside the point. In such legal systems, we're bound to conclude, these officials lack any such disability and they therefore possess (1).

However, it's also true that some legal systems are ones where these superior officials lack this power. They lack it by virtue of certain disabling *constitutional* provisions. And indeed, this type of consideration is seen by Hart and others as imposing a limitation on the scope of his Choice Theory of rights.[25]

Does it? Disabilities correlatively entail immunities. To claim that no state official can waive compliance with a criminal law duty is to claim that any such official is encumbered with a disability which is unwaivable by the holder of the correlative immunity. For brevity's sake, let's refer to any such immunity – any immunity whose correlative disability cannot be waived by that immunity's holder – as an *unwaivable immunity*. Can there *be* unwaivable immunities?

Like ordinary citizens, subordinate state officials are standardly

---

[25] Hart, *Essays on Bentham*, 188–93. For example, the Fourteenth Amendment to the American Constitution disables state legislatures from denying equal protection of the laws to any citizen.

disabled from waiving compliance with criminal law duties. Thus Yellow, a subordinate state official, holds a disability to waive a person's duty not to rob. Yellow's superior, let's call her Black, therefore holds an immunity against Yellow's doing so. Can Black waive her own immunity? What would be implied in denying her the power to do so? For Black's immunity to be an unwaivable one she, in turn, would have to be encumbered with a disability: namely, the disability to waive Yellow's disability. But if Black does hold such a disability then some still more superior official, call him Green, must hold an immunity correlative to Black's disability.[26]

We could, I suppose, continue indefinitely adding such epicycles to this line of reasoning by imagining that Green's immunity too is unwaivable and identifying yet another even more superior official, Orange, who in turn holds the immunity correlative to Green's thereby entailed disability. And so on. Let's not do that. For the sufficiently unmistakable point here is that wherever we decide to stop this otherwise infinite regress, it can be stopped only by an immunity which *is* waivable. Unwaivable immunities (eventually!) entail waivable ones. So, yes, there can be unwaivable immunities. But what there can't be are unwaivable immunities without there also being a waivable one. And the waiving of that one renders waivable whatever (otherwise unwaivable) immunity entails it.

What this demonstrates is that state officials' disabilities cannot be absolute ones. An official has a disability only so long as a superior refrains from waiving it. And even if a constitution disables some superior official from waiving it, there must be some still more superior official in a Hohfeldian position to release him from that disability. Hence that still more superior official controls (1) and is not disempowered from either conferring it on or withholding it from a subordinate. In most cases, of course, ordinary citizens can be presumed to be (third party) beneficiaries of this more superior official's withholding, from subordinates, the power to waive compliance with such criminal law duties as those not to rob.[27]

So the inference to be drawn is *not* that Choice Theory rights are absent from criminal and constitutional law. On the contrary, they are

---

[26] Cf. MacCormick, "Rights in Legislation," 195–6, for an acknowledgement that immunities which are unwaivable thereby entail the presence of disabilities in the immunity-holders themselves. Whereas a waivable immunity implies a single relation between two persons, an unwaivable immunity implies a pair of relations between three persons.

[27] This may not be true of all criminal law duties; see n. 15, above, for examples of some possible exceptions.

very much present in it and are to be found fairly high up in the hierarchy of state officials. Just how high up will depend on whether the legal system contains a constitution and, if so, what its particular provisions are. Hence the general point stands: namely, that no conceptual distinction exists – with respect to the presence or absence of Choice Theory rights – between the relationship of superior to subordinate state officials and, say, the relationship of superior to subordinate officers in a private corporation. The latter uncontestedly offers no resistance to the ascription of (civil law) rights. Nor therefore should the former, as regards ascriptions of (criminal law) rights.[28]

Where does all this leave us, with regard to the rival theories of rights? Not only does the Choice Theory model succeed where the Benefit Theory model fails: namely, in describing the jural relations pertaining to third party beneficiaries of correlative duties. It's also perfectly capable of describing the conduct-constraining implications of criminal and constitutional law: that is, those sets of jural relations which have sometimes been said to elude its analytical grasp. It thus appears able to withstand the criticisms standardly levelled against it and to offer an account of rights that is of notably greater generality than that advanced by the Benefit Theory. So although the following sections will reveal a significant additional reason for favouring the Choice Theory, I shall take the foregoing arguments as sufficient to vindicate its central thesis that rights are claims or immunities to which are attached powers of waiver and enforcement over their correlative constraints. Hereafter, our concern will be chiefly with first-order rights, i.e. claims.

---

[28] Anticipations of this general argument are to be found in: Holland, *The Elements of Jurisprudence*, 125–7; Gray, *The Nature and Sources of the Law*, 19–20, 79–83; Williams, *Salmond on Jurisprudence*, 264–5.

(B) LIBERTIES AND DUTIES

If the Choice Theory is correct, then all rights are indeed exercisable: all rights entail control over the duties of others. What we want to know now is how this feature of rights supports my earlier suggestion that rights thereby prescribe interpersonal distributions of pure negative freedom. The connection is not immediately obvious. For although a person may be said to have the *freedom* to do something, Glanville Williams correctly remarks that "No one ever has a right to do something; he only has a right that some one else shall do (or refrain from doing) something. In other words, every right in the strict sense relates to the conduct of another."[29] Of course, one freedom which my rights *do* assign to me (or my agents) is the freedom to do acts enforcing the correlatively dutiful conduct of others. If you have a duty to pay me five pounds, then my exercisable claim that you perform this act empowers me to secure the prevention of your not paying and entitles me to your non-interference in my so doing. My right assigns to me the pure negative freedom to curtail your pure negative freedom.[30]

But although the freedom to do duty-enforcing acts is one sort of freedom assigned by rights, it's neither the only nor arguably the most important one. And this is the point of Williams's remark. For as was noted earlier, we often speak of our having the right to do certain acts ourselves. Williams's point, like Hohfeld's mentioned earlier, is that what we casually refer to as our *right* to do these acts (e.g. wear mis-matched socks) is more precisely and discriminatingly denoted as a *liberty* to do them.

And not all our liberties represent assignments of freedom. For although they signify our lack of a duty not to do those acts, what they don't imply is that others are duty-bound not to prevent us from doing them. Other persons may well have liberties (and even duties) to do certain acts which interfere with our wearing mis-matched socks, even

[29] Williams, "The Concept of Legal Liberty," 139.

[30] Strictly, my being assigned the pure negative freedom to do this preventing act requires not only that I am vested with the power (and hence liberty) to do it but also that others have duties to refrain from interfering with my doing it. The conditions under which this latter requirement is satisfied are those of what I call "rights-compossibility" and form the developing central theme of this chapter.

though we are at liberty to wear them. You may have a duty, or only just a liberty, to do my laundry. So all my mis-matchable socks may be locked away soaking in your washing machine.

Indeed, our exercise of our liberties may be restricted by our own duties. I'm at liberty to read the entire *Encyclopaedia Britannica*. That is, I have no duty specifically enjoining me not to read it. But I may have child-rearing and other duties which are so extensive as effectively to preclude my exercising that liberty: duties which, when enforced by those holding the rights correlative to them, leave me nowhere near enough freedom to exercise that liberty and read all those instructive volumes.

While it's therefore true that my exercise of a liberty is not protected by others having duties specifically enjoining them not to interfere with that exercise, it can also be true that the duties they do have may sometimes be such as effectively to rule out such interference. I'm at liberty to play patience in my house with my pack of cards. Other persons have no specific duty to forbear from interfering with my playing patience and I therefore have no strict right (claim) to that forbearance. But the many specific forbearance duties which they do have (and my correlative rights) with respect to my physical person, my house and my cards would normally suffice to imply the impermissibility of their interference with my playing patience at home and, hence, would assign me the freedom to do so.

These differences in the permissible obstructability of various liberties are nicely captured in Hart's refinement of the picturesque and important Benthamite distinction between *naked* and *vested* liberties. (Bentham himself referred to them as types of rights.)[31] A vested liberty is one surrounded by a "protective perimeter" formed by others' duties which, though not specifically correlative to any right in the liberty-holder to exercise that liberty, nonetheless effectively prohibit their interference. The patience playing is a vested liberty. A naked liberty lacks such protection, though it's rarely without any protection. I have a naked liberty to make calls from a public pay-phone. This liberty is surrounded by a rather more penetrable perimeter which both allows me to make the calls and allows others to prevent me from doing so by using that phone themselves, though not by assaulting me, taking my coins and so forth.

Now as every sensible nanny knows, vests provide considerable but not complete protection against the cold. Evidently the nakedness or

[31] Hart, *Essays on Bentham*, 171–3.

vestedness of a liberty, where liberties are described in terms of *types* of action, is a matter of degree. How protective or penetrable such a liberty's perimeter is must depend on the technical availability of interfering actions (you might block my call by dialling the number of my payphone), on the extent to which forbearing from them figures in others' duties, and on the nature of one's own enforceable duties.

On the other hand, and as will presently be shown, liberties to perform particular acts (act-tokens) are more readily classified as either naked or vested. In this regard, we can say that a vested liberty is *internal* to a person's rights – contained by them because protected by their correlative duties – while a naked liberty is *interstitial* to respective persons' rights, suspended in whatever action-space is left between them. Vested liberties exist in one-man's land; naked liberties inhabit no-man's land.[32]

A set of rights assigns an interpersonal distribution of freedom. In conferring vested liberties as well as waiver and enforcement powers on right-holders, it prohibits some preventions and licenses others. But not all putative sets of rights are possible ones. We can best examine the reasons for this by considering the practice of promising.

Promises create rights. However, as we'll presently see, not all promises create rights and not all rights can be created by promises. Why should promises be kept? Should they be kept? These questions have engaged legal and moral philosophers for centuries. And while, in a manner of speaking, there is broad agreement on the appropriate answer to the second question – namely, "sometimes" – the first has met with a more varied set of responses. Promises create duties or should be kept, it is said, because there's a basic moral rule enjoining promise-keeping; or because it's part of the meaning of "I promise" that I incur a duty to keep my promise; or because the disappointed expectations consequent on promise-breaking result in a net surplus of harm over benefit; or because promise-breaking has the effect of eroding the institution of promising, an effect which either is on-balance detrimental or cannot consistently be willed by the promise-breaker.

Happily, we're not here called upon to supply an answer to either of these questions. For while those promises that create rights do indeed do so by creating duties, the reasons why they do so follow analytically from the nature of rights and don't consist in ethical or meta-ethical claims. Whether the promises that create rights should be kept is thus a question whose answer is identical to that offered in response to the

---

[32] See generally, Williams, "The Concept of Legal Liberty."

more general question of whether rights should be respected. And this is a matter which will be considered in the chapter on justice.

The oddity of the idea that an act of will can be self-obligating has been much remarked since Hume. For it's clear that mere resolutions or declarations of intention are not promises.

> One may resolve to do something while yet retaining complete moral freedom to change one's mind. If a promise is created by an act of will, therefore, it must be some act by which we intend to obligate ourselves. The very nature of such an act is, to most people, something of a mystery; and, in any event, all this totally fails to explain *how* the will can obligate itself. For what the will decides upon today, the will may (it seems) decide against tomorrow.[33]

A great deal has been written about the nature of these acts of will, the sorts of beings who can perform them, and what is to count as evidence of their occurrence. But, again fortunately, it's unnecessary to take a view on these perplexing issues to establish that promises can create rights by creating *correlative* duties. For virtually all models of rights simply presuppose that there can be such acts of will and that they can effect duties. In confining our attention to those duties which are correlative to rights, we can explain *why* an act of will is capable of creating them by indicating *how* it does so.

That it can do so is apparent in the light of the analytical truth that an act of will can *extinguish* a correlative duty. For as we've seen, your right that the florist deliver flowers to a wedding entails both his duty to do so and your power and liberty to waive or extinguish that duty (or to forgive its breach). That is, by an act of choice or will you can cause it to be true that no such duty exists.

And yet this does not fully answer the problem posed in the previous quotation: "What the will decides upon today, the will may (it seems) decide against tomorrow." Evidently then, what demands explanation is why the will *may not* – lacks the liberty to – reverse its decision. How does one lose the liberty to decide against what one previously decided for? If you can unilaterally extinguish the florist's duty today, why may you not unilaterally resurrect it tomorrow?

As was noted earlier, any action which we have a power to do we also have a liberty to do. Having a power to demand, proceed for or

---

[33] Atiyah, *Promises, Morals and Law*, 17. Cf. Hume, *A Treatise of Human Nature*, 516–25.

enforce compliance with a duty entails that we may do so. Recalling the Hartian classification of powers, we can see that exercises of some of them necessarily preclude exercises of others. If you exercise your power and liberty to waive the florist's duty, you thereby preclude your exercise of the power and liberty to demand his compliance with it. In thus extinguishing his duty, you extinguish your right which is correlative to it. Since your power to demand his compliance comes attached to that right, it is extinguished along with the right.

Of course it's true that, if you've since regretted your decision to waive, you can still beg or cajole him to deliver the flowers. But you can no longer demand it as a matter of duty. What your waiver has done is to restore to him the power and liberty to decide whether the flowers should be delivered. In addition to a liberty *to* deliver the flowers – a liberty which the florist held prior to your waiver – he now also has a liberty *not to* do so. With respect to delivering the flowers, the florist now has what Hart calls a "bilateral liberty."[34] Having this liberty and power (or *pair* of liberties and powers), he now has a right which he had before taking your order: namely, the right to dispose of the flowers as he wishes or, more exactly, the right correlative to your now-resumed duty not to interfere with his so doing.

Thus it's not difficult to see how an act of will, a promise, creates a correlative duty. In originally taking your order, the florist was exercising a variety of liberties and powers and thereby precluding the exercise of (and extinguishing) others. He was waiving your duty not to interfere with his disposition of the flowers, conferring on you the power to decide whether the flowers should be delivered, extinguishing his liberty not to deliver the flowers and so forth.

So the question of why the will cannot decide against what it previously decided for is answered, in the case of correlative duties, in the following manner. If, before the florist and you entered into the contract, he had the power to decide that *you* should decide whether he should deliver the flowers, and if he then exercised that power, then (in the absence of your waiver) it cannot be the case that *he* now has the power to decide whether he should deliver the flowers. If he nonetheless claims this latter power, he must deny that he exercised the former one. And *ex hypothesi* that denial is untrue.

To further clarify this point and to facilitate the presentation of subsequent arguments, I now invite the following modest thought-experiment. Imagine that persons are each asked to write down on slips of

---

[34] Hart, *Essays on Bentham*, 166–7.

paper – called "duty-slips" – their names and every action they can do. Each action is to be temporally specified and entered on a separate duty-slip. And each duty-slip consists of two attached pieces of paper: a top copy labelled "Liberty Not To" and a detachable carbon duplicate labelled "Liberty To."

When Red undertakes a correlative duty to Blue – makes a promise – he hands Blue the top copy of the duty-slip for the action promised, retaining the carbon duplicate. If Blue subsequently returns this top copy to Red, the latter can be said to have both a liberty to, and a liberty not to, do that action: Red would have a bilateral liberty with respect to that action (as he did before making the promise). However, if the top copy is not returned, Red has the liberty to do that action but he also has a duty to do it, i.e. lacks the liberty not to do it.[35] For as Williams observes, "The statement 'You are at liberty to leave' does not imply the statement 'You are at liberty to stay.'"[36] All persons' rights would thus appear to consist in those duty-slips of others of which they hold the top copies. And all persons' correlative duties would be represented by those of their own duty-slips of which they hold *only* the carbon duplicates.

This serviceable metaphor comes equipped with lemmas and codicils. First, actions consist of forbearances as well as performances. Suppose there's an action B which is described as the forbearance from doing action A. Evidently when Red hands Blue the top copy of his duty-slip for A, he must also be understood to be giving her the top copy of the duty-slip for *not-B*. For simplicity of exposition, we'll simply assume that persons make logically consistent adjustments, in their dispositions of duty-slips, to take account of the multiple permutations engendered by such forbearances and negations.

Second, it should not be assumed that all the top copies one holds, of others' duty-slips, are acquired through promising or some other form of discretionary transfer. For I shall argue later that this indeed cannot be so.

Third, nothing has been or will be said about what counts as handing or returning a top copy to someone. Specifying the requisite features of such acts of will lies beyond both my competence and our present concerns.

Nor, finally, have we considered what sorts of beings are eligible to

---

[35] Blue's return of the top copy counts as waiving the duty if it occurs prior to the action-time specified on the duty-slip. Alternatively, returning it after that time and after Red's non-compliance with the duty signifies Blue's forgiving the duty's breach.

[36] Williams, "The Concept of Legal Liberty," 133.

complete or receive duty-slips. Something more will be said about this in the sixth and seventh chapters.

Bearing these qualifications in mind, we might reasonably suppose that a person's collection of duty-slips – his own and others' – would provide an exact inventory of his rights, correlative duties and bilateral liberties. A central theme of my argument is that this would be a serious mistake. For the conditions so far laid down are insufficient to imply such an inventory. Red's possession of only his carbon duplicate for A is not only insufficient to guarantee that his doing A may not be permissibly prevented by another person. It's not even sufficient to guarantee that such interference cannot be an exercise of a right.

How can this be so? Surely if Red has only the carbon duplicate – and Blue the top copy – of Red's duty-slip for A, then Red's doing A is something which he has a liberty and a duty to do and which Blue has a right that he do. How then is it possible that *White* can have a right to, and a power to enforce, Red's not doing it? This can't be accounted for by supposing Red to have made logically inconsistent dispositions of his duty-slips, since we ruled that out in our first qualification above. White does not hold the top copy of Red's duty-slip for not-A. That is, White's right against Red is not specifically one to Red's forbearance from doing A. Nor, therefore, does Red have any such correlative duty to White.

Yet Red has *some* kind of duty correlative to a right in White – White holds the top copy of *some* duty-slip of Red's – such that White is empowered to demand and enforce Red's performance of an action, the doing of which precludes Red's compliance with his correlative duty to Blue. And conversely, Blue's right is thus one that empowers her to prevent Red's compliance with his duty to White, since that compliance involves Red not doing A and Blue's top copy entitles her to Red's doing A. It would seem that one of the top copies held by either Blue or White is not worth the paper it's printed on. It is not a valid right.

Red's problem – and consequently either Blue's or White's as well – is that he is subject to *incompossible duties* and Blue and White are thereby vested with *incompossible rights*. The fault lies, perhaps, not so much with Red as with the person who designed the duty-slips. For in his haste to foster accuracy and clarity in normative judgement by instituting the duty-slips system, he has under-specified the kinds of information required to complete the slips, with the consequence that the information supplied is insufficient to facilitate their consistent mutual adjustment.

As described thus far, that system appears to guarantee that Red's duties will necessarily be such that he may exercise at least one of (i) the liberty to do A, and (ii) the liberty to do not-A: that his doing at least one of these actions must be permissible and not impermissible. Yet the joint implication of Blue's and White's rights is that this is not so and, hence, that there is nothing Red can do that will not be a breach of duty. Whichever action he does will be both permissible and impermissible.

It's possible, of course, that the system's designer is not particularly bothered about this. Confronted with Red's problem, he might casually dismiss, as no concern of his, the fact that his system allows persons to be in contradictory positions, thereby rendering their duty-slips worthless. But this seems an unlikely response since the avoidance of such contradictions was his very purpose in designing them.

And moreover, it's a response unlikely to be endorsed by *Adjudicator* who is charged with the task of upholding both Blue's and White's rights and everyone else's. For she shares with many others a strong aversion to what Hart has aptly labelled "the Nightmare," and is unenthusiastic about the prospect of having it inflicted upon herself.

> The Nightmare is this. Litigants in law cases consider themselves entitled to have from judges an application of the existing law to their disputes, not to have the law made for them ... The Nightmare is that this image of the judge, distinguishing him from the legislator, is an illusion ... that judges make the law which they apply to litigants and are not impartial, objective declarers of existing law ... [but rather exercise] what Holmes called the "sovereign prerogative of choice."[37]

The existing law, putatively embodied in the duty-slips system, is that one ought to do – and another may prevent one's forbearance from doing – any action for which one holds only the carbon duplicate. Conscious of the truth that "ought implies can," Adjudicator knows that by upholding Blue's right she will be denying White's (and *vice versa*), thereby altering the existing law and incidentally affirming the contradiction that compliance with one's duty is not obligatory. What, then, must she do to avoid the awesome burden of exercising the sovereign prerogative of choice?

The answer, of course, is that she must call for the reform of the duty-slips system. But what sort of reform should she demand? Several possibilities suggest themselves. One is simply to do away with duty-

[37] Hart, *Essays in Jurisprudence and Philosophy*, 126, 127, 134. Hart associates the nightmare with some of the doctrines of Legal Realism.

slips altogether – or what amounts to the same thing, require that no one hold another's top copies – and thereby inaugurate a Hobbesian state of nature in which none has correlative duties or rights and all have bilateral liberties with respect to any action. White, for example, might well find this preferable to a situation in which Blue's right is judicially upheld against his own claim on Red: a judicial decision which is tantamount to denying that White holds a top copy from Red.

Since the reasons for rejecting such a reform can only be moral rather than philosophical ones,[38] I shall leave aside any further consideration of it here. Suffice it to say that Adjudicator is only marginally less interested in this possibility than in Hobbes's proposal for avoiding it. This consists in having each person complete his set of duty-slips and then surrender *all* top copies to one and the same agency (ideally, a single person) called "Leviathan."[39]

Leviathan may, of course, choose to be liberal and hand back a great many top copies to his subjects: that is, he may confer numerous bilateral liberties upon them. But he knows that if he is excessively liberal in this sense, he will by degrees reinstate the Hobbesian state of nature. Alternatively, such liberality can result in his having to spend most of his time at the bothersome task of exercising Holmes's sovereign prerogative of choice, arbitrarily adjudicating between mutually contradictory claims, since his subjects are likely to engage in transferring these returned top copies amongst each other and thereby frequently to get themselves into difficulties like that of Red, White, and Blue. Exercising prerogative choice is, he feels, acceptable as an occasional necessity but not as a full-time occupation.

However, what finally convinces Adjudicator that even a non-liberal Leviathan isn't the remedy she seeks is her realization that it too would fail to preclude the creation of incompossible duties and rights. For even if Leviathan were to hand back few or no top copies to his subjects, there's no reason why Red could not find himself in a predicament essen-

---

[38] A plausible but inconclusive reason is offered in ch. 5; see p. 184.

[39] Strictly speaking, what Hobbes proposes is more complicated than this. It is, at least for a "sovereign by institution," that each person somehow gives to every other person a top copy of that duty-slip – sometimes considered a blank cheque – which pertains to the action of "withholding from Leviathan any top copy he/she/they may demand." (Arguably, what a Hobbesian "sovereign by acquisition" gets is this top copy directly.) Thus as Hobbes suggests, collaborative disobedience to Leviathan is almost necessarily impermissible. For even if Red, White, and Blue reciprocally waive their duties to one another to obey Leviathan – hand back to each other the aforesaid top copies – they continue to owe what is substantively the same duty to everyone else, including the person or group designated as Leviathan, i.e. in his/her/their private capacity.

tially the same as his present one. The duty-slips, as presently drafted, would still be such as to permit his having many mutually incompatible duties – albeit duties which may all be owed to one and the same person (namely, Leviathan) rather than to Blue and White and others. And while, doubtless, Leviathan could cope with such predicaments by simply waiving some of these conflicting duties, he wouldn't relish the prospect of spending all his waking hours making such arbitrary decisions, much less that of futilely withholding top copies which must then be handed back. If what's wanted is some means of escape from such perpetual retrospective legislating – from the embarrassment of declaring duties non-obligatory – Leviathan is no vehicle.

Evidently the general problem of incompossibility cannot be solved by a reallocation of duty-slips. Short of cutting the Gordian knot by returning to Hobbes's state of nature, Adjudicator's elusive reform must be sought in the design of the slips themselves. What, precisely, is wrong with them as they stand? To identify their present deficiency, we need to retrace our steps a bit and examine the contents of Red's duties to Blue and White.

The scene is Adjudicator's parlour, and the *dramatis personae* include Red, White, and Blue as well as Adjudicator herself. In evidence of their (competing) claims, Blue and White have each submitted their respective top copies of Red's duty-slips. Blue's top copy reads "Liberty Not To – deliver flowers to wedding W on 26 February 1975 at four o'clock p.m." And White's top copy reads "Liberty Not To – return his van to White upon demand." Having authenticated Red's signature on both top copies, confirmed that Red is in possession of the corresponding carbon duplicates and established that neither top copy was ever returned to Red, Adjudicator further ascertains that the use of White's van had turned out to be Red's only means of delivering the flowers at the prescribed time. Understandably annoyed with Red, Adjudicator asks him how he could possibly have taken on *both* of these duties.

"Well your honour," Red explains, "on 19 February 1975 White agreed to loan me his van on condition that I give him the top copy he has now submitted to you. I checked through my collection of duty-slips, discovered that I still possessed the requested top copy, gave it to White and duly borrowed his van. The next day, Blue approached me and asked whether I was still in possession of the top copy she has now submitted to you. Since I did still have it and wished to accommodate her, I gave it to her. That's the whole story."

"Yes, obviously that's the story," responds Adjudicator impatiently, "but it's not the answer to my question. What I want to know is how a *reasonable man* – I presume you count yourself a reasonable man –

could, in these circumstances, have undertaken that duty to Blue? How did you imagine you were going to be able to meet both your commitments?"

"To tell the truth, your honour, I've never been very strong on the imaginative side," replies Red. "But I do know my station and its duties. And what's more, I know my rights and liberties too. I have my collection of duty-slips to keep me informed about all these things. Presumably even unimaginative people can have rights and bilateral liberties. My duty-slip for Blue made absolutely no mention of White's van. That aside, it seems to me quite unreasonable to have expected that White would request the return of his van that soon after loaning it to me, since he never had in the past. How was I to know that he intended, that very afternoon, to use it for a round-the-world sea voyage? Would a reasonable man be expected to have ascertained White's plans and, even if so, to have credited them?"

And Red continues: "It's not as though even simultaneous duties are invariably incompossible. Last night, for instance, I was committed to spending the whole evening babysitting for a neighbour *and* to phoning a business associate at nine o'clock. And I succeeded in performing both of these duties. Mind you, it was a near thing, so far as incompossibilities go. Because while there's clearly no problem about phoning and babysitting at the same time, my neighbour has a standing commitment to his sister whereby she can come over and use his phone whenever hers is out of order. And as luck would have it, she turned up last night at eight-forty-five needing to make an urgent call and brandishing the top copy her brother had given her. Fortunately, she completed her call in the nick of time, saving me and my neighbour from a disastrous incompossibility."

At this point, White interjects: "I really must protest at any attempt to implicate my travel plans in Red's breach of his duty to Blue. Even if I had postponed my departure and let Red use my van for the rest of the afternoon, he would still have been unable to deliver the flowers. At around four o'clock I happened to be passing by the area where the wedding was to be held and observed that all access to the building had been cut off by a solid line of marching demonstrators, exercising what I assume were their liberties of assembly and expression to protest against the bad weather we've been having lately. Presumably Red's duties also include ones not to cause these people the sort of bodily injuries that would have inevitably resulted from his attempting to get through this demonstration in the van to deliver the flowers at the agreed time."

"It does rather begin to look," Adjudicator wearily concedes, "as though Red's duty to Blue was not fulfillable, perhaps not even by a reasonable man. So there's not much point in reproving him further, and I suggest that we conclude these proceedings by simply requiring Red to compensate Blue for failing to comply with the delivery duty."

To which Red, brightening noticeably, replies: "Just one point, your honour. I don't really see why I owe Blue compensation. Surely a non-fulfillable duty is not a duty at all. Ought implies can and cannot implies not-ought. And if I had no duty to Blue, I couldn't possibly have committed a breach of any such duty. Nor, therefore, do I owe her any compensation."

Utterly baffled, Adjudicator adjourns the proceedings indefinitely and retires to bed, steeling herself for the Nightmare.

(C) COMPOSSIBILITY AND DOMAINS

The temptation to dismiss what we have here as *merely* a problem of remediably imperfect knowledge is very great and should be resisted. On the face of it, one might think that if Red had informed himself of White's travel plans and the intended demonstration, he wouldn't have undertaken his duty to Blue. Against this, four things can be said. First, White may not have made his plans until after Red incurred his duty to Blue. Second, and even if the plans were made before then, it's not clear (as Red remarked) that a reasonable man would have regarded such plans as likely to be executed: vans are not noted for their seaworthiness and it might be reasonable to expect that this fact would come to White's attention before Red was asked to return the van. Third, and similar to the first, the demonstration may have been a relatively spontaneous occurrence and thus one of which Red could not have known when he made his contract with Blue. Finally, and even if these things had been knowable at the relevant time, *Blue*'s having informed herself of them would have been as sufficient as Red's doing so, to avoid the creation of that non-fulfillable duty. A cynic might even speculate about the possibility that Blue *did* know of these forthcoming events and saw her engagement of Red's services as a painless way to a quick profit, via a compensation award.[40] Certainly, the foreseeability of a duty's non-fulfillability – treating it as merely an information problem – provides no basis for any resolution of the incompossibility, since it crucially fails to locate responsibility for the absence of that foresight as between right-holder and duty-holder.

That said, the suggestion that more information is a prophylactic against incompossibilities does contain an important grain of truth. But this information is not specifically about future intentions, as such. And moreover, it's information which would need to be entered on the duty-slips constituting a set of compossible rights.

To discover the general nature of this information, we need to probe a little deeper into our description of the present incompossibility. As noted earlier, a duty to do an action implies a liberty to do it (and the

---

[40] Along similar lines, a cartoon in the *New Yorker* (17 August 1981) depicts a hopeful debtor explaining his overdue loan to an irate bank manager: "Frankly, when I took out the loan I sincerely believed we'd all be blown to hell before it came due."

absence of a liberty not to do it). I'll occasionally refer to liberties which one has a duty to exercise as *committed* liberties.

Now, reverting to the important Benthamite distinction mentioned previously, we can see that the source of Red's difficulty is that his committed liberty to deliver the flowers is a *naked* liberty rather than a *vested* one. Like my liberty to use the pay-phone, his liberty to deliver the flowers is surrounded by a highly penetrable perimeter: penetrable, in this instance, by the demonstrators' exercise of their liberties, of their rights (and powers to enforce) that Red cause them no injuries and by White's exercise of his right to (power to enforce) Red's return of the van.

Like other naked things, unvested liberties are exposed to the numbing effects of cold fronts: in the case of liberties, to the obstructive impact of others' exercises of their powers and liberties. This is not to say that all naked liberties are numbed liberties. Immediate examples are the demonstrators' liberties of assembly and expression. These are presumably not vested liberties inasmuch as there are certain actions which others might permissibly perform – like mounting an obstructive counter-demonstration in favour of bad weather – that could restrict the demonstrators' exercise of their liberties.

Nevertheless the salience of nakedness, in the creation of incompossibilities, is clear enough. Any duty which depends for its fulfilment on the exercise of a naked liberty stands in danger of being non-fulfillable due to that liberty being numbed. And it's important to emphasize that such numbing can occur by virtue of an entirely permissible and even obligatory action. That is, we are *not* here talking about a duty being non-fulfillable because another duty was breached: a non-fulfillability that, whatever other problems it poses, does not give rise to any problem of incompossibility. If the only reason for Red's failing to deliver had been that Black struck him on the head and left him unconscious on 26 February, Adjudicator would have made short work of any charge brought by Blue: by awarding compensation to Blue against Black (assuming that Black is under an unwaived duty not to strike Red on the head).[41] On the other hand, a duty which can only be fulfilled by traversing the no-man's land of naked liberty is necessarily a candidate for incompossibility with other duties.

---

[41] The procedure would be more indirect than this. Blue would be awarded compensation against Red for his failure to deliver. And Red would be awarded compensation against Black for the losses and injuries the latter had caused, including Red's compensation to Blue.

Candidacy, of course, does not imply election. Being numbable, a naked liberty may yet escape numbing. And if there is a duty requiring its exercise, its not being numbed leaves that duty fulfillable and thus compossible with other duties. The duty-holder may have the good luck to be unobstructed by others from exercising that naked liberty. That is, others may choose to fulfil their duties and exercise their powers and uncommitted liberties in ways which contingently involve no obstruction of his duty-fulfilment.

But no requirement that they so choose is thereby implied. And it's entirely possible that their duties are of a sort that no such choice is open to them. No-man's land may be a vanishingly small place, even for the accommodating. Whether the demonstrators were at liberty to hold their march elsewhere than in the path of Red's duty-fulfilment is an open question. Whether they had a duty to do so is not. Indeed, for all we know, they may have been duty-bound to hold it exactly when and where they did.

Recall our quarry. What we're concerned with here is to relieve Adjudicator of the worry of undergoing the Nightmare. We want to know what must be true of a set of rights for it to be a compossible set. That persons who happen to have the requisite latitude will opt to fulfil their duties and exercise their powers and uncommitted liberties in ways which don't obstruct the fulfilment of others' duties is, even when true, not a truth about a set of rights. It's an empirical prediction of general affability: a prediction from which, if plausible, Adjudicator may admittedly take some comfort.

But it won't suffice for her relief, since she knows that persons' duties can be such as to deprive them of this latitude: that is, deprive them of any practical option which is both permissible and non-obstructive of Red's duty-fulfilment. Rushing out of the train station, you may need to take the only taxi available to get to your suburban appointment on time – the very taxi I need to get to my city-centre appointment on time. The two persons to whom we respectively owe these jointly non-fulfillable duties of punctuality thus have incompossible rights.

Nor is there any obvious general restriction on the kinds of liberty persons can have, the kinds of action (act-types) they may perform, that would ensure the compossibility of duties requiring the exercise of liberties which are naked. The remedy can't be said to lie in subjecting persons to a general duty not to create duties which require the exercise of naked liberties. There is, to be sure, some validity in this suggestion. But as it stands, it's wrongly formulated. For, in the first place and as was emphasized earlier, not all our duties are ones which we *create*:

some exist independently of our promises or other acts of will.[42] A general duty not to commit naked liberties wouldn't ensure the compossibility of uncreated duties. Secondly, what would be the status of this over-arching general duty? Is it correlative to a right and, if so, to whom could it conceivably be owed? More problematically still, the vests of non-naked or vested liberties are themselves *constituted* by duties: namely, those forming the impenetrable perimeters surrounding them. What ensures that these perimeter duties are compossible? So some re-working of the thought behind this suggestion is called for, and will presently be supplied.

The upshot of this is simply the confirmation that naked liberties can always be permissibly numbed and there is no way of designing a set of rights that will alter this fact. Whenever the exercise of a naked liberty is obligatory, Adjudicator is destined to spend another sleepless night. What she therefore seeks is the condition for a set of rights to be *categorically* compossible. She wants an assurance that the compossibility of correlative duties is guaranteed by their content and is not precariously dependent on the incidence of (or scope for) affability in society. And this means that one object of our quest is the sort of clothing which a liberty needs in order to be decently vested and immune to permissible numbing. For the correct thought, underlying the wrongly formulated suggestion canvassed in the previous paragraph, is that it's those duties requiring the exercise of only vested liberties that alone are categorically compossible duties, correlatively entailing categorically compossible rights.

A vested liberty is one surrounded by an impenetrable perimeter. This consists of various duties in all persons other than the liberty-holder not to interfere. These duties, it will be recalled, are a set of obligatory forbearances which, though not specifically ones of not obstructing the exercise of that particular liberty, nonetheless are such as jointly to imply the impermissibility of any action that would obstruct it. (The set of others' various duties, protecting me from permissible interference with my playing patience in my house with my cards, was the example offered earlier.)

Now, since (i) a right is entailed by a correlative duty, and (ii) a set of categorically compossible rights is entailed by a set of categorically compossible correlative duties, and (iii) such duties are ones involving the duty-holder's exercise of only his vested liberties, and (iv) vested liberties imply duties of forbearance in others, it follows that *a set of categorically compossible rights implies the presence of rights in duty-*

---

[42] Hobbes apart, most persons would say this is true of, for example, our duties not to assault others.

holders: namely, rights correlative to those forbearance duties that conjunctively form the perimeters surrounding any duty-holder's vested liberties. A duty-holder who lacks any rights is one whose liberties are all
naked and whose duties may thus be incompossible either with one
another or with those of others or both. Red lacked a vested liberty to
cross the path of the demonstrators because they held no duties – correlative to rights in him – jointly sufficient to prohibit their obstruction
of his passage.

The profile of a rather intricate normative structure begins to emerge.
Holders of categorically compossible duties are right-holders against
whom others hold rights. Other persons' duties to Red, forming the perimeter of his vested liberty to do A, are necessary conditions of his duty
to do A being categorically fulfillable. By the same token, the categorical
fulfillability of those perimeter duties implies their compossibility. And
this in turn implies a further set of perimeters surrounding the committed
liberties to be exercised in fulfilling that first set of perimeter duties. And
so on. Each vested liberty is vested by virtue of its being protected by a
perimeter of others' vested liberties.

If White's doing B would prevent Red's doing A, then the perimeter
of Red's vested and committed liberty to do A includes White's duty to
forbear doing B. But for Red's doing A to be a member of a set of categorically compossible duties, others must have a duty to forbear doing C,
since C would prevent White's forbearing B and this would result in the
penetration of Red's perimeter and the prevention of his doing the obligatory A. If someone were at liberty to do C – or worse, had a duty to do
C – Red's and White's respective perimeters would be permissibly penetrable and their respective duties would be permissibly obstructable. A
perimeter is impermissibly penetrable, categorically impenetrable, only if
there are other categorically impenetrable perimeters.

How can we even begin to capture the complexity of this densely
webbed structure of serially implied perimeters? What is the general
character of the duties, and their correlative rights, constituting such a
structure? I'm going to call the set of vested liberties contained by each
person's set of perimeters his *domain*. What we want to know, then, is
what these domains must be like – by what sort of rights must they be
constituted – to guarantee the compossible exercise of the liberties they
respectively contain. Since Red's domain contains his vested liberty to
do A, it's partly constituted by his right that White forbear B. To discover what sort of right this is, we therefore need to examine the
relationship between A and B.

White's doing B is an action which penetrates the perimeter of Red's
liberty to do A. The latter action's occurrence would be rendered imposs-

ible, is *prevented*, by the occurrence of the former. This relation of prevention between two actions was discussed at some length in the previous chapter. As we saw there, a relation of prevention obtains between
two persons' actions which are incompossible. That is, these actions are
incapable of jointly occurring if there is a partial coincidence between
their *extensional* descriptions – if those actions simultaneously have at
least one, but not all, of their physical components (objects or spatial
locations) in common.[43] Conversely, if the set of the physical components of Red's doing A does not intersect with that of White's doing B,
the latter cannot be said to prevent the former. But since, *ex hypothesi*,
the latter does prevent the former, the two actions have at least one such
component in common. They conjunctively suffer from what I previously referred to as "extensional overlap."

For Red to have a vested liberty to do A, his right to White's forbearing B must therefore imply a right against White's simultaneous possession of those common physical components. And since that liberty is
vested, there must be a similar right against every other person as well.
In short, what Red has is a right to the physical components of his
doing A.

The rights constituting a person's domain are thus easily conceived as
property rights: they are (time-indexed) rights to physical things. A set
of categorically compossible domains, constituted by a set of property
rights, is one in which each person's rights are demarcated in such a way
as to be mutually exclusive of every other person's rights. Pending
further clarification, we'll interpret this to mean that no two persons
simultaneously have rights to one and the same physical thing. Let's call
domains constituted by such property rights *title-based* domains.

At last we're in a position to formulate what's wrong with the current
design of the duty-slips. The sets of rights that derive from the allocation
of their top copies are not property rights and don't constitute title-
based domains. Rights arising from the current duty-slips are claims to
other persons' performance of *intensionally described* actions (albeit
ones which may have some incomplete extensional specification). And
as we saw in the previous chapter, the intensional descriptions of any
two actions imply nothing about whether they are events which can
jointly occur. Whether my seeing a film tomorrow afternoon, and your
wrecking a building then, are or are not jointly performable actions
depends *inter alia* on whether the building you are to wreck is the cinema
I'm to attend. If it is and if we each have a duty to do these actions,

---

[43] Being the actions of two different persons is sufficient to ensure that they do not have
all their physical components in common.

those two duties are incompossible and so are the respective rights which they correlatively entail.

A set of title-based domains is a categorically compossible set because the rights constituting it are correlative to duties enjoining extensionally differentiated acts. On the other hand, a set of domains constituted by rights correlative to only intensionally described obligatory actions – actions whose several descriptions are thus not fully reducible to differentiated extensional ones – consists of what we may call *purpose-based* domains. The obligatory actions entailed by them are act-types and not act-tokens. A set of purpose-based domains cannot satisfy the requirement of being categorically compossible.

We should briefly pause here to notice how this reveals and explains yet another serious shortcoming in the Benefit Theory of rights. That rights, as modelled by that theory, unavoidably generate incompossibilities is not much disputed by its proponents. Jeremy Waldron, for example, acknowledges that "if rights are understood along the lines of the Interest [Benefit] Theory . . . then conflicts of rights must be regarded as more or less inevitable."[44] This is not surprising. Recall that, according to this theory, persons may be said to have a right if and only if some aspect of their wellbeing (some interest of theirs) is sufficiently important in itself to justify holding other persons to be under a duty.[45] Whereas Choice Theory duties are identifiable solely by virtue of their controllability, what is distinctive of Benefit Theory duties is that they all have the same general *content*: all actions enjoined by them have the purpose of servicing these important interests. And there are evidently no reasons to suppose that any two such services need be jointly performable, as well as many reasons to suppose that frequently they are not. The important interests persons have both in privacy and in free expression are, as we know, ones which cannot invariably be jointly serviced. Nor, tragically, can the vital interests several persons may each have in gaining access to some scarce medical resource. As Waldron shows, neither *intra*-right nor *inter*-right incompossibilities – conflicts between correlative duties of the same or different act-types – can be avoided under the Benefit Theory.

Returning then to the deficiencies of the duty-slips as currently designed, we see that what's wrong with them is that the domains they generate are constituted by purpose-based rights. Lacking full extensional specification, they fail to confer impenetrable perimeters on per-

---

[44] Waldron, "Rights in Conflict," 503. Waldron advances a case for the Benefit Theory in *The Right to Private Property*, 79–101.
[45] Cf. Raz, *The Morality of Freedom*, 166.

sons vested with correlative duties. They fail to partition what we might compendiously call *action-space*, severally assigning control of particular portions of it in such a way as to ensure that all committed liberties are jointly exercisable and impermissibly obstructable. It's precisely because a set of title-based domains *does* make such partitions and assignments that the rights constituting it prescribe (as was suggested at the outset of this chapter) an interpersonal distribution of pure negative freedom.

Hence the traditional Lockean view – that all rights are essentially property rights – far from being merely a piece of bourgeois ideology, actually embodies an important conceptual truth. In this vein, Hart correctly observes that "Rights are typically conceived of as *possessed* or *owned* or *belonging to* individuals, and these expressions reflect the conception of moral rules as not only prescribing conduct but as forming a kind of moral property of individuals to which they are as individuals entitled."[46] Accordingly, a reformed set of duty-slips will include full extensional specifications of the action to which each slip pertains. And each person's domain, as constituted by his set of others' top copies, will thus consist of a set of specified extensional elements that does not intersect that of any other person.[47] In order to have an impermissibly obstructable duty to Blue to deliver flowers, Red will need to have, *inter alia*, a vested liberty to use White's van at the appointed time as well as a vested liberty to gain access to the building where the wedding is to occur. And the top copies Red respectively holds from White and others will indicate as much. Of course, the top copies Red receives from White will themselves be underwritten by top copies which White in turn holds from others, and which conjunctively render White's liberty to use the van a vested one – a temporal slice of which he conveys to Red in loaning the van to him.

And yet the Lockean view does seem peculiar. We can readily see the sense in calling White's right to the van a *property* right. Much the same is probably acceptable for Red's temporary right to it. But isn't it a bit Procrustean – a rather tendentiously strained departure from ordinary usage – to regard the sort of right which Blue holds as a property right? It is, after all, only a right that Red deliver flowers. In what sense does it confer on Blue an entitlement to exercise the kind of control over physical things that White and Red have?

That it does confer the same kind of control is, perhaps, most readily

---

[46] Hart, "Are There Any Natural Rights?" 182. Hart, perhaps, here intends a more figurative interpretation of "property" than the one I am suggesting.

[47] One of the important conditions ensuring such non-intersection is the subject of the next section.

seen if we consider that Blue could in turn promise to *Brown* to have Red deliver the flowers. That is, Blue could incur a duty not to exercise her power and liberty to waive Red's delivery duty. And she would thereby be incurring a duty to exercise her power and liberty to demand – and if necessary enforce – that Red deliver. We've already seen that, for a duty to be a categorically fulfillable (impermissibly obstructable) one, the committed liberty exercised in its fulfilment must be a vested one. Just as White's duty to loan the van confers a (temporal slice of White's) vested liberty on Red, so too does Red's duty to Blue confer upon her a (temporal slice of Red's) vested liberty with respect to the physical components of the action of Red delivering the flowers.

The apparent distinction between the two cases is that the perimeter of the first vested liberty consists solely in duties of forbearance in all persons including White, whereas the perimeter of the second consists both of these forbearance duties and also a duty of performance in Red himself. But this is a distinction without a relevant difference. For Red's performance, like any action, can be extensionally specified. And again like any performance, it can be re-described as a forbearance: namely, Red's forbearing from not delivering the flowers. What Blue holds can thus be construed as a property right in the extensional elements of Red's delivering the flowers. It is a right, conferred by Red on Blue, constituted by duties of forbearance in others but also, and most pertinently, in Red.

Like most actions, Red's delivering the flowers involves a host of physical elements, not the least of which is Red's person itself. Doubtless we are loath to grant that others' duties confer property rights in their persons, even of a temporary sort, upon those to whom these duties are owed. Kant's reduction of the marriage contract to "a mutual lease of sexual organs" may be distasteful to many and, in an increasing number of legal systems, simply mistaken.[48] Nevertheless Blue's duty to Brown, to have Red deliver the flowers, can be impermissibly obstructable only if Blue has a vested liberty to control these elements: if necessary, by enforcing Red's delivery. For if Blue *lacked* this vested liberty to use Red's person to secure the delivery – and others, including Red, lacked duties not to obstruct the exercise of that liberty – some such obstruction would be permissible. And were it to occur, Blue's duty to Brown would thereby be non-fulfillable and thus (contradictorily) non-obligatory. Cannot implies not-ought. So *all* rights in a set of compossible rights may be regarded as property rights. They imply all other persons' duties

---

[48] Cf. Cohen, *Reason and Law*, 120. This reduction is suggested in Kant, *The Philosophy of Law*, 109–11. The reduction is mistaken in those legal systems which reject the doctrine that there can be "no rape in marriage."

of non-interference with the right-holder's use of certain physical things for certain limited or unlimited periods of time.[49]

This argument, to be convincing, cannot afford to ignore the two apparently adverse aspects of ordinary and legal usage that confront it. The first is that property rights are commonly understood as rights *in rem*, rights in things "against the world." As such, they correlatively entail only those duties which are owed by all others *directly* to the right-holder. And White's duty not to obstruct Red's flower-delivering use of the van is not one owed directly to Blue but rather to Red. Indeed, insofar as the traditional distinction between rights *in rem* and rights *in personam* has been challenged, that challenge has generally consisted in the proposed reducibility of the former to the latter, rather than the reverse reducibility suggested here.[50]

The grounds and motivation for that challenge are certainly sound enough. The motivation, shared by the present account, is simply one of clarity and intellectual economy: to secure a uniform conceptual model of all rights, one that is independent of their varying contents. And the grounds are the undisputed fact that all rights entail duties owed to some persons by other persons. That is, no rights entail duties owed by things! Accordingly, it's been argued that the difference between *in rem* and *in personam* rights is best seen as one of degree, with the former simply entailing correlative *in personam* duties in many more persons than the latter. Arguing for this reduction, Hohfeld observes:

> Assuming that the division represented by *in personam* and *in rem* is intended to be mutually exclusive, it is plausible enough to think also that if a right *in personam* is simply a right against a person, a right *in rem* must be a right that is *not against* a *person*, but *against* a *thing* ... Such a notion of rights *in rem* is, as already intimated, crude and fallacious ... [Thus] Mr. Chief Justice Holmes, in *Tyler v. Court of Registration*: "All proceedings, *like all rights*, are *really against persons*. Whether they are proceedings or *rights in rem* depends on the *number of persons affected*."...
> What is here insisted on, – i.e. that all rights *in rem* are against persons, – is not to be regarded merely as a matter of taste or preference for one out of several equally possible forms of

[49] The suggestion that rights to others' services amount to property rights in their bodies is also to be found in Gibbard, "Natural Property Rights," 77, and Arneson, "Property Rights in Persons," 202.

[50] Cf. Kelsen, *General Theory of Law and State*, 75–6; Hohfeld, *Fundamental Legal Conceptions*, 67–85.

statement or definition. Logical consistency seems to demand such a conception, and nothing less than that.[51]

Hohfeld suggests that a more perspicuous characterization of what is intended in the traditional *in personam–in rem* distinction can be better expressed by referring to the former as "paucital" and the latter as "multital" rights. These terms capture the idea that an *in personam* right avails uniquely against one definite person, whereas an *in rem* right is always one of a large class of duplicate rights respectively availing against separate persons who constitute a large and indefinite class of persons. Hence Hohfeld would regard Blue's right that Red deliver the flowers as paucital, and White's right to the van as multital, inasmuch as the latter correlatively entails the same forbearance duties in countless persons who must each thereby respect White's ownership of it. On this account of the matter, *in rem* (property) rights are merely *in personam* rights duplicated and multiplied, and the former may thus be conceptually reduced to the latter without loss of meaning.

Opposed as this suggestion appears to be to the account I've offered, it is not so in fact. For I have not claimed that Blue's right, that the flowers be delivered, *correlatively entails* duties in everyone else. It correlatively entails a duty only in Red. What I have suggested is that this right, if it is a member of a compossible set of rights, *implies* duties in everyone else. The duties it implies in them are those which constitute White's, and in turn Red's, serially impenetrable perimeters surrounding the vested liberties they exercise in fulfilling their respective duties to Red and Blue. These perimeter duties *are* ones correlatively entailed by rights in White and in Red, each of whom conveys – indirectly and directly – a temporal part of those perimeters to Blue. White conveys this to Red in undertaking to loan Red the van. And Red in turn conveys to Blue part of what White conveyed to him, along with the various perimeter forbearances he is already owed directly by all other persons. It is this set of perimeter duties that makes Red's committed liberty to deliver the flowers a vested one and his exercise of it impermissibly obstructable by all others.

It's certainly true that, if Red fails to deliver the flowers because White repossesses the van before the expiry of the loan, Blue's complaint cannot lie against White because Blue has no borrower's right against White. But Blue does have a right against Red, and White does owe a lender's duty to Red. So my claim is that, in a compossible set of rights, Blue's right *implies* White's duty even though it doesn't correlatively

---

[51] Hohfeld, *Fundamental Legal Conceptions*, 75–6.

entail it. In this sense, Blue's apparently paucital right can plausibly be regarded as something akin to a multital one – a property right – since it not only entails a duty in Red, but also implies a duty in White and, through him, in everyone else. Red, White, and everyone else are under various duties that imply the impermissibility of their doing actions obstructing the flower delivery. If any such obstructive actions *were* permissible, some persons' relevant perimeters would be permissibly penetrable and their committed liberties would be naked and not vested. Some of their rights would be incompossible.

The second and more informal reason for resisting the Lockean construal of all rights as property rights lies in our common inclination to regard property rights as licensing a wide discretion in right-holders' dispositions of whatever they have property rights to. Pretty clearly, Blue's flower-delivery right doesn't give her very much scope in this respect. This point is nicely displayed in a report of a recent case before the European Court of Justice. The plaintiff, Mrs Liselotte Hauer, appealed to the European Court of Human Rights against a legislative prohibition on one use of her agricultural land, on the grounds that this measure violated the right to property enshrined in the European Convention for the Protection of Human Rights and Fundamental Freedoms.

> The interesting issue for the Court was whether the prohibition on new planting of vines should be classified as an expropriation or merely as a restriction of the right of property. The Court did not find the question difficult to answer. The individuals affected by the prohibition were not being deprived of their property. They remained free to keep them for themselves or to transfer them to others. The content of the right was being reduced only to the extent that temporarily one particular form of enjoyment was being precluded, namely the planting of vines.[52]

Our concern here is not to ask whether the Court's reasoning was sound.

---

[52] "Euro-debate over the citizen's right to property," *Financial Times*, 6 October 1980. A similar issue arises in American law in respect of whether state regulation of the use of property counts as a "taking" under the Constitution's Fifth Amendment which states: "Nor shall private property be taken for public use, without just compensation"; see Pilon, "Property and Constitutional Principles," for a discussion of the case of *Lucas v. South Carolina*; also Becker and Kipnis (eds), *Property: Cases, Concepts, Critiques*, 48–65, on the cases of *Kaiser Aetna v. United States* and *Robins v. Pruneyard Shopping Center*. More generally, see Epstein, *Takings*.

For it's not very profitable to ask for the number of forms of enjoyment that need to be removed, and for how long, before a person can be said to have been expropriated or denied "the" property right in a thing.

That there is indeed no essence of property rights to be found along these lines has been ably demonstrated by A. M. Honoré, who identifies no fewer than eleven general forms of enjoyment – "standard incidents" – which can pertain to the ownership of an object.[53] It's true that, with respect to some kinds of object, some of these incidents are of vastly greater importance than others. And it's also true that with some objects not all these incidents can apply, while with others not all of them can be individuated.[54]

The inclination to regard property rights as licensing a wide range of unencumbered dispositional choices arises from the fact that our ordinary use of that phrase tends to reflect what Honoré calls the "liberal concept of full individual ownership": that is, one which locates all or most of the standard incidents pertaining to an object's ownership in a single person. From what we've seen about the rights of White, Red, Blue, Brown, and Mrs Hauer, there can be little doubt that Adjudicator's labours would be considerably lightened if the liberal model were generally prevalent in practice: if such ownership incidents in a thing as those to possess it, use it, manage it, transmit it, destroy it, and secure its income, were all claims, powers, and vested liberties held by one and the same person. Unfortunately, for Adjudicator at least, this is often not the case. Nor is there any conceptual reason why it need be. (If there were, many contractual rights would be inconceivable!) The partition of ownership in a single object, and the dispersal of its several incidents among different persons, are commonplace features of property rights.[55]

The European Court's reasoning was therefore correct if what was thereby intended was simply that, in not being deprived of the incidents of possession and alienation, Mrs Hauer still held *some* property rights

---

[53] Honoré, "Ownership," 123–4. Perhaps only nine of these incidents should be regarded as forms of "enjoyment" since two of them – prohibition of harmful use and liability to execution – are respects in which an owner may *not* enjoy his property.

[54] Cf. L. Becker, *Property Rights*, 18–22.

[55] Cf. Lawson, *Introduction to the Law of Property*, chs v–x. Thus Joshua Cohen, "The Economic Basis of Deliberative Democracy," 49, suggests that the question "*Who* should have the bundle of rights that comprises the ownership of capital?" is one which "should be criticized, not answered. Arguments in social philosophy should not premise a highly unified conception of property and confine our attention to different ways of shifting the bundle around. A more suitable procedure is to "unbundle" ownership, and then to consider the different ways of distributing the rights that comprise it."

in "her" land.[56] By the same reasoning, Blue's right to Red's flower-delivery amounts to *a* property right in the physical elements of that action. She, along with Red and White, each have temporally differentiated titles to some of the same objects and, in that sense, their respective titles each entail encumbrances, one upon the other. The compossibility of all the rights in a set, though it requires that these rights be property rights – titles to the disposition of physical things, implying forbearance duties in all others – does not require that they be modelled on the liberal concept of unencumbered full ownership of a single object by a single person. Extensional differentiability is the necessary and sufficient condition of their being compossible. And extensional differentiability does not require full liberal ownership.

Nonetheless, an important insight underlies our casual mis-identification of property rights with full liberal ownership. For as was noted previously, it's not always possible to individuate or partition all the standard incidents of ownership with respect to every kind of object. Which of them can be individuated and partitioned may partly depend, *inter alia*, on current technical knowledge and other highly variable factors. Things commonly regarded as purely consumption goods, kinds of income, may be discovered to have productive uses and thus come to be alternatively regarded as capital. Similarly, managing the use of a thing and destroying it are not always readily distinguishable. These considerations pose no incompossibility problems in a set of rights where all incidents in a thing are liberally owned by one and the same person.[57]

But where this is not the case – where the several incidents of possession, alienation, use, management, income enjoyment, and destruction applying to one and the same thing are severally owned by different persons – obvious difficulties can arise. For any adjudicatory decision as to which of them may do what with that thing may unavoidably presuppose some intensional (e.g. functional) judgement about what that thing is *for*. That is, it may *pre*judge precisely what is at issue between two rival litigants.[58] Bibliophiles may not see eye-to-eye with paper recyclers; a human cadaver is sometimes regarded differently by persons

---

[56] Others would then be said to be held by state officials.

[57] Though it may confront the person involved with very serious emotional and moral dilemmas.

[58] Epstein, *Takings*, 69–70, suggests that such decisions appear "to embrace a teleological view of inanimate objects." More generally, see Simmonds, "Epstein's Theory of Strict Tort Liability," 114–16, on the instrumentalist tendencies characteristic of modern public law to intrude into private law adjudication.

awaiting transplants than by the deceased's survivors; and property-developers are not invariably on the best of terms with countryside ramblers. The avoidance of adjudicatory prejudgement here crucially turns on the extensional differentiability of owned incidents, on their not being irreducibly intensional in description.

Before concluding this section and leaving Adjudicator to get on with the indicated reform of the duty-slips system, it may be worthwhile to notice one further implication that follows on from the previous point. For with the insertion into a duty-slip of a complete extensional specification of the action to which that slip pertains, it can be at best superfluous, and at worst misleading, still to include that action's *intensional* description. The case of Red's delivering the flowers to the wedding is probably somewhere near the superfluous end of this scale. Red will be fulfilling his duty to Blue regardless of whether his performing that *ex*tensionally described action is intensionally described as delivering flowers to the wedding, or mischievously provoking a disruptive allergic reaction in the pollen-sensitive bridegroom, or desperately escaping the gossipy conversation of his shop-assistant, or whatever.

But consider the case of a private nurse, Yellow, incurring a duty to make his seriously-ill patient, Green, comfortable. There is evidently an indefinitely large number of extensionally quite distinct actions that could all satisfy the description of "Yellow's making Green comfortable." These may range from helping him to sit up in bed to taking him for a walk in the park to accompanying him on a long sea voyage. Of course, there's no reason why Yellow's duty cannot include all of these actions and more. But the potentiality here, for incompossibilities, is plain enough. If Yellow has even a fraction of the average person's assortment of other duties, and if Green suffers any discomfort from Yellow's inattention, it seems quite likely that Adjudicator is again going to have her hands full. Only a set of extensional specifications (explicit or implicit) of the actions owed by Yellow to Green will preclude this possibility.

None of this should be taken to deny what is obviously true: namely, that intensional descriptions of owed actions often serve as perfectly adequate *surrogates* for extensional specifications. But they can do so precisely because and to the extent that duties to do those actions exist against a background of reasonably well-partitioned property rights. Certainly a world devoid of the linguistic and other conventions that facilitate such surrogacy would, to say the least, be cumbersome in the extreme. So all that's being argued here, with the metaphor of the duty-slips system, is that these intensional descriptions *must be* such surrogates: in the event of litigation, they must be translatable, however tediously, into extensional specifications.[59]

To say all this is to say no more (and no less) than that, in a compossible set of rights, all rights are *funded*. The sets of resources respectively required for the performance of each of their entailed duties are specifiably distinct from one another.

For if they are not, if a set of rights is incompossible, then Adjudicator will have in effect to supply such specifications *ex post*. She will have to exercise Holmes's sovereign prerogative of choice, thereby making law rather than merely applying it. Adjudicator would thus become Leviathan. In that nightmarish circumstance, some persons would not have the rights and duties indicated in their duty-slips. Rights would not entitle and duties would not obligate. For like many other things, rights have costs. And these costs are the impossibility of other rights. Any assignment of rights that is uninformed by this fact ultimately assigns those rights to no one but Adjudicator.

---

[59] Thus Fred Miller, "The Natural Right to Private Property," 275, contends that "All serious issues of public policy eventually turn on questions of property rights." Cf. Nozick, *Anarchy, State and Utopia*, 238: "The major objection to speaking of everyone's having a right *to* various things such as equality of opportunity, life, and so on, and enforcing this right, is that these "rights" require a substructure of things and materials and actions; and *other* people may have rights and entitlements over these. No one has a right to something whose realization requires certain uses of things and activities that other people have rights and entitlements over. Other people's rights and entitlements to *particular things* (*that* pencil, *their* body, and so on) and how they choose to exercise these rights and entitlements fix the external environment of any given individual and the means that will be available to him . . . No rights exist in conflict with this substructure of particular rights. Since no neatly contoured right to achieve a goal will avoid incompatibility with this substructure, no such rights exist. The particular rights over things fill the space of rights, leaving no room for general rights to be in a certain material condition."

I previously referred to the intricate normative structure formed by categorically compossible rights and signified by the concept of a set of title-based domains. The extensionally differentiated character of these domains, constituting this structure of compossibility, is needed to ensure that there's no extensional overlap between committed liberties. But in this regard, there is an important question which we've so far not addressed. What is it that ensures that the extensional specifications of the titles constituting each person's domain actually can be differentiated from those of every other person's domain? What conditions guarantee that physical object P does not figure simultaneously among the titles of both Red and Blue?[60] Or for that matter, Red and Blue and White and Orange and . . . N? Why is there only one person, rather than one hundred thousand, entitled to dispose of P at time T_6?

These questions may seem footling. In one sense, the answers to them are already implicit in much of what has gone before. Suppose P is the van. The reason why Blue alone has a title to the van at T_6 runs like this: White had a title to the van for T_3–T_n; he then undertook a duty to loan Red the van, thereby giving the latter a title to it for a certain period, say T_5–T_8; and Red then undertook a duty to Blue to deliver flowers at a certain time within that period, thereby giving Blue a title to it for T_6.

All this is pretty straightforward. White and Red successively transfer temporal slices of their titles to the van, leaving themselves with the residual untransferred slices.[61] If challenged to *vindicate* her T_6 title, all Blue would apparently have to do is cite both Red's title and his duty to her. Perhaps, if pressed by her challenger, Blue would also need to cite White's title and his duty to Red. Surely that would suffice.

Or would it? What if the challenger persisted, by querying White's

---

[60] In referring to P as a physical object, I don't wish to overlook Honoré's previously mentioned point about the fragmentability and interpersonal dispersability of rights in a single physical object. P should therefore be strictly understood to be any owned *incident* among the various rights pertaining to a single physical object, provided of course that it's extensionally differentiable from the rest. For expository simplicity, I shall treat P as a single physical object.

[61] Equally we can describe White's (Red's) title for T_3–T_n (T_5–T_8) as a *set* of titles – for T_3, T_4, T_5, etc. – some members of which are transferred.

title? Evidently *Blue's title is only as vindicable as White's*. Suppose Blue is able to produce a bill of sale indicating that White purchased the van from Black at T_2. Will this finally silence her challenger?

It may. Whether it does will partly depend on the challenger's estimation of Black. It is reported that, at the turn of this century, newly arrived immigrants to New York City were frequently the hapless victims of confidence tricksters who successively "sold" the Brooklyn Bridge to as many of them as possible, on the strength of its being an obviously lucrative investment. Blue's challenger may want some assurance that Black was neither a confidence trickster nor a hapless victim of one. Suppose Blue is able to produce evidence that Black was, in fact, the manufacturer of the van. Will this provide the requisite assurance? Again, not necessarily. For Blue must still satisfy her challenger that Black owned the various factors that went into the van's manufacture. *Blue's title is only as vindicable as Black's*.

What this cautionary tale suggests is that the structure of a set of compossible rights has a diachronic as well as a synchronic dimension. The set must have a well-partitioned history as well as a well-partitioned topography. Its having this history is a simple consequence of the conceptual fact, established earlier, that rights are exercisable. Compossible sets *derive* from compossible sets via right-holders' controlling choices. If Pink, as well as Black, claimed to have a T_1 title to the van's component factors, he might well contest Blue's T_6 title. Vindicable titles imply previous vindicable titles from which they derive.

It's this relation of derivation that underlies the *historical* dimension of compossibility. But the ways in which titles derive from other titles are, in some cases, more complex than might at first appear. To get a grip on this complexity and to complete our account of rights-compossibility, we need first to be a bit more precise about titles. A title is a (time-indexed) two-term relation, subsisting between a named person and a named physical object. As we've seen, it's a relation which vests that person with rights which imply duties of forbearance from disposing of the named object in all other persons. I'll say that titles are *extinguished* when either of the terms in the relations they denote – the person or the object – is changed. And I'll speak of the titles resulting from that change as ones which are *created*.

There are, then, two basic ways in which titles are extinguished and created: change of person and change of object. The first and simpler of these consists in the title-holder transferring ownership to another person, for part or all of the period covered by his title. In the present case, say, Black's title to the van is extinguished and White's title to it is created. And all those persons who previously owed forbearance duties to Black in respect of the van thereby have those duties extinguished and, in their place, they (now including Black but excluding White) become subject to created duties owed to White in respect of the van.

Thus both titles and the forbearance duties implied by them can be said to have *pedigrees*. Their derivation can be traced back through a series of extinguished titles and duties which are their *antecedents*. Grey has a duty to forbear from using the van now that it's White's because (i) Grey previously owed the same forbearance duty to Black, and (ii) Black extinguished that duty, replacing it with the one owed to White.

The second and more complex form of title extinction and creation consists of a change in the object named in the title. Suppose that Black, instead of selling his van to White, decides to disassemble it irreversibly. Assuming that his title to the van is not encumbered by any other persons' claims that imply the impermissibility of his doing so – the simplest example of such an encumbrance being another's vested liberty to use the van at specified future times – it follows that he has a vested liberty to disassemble it.[62] Clearly at some point in this permissible act of disassembly the van ceases to be a van, i.e. ceases to be the kind of object named in Black's title. Precisely which point this is must be largely a matter of linguistic conventions.

But what is *not* a matter of convention is that Black holds (created) titles to the disassembled components. For suppose Black begins by detaching a door-handle from the van's body. If his title to the van were not to entitle him to its components, over which of these two disjoined parts might his ownership lapse? With respect to which of them could other persons cease to have forbearance duties? The answer plainly is "neither." His vested liberty to disassemble the van entails that his detaching the handle, his melting it down, his detaching the chassis from the body, etc., are all impermissibly obstructable. Hence, since Black is exclusively entitled to dispose of these components at these points, and since there is the aforesaid absence of others' encumbering claims, there are *ex hypothesi* no reasons why his ownership of the van's components could lapse at any further point of disassembly. Thus Grey owes duties to Black to forbear from using any of the van's components because (i) Grey previously owed a forbearance duty to Black in respect of the van itself, and (ii) Black extinguished that duty by replacing it with ones in respect of the several components.

---

[62] This absence of encumbrances does not, of course, exclude others' rights against his driving the van into *their* front parlours, his tossing unwanted components into *their* gardens, etc., since we are assuming extensionally differentiated domains.

The same line of reasoning applies equally to a reverse form of title-change due to object-change. If instead of disassembling the van, Black decides to turn it into a bronzed statue, and if he holds similarly unencumbered titles to the bronzing paint, marble plinth, etc., which he attaches to the van, he thereby extinguishes a set of titles to these several objects and creates a title to a single new object.

A closely related argument is at work in Locke's famous "acorns and apples" example which, however, is principally deployed by him to support a far more problematic claim about the creation of titles to previously unowned objects.

> He that is nourished by the acorns he pickt up under an Oak, or the Apples he gathered from the Trees in the Wood, has certainly appropriated them to himself. No Body can deny but the nourishment is his. I ask then, When did they begin to be his? When he digested? Or when he eat? Or when he boiled? Or when he brought them home? Or when he pickt them up? And 'tis plain, if the first gathering made them not his, nothing else could.[63]

Commentators have not always been sufficiently careful to disentangle the two claims being urged here. For what is correct in this argument is its implicit suggestion that transformations by their owners, of owned physical objects, do not alter the personal location of titles to their physical derivatives. If the gatherer has a title to his (unnourished) body, and *if* he has a title to the acorns or apples, then he has a title to his nourished body – just as Black has a title to his statue. What is not necessarily correct here is Locke's main contention that gathering, or any of the other actions mentioned, creates a title to what is gathered. For this, as we shall see, raises very deep problems about the foundations of a set of rights: problems to be discussed at some length in the last two chapters.

Our present concern, however, is simply to establish that titles and duties derive from their immediate antecedents by the exercise either of powers to transfer ownership or of vested liberties to transform owned objects. To vindicate a title, one must refer both to previous vindicated titles and to exercises of powers or liberties attached to them. The forbearance duties implied by any title are vindicated in the same way. They, like the titles which they mirror, symmetrically possess mutually consistent causal and proprietorial pedigrees.

It's the consistency of these pedigrees – these chains of vindication – that constitutes the historical dimension of a set of compossible rights

---

[63] Locke, *Two Treatises of Government*, 306.

and guarantees the extensional differentiability of every right in that set. That is, it ensures that not more than one person holds the title to one particular object at the same time and that all other persons have the corresponding compossible duties. As was said above, the structure of compossibility is historical as well as topographical. Regrettably, I find myself unable to devise a suitably graphic metaphor for capturing the multi-dimensional complexity of this partitioning structure.

Before concluding this chapter, we should take note of two further implications of the historical dimension of rights-compossibility. The first is this: the fact that compossible rights do have histories shows what's wrong with any principle that purports to constitute a set of rights *solely* on the basis of what Nozick calls an "end-state" or "patterned" criterion.[64] What's wrong with such a principle could indeed be described as its failure to take rights seriously. For whatever sort of entitlements it may be thought to constitute, these cannot be understood as rights inasmuch as they lack the powers and liberties attached to rights, the exercise of which produces the kind of histories sketched above.

Suppose there's a principle assigning equal Ps to Red and Blue. If this is an end-state or patterned principle, their respective titles are encumbered by duties in each of them not to transfer or transform (including consume) more Ps than the other, since such activities destroy the parity mandated by that principle. To whom could these duties be owed? Could Red and Blue owe them to each other? If so, then Blue must be said to have a right correlative to that duty in Red (and *vice versa*). But if she indeed has this right, it must empower her to waive Red's correlative duty to her. That is, it must be possible for Blue to confer upon Red a liberty to use his Ps in ways which could result in some deviation from this parity. But the principle constituting that right, in prescribing distributive equality, contrarily implies that Red cannot have that liberty and, hence, that Blue cannot have that power. And this same contradiction arises regardless of where (in whom) rights correlative to such duties are located.

The second implication is this: like all good things, every vindication-

---

[64] Nozick, *Anarchy, State and Utopia*, ch. 7. An end-state criterion requires a particular proportional relation to obtain directly between persons' titles. A patterned criterion requires their titles to bear a proportional relation to the presence of a particular variable (need, productivity, caste, etc.) in them. We might say that to ascertain whether a set of holdings conforms to an end-state criterion requires only a snapshot of it. Conformity to a patterned criterion requires two snapshots: one of the set of holdings and one displaying the incidence of the stipulated variable. And conformity to Nozick's historical entitlement criterion requires a movie which records the set's history.

chain must come to an end. All sequences of antecedent titles and duties must terminate in a set of *ultimately antecedent* titles and duties. I'm going to call this a set of *original* rights and duties. The vindicability of any current right or duty clearly depends upon the vindicability of its original antecedents. What's therefore equally clear is that the vindication of original rights and duties can involve no historical reference: being original, they cannot derive from exercises of powers and liberties attached to antecedent rights because there are no rights antecedent to them. Yet, being rights and duties, they must be constituted by some rule or principle. It's this rule that supplies *their* vindication and a formulation of its general content will be presented in the sixth chapter, on justice.

Pursuing a similar line of thought, many writers have concluded that original rights and duties must be ones pertaining only to the ownership of raw natural resources.[65] This, because all objects named in current titles and corresponding forbearance duties either are, or are the physical derivatives of, natural resources.

The problem with this view is that no analogous claim can be made about the *persons* named in those titles and duties. Red's current duty to respect White's title to the van has its antecedent in – is vindicated by reference to – his previous duty to respect Black's title to the van, since Black sold the van to White. But it's not clear how a duty to respect White's title can similarly be ascribed to *Orange*, who came into existence only after that sale and who therefore never had a previous duty to respect Black's title. Hence Orange's duty to respect White's title, if he has such a duty, lacks an antecedent and must be an original one. And then so must White's correlatively entailed right against Orange.

Observe how this confronts the aforesaid view with a serious dilemma. For if Orange and White do respectively have this original duty and right, then original duties and rights cannot be ones pertaining solely to natural resources. The van is not a natural resource. On the other hand, if Orange does *not* have this duty nor White this right, it's unclear in what sense White can be said to have the title to the van, since property rights – as rights *in rem* – entail forbearance duties in all other persons, including Orange.

It follows that the compossibility requirements, as developed so far, govern ascriptions of rights and duties only to sets of *entirely concurrent persons*. Their extension to the rights and duties of only partially concurrent persons profoundly impairs many erstwhile accounts of original rights, and has significant ramifications for the rights derivable from original rights.

---

[65] And to persons' bodies, on which more in chs 7 and 8.

That the "generations problem" poses special difficulties for theories of justice is now widely acknowledged. In the last two chapters I'll try to show how a yet-to-be-formulated principle of justice, in conjunction with our compossibility requirements, copes with these difficulties. Before that, however, we need to explore the relations between any principle of justice and other moral rules. And to do this, we must first turn our attention to several pertinent aspects of moral reasoning.

4
Moral Reasoning

Trivially, moral reasoning is reasoning about moral actions. And moral actions are ones directed at those amongst our various ends which we believe should be pursued and sustained by everyone and ought not to be obstructed or abolished by anyone.[1] One such end may be justice: the requirement that moral rights be respected. To find out what that requirement is, to discover what justice demands of us, we need first to attend to two kinds of consideration.

In the next chapter we'll be looking at an important aspect of how we go about selecting the actions to secure our ends, including our moral ends. That is, we'll be looking at the structure of our thinking about *means*. Economic reasoning concerns, so to speak, some aspects of the supply side of moral actions (as well as non-moral ones). For the moment our concern is with the demand side: with certain general features of our moral judging and, especially, with the structure underpinning our judgements that particular actions are right or wrong, permissible or impermissible. One way of exhibiting this structure is to examine a number of Blue's problems.

Blue's chief problem is that every moral judgement she makes, along with her reasons for making it including the circumstances occasioning it, are reported to Adjudicator's superior – a pedantic and rather censorious computer called *Evaluator*.[2] What's particularly unattractive about

---

[1] In speaking of "ends," I'm not here prejudging the issue of deontological versus teleological or consequentialist views of morality in favour of the latter. This is discussed below (section (d)).

[2] The precise nature of the relationship between Evaluator and Adjudicator, between the general structure of moral reasoning and the sub-structure of moral rights reasoning, will be clarified in ch. 6.

Evaluator, apart from the very fact of his being a self-appointed auditor of Blue's moral deliberations, is his resolute refusal to respond to any of Blue's judgements other than those which are unsound. Her acceptable judgements, often agonizingly and painstakingly arrived at, evoke not so much as a murmur from Evaluator who hums along with sublime indifference. But when an unsound judgement is fed into the machine, all hell breaks loose. Bells ring, sirens scream and a big chartreuse neon sign flashes the eternally exasperating message, "This does not compute." Worse still, this pandemonium doesn't stop until Blue has revised either that unsound judgement or all those previously recorded judgements and reasons with which it is inconsistent.

Like most of us, Blue prefers a reasonably tranquil life. And so, unable to elude this albatross of a computer, she takes to studying moral philosophy in the vain hope of silencing her tormentor forever.

Sooner or later in her reading, Blue is going to come across that most familiar of examples in modern moral philosophy, the story of Sartre's student.[3] This case is one of moral *conflict* or *dilemma*. Sartre's student was confronted with a choice of going to England to join the Free French Forces in their efforts to liberate France from Nazi rule, or remaining in France to care for his severely ill mother. Evidently there are weighty moral reasons supporting the pursuit of each of these courses of action. Yet only one, either one, could be pursued.

As with the previous analyses of freedoms- and rights-compossibility, examining the circumstances of jointly unperformable actions can be a quite effective instrument for excavating some conceptual features of, in this case, moral reasoning.[4] Which aspect of those circumstances concerns us here? Note that Sartre's student was not (merely) deciding what to do, but rather what he *ought* to do. His judgement was to be a moral one of the form "I ought to do A," and neither a prediction ("I shall do A") nor an expression of resolve ("I will do A"). Blue, of course, is only a spectator of the student's predicament. Nevertheless, since her own moral commitments are not so very different, she too finds the choice dilemmatic and her judgement will therefore also be moral in form. Consequently the report received by Evaluator, in enumerating Blue's reasons for making the judgement, will have to refer to some statement containing the term "ought." Otherwise the pandemonium will start, inasmuch as Blue will have invalidly inferred an "ought" conclusion (her judgement) from premises (her reasons) devoid of any "ought."

Suppose Blue judges that what the student ought to have done is to have gone to England to join the Free French. The reasons for this judgement will include a number of reported empirical claims having to do with the facts of the German invasion and occupation, the overthrow of the French state and the Free French Forces' campaign to restore that

---

[3] Sartre, *Existentialism and Humanism*, 35–6.

[4] The use of dilemmas to illuminate a broad range of issues in moral philosophy is indicated in, among many sources, Castaneda, *The Structure of Morality*, 52; Chisolm, "Practical Reasoning and the Logic of Requirement," 1–2; Gowans (ed.), *Moral Dilemmas*; Hare, *Moral Thinking*, 26; Sinnott-Armstrong, *Moral Dilemmas*; Stocker, *Plural and Conflicting Values*; Bernard Williams, *Problems of the Self*, 166, and *Moral Luck*, 72.

state. But these reasons will also refer to a universal moral or prescriptive claim – a rule – to the effect, say, that one ought to repel foreign aggression. Let's call this moral rule the *Patriotism* rule. Why are the empirical claims described as "reported" whereas the Patriotism rule is described as "referred to"? This is because the Patriotism rule is already on file in Evaluator's memory banks, whereas the facts about what's going on in the world are not. Evaluator is not an avid newspaper reader. He is, however, a meticulous recorder of Blue's moral commitments. And Blue must already have a commitment to something like the Patriotism rule for a choice like that which confronted Sartre's student to constitute a moral dilemma for herself as well. Were she no believer in patriotism, she could hardly find herself exercised by such a choice.

Is the report as described sufficient to keep Evaluator quiet? Possibly not. For it goes on to include the facts about the student's mother and her need for her son's constant presence. And it further remarks that Blue's judgement, that the student ought to have gone to England, implies that he ought not to have remained in France with his mother. This appears to threaten an eruption on the part of Evaluator because it's inconsistent with the *Familial Devotion* rule, also on file with Evaluator, which is the other horn of Blue's (and the student's) dilemma.

The rest of this chapter is going to be concerned with various conceptions of what will make the report sufficient in the respect indicated. What is it that's needed to render Blue's moral judgements consistent with her avowed commitments? What will keep Evaluator quiet? We'll call Blue's set of commitments – the collection of moral rules she affirms – her moral *code*. And what we want to know is how this code must be organized, structured, so that she can comply with it in her moral judging. Leonard Nelson remarks:

> It happens to us often enough that these rules fail us. We find ourselves in situations not provided for in this set of rules, or in situations in which a given rule is applicable but in which we feel ourselves justified in violating the rule. This second situation occurs whenever there is a conflict between one rule and another ... The decision as to which of these rules is to be given preference cannot lie in either of the two rules in question. In the case of such conflict one moral rule must be waived in favour of another; here we require a principle of selection enabling us to know which rule we are to waive and which we are to uphold.[5]

---

[5] Nelson, *Critique of Practical Reason*, 116, quoted by Chisolm, "Practical Reasoning and the Logic of Requirement," 1–2. For reasons to be offered presently, it's difficult to

What distinguishes the aforementioned various conceptions from one another are their differing accounts of such selection principles.

According to one view, however, there simply are *no* rules or principles for selecting among primary or basic moral rules. (We are, provisionally at least, treating the Patriotism and Familial Devotion rules as primary moral rules.) Characterizing this view as "intuitionism," John Rawls observes: "Intuitionist theories, then, have two features: first they consist of a plurality of first principles which may conflict to give contrary directives in particular types of cases; and second, they include no explicit method, no priority rules, for weighing these principles against one another."[6] In the course of defending intuitionism against Rawls and others, J. O. Urmson has usefully distinguished three broad types of theory concerning the structure of moral judging. *Mononomic* theories (such as utilitarianism) hold that there's no plurality of first principles or primary rules, that there's only a single primary rule, and that all moral judgements are inferable from it. *Hierarchical* theories allow that there can be a plurality of primary rules, and assert that these are ordered by priority rules (which may include ones mandating decision procedures). And *intuitionist* theories, following Rawls's description, also embrace the plurality of primary rules, but deny that these are ordered.

In his defence of mononomism, John Stuart Mill famously contended that

> There must be some standard by which to determine the goodness
> or badness, absolute and comparative, of ends or objects of desire.
> And whatever that standard is, there can be but one: for if there
> were several ultimate principles of conduct, the same conduct
> might be approved by one of those principles and condemned by
> another; and there would be needed some more general principle,
> as umpire between them.[7]

Endorsing the plurality of primary moral rules and thereby rejecting mononomism, Urmson urges against hierarchical theories that "If it be recognized that there is a plurality of primary moral reasons for action, the complexity of many situations seems to me to make it implausible to suppose that we are guided . . . by any decision-procedure when we

---

make sense of the first sort of situation referred to by Nelson, if this is to be understood as different from the second.

[6] Rawls, *A Theory of Justice*, 34.

[7] Mill, *A System of Logic*, 547–8. In his *Autobiography*, 164, Mill denounced intuitionist moral theory as "an instrument devised for consecrating all deap-seated prejudices."

weigh up the pros and cons."[8] Let's adapt Urmson's terminology and call any codes containing a plurality of primary rules, whether hierarchical or intuitionist, *polynomic* ones.

Blue's code, in containing at least two primary rules (Patriotism and Familial Devotion), is a polynomic code. This is why she's in grave danger of being at the receiving end of an Evaluator outburst, unless her judgement in the case of Sartre's student can be construed as rule-governed: that is, priority rule-governed. In order to show that Blue can avoid Evaluator's wrath, I propose to argue for two claims: (i) that some of the considerations brought by intuitionists, against the plausibility of priority rules in polynomic codes, are ones which make sense only from a mononomic perspective; and (ii) that while mononomic and hierarchical theories can be correct accounts of coherent moral judgement, intuitionism cannot.

It should immediately be acknowledged, however, that there's one presumably unintended sense in which Urmson's scepticism about priority rules must be correct. For evidently if Blue had *already adopted* a priority rule ordering the primary Patriotism and Familial Devotion rules, she could not strictly be said to be in a dilemma when, subsequent to that adoption, she finds herself contemplating the student's choice. The right action, the judgement of what ought to have been done, would be unambiguously implied by her moral code. And in that sense, she would be "guided" by it. Or if she weren't, Evaluator would sound the alarm.

Nor, to say the least, is it inconceivable that she could have adopted such a priority rule beforehand. After all, she has already contemplated the possibility of familial and patriotic exigencies, in adopting primary rules for them. There's no reason why such prescience, or even just a bit of rational reflection, might not have led her to anticipate the further possibility of these two kinds of circumstance occurring conjunctively, and thereby induced her to adopt a priority rule. Or equally, if Evaluator were only a little more inclined to approach his task constructively, and to be less exclusively censorious, he would have advised Blue that the danger of such conjunctive eventualities is a logically entrenched feature of any polynomic code such as her own.[9] Obviously there's no logical necessity that Blue have anticipated this prospect, much less, that Evaluator have forewarned her of it. And in fact, they haven't.

---

[8] Urmson, "A Defence of Intuitionism," 119.

[9] Thus Gowans, *Moral Dilemmas*, 13, is mistaken to claim that, because "it may be that a plurality of principles never conflict," the existence of such a plurality "does not entail" that they *can* conflict.

But Urmson's contention does not and, indeed, cannot rest upon the accidents of Blue's shortsightedness and Evaluator's bloody-mindedness. It's situational *complexity* – not *novelty* – that is said by Urmson to render implausible our being guided by priority rules. For if the novelty of situational circumstances were to be regarded as so salient an aspect of our moral judging, it would be implausible to suppose (as Urmson does suppose) that it could be informed by any rules at all, even primary ones.

What is it, then, that makes a situation a complex one? Urmson's correct suggestion is that this is due to its being inhabited by pros *and* cons. How do we know that a situation's inhabitants include pros and cons? How do we identify them? Quite clearly, the pros of a situation are those of its empirical circumstances that are of a kind cited in some affirmed primary rule as occasioning a duty to perform a particular sort of action. Conversely, the cons are circumstances of that situation that, in conjunction with the provisions of an affirmed primary rule, imply that one ought not to perform that sort of action. With respect to the action of Sartre's student leaving France and going to England, the pros are the German occupation and the Free French campaign while the cons are his mother's need for his presence. So far as Blue's moral commitments are concerned, these circumstances exhaust the list of pros and cons inhabiting that situation.

Among the manifold features of any situation, the only ones which are relevant for moral judgement – which count as pros and cons – are (all) those of types which figure in our primary moral rules. What other facts could be relevant? When one surveys the features of a complex situation it's not the case that, having identified all the primary rules that bear on it, one then goes on to search for pros and cons. These are not different sets of data. Beyond the kinds of circumstance indicated in those primary rules, there is no additional relevant information about the situation to be intuited or, as Aristotle would have it, "perceived."[10] Hence what intuitionists refer to as "weighing up the pros and cons" or "judging the case on its merits" can amount to nothing other than the identification of a priority rule which orders the conflicting primary ones.[11]

---

[10] Aristotle, *Nicomachean Ethics*, 47; cf. Hare, "Relevance," 75.

[11] This may seem too quick. For a common response is to ask "What if the contribution Sartre's student can make to the Free French campaign is slight, while the service he can render to his mother is considerable?" I'll argue below that, *if* one deems such proportional considerations to be morally relevant, this can only be due either to one's code being mononomic or to the greater plurality of its primary rules, and *not* to the absence or inapplicability of priority rules.

But what, it may be objected, does the phrase "identifying a priority rule" really signify? Does it suggest, implausibly, that this rule already and necessarily exists as a long-confirmed member of the code in question? No. The argument for the presence of priority rules in polynomic codes has nothing to do with genealogical facts about codes, the historical sequence and psychological conditions in which they acquired their rules. It consists, rather, in claims about the logical coherence of codes and about the meaning of moral terms like "ought."

"Ought," when used in the expression of a moral judgement – a judgement about the rectitude of a particular action or policy – implies the universalization of that judgement. That is, it implies a rule. My statement that "You ought to tell me what you believe to be true about this matter" would not be understood as a moral judgement if, in the absence of countervailing considerations, I would dissent from the universal statement that anyone similarly placed ought to be honest. Of course, there can be situations inhabited by countervailing considerations which tell in favour of a judgement that you ought to be dishonest. But for those considerations to do so, they must themselves be of a sort covered by a moral rule. Believing in honesty, we can nonetheless endorse an instance of dishonesty as the right action, but only for other overriding moral reasons. And the overridingness of those reasons is evidently not implicit in the reasons themselves. It cannot be self-conferred but is, rather, an implication of a priority rule.[12]

Blue's moral judgement in favour of Sartre's student going to England trivially implies that it's not the case that he ought to have remained in France. The universalization of this judgement is itself a rule which states, in effect, that "In situations where patriotic and familial exigencies arise conjointly, and where it's possible to respond to either but not both of them, one ought to respond to the patriotic one." And its extensional equivalent is "Accord priority to the Patriotism rule over the Familial Devotion rule." In delivering the aforesaid judgement, Blue is adopting this priority rule and incorporating it into her code. Were she to reach a different judgement in another similar case, Evaluator's clamour would not abate until Blue had either (i) revised this latter judgement, or (ii) revised her code (by altering the priority rule) and reversed her judgement in the case of Sartre's student.

We can now see what's wrong with the intuitionist account of moral judgement. Intuitionist codes are incoherent because they are inherently *incomplete*. Such codes contain rules implying that action A_1 is obligatory in circumstance C_1, and A_2 in C_2. But they lack any rule covering

---

[12] In the chapter on justice I shall suggest one qualification of this latter claim.

what ought to be done in a situation where both C_1 and C_2 obtain and where either, but not both, A_1 or A_2 can be done. Hence an adherent of such a code is licensed to deliver a pair of mutually contradictory judgements about which actions are obligatory and non-obligatory in that situation. The code's incompleteness and consequent capacity to generate judgemental contradictions consist in the fact that it contains more than one rule *pertaining* to that sort of situation, but no rule *governing* it. And if the prioritized judgement made by that code's adherent is thus held not to imply a universal rule, it must fail to qualify as a moral judgement.[13]

[13] This seems to be conceded by Sen and Williams, *Utilitarianism and Beyond*, 17–18, who, while denying that rationality in moral codes in itself requires completeness, allow that rationality in particular moral judgements may do so.

That, the intuitionist might reply, is all very well in theory. Perhaps it is the case that polynomic codes lacking priority rules can generate judgemental contradictions. But that doesn't prove that such codes don't exist: those of Sartre's student and Blue show that they do. Indeed, we could hardly make sense of the notion of someone being in a moral dilemma – the notion with which this chapter began – unless his moral code was polynomic and lacked priority rules. The very possibility of dilemmas implies the non-necessity of priority rules.

This argument from the brute fact of dilemmas is a powerful one but its force is misdirected. It is, I suggest, better understood not as registering a reservation about the prioritized structurability of moral codes but rather as pointing to certain epistemic facts about primary moral rules. Historically, as Urmson notes, ethical intuitionism has been alternatively or additionally regarded as a theory about the *source* of our basic moral beliefs: viz. that these are a form of uninferred or self-evident knowledge.[14] Whether such a view is ultimately plausible is beyond my competence to assess. But its insight, that our conceptions of what is of *fundamental* moral worth are not derivative from nor gainsaid by systematized empirical knowledge, serves to illuminate the conditions necessary for the occurrence of dilemmas.

There is an important analogy here with geometry. Insoluble geometrical problems can occur for anyone whose geometry lacks a postulate concerning *parallel lines*. And moral dilemmas can occur for anyone whose polynomic code lacks priority rules. The non-necessity of parallel lines postulates closely resembles the non-necessity of priority rules in several salient respects. In order to display this resemblance and its implications more clearly, I want first to look at some conditions under which dilemmas *cannot* occur. Consider three questions:

1   Can all dilemmas be precluded from occurring?
2   Can any dilemma recur?
3   Are some dilemmas necessarily precluded from occurring?

---

[14] Urmson, "A Defence of Intuitionism," 111–12; cf. Williams, *Ethics and the Limits of Philosophy*, 93–5.

Showing that the answer to the first and third questions is "yes" and that the answer to the second is "no" will, I hope, help to indicate the proper significance of the reality of moral dilemmas.

Can all dilemmas be precluded from occurring? The reasons for this question's affirmative answer are straightforward enough and were alluded to previously. A necessary condition of a situation's confronting someone with a dilemma is that the primary rules conflicting in it are ones which he already affirms. Now, whatever may be the complex epistemic processes whereby persons determine the kinds of circumstance occasioning *primary* moral judgement – whether it be through conditioning, instruction or direct intuition – one thing is clear: determining the kinds of circumstance occasioning *prioritized* moral judgement is no more than a matter of simple inference, and requires neither broad experience of the world nor a vivid imagination. Evaluator, who possesses neither of these, would not be regarded as a great seer were he to identify these eventualities to Blue. And were he to do so, or were Blue to do the inferences herself, she need never encounter a dilemma.

Can any dilemma recur? It's difficult to see how it could. Having considered the case of Sartre's student and reached the judgement that he ought to have joined the Free French, Blue thereby added the implied priority rule – Patriotism over Familial Devotion – to her moral code. Were she to encounter another similarly situated person, we should expect and Evaluator would demand the delivery of a similarly prioritized judgement. To this it's sometimes been objected that no two situations are ever exactly similar. But this objection is self-refuting and its proponents can fairly be accused of trying both to have their cake and eat it. For in the first place, the objection is idle unless supported not merely by an assertion of any two situations' mutual dissimilarities, but also by a claim that at least some of these dissimilarities are morally relevant. However, this latter claim can mean nothing other than that the set of conflicting moral considerations or primary rules pertaining to that second situation is non-identical with that in the first. In which case, it's simply false that the second dilemma is the same as, or a recurrence of, the first one. Relevantly different situations constitute different dilemmas, not recurrences of previous ones.

Are some dilemmas necessarily precluded from occurring? A dilemma is necessarily precluded from occurring, we'll say, if the type of situation constituting it is necessarily covered by a particular priority rule. And a situation is necessarily covered by a particular priority rule if the content of that priority rule is uniquely inferable: that is, if that rule can already be attributed to a code, even though its adherents may never even have contemplated it, much less affirmed it or delivered a judgement of which it is the universalization. As we'll see, polynomic codes can contain many such *inferable* priority rules and it's this fact that makes them like geometries. Inferable priority rules are like a geometry's theorems. But not all priority rules are inferable. Blue's "Patriotism over Familial Devotion" rule, as presented thus far, is not an inferable one. Under what conditions would it be an inferable one?

Suppose Blue's moral code contains a third primary rule, *Promise-keeping*. The presence of this primary rule implies that, for the code to be coherent, it must contain at least two other priority rules. (In fact, as will be seen presently, it must contain nine priority rules altogether.) These two priority rules respectively govern situations in which there's a conflict between either the Patriotism and Promise-keeping rules or the Familial Devotion and Promise-keeping rules. Suppose these priority rules enjoin "Patriotism over Promise-keeping" and "Promise-keeping over Familial Devotion." Then, according to the rational choice condition of *transitivity*, the code *must* contain the rule "Patriotism over Familial Devotion." That is, we can infer this priority rule from the other two priority rules.

The presence of transitivity in the priority rules of a coherent moral code should not, of course, be taken to imply that this condition is reflected in all forms of rational choosing.[15] Alex Michalos explains:

> The importance of [non-transitivity] may be seen by considering the combat superiority of ships. It so happens that destroyers tend to be superior to submarines, submarines tend to be superior to battleships and battleships tend to be superior to destroyers. Thus, if one had to bet on the outcome of certain battles, one would be wise to prefer a destroyer over a submarine, a submarine over a battleship and a battleship over a destroyer ... [somewhat similarly] x might prefer apples to bananas and the latter to cherries on the basis of their taste, but cherries to apples on the basis of their price.[16]

Non-transitivity makes perfect sense in these preference relations because, in each example, there is a plurality of more fundamental con-

---

[15] One reason why transitivity (A>B, B>C, A>C) is considered a *prima facie* condition of rational ordering is that non-transitivity (A>B, B>C, C>A) implies the mutual contraries AB>BC and BC>AB.

[16] Michalos, *Foundations of Decision-Making*, 29–30. And thus, following the previous note, informed gamblers would be uncertain whether to bet on a fleet of destroyers and submarines in combat against one of submarines and battleships.

siderations with respect to which the relative preferences for the three different types of ship and fruit are purely instrumental. In the former case these are different (unnamed) dimensions of combat superiority and in the latter they are taste and economy.[17] And these more fundamental considerations can themselves be ordered. But when it comes to priority relations between primary moral rules, there *ex hypothesi* can't be more fundamental moral considerations to determine those relations instrumentally since, if there were, those rules would *ipso facto* not be primary ones.

So one condition necessary for the inferability of the "Patriotism over Familial Devotion" priority rule is the presence in Blue's code of another primary rule. A second condition is the presence of other already determined priority rules. These need not be the two mentioned above. If the code contains three primary rules, it's capable of generating no fewer than *nine* kinds of conflict situation: that is, six kinds of conflict more complex than those between only two primary rules. This greater complexity is due both to the greater number of rules in conflict and to the fact that, among the jointly unperformable actions available in such situations, there can be some that each comply with the demands of more than one primary rule.

All the possible kinds of conflict situation for a code containing Blue's three primary rules are set out in table 4.1. For brevity, I employ the following notation: P, PK, FD, for actions respectively compliant with the Patriotism, Promise-keeping and Familial Devotion primary rules; (+) for actions conjunctively compliant with more than one primary rule; "or" for alternative or jointly unperformable rule-compliant actions; and (>) for "has priority over."

Table 4.1

		1	2	3
	(a)	P or PK	PK or FD	P or FD
Levels of		4	5	6
complexity	(b)	P or PK+FD	PK or P+FD	FD or P+PK
		7	8	9
	(c)	P+PK or P+FD	P+PK or PK+FD	P+FD or PK+FD

[17] The classic account of intransitivity as being a consequence of a plurality of more fundamental considerations is given in May, "Transitivity, Utility and Aggregation in Preference Theory'; cf. Edwards, "The Theory of Decision Making," 44–7; von Wright, *The Logic of Preference*, 22–3; Pettit, "Decision Theory and Folk Psychology," 163.

The dilemma faced by Sartre's student is represented in 3. We've seen that Blue's priority rule for this kind of conflict is an inferable one if the previously mentioned priority rules for situations 1 (P>PK) and 2 (PK>FD) are already present in the code. Alternatively, it would be equally inferable from a rule conferring priority on P in 4 or on P+PK in 8.[18]

In general, just which and how many priority rules are inferable depends upon which priority rules are already (non-inferably) present in the code. Thus, for example, if the previously mentioned rules for 1 and 2 are already present, then all the remaining priority rules except that for 4 are inferable. And much the same is true if the only priority rules already present are ones on the second or third level of complexity. Since there's no reason why the conflicts initially contemplated or encountered by Blue need be of the simpler first-level sort, we cannot say *a priori* which priority rules will be inferable. But what we can say *a priori* is that some, indeed most, will be inferable and that these are ones which can therefore be attributed to Blue's code even though she may (as yet) have neither directly affirmed them nor made prioritized judgements of which they are the universalizations.[19]

The membership status of inferable priority rules, in Blue's moral code, is as respectable as that of any directly affirmed or judgement-implied priority rule inasmuch as judgements inconsistent with them will provoke the same adverse reaction from Evaluator as would be forthcoming for a judgement inconsistent with the latter. And since situations governed by an inferable priority rule are describable as ones necessarily covered by a priority rule, what would otherwise constitute dilemmas in those situations are – in answer to our third question – necessarily precluded from occurring.

Are we really warranted in ascribing such a high incidence of inferability to the set of priority rules in a polynomic code? Consider the following suggestion as to why third-level priority rules are *not* inferable from first-level ones. It could be the case that a particular action which is conjunctively compliant with the two lower-ranked primary rules (Promise-keeping and Familial Devotion) is morally better than one conjunctively compliant with the two higher-ranked primary rules (Patriotism and Promise-keeping) because an important additional

---

[18] Triadic conflict situations (e.g. "P or PK or FD," "P+PK or P+FD or PK," etc.) are reducible to sets of the dyadic ones indicated.

[19] Each increase in the number of primary rules exponentially increases the number of possible kinds of conflict. A code with four primary rules generates fifty-three possible kinds of conflict, distributed over six levels of complexity. From a strict ordering of four primary rules (A>B>C>D), one can infer no fewer than forty of the remaining forty-nine required priority rules.

feature may exist in instances of the former conjunction that is lacking in the latter. Hence the first-level ordering P>PK>FD need *not* imply the priority rule P+PK>PK+FD in situation 7 on the third level. The motivation for this suggestion is somewhat analogous to the economist's concept of "complementary goods" – goods which, like bread and butter, are of greater aggregate value when secured together than when secured separately.[20]

Since this suggestion will also have a significant bearing on our later discussion of non-polynomic codes, it's doubly useful here to ascertain whether it can be true of polynomic ones. Let's do this by constructing an example that further complicates the predicament of Sartre's student and that again calls for a judgement from Blue. Suppose that, in addition to his conflicting commitments to his mother and the Free French, the student had promised assistance to a friend serving in the Resistance should the latter ever need to escape France. And we'll further suppose that the day came when, on the run from the occupying forces, the friend presented himself weary and wounded and invoking the promise. Prevailing circumstances and the student's resources were such that there were only two ways to arrange his friend's escape: either he could expensively bribe a border official to let his friend cross into nearby Switzerland; or he would have to accompany him on the considerably more arduous journey across France to a Channel port where they could get a fishing boat to take them to England. The first option would preclude the student's ever getting to England, while the second would rule out staying with his mother.

On the face of it, this looks like a clear choice between either Promise-keeping + Familial Devotion or Patriotism + Promise-keeping (situation 8, above). And given the first-level priority rules mentioned above, we might be inclined to think that Blue's code commits her to the latter alternative. However, on the suggestion we're examining, there could be something more to be said for the former that would be weighty enough to reverse this implied priority. Thus one might point to the fact that the friend's health is so poor that it would be far more *compassionate* to fulfil the promise by enabling him to slip across the nearby border than by dragging him all the way to England. This is surely a not unreasonable argument.

Nevertheless what we want to know is whether, and if so how, Blue can consistently accept it as decisive. Evidently she can if, among other things, compassion is deemed a relevant feature of situations occasioning

---

[20] I owe this objection to Amartya Sen.

moral judgement. But from what we know of Blue's code so far, it's not. There is no Compassion rule (C) in Blue's set of primary rules and, consequently, she must expect a noisy reaction from Evaluator if she allows this consideration to count – let alone, be decisive – in her judgement. Of course, she's not absolutely debarred from doing so, provided that she's prepared to add the Compassion rule to her list of primary rules and to make the appropriate additions and alterations to her set of priority rules. And these amendments will further entail alterations in all those of her previous moral judgements which neglected attendant considerations of compassion and are thus inconsistent with the revised set of priority rules consequent upon the adoption and ranking of the Compassion rule.

Now there's certainly no reason why Blue cannot make these changes. Indeed, such changes and reappraisals are very much the stuff of many processes of moral learning, a good deal of which takes place in the school of moral dilemmas. But this in no way embarrasses our structural claim that, in a code containing only three primary rules, third-level priority rules are inferable from first-level ones. For if Blue's code does contain the Compassion rule, it's a code containing four rather than three primary rules. And the proposed priority rule governing the conflict situation just described – PK+FD+C>P+PK – is located on that code's fifth, rather than its third, level of complexity. A high incidence of inferability similarly attends the set of priority rules in a four-primary-rules code.[21]

We're now better placed to see the geometrical analogy. Geometries consist of a set of propositions which serve as premises in the solution of particular geometric problems. Five of these propositions are postulates – uninferred principles – from which the others, theorems, are inferred. But although the first four of those postulates (initially systematized by Euclid) are generally taken to be necessary or self-evident truths, since the last century it has become clear that Euclid's fifth postulate – about parallel lines – cannot be. Nor, however, is this status enjoyed by any of the alternative parallel lines postulates severally embraced by non-Euclidean geometries. Different parallel lines postulates thus generate different sets of theorems, different geometries, each of which is an internally coherent body of propositions.[22]

Whether, as some intuitionists would have it, our primary moral rules are self-evident in the way that the first four geometrical postulates are,

[21] Cf. n. 19, above.
[22] Cf. Reichenbach, *The Philosophy of Space and Time*, ch. I; Barker, *Philosophy of Mathematics*, ch. 3.

is fortunately not our concern here. In any case, while certain elementary moral judgements, like the solutions to simple geometrical problems, can be got with the aid solely of these basic propositions, answers to more complex and common moral or geometrical questions cannot. These answers are available only from priority rules or, in geometry, from a parallel lines postulate and the theorems derivable from it. A polynomic code's non-inferable priority rules are thus epistemically similar to a geometry's parallel lines postulate: they are needed but their content is logically indeterminate. Once determined, determinate priority rules are inferable from them, just as the content of many geometrical theorems is inferable from a parallel lines postulate. So the analogy between a geometry and a polynomic code consists in the fact that they each contain three corresponding types of proposition: (i) the first four Euclidean postulates and the set of primary moral rules; (ii) a parallel lines postulate and a set of non-inferable priority rules; and (iii) a set of theorems and a set of inferable priority rules derived from (ii).[23] *Completeness*, i.e. the presence of (ii) and (iii), is a rational requirement of both structures in the sense that many questions formulated in terms of the propositions included in (i) cannot be answered – constitute dilemmas – in the absence of the propositions in (ii) and (iii).

[23] The limit of the analogy arises in (iii) inasmuch as a geometry's theorems may be infinitely numerous, whereas the number of inferable priority rules is strictly constrained by the number of primary rules and is zero in the case of a code with only two primary rules.

(C) QUALITY AND QUANTITY

Having taken so much trouble to erect this polynomic structure, let's now see what could be done to collapse it. One piece of heavy equipment that can be wheeled on for this operation is an item called the *Moral Judgement Machine* (MJM), whose specifications will be described presently. The inventor of MJM, like intuitionists, was deeply impressed by the complexity of many situations occasioning moral judgement. And while he recognized a structured set of priority rules as one kind of rational response to such complexity, he nonetheless found it unsatisfying – as perhaps intuitionists might – inasmuch as it appears to subdue that sort of complexity only by introducing another. But MJM's inventor was very far from being a card-carrying intuitionist. For although some of his objections to priority rules are shared by intuitionists, the conclusions he drew from them are radically different from theirs. The appropriate response to moral complexity, he maintained, is neither a polynomic hierarchy of priority rules nor an intuitionist resignation to ever-recurring dilemmas, but simply *mononomism*. How did he think this bold move would help? And how, in any case, is it to be motivated?

The first step is plausible enough. Returning to Sartre's student, we'll now suppose that the choice before him was not between a patriotic act and one of familial devotion, but rather between two mutually incompatible acts of familial devotion: say, caring for this unwell mother or helping his sister to escape arrest by the authorities by accompanying her abroad. Evidently this dilemma, consisting in a conflict between two applications of the same primary rule, is not going to be resolvable by reference to the sort of priority rule we've been examining. Nor, however, should this be taken to indicate the limitations of priority rules or polynomic codes generally. For "ties" of this kind, since they occur with respect to one and the same primary rule, are an ineliminable possibility in any kind of code, even mononomic ones. Conflicts between duties displaying no morally relevant difference cannot be resolved in any rule-governed way.[24] And so far, at least, the only types of morally relevant

---

[24] I ignore the uninteresting fact that polynomic codes, and perhaps mononomic ones too, could contain a rule mandating a tie-breaking decision-procedure such as coin-flipping.

difference we've considered have been *qualitative* ones: differences between the types of action in conflict.

But suppose that the devotional service the student could have rendered to his sister was *greater* than what he could have done for his mother. I'll defer, for the moment, any discussion of what "greater" could mean here since this question lies very much at the heart of the move we're about to explore. Let's just provisionally imagine that we have some notion, not only of what constitutes an act of familial devotion, but also of what would make one act exhibit *more* of this feature than another such act. On this basis, it seems plausible to say that the student ought to have favoured his sister, that since familial devotion is a morally good thing more of it is better than less.

Now we wheel on MJM. Ostensibly, MJM is a sort of game: a machine for testing a person's capacity to deliver consistent moral judgements, whatever and however numerous his primary rules happen to be. As such, it's much beloved of Evaluator for whom players' frailties and computational ineptitudes furnish countless opportunities to exercise his censoriousness. The machine has two basic components: a *situation device* and a *constraint mechanism*. At various intervals, the situation device ejects one or more coloured balls on to a partially enclosed tray. These balls each represent an action of a kind cited in a primary rule as obligatory. A player's removal of a ball from the tray signifies his judgement that that action ought to be done. The balls are variously painted in the primary spectral colours: red, orange, yellow, green, blue, indigo, violet. Each colour is the counterpart of a different primary moral rule. And the simple ordering of primary rules – expressed in first-level priority rules – is replicated in this spectral sequence, with red balls corresponding to the highest-ranked primary rule, orange to the second-highest, and so forth. Thus, in Blue's code for example, red balls are acts of patriotism, orange balls of promise-keeping and yellow balls of familial devotion.[25]

MJM's other component, the constraint mechanism, is as simple as it is (usually) tight-fisted. It consists of two parts: a screen which flashes a number whenever the situation device ejects balls on to the tray; and a small turnstile which prevents players from removing more balls than the number on the screen. In more advanced versions of the game, which need not trouble us for the moment, the constraint mechanism also limits

---

[25] Players with codes containing more than seven primary rules are accommodated with balls of colours intermediate between the primary spectral ones. Those like Blue, whose codes contain fewer than seven primary rules, are entitled to ignore balls of colours lower in the sequence.

the possible combinations of balls which players may remove. Suffice it to say that the number of removable balls is rarely as great as the number ejected. So players usually have to make hard choices.

Novices, however, get started off gently. On the first round, the situation device ejects only one ball. And the constraint mechanism, in an uncharacteristic paroxysm of generosity, flashes 10. The next round is hardly more taxing, with a red and a yellow ball being ejected, only one of which can be removed. Nor is Blue much exercised even by the third round, involving a choice of any pair of a red, an orange and a yellow ball.

But honeymoons can't last forever, and MJM soon gets down to business. That is, it gets down to its inventor's business, which is to advertise the attractions of mononomism. The first move in this direction is to present Blue with the new dilemma we previously constructed for Sartre's student: the choice between caring for his mother and helping his sister escape. Two balls are ejected by the situation device, while the constraint mechanism flashes 1. The difference between this round and the easygoing honeymoon rounds is that one of the balls is big and the other little, while both are of the same colour (yellow). Previously, all the ejected balls had been of the same size. Or so it had seemed to Blue, who hadn't really paid much attention to their sizes since their colour differences appeared to be all that mattered, and all that was needed, in order to arrive at a judgement about which should be removed.

Now Blue is perplexed. She ponders the choice, examining the balls very closely in an effort to detect some slight difference of shading between them. But finding none, and pursuing the plausible line of reasoning we rambled down earlier, she cautiously removes the big one, all the while glancing nervously over her shoulder at Evaluator.

Evaluator remains silent. Relieved and emboldened by her success, Blue sails confidently through the next half dozen rounds which present her with no new conceptual problems and appear to be mere variations on the same theme: any one of a big red, a little red and a big orange; any pair of two big oranges, a little orange and two big yellows; any triple of a little red, a little orange, a big yellow and three little yellows; and so forth. It's not until the eleventh round that Blue's casual mastery comes to an abrupt halt.

For with a constraint of only one ball removable, the situation device has ejected one little red and one big orange. Blue is well and truly shaken. Can it really be that a little bit of patriotism is morally better than a big promise-keeping? Blue's natural initial response is to deploy the standard reinterpretive tactics of hard-choice-avoidance: she squints at the tray in an effort to make the little red ball disappear altogether;

she ransacks physics books in the hope of discovering a casuistry implying that big oranges are simply little reds enlarged;[26] finally, in heroic desperation, she tries to remove both balls from the tray. All to no avail. What is to be done?

Rather than answer this question immediately, let's hedge for a while and look at several other possibly pertinent questions. One of these asks what sort of priority rule has in fact been instanced by Blue's judgements up till now. In choosing the big yellow over the little one, wasn't she affirming that "big is better"? And wasn't the same rule implicit in many of her subsequent judgements? In which case, won't Evaluator make a fuss if she now chooses the little red over the big orange?

It's certainly true that Blue followed *some* big-is-better rule, since Evaluator will most assuredly come down on her like a ton of bricks should she ever choose a little yellow over a big one or, for that matter, a little ball of any colour over a big one of the same colour. But at least so far, none of Blue's judgements can be said to instance an *unqualified* big-is-better rule. Nor, however, is any of them inconsistent with such a rule. Her earlier prioritized judgements, though doubtless involving the regret appropriate to all occasions of forgone valuable ends, nevertheless spared her one sort of anguish: they were equally compatible with an unqualified big-is-better rule and with the qualitative priority rules represented by the spectral colour sequence. Now she seems to have come to a parting of the ways and to be having to make a choice between these two alternatives.

At this point, MJM's operator (whom we'll call *Operator*) volunteers some not entirely disinterested advice. Not entirely disinterested, because Operator is a lifelong disciple of MJM's inventor and a convinced mononomist. "Look," he says to Blue, "I really understand your predicament. You think that both patriotism and promise-keeping are morally important and that the former is more important than the latter. You also agree that a big act of patriotism is more important than a little one, and that the same is true with respect to promise-keeping and familial devotion. At the same time, you obviously have qualms about becoming a *fanatical* patriot. I applaud both your reasonableness and your scruples. So why not do the following? Keep your qualitative priority rules – red over orange over yellow – but reform them slightly with a big-is-better rule. In other words, double your present set of primary rules from three to six and rank them so that, in terms of MJM, they assume this order: big red over big orange over big yellow over little red

---

[26] Would that further imply that big indigos are lesser reds enlarged still more?

over little orange over little yellow. I don't know what sorts of moral judgement you may have made before you started playing MJM but, if you're lucky, they might well be consistent with this ordering anyway. In which case, Evaluator won't force you to revise them. Even if you do have to revise some of them, that shouldn't prove insuperably difficult. In any event, this reform will serve to extricate you honourably from the present round."

Blue provisionally adopts this suggestion. Operator then proceeds to give her a few easy rounds of choices between big and little balls of varying colours, enabling her to become fairly adept at practising the new semi-quantified set of primary and priority rules. Once Blue's confidence is restored, however, Operator's next two moves are entirely predictable. On the next round, a constraint of one ball removable is imposed on a choice of three balls: one little, two big, and all of them red. The novelty is that one of the big balls is *bigger* than the other big one.

A vague sense of foreboding overtakes Blue as she absorbs this discovery that balls can come in more than two sizes. "*How many more?*" she wonders uneasily as she contemplates further proliferations of semi-quantified primary rules and exponential proliferations of priority rules. But putting these worries aside for the moment and turning to the choice at hand, Blue removes the biggest red ball on the eminently reasonable grounds that, if big is better than little, then bigger is better than big and *a fortiori* biggest is best. (Evaluator remains silent.)

The *coup de grâce* is not long in coming. For on the following round, Blue's worst fears are realized inasmuch as she is constrained to pick one ball from among a big red, a bigger orange and a still bigger yellow. Angry and frustrated, she turns on Operator: "This is all *your* fault", she remonstrates. "*You* led me down this garden path with that infernal machine. Before I started playing this game, consistent moral judging was painful but at least it was possible, and it was gradually getting easier. Now you throw constantly varying magnitudes at me, complicate my priorities incomprehensibly and present me with an unending series of dilemmas. Life was infinitely simpler than it promises ever to be under your quantified scheme and I am therefore rescinding my adoption of your big-is-better rule and all that it entails."

Long experienced in coping with such outbursts, Operator responds in his most soothingly therapeutic manner: "I do see your point, I assure you. But you really mustn't do anything hasty. In the first place, it was on your own initiative and prior to my advice that you chose a big yellow over a little one. Second, as to the constant variation in ball size, life is just like that and it has nothing to do with my wishes or MJM.

You can't honestly expect all morally good actions to come neatly wrapped up in only two standard sizes, much less only one. But third, and here's the good news, you're quite mistaken to claim that a quantified scheme is more complicated than your earlier purely qualitative one. In the last round you clearly perceived that biggest-is-best is the natural extension of big-is-better. With the achievement of that insight, you reached the summit of moral wisdom. No further dilemmas lie in your path. All you need ever do from now on is simply select the biggest ball, or biggest combination of balls, removable under the constraint mechanism. In the present round, this would be the yellow one. Of course, you will encounter the occasional 'tie,' but since that can happen under any kind of structure there's no point in worrying about it. We'll even supply you with a coin to flip on such occasions."

Blue listens to this and slowly regains her composure, but remains suspicious of Operator's solicitude. "If I understand your proposal," she ventures shrewdly, "the colours of the balls – the *kinds* of act they represent, let alone their ordering – will no longer matter at all. It will be as if the balls were colourless, when all that counts is their size."

"Exactly!" exclaims the beaming Operator, gratified at his impending convert's rapid progress. "Look, I'll show you." And so saying, he pushes the biggest-is-best button on the MJM and activates the situation device. The sound of balls being ejected is heard, the number of balls removable is flashed on the constraint mechanism screen, *but no balls appear*. "Just a minor technical hitch," Operator apologizes, "I shan't be a moment." And he slips away to make a few adjustments. Upon returning, he re-activates the machine but again no balls appear.

Sensing a momentary shift in the balance of forensic power, Blue decides to take a bolder line. "Of course there are no balls there," she scoffs. "Colourless balls can't exist or, if they can, they certainly can't be seen. How can there be acts, whether of one size or many, which are not acts of particular kinds? This absurd assumption has bedevilled discussions of utilitarianism for an embarrassingly long time. But even Bentham, when he brought down the mononomic tablets and told us to do that act which is biggest (with respect to a composite magnitude of intensity, duration, certainty, propinquity, fecundity, purity and extent), wasn't referring to just any kind of act but rather, in his case, to only those which promise to produce happiness.[27] You, Operator, seem to be as suggestible as I, in so quickly accepting my sophistry that a judgemental concern exclusively with the size of balls implies their possible

[27] Bentham, *An Introduction to the Principles of Morals and Legislation*, 38–40.

colourlessness. All that it implies is the absence of any *difference* of colour among them, i.e. that they are all the same colour. God knows what sorts of act one would be choosing and rejecting if one had to select from colourless balls. There could be no way of distinguishing those that have at least some moral value from those that haven't."

"Fine, fine," Operator retorts impatiently, annoyed that Blue's conversion might be slipping from his grasp. "We'll make the balls all the same colour. No problem." A few more adjustments are made, MJM is activated once again, and all the balls come out the same colour – *indigo*.

"*Indigo*! What's indigo?" chortles Blue.

"Why should you care? What's the difference?" counters Operator. "You've got what you wanted: balls which are all identically coloured. Just get on with it and select the biggest."

"Yes, but how do I know that I have to choose at all here, let alone in a rule-governed way? How do I know that indigo balls represent *moral* alternatives? Maybe they're only alternative physical exercises or concert attendances. Fitness and culture may have moral value for some, but not for me. For me, they're simply objects of preference, like ice-cream flavours, and my choices among them are not universalized (i.e. rule-implicating) judgements. So I repeat: What kind of acts are indigo balls?"

"Look," says Operator, "if you're going to be fussy, we can change all the balls to red."

"Ah, if only it were that simple," sighs Blue. "As a matter of fact, I tried something like that myself back in the eleventh round when I had to choose between a big orange and a little red. I hoped, indeed prayed, that there might be some basis for construing promise-keepings as patriotic acts. But while it's doubtless true that *some* promise-keepings are patriotic, I failed to find any grounds for believing that this is invariably so. Sartre's student's "escape to Switzerland option,' which I considered previously, is a case in point. W. V. O. Quine is certainly correct to say that

Ethical axioms can be minimized by reducing some values causally to others: that is, by showing that some of the valued acts would already count as valuable anyway as means to ulterior ends... Causal reduction can serve not only in thus condensing the assumptions but also in sorting out conflicts.[28]

---

[28] Quine, *Theories and Things*, 64.

But he's equally right in immediately cautioning that this works only 'to the extent that we can reduce moral values causally to other moral values' and that 'there must remain some ultimate ends unreduced.' Of course, if by 'some' he means more than one, his caution may be slightly overstated: I don't want to claim that mononomism is impossible, that there *must* be a plurality of ultimate ends or primary rules. But you've so far given me no reason to subscribe to your diametrically opposed view. And you still haven't told me what indigo acts are."

"Well," replies Operator gracelessly, "I suppose they can be anything you fancy. A lot of players seem to construe them as happiness-producing acts. Others reckon they're desire- or preference-satisfiers or even regret-minimizers. And some players, with more metaphysical leanings, tend to regard them as self-developers or organic-unifiers. It really makes no difference to me. All I'm interested in is getting your moral judging on to a sound rational footing and saving you from having to become a fanatical patriot. And look at the thanks I get!"

"A reasonable aspiration," concedes Blue. "I don't much relish fanatical patriotism. But at the same time, it's beginning to look as though *some* kind of fanaticism is well-nigh unavoidable. And what I don't see is why it needs to be what is in fact the rather streamlined version you're trying to foist on me, much less, why it should be a fanatical commitment to happiness-production, preference-satisfaction or any one of those other items you mentioned. If I believed any of them to be of intrinsic moral worth, I would of course include it among my primary rules. I might even assign it a high priority relative to some of my other primary rules. But this would still be a far cry from regarding it *alone* as being morally valuable, with all other putatively primary rules as just so many instrumental subsumptions of it. This would still be a far cry from mononomism. In short, while we agree that pure intuitionism is a non-starter (or, more precisely, a non-finisher), I'm not convinced that my moral geometry is fully replaceable by your moral arithmetic."

"But that's exactly the point!" exclaims Operator. "In fact, I couldn't have put it better myself. To do geometry you have to do arithmetic, whereas the reverse is not true. If you can solve moral problems with arithmetic alone, why complicate matters by also bringing in geometry?"

"The geometry," retorts Blue, "comes in through the very same epistemic door as your arithmetic. You have to let *something* in – be it happiness-production or whatever – to orchestrate your numbers: they don't just grind away on all acts indiscriminately. The basic difference between you and me is that you want to close that door after only one primary rule has arrived, while I incline to less sectarianism in these matters. I know my parties must seem to you to be pretty motley affairs.

And it's also true that I have to include some policemen (priority rules) among my guests to stop things getting out of hand. But I assure you that we are as orderly, and as capable of consistently handling complex situations when they arise, as you are."

"*Touché*, my polynomic friend!" applauds Operator. "Encountering so formidable an adversary is such a rare experience these days that I'm almost tempted to agree with you. But not quite. And thus I fear I must now wheel on my clincher which, if you don't mind, I'll introduce with a brief cautionary tale. Last week we had another polynomist in to play MJM, only this poor chap – called *Poor Chap* – had come along freighted with what he took to be no fewer than *thirty* fully-fledged, independent primary rules. (You can imagine the size of the priority rule-book he was carrying around with him!) I shan't bore you with the full list but it included your three, along with such old favourites as Benevolence, Honesty, Clemency, Chastity, Courage, Prudence, Temperance, Humility, Courtesy, Creativity, Justice, Geniality and so forth. Frankly, I was pretty worried about finding enough colours to accommodate him, and asked if he could possibly make some reduction. But he adamantly refused on the same grounds as you offered earlier, viz. that although acts of one of these kinds might sometimes also be acts of another of them, one couldn't presume this to be invariably so. At any rate, we somehow managed to replicate his full range of primary rules and started putting him through his paces.

"Where we got him was on the first big-is-better round. You remember it, don't you – the one with two yellow balls, one little and one big? (Coincidentally, yellow was Familial Devotion for him too.) Anyway, he was taking simply ages over it and I thought I'd better give him a hand, little dreaming that we would bag him so early. It seems he was having trouble conceiving of a moral analogue for balls being of different sizes: he wasn't sure what could be meant by larger and smaller acts of familial devotion. So I borrowed your last fabricated example using Sartre's student, where the choice lies between caring for the unwell mother and helping the sister to escape the authorities. And I put it to him that while the mother's need for his care could hardly be doubted, the sister's risk of imprisonment, torture and possibly execution made it plain that her rescue would be the greater act of familial devotion.

"To all this Poor Chap listened most attentively – a very earnest fellow – and after much deliberation he reached for the big yellow. It was then that I made my move. Staying his hand, I asked him why he was choosing the big over the little rather than, say, first flipping a coin. 'Obviously on the grounds that a greater act of familial devotion is better than a lesser one,' came his impatient reply. 'But why,' I asked, 'do you think that helping the sister is the greater one?' 'For the very reason you suggested,' was his response: 'the sister's need, threatened unhappiness – call it what you will – is greater than the mother's.' 'In other words,' I said, 'you think that greater acts of familial devotion are greater, and therefore better, because they are are greater acts of *benevolence*.'

"Well as you can imagine, Blue, this revelation took him rather aback. And it didn't take very long for me to show him that considerations of benevolence were what lay behind a good many of his judgements, about greater and less, with respect to most of his other primary rules. Bigger and smaller acts of inclemency, promise-breaking, injustice, dishonesty, discourtesy and so forth all turned out to be bigger or smaller according to the relative amounts of suffering or unhappiness he expected them to cause. Regrettably our session ended before I was able to perform this reductive exercise on all his primary rules. But I can assure you that he went out with fewer of them than he brought in. And I look forward to completing the job at next week's session.

"In short, I think you're quite unfair to characterize mononomism as a narrow sectarianism that arbitrarily closes the door on all but one primary rule. The general point is surely this: mononomic reduction is achieved, not by some exogenous Procrustean imposition of a single value on a plurality of values, but rather by showing that some feature endogenous to each of those values – that feature which enables us to know when more or less of that value is at stake – points to a single subsuming value that commensurates the rest. Let me conclude, then, by simply reminding you that you too chose the bigger yellow ball, and it wasn't by flipping a coin."

"I guess it's my turn now to be almost, but not quite, tempted into agreement," responds Blue after a long and reflective silence. "I do, of course, see that it's possible to overload oneself with primary rules or values: that is, to imagine that acts of a certain kind are intrinsically valuable whereas, when it comes down to it, one realizes that they're valuable only because they're instances of another valued kind of act. But I don't think you've shown this to be what was involved in either my own or Poor Chap's big yellow choice, though for different reasons in each case.

"In his case, your proposed reduction implies not only that an act is one of greater familial devotion when it's one of greater benevolence, but also that an act of zero benevolence is one of zero familial devotion. This is patently false. Suppose Poor Chap sees it as his duty annually to place flowers on his relatives' graves. And suppose there's no one else who even knows about this, much less cares. It seems to me that such acts, while in no way describable as benevolent, could hardly be other

than ones of familial devotion. And his duty to perform them would be
so justified by him. So there are two significant respects in which you
misled Poor Chap by assimilating his choice between the two yellows to
the mother–sister case. First, the mother-caring act and the sister-helping
act are, for him, both *morally composite* ones: they each instance two
of his primary rules – familial devotion and benevolence – rather than
only one. Consequently that case would have to be replicated by shifting
MJM on to a more advanced level of play: the situation device would
need to eject two yellow balls but also two balls of whatever colour, say
indigo, stands for benevolence; and the constraint mechanism would
have to allow the removal of either pair of the correspondingly combined
yellow and indigo balls."

"But surely that would involve double-counting," interjects Operator.
"I take it you're not disputing that sister-helping is the more benevolent
of the two acts and that its analogue would therefore be a bigger one of
these two proposed indigo balls. And as this would be paired with the
bigger yellow, and as the bigger yellow is bigger precisely because it
represents the more benevolent familial devotion act, the addition of
benevolent indigo balls is otiose since the choice comes out the same."

"That, my friend, is a typical piece of mononomic question-begging,"
replies Blue. "For a polynomist, it can make a judgemental difference
whether an act is a morally simple one, instancing only one primary
rule, or a morally composite one. A morally composite act is on a higher
level of complexity than a simple one, in any situation of conflict with
other acts. And this brings me to the second way in which you misled
Poor Chap. You simply assume that because sister-helping is more benevolent (is a bigger indigo) than mother-caring, its analogue is a bigger
yellow. Now I readily concede that sister-caring's greater benevolence
makes it an act of greater familial devotion than it would be if it were
less benevolent: benevolence *is* a natural dimension of familial devotion.
But the grave-flowers example shows that it's not the only such dimension. And it's entirely possible that mother-caring could have exceeded
sister-helping in some other natural dimensions of familial devotion. In
which case, the yellow ball representing the former might have been at
least as big as that representing the latter, even though the latter's indigo
is bigger than the former's. Benthamite happiness, for instance, remains
a multi-dimensional affair. Bentham does not say that the act promising
the most happiness is the one promising the most enduring happiness.

"Of course, the multi-dimensionality of certain kinds of act doesn't
imply that the presence and extent of these variable dimensions in any
particular act, and even the appropriate ways of aggregating them into
a single magnitude, are not matters of ascertainable fact. I'm prepared

to allow that how much familial devotion an act displays, or at least whether it displays more such devotion than another act, is itself a non-moral question, albeit of a quite complex sort. But to vindicate monon-omic reduction in the way you suggested, you need to contend for much more than this. To prove that all valued acts are commensurable by virtue of something endogenous to them, you have to show that all valued kinds of act exhibit only the same set of natural dimensions and that these are naturally aggregated in the same way. The grave-flowers show that this is not necessarily true.

"It's true that benevolence is a dimension which figures significantly in a good many kinds of act enjoined by standard primary rules, as is prudence. It's also true that benevolence and prudence are commensur-able as pursuits of wellbeing. But consider, for instance, what makes one act of dishonesty more dishonest than another. One factor is doubtless their differential impact on the wellbeing of others and also, perhaps, of their perpetrators: 'white lies' are small dishonesties because of their presumed harmlessness to others. Another factor, however, is the differ-ence between their respective distances from what their perpetrators believe to be true. When a journalist lies about the number of people he knows to have been killed in a massacre of one thousand villagers, he tells a bigger lie if he reports a dozen dead than if he reports a hundred dead.

"We can certainly compare an act of familial defection with one of dishonesty in terms of their wellbeing dimension, i.e. which one causes more suffering. But this wouldn't tell us which one is bigger. And it would seem that, as with the veracity dimension of dishonesty, all other valued kinds of act like courage, creativity, justice, chastity and so forth possess *sui generis* dimensions and ways of aggregating them. It's surely this fact that accounts for their being different kinds of act and not all the same kind of act: recall the colourless balls fiasco, showing that you too must distinguish between kinds of act. Creativity and compassion, you reported, are primary values for Poor Chap. How do you propose to show him that an act of symphony-composing is bigger or smaller than one of kidney-donation? It's no use saying that one is bigger than the other because it produces more wellbeing or preference-satisfaction or self-realization or organic unity. Just as it makes no sense to say that a pint of milk is bigger than a yard of ribbon because it's heavier or more nourishing or fills a greater amount of space. A cube can have both a larger surface area and a smaller volume than a sphere. Which would then be bigger?[29]

[29] Cf. Brown, "Incommensurability," 5–10.

"In my own case, it is fair to assimilate the mother–sister choice to that between two yellows alone. Not, however, because of reducibility, but rather because benevolence is not one of my primary rules. Acts of benevolence which aren't directed at one's relatives (and which aren't instances of promise-keeping or patriotism) might well be undertaken by myself and others but, unlike Poor Chap, I wouldn't regard them as having moral value. I accept that if, in aggregating the variable dimensions of the sister-helping act, its greater benevolence isn't outweighed by the magnitude of some other dimension of familial devotion in the mother-caring act,[30] then sister-helping is a bigger yellow – a better act – and ought to be the one chosen. It would be silly to deny this, just as it would be even sillier to deny that helping *two* similarly situated sisters would be a still better act. But this natural commensurability of acts of the same kind can't be extended in the way you suggest to a natural commensurabilty of acts of different kinds. The sort of *continuity* that mononomism supposes to exist between qualitatively different objects of choice is simply not a necessary feature of moral values."[31]

[30] One such other dimension typically is genealogical proximity to one's nuclear family.
[31] *Continuity*, as a requirement of rational choosing, is centrally discussed in the next chapter (sections (b), (c)).

"Well," replies Operator despondently as he prepares to shut up shop for the day, "I guess I'm going to have to abandon you to your deontology and let you get on with doing the fanatically patriotic thing, whatever the consequences."

"Wait a moment," says Blue. "That's a rather heavy indictment and I think I want to reject each of the three charges in it. In the first place and as I earlier insisted, the idea of a mononomist condemning polynomists as moral fanatics strikes me as little short of ludicrous inasmuch as his complaint is directed precisely at their unwillingness to disregard all but one kind of consideration – be it happiness-production or whatever – in making moral judgements. I shan't now tax you with any juvenile word-play on the etymological affinity between 'mononomia' and 'monomania,' nor with the latter's relation to fanaticism, since I've conceded that mononomic codes are perfectly coherent moral commitments. But not the only ones.

"Second, I can't see where the deontology charge is coming from nor, I confess, what exactly it amounts to.[32] If, by that term, you mean the view that certain actions are intrinsically bad, then there's no difference between a mononomic and a deontological code: sub-maximizing happiness prospects is intrinsically bad in the same sense as promise-breaking is. If you mean a view that denies that one bad action can be inferably worse than another, i.e. that denies the possibility of a rule-implied judgement favouring one over the other, then you're talking about intuitionism, which we both reject. My prioritized polynomism, in singling out a particular action (from amongst several jointly unperformable valuable alternatives) as the one which ought to be done, in no way implies that its doing has no moral cost but only that doing any of the others has a worse moral cost. And if you mean a view denying the possibility of exceptionless moral rules – asserting that all valued acts are merely *prima facie* obligatory – then that too fails to describe my code, which contains exceptionless priority rules.

"I suppose however (and this brings me to the third item) that what you intend in this charge of deontologism is what's covered by your

---

[32] Here I rely upon the characterization of deontology offered by Frankena, *Ethics*, ch. 2.

further claim: that I'm morally committed to doing certain actions, e.g. patriotic ones, *whatever the consequences*. Here again I fail to see a difference from mononomism which can equally be described as committing its adherents to do the prospectively maximizing act regardless of the consequences. You might object that there simply are no other relevant prospective consequences. But that would be question-begging, since which ones of an act's various prospective consequences are relevant depends entirely on what (and thus, how numerous) one's primary rules are. Conversely, you might complain that my prioritized polynomism forces me to discount (in complex situations) certain prospective consequences – such as a broken promise or a familial defection – which I myself acknowledge as morally significant. But this is just the point about moral cost over again, and you too are forced to discount those disjunctively attainable increments of mononomic value whose realization would preclude maximization: you have frequently to forgo some particular productions of happiness or preference-satisfaction in order to secure a prospectively greater amount of others.

"In short, I think my consequentialist credentials are as impeccable as yours. And quite frankly, I've never really fathomed what it is that's been fought over so long between deontological and teleological or consequentialist armies of moral philosophers. Thus I'm inclined to agree with R. M. Hare who argues that

> The distinction between deontological and teleological theories is a false one. It is not possible to distinguish between a moral judgement made on the ground of the effects of an action, and one made on the ground of the character of the action itself; it is possible to distinguish only between different sorts of intended effects.[33]

---

[33] Hare, *Freedom and Reason*, 124; also *The Language of Morals*, 56–8, 68–70. An example traditionally favoured by proponents of this allegedly irreconcilable opposition is the case of promise-keeping. Thus someone who affirms promise-keeping as a primary rule is said to be debarred, at risk of trivialization, from consequentially justifying a particular promise-keeping act as one which brings about a kept promise. Whereas it's open to the teleologist/consequentialist non-trivially to justify that act on the grounds that it brings about happiness, preference-satisfaction, self-realization or whatever. The trouble with this line of argument is that it tendentiously shifts between two distinct levels of act-description. For what the former ought to say is not that its bringing about a kept promise is what justifies this *act of promise-keeping*, but rather that its bringing about a kept promise is what justifies this *act of repaying Smith his five pounds*. Any justification, including characteristic consequentialist ones, can be trivialized by describing the *justificandum* (the act to be justified) in the same terms as are employed in the rule justifying it.

The real battle is, on the one hand, that between intuitionists and their opponents, over whether it makes sense to hold that one good (bad) action is *inferably* better (worse) than another. Here we agree that it *does* make sense and that the intuitionists are therefore mistaken. On the other hand, there's the reducibility issue between polynomism and mononomism: an issue which in one sense is unresolvable and in another sense must be decided in favour of polynomism. In favour of polynomism, insofar as the latter is understood as affirming – whereas mononomists must erroneously deny – that more than one kind of action *can be* of primary moral value.

"Of course, some polynomists go on to say, without possibility of proof, that more than one kind of action *is* of primary moral value. But in this contention they are forensically no worse placed than mononomists who similarly lack any proof of the valuable status of their single primary rule and who, in any case (as you've already indicated), tend not to agree on what that rule is. So whatever may be the relative merits of polynomism and mononomism, they have nothing to do with any differential regard for the consequences of actions. The chief difference between the two structural views consists in this: that all mononomically *better* acts/sets of consequences are naturally describable as *bigger* ones, whereas this is not invariably true of those which are polynomically better."

Let's give this by now rather stilted dialogue a rest, and consider more closely the relation "polynomically better." For a polynomist, one action can be better than another (which I'll call "worse") in any of several different ways. And a polynomic code can incorporate more than one of these in its structure of priorities.[34]

The simplest form of one act's being better than another is, of course, that which the mononomist regards as the *only* such form: namely, that the better act is of the same valued kind as the worse one and is measurably bigger than it, by virtue of its measurably greater extensive qualities or a numerical derivative of them. For Blue, helping the student's sister is *ceteris paribus* a polynomically better instance of familial devotion than caring for his mother because the suffering averted in the former case is measurably greater than in the latter, and averting suffering on the part of family members is a natural dimension of familial devotion. I suppose that, in principle, a polynomist is entitled to ignore such quantitative differences between acts of the same primary-valued kind, and

---

[34] Analyses of the formal properties of the ordering relation "better than" can be found in: Rennie, "On Hare's 'Better'"; Smyth, "The Prescriptivist Definition of 'Better'"; Castaneda, "'Ought' and 'Better'"; Silverstein, "A Correction to Smyth's 'Better.'"

to regard any complex situation in which they're jointly unperformable alternatives as a "tie," warranting only a coin-flipping. But this seems such an unreasonable attitude as to deserve little consideration.

Some recent arguments suggesting that it's *not* an unreasonable attitude, and that a bigger act may even be *worse* than a smaller one of the same kind, arise out of considerations of what has come to be called "agent relativity." Bernard Williams proposes a situation in which A, who affirms a promise-keeping rule, knows that by keeping a particular promise he's made he'll be providing several other persons with inducements to break promises they've made. Williams argues that keeping his promise can nonetheless be the better thing for A to do and, hence, that the lesser amount of promise-keeping that his so doing brings about is not a sufficient reason for denying that A's keeping his promise is the better act.[35] The plausibility of this argument fails, however, to tell against the aforementioned charge of unreasonableness, since the two alternative actions confronting A evidently are (and are implicitly treated by Williams himself as being) of two relevantly different valued kinds: only a mononomist is bound to deny this. Hence they must implicate two different primary rules, and cannot be construed as merely quantitatively different instances of one and the same valued kind of action. The first of these rules, and the one to which Williams's suggestion would attach priority, runs to the effect that "one should keep one's promises," while the second enjoins that "one should promote the keeping of others' promises." There's no reason why a polynomic code cannot contain both these primary rules and this prioritization of them, just as there's no reason why such codes cannot contain distinct rules respectively covering uxoricide and (other forms of) homicide.[36]

A second form of "polynomic better" is the purely qualitative sort canvassed in the earlier part of this chapter: namely, that the better act is of a primary valued kind different from and higher ranked than that of the worse act. Thus, in Blue's code, a patriotic act is better than a promise-keeping.

What about the problem of little patriotisms versus big promise-keep-

[35] Williams, "Consequentialism and Integrity," 25–6; see also his well-known "Jim and the Indians" example in Smart and Williams, *Utilitarianism: For and Against*, 98ff.

[36] Whether, more generally, this furnishes the basis for a reduction-without-remainder of agent relativity is a matter about which I'm uncertain; see also the discussion of "a right to do wrong," ch. 6, section (c). My conjecture is that arguments for the agent relativity–agent neutrality opposition as a structural feature of morality (like those for the deontology–consequentialism opposition) are often responses to the moral counter-intuitiveness many find in mononomic codes, and not to the inadequacies of agent neutrality (or consequentialism) *per se*.

ings? Is a polynomist like Blue logically debarred from regarding the latter as better than the former? I've argued that no sense can be given to the claim that either of these is bigger than the other. On the other hand, we have Operator's (ultimately unhelpful) initial suggestion that Blue could double her set of three primary rules by dividing all patriotisms, promise-keepings and familial devotions into two size categories and, while still maintaining her qualititative ordering (P>PK>FD) within each size category, assign priority to any big act over any little one regardless of the kinds of act they are. It will be recalled that this suggestion quickly proved useless because acts of any one kind can come in indefinitely many sizes. Nevertheless, there's a viable adaptation of this proposal that is available to Blue and that would bring parts or all of her code closer to mononomism while still preserving an important distance from it.

It's not open to Blue to say that a big promise-keeping is bigger than a little patriotism. But it is open to her to say that any promise-keeping over a certain size on the promise-keeping scale has priority over, is better than, any patriotism under a certain size on the patriotism scale. That is, it's consistent with her polynomism to impose an *exogenous* commensurablility on some or all primary-valued kinds of act: she could assign numerical weightings – say 8, 4, 2 – to patriotism, promise-keeping and familial devotion, respectively. And these, multiplied by the measurable size of any act of these kinds, would yield a number representing its moral value and hence deliver an inferable judgement as to which one of two jointly unperformable actions (of different primary-valued kinds) is better. Note, however, that we could still not say that this better act is *bigger* than the worse act. Suppose the sizes of two acts, a patriotism and a promise-keeping, are naturally measured as 3 and 12 respectively. The fact that an application of the above weightings would respectively assign them moral values of 24 and 48 doesn't entitle us to say that the promise-keeping is twice as big as the patriotic act, though it is twice as morally valuable. For the weightings, and any number derived from their manipulation, reflect no natural or endogenous feature common to those two acts, but rather a basic moral decision.[37]

Perhaps not an unconstrained decision. For Blue's simple qualitative ordering, P>PK>FD, indicates that if she does incorporate such a set of numerical weightings, the highest of these weightings must be assigned to P and the lowest to FD. (What it doesn't determine is the precise magnitude of the weightings.) This fact may be sufficient to enable Blue

---

[37] Cf. Sen and Williams, *Utilitarianism and Beyond*, 21.

to reduce what would otherwise be the greater propensity of such a code to generate "ties." Suppose the sizes of a patriotism and a promise-keeping are naturally measured as 3 and 6 respectively. An application of the above weightings would assign them each a moral value of 24. Is it plausible that Blue would regard this as a coin-flipping occasion? I've offered no purely conceptual arguments against her doing so, just as I've offered no such argument against a refusal to assign moral significance to quantitative differences at all, i.e. between acts of the same primary-valued kind. Nonetheless, the implausibility of the latter strongly suggests the implausibility of regarding the numerically weighted equality as a "tie." For in a case where a patriotism and a promise-keeping both have a moral value of 24, it seems reasonable to think that Blue would regard her simple qualitative ordering as decisive and would judge the patriotism to be the better act.

Does such numerical weighting amount to mononomism? It's true that adherents of a polynomic code structured *entirely* in this fashion can be described as engaged in a maximizing enterprise in their moral judging. But the only thing they can be said to be maximizing is, trivially, moral value. And this deeply distinguishes them from mononomists who, though also maximizing moral value, are doing so *by* maximizing some measurable descriptive magnitude. Or to put the matter another way, the mononomist's maximizing act is a maximizing act regardless of whether it's valuable, whereas the polynomist's is not. For the mononomist, best means *most*. For the polynomist, best means (only) *best*.

Even if Blue were not to impose any element of such exogenous commensurability on her primary values, and were consequently to eschew the sorts of inter-qualitative trade-offs it mandates, there would still be some scope for a certain (non-quantitative) type of trade-off between acts of different primary-valued kinds. Recall the table of nine complex situations generated by her three-primary-rules code (table 4.1, repeated here).

Table 4.1

		1	2	3
	(a)	P or PK	PK or FD	P or FD
Levels of		4	5	6
complexity	(b)	P or PK+FD	PK or P+FD	FD or P+PK
		7	8	9
	(c)	P+PK or P+FD	P+PK or PK+FD	P+FD or PK+FD

It was noted previously that if the priority rules for situations 1 and 2 are (non-inferably) determined as P>PK and PK>FD, then all the remaining priority rules *except that for 4* are inferable. That is, the fact that patriotism is the highest ranked primary value does not, of itself, imply that a patriotic action is better than one which combines promise-keeping with familial devotion. It's equally consistent with those first-level rankings that the latter action is better than the former, and no quantification is presupposed in affirming that conjunctions of the two lower ranked primary values have priority over the highest ranked one.

Suppose, however, that Blue's commitment to the superior value of patriotism is such that she affirms the priority rule P>PK+FD in situation 4. Then we should describe that rule as one implying the *lexical* priority of patriotism. Patriotism's enjoying lexical priority entails that, if Blue *were* to adopt a set of numerical weightings for commensurating her primary rules or values, the weight assigned to patriotism would be *infinity*. And consequently no acts of promise-keeping and/or familial devotion, regardless of how big they were, would be as valuable as any act of patriotism, however little. Its lexical priority would have the effect, so to speak, of immunizing patriotism against trade-offs with other values and would imply that all patriotic acts are better than their valued alternatives, whatever they may be.

Lexical priority can be assigned to more than one primary value in a polynomic code. In such cases, of course, it makes no sense to regard the two or more primary values involved as *each* being infinitely weighted. One will be so weighted, and may therefore be described as enjoying *lexical primacy*, in precisely the same sense that the word "a" enjoys the first place in any dictionary. Other values enjoying lexical priority are serially ordered after the lexically prime one: acts enjoined by them, regardless of their size, are better than any acts enjoined by non-lexically-prior values and also have priority, one over another, according to the place of their respective lexically-prior values in the serial order[38] (just as "aardwolf" precedes "abaca" in the dictionary, where words are ordered alphabetically and ones beginning with the same letter are sub-ordered by reference to their second letter, etc.).

[38] This is oversimplified. In fact, one can have ordered sets which include some exogenous weightings and in which the rank of some lower ranked member has lexical status whereas that of a higher ranked member doesn't. In the ordered set a>b>c>d>e, it's possible that only c's rank has lexical status. This would allow trade-offs between varying weighted amounts or combinations of a, b, and c, but would immunize c against any such trade-offs with d and/or e. On lexicographic orderings, see: Hargreaves Heap, Hollis, Lyons, Sugden, and Weale, *The Theory of Choice*, 330–2; Anderson, Deane, Hammond, McClelland, and Shanteau, *Concepts in Judgement and Decision Research*, 144.

Polynomic codes, as was remarked above, can imply the "betterness" of actions in any of the senses just outlined and can embody several of them. It seems very likely that such codes would ascribe betterness to one of two acts of the same valued kind and differing only in size. It's also probable, especially in codes containing a large number of primary rules or values, that some set of rough weightings is deployed to commensurate jointly unperformable actions of different valued kinds.[39] And as will be argued in the chapter on justice, any polynomic code containing a rule for rights *must* incorporate an element of lexical ordering into its structure of priorities.

[39] Perhaps this is what happens in the much discussed problem of "innocent shields"; cf. Nozick, *Anarchy, State and Utopia*, 34–5, and Kagan, *The Limits of Morality*, 138–44. Innocent shields (e.g. hostages chained to the front of aggressors' tanks) pose a problem because they represent a conflict between two standardly affirmed primary moral rules: one which permits (prohibits the prevention of) killing in self-defence, and one which prohibits killing innocent persons. Presumably the judgements delivered in such tragic cases implicate polynomic codes that either simply rank these two rules relative to one another, or also weight them.

5
Economic Reasoning

Impossibilities, due to incompossibilities, are closing in on us. Some freedoms preclude others. Some rights are incompatible with others. Not all
morally valuable actions are jointly performable. So this seems as good
a point as any to turn to the teachings of what Thomas Carlyle called
the "dismal science" in an effort to learn more about having to choose
among desirable but mutually exclusive alternatives.[1] At the beginning
of the previous chapter I suggested that, if moral reasoning is concerned
with the demand-side of moral actions, economic reasoning exhibits certain structural aspects of their supply. Economic reasoning is reasoning
about the *means* to moral as well, of course, as other ends. And broadly
speaking, the bad news has been that these means are in short supply.

What would life be like if they were *not* in short supply? This is a
question to which we'll not devote much attention, not least because its
meaning is exceedingly obscure. If the supply of means – as conditions
of those effects which are ends – were sufficient for our ends, it would
be trivially true that those ends themselves exist or are already secured.
In that happy circumstance there would be no conceptual room for
describing any piece of behaviour as purposive nor, indeed, as action.
Alternatively, such worlds are often proposed by science-fiction writers
(but alas, not only by them) and are portrayed as Disneylands where
merely *wishing* for an end is sufficient to bring it about.

> When you wish upon a star,
> Makes no difference who you are,
> Anything your heart desires
> Will come to you.

[1] This chapter has greatly benefited from the advice of Ian Steedman.

If your heart is in your dream,
No request is too extreme ... (etc.)[2]

Situations where all ends are already present, or where their presence requires only that it be wished for, do not occasion the sorts of problem discussed in this book nor, perhaps, any other sort of problem.

The problem that does interest us here is typically conveyed in claims of this form: "That course of action, though morally desirable, is economically impossible." Now as is well enough appreciated, impossibilities come in many shapes and sizes. For instance, my drawing a square circle is logically impossible. And my eating the whole of Mount Everest, even when I'm very hungry, is physically impossible. What kind of impossibility is economic impossibility? The normal reason for judging some kinds of event (actions are events) to be impossible is that their occurrence would violate a law which is held to be true. Such events are presumed to be ones that cannot happen. Are actions that violate economic laws much like squaring circles and eating Mount Everest in this respect? In setting out to secure our ends, do we ignore such laws at our peril, as we assuredly do when it comes to logical and physical laws?

> Physics and chemistry give us a sense of the possible by formulating laws ... They tell us what we can't do anything about; consequently they tell us what we have to do to achieve our purposes ... If economics is a science like physics or chemistry, then we ought to expect it to tell us about similar constraints. There are real problems in thinking of economics as an exact parallel to the physical sciences. In particular, the kinds of constraint spoken of by economic theory turn out, with a few exceptions, to be self-imposed constraints. This is certainly not something you could say about the law of gravity.[3]

An important constraint on Red's securing his ends is that other persons are engaging in the same sort of enterprise. In non-Disneyland worlds, their respective sets of ends are mutually competitive inasmuch as many of them can be achieved only at the cost of the non-achievement of others. It is these incompossibilities, and the pattern of interpersonal

---

[2] This song (lyrics by Ned Washington, music by Leigh Harline), which eventually became the theme of the *Disneyland* television programme, made its first notable appearance in the wonderful 1940 Walt Disney film *Pinocchio* where it was sung by Jiminy Cricket whose nose, oddly enough, never grew longer with the singing of it.

[3] Dyke, *Philosophy of Economics*, 130–1.

relations to which they give rise, that are said to be governed by the laws of economics.

At the heart of economic science lies its chief theorem, the *Law of Demand*.[4] It states that demand functions are geometrically represent-able as *negatively inclined* curves. In more everyday language this means that persons choose less of one valuable thing if the amount of other valuable things, to be forgone in securing more of the former, increases. The higher the price of a good or service is, the lower is the sought quantity of it, and *vice versa*. What we want to know, then, is why a person's choices have this negatively inclined quality. What reasons are there for thinking that individuals' purposive behaviour displays what I'll call the *NI factor*? Why is that behaviour price-sensitive? And in what sense does this fact give rise to a "constraint" on the achievement of persons' ends?

[4] Or more precisely, the Law of Compensated Demand. The reasons for this refinement will emerge in section (c), below.

Historically a principal, though now largely discredited, reason for regarding persons as negatively inclined choosers has been their alleged *egoism*. Economic man, we were sanctimoniously assured, is selfish man. His choices are confined to maximizing his own satisfaction. Of course, if "maximizing his own satisfaction" means no more than securing the optimal realization of his ends, then the historical characterization is true.

But it's also trivial, inasmuch as it excludes no conceivable choice and extends its coverage even to the conduct of saints whose ends are often solely the wellbeing of others. If, on the other hand, "satisfaction" is not given this purely formal interpretation and is taken (as it often has been) to refer to some particular end, perhaps personal pleasure, then the historical characterization is simply false. Economizers need not be hedonists. As Lionel Robbins remarks,

> The distribution of time between prayer and good works has its economic aspects equally with the distribution of time between orgies and slumber ... So far as we are concerned, our economic subjects can be pure egoists, pure altruists, pure ascetics, pure sensualists or – what is much more likely – mixed bundles of all these impulses ... Economics is not concerned with any ends *as such* ... It takes the ends as given in scales of relative valuation, and enquires what consequences follow in regard to certain aspects of behaviour.[5]

The "science of making choices," as economics has sometimes been called, does not rest upon any assumptions about the content of the ends choosers entertain. And the truth of its laws is, in this respect, held to be independent of any particular motivational theory or moral code. The choice axioms from which the NI demand theorem is deduced are said to express no more than the requirements of choosing rationally in circumstances where one's options consist of "scarce means with alternative uses."[6]

[5] Robbins, *An Essay on the Nature and Significance of Economic Science*, 26, 95, 30.
[6] Robbins, *An Essay on the Nature and Significance of Economic Science*, 16.

Unfortunately, space does not permit any extensive examination of the extremely interesting question as to whether or in what sense the axiomatized requirements of rationality and the economic theorems deducible from them can be viewed as *causal* constraints on choosers, particularly in their interactions with one another. Can reasons be causes? This question continues considerably to exercise philosophers and economic methodologists, and it encompasses deep problems about the status of functional and game-theoretic explanations.[7]

Nor, in investigating these axioms, are we going to be deflected by the large body of literature that decries the heroic unrealism of assuming that persons do in fact choose rationally. Doubtless, choosers are not invariably perfectly rational. But our concern, however heroic, is with what they would be like if they were and whether, if they were, they would make NI choices. We can take it, I think, that whatever may be the correct answer to the causality question, the rationality of NI choosing is at least a necessary condition of regarding economic laws as structuring the constraints imposed by scarcity on our chosen activities. So the main story to be told in this chapter might be called "Red Meets the Axioms."

Not all of these are first encounters. For in the previous chapter we saw that rationality implies a number of restrictions on moral choosing. And if moral actions are at least a subset of economically constrained actions, we should not be surprised to find these same conditions present in economic reasoning. Among them are the requirements that, in any situation of choice between mutually exclusive valued options, (i) the options are ranked in an ordering, (ii) this ordering ranks all possible pairs of options (completeness), and (iii) the ranks of the options in any pair of options are consistent with the ranks of the options in every other pair (transitivity).

The set of axioms also includes a further ordering requirement – the axiom of dominance – which was previously suggested as a likely element in polynomic moral codes, as well as a necessary aspect of mononomic ones. This is that a superior rank is assigned to that one of any two options that differs from the other only in its greater quantity and not in kind. A big yellow, it will be recalled, is superior to a little yellow; and a big yellow–little red combination is inferior to a big yellow–big red combination.

But the axioms detailed so far, though sufficient for moral ordering,

---

[7] Cf. Hollis and Nell, *Rational Economic Man*; Rosenberg, *Microeconomic Laws*; Lewis, "Causal Decision Theory"; Eells, *Rational Decision and Causality*; Jeffrey, *The Logic of Decision*; Bacharach and Hurley (eds), *Foundations of Decision Theory*.

are insufficient to imply an ordering that yields NI choices. If these were the only axioms of economic choice theory, there would be no grounds for thinking that a morally desirable choice can be any different from an economically possible one nor, therefore, that economic laws constrain moral choosing. The ordering requirements of completeness, transitivity and dominance would lead Red to make the same practical response to any choice situation confronting him, regardless of whether it's viewed as one of economic scarcity or of moral conflict. Clearly then, the set of axioms needed to generate NI choices must be more stringent, more extensive, than those governing moral choice.

To explore these additional axioms and assess their significance, I'll again introduce several *dramatis personae*. Their appointed task is to save Red from the pitfalls of attempting the economically impossible. These characters include an eminently sensible cartographer whom we'll call Archimedes, along with his assistants, Ordinate and Abscissa – two shopkeepers who respectively dispense quantities of O and A which are means to Red's ends. What they aim to do is take Red's ordering of his options and exhibit it on a diagram, called an *indifference curve map*, the topographical features of which are drawn in accordance with the complete set of economic axioms. Furnished with this map, Red will find that the best option for him in each choice situation is fully and uniquely determined, and that this set of best options is representable as an NI function.

Archimedes begins the construction of this map by illustrating the graphic implications of the axioms we've already discussed. Red's options are construed as a set of bundles packed by Ordinate and Abscissa: that is, as collections of varying quantities of O or A or, more commonly, combinations of them. These collections are represented by points on the map (figure 5.1 opposite), and every possible point on the map represents a different collection. Red's choosing an option consists in his selecting a bundle. Bundles are conveniently labelled "B" and, in figure 5.1, six of these have been so marked. The quantities of O and/or A contained in a bundle are respectively identified by referring to how far "north" it is on the map (as measured by Ordinate) and how far "east" it is (as measured by Abscissa), with these quantities increasing as one travels further in these directions. Thus B_1 contains only O and B_3 only A, while the remaining four bundles contain different combinations of O and A.

Red satisfies the completeness axiom inasmuch as all these bundles, as well as every other bundle on the map, have been assigned ranks in his ordering. And he meets the transitivity requirement by having ensured that all his pair-wise rankings are mutually consistent. Hence if

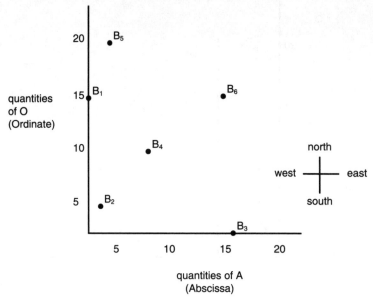

Figure 5.1.

$B_1>B_2$ and if $B_2>B_3$, then $B_1>B_3$. But these two axioms, in themselves, imply nothing about which bundles actually outrank which (much less, which of them are in Red's set of best options) across a wide range of alternative choice situations.

The axiom of dominance begins to discipline the field a bit. To illustrate its contribution to organizing Red's ordering, we fix our attention (in figure 5.2 overleaf) on one bundle, B_4, and divide the surrounding option set into four quadrants. What the dominance axiom tells us is that the entire set of bundles is partitioned into three proper and disjoint subsets whose respective members are quantitatively either bigger or smaller than B_4, or neither. All bundles in the northeast quadrant contain more O and/or A (and no less of either) than B_4. They are thus unequivocally bigger, and hence better, than it. Precisely the converse is true of the southwest quadrant's bundles. So B_4 may be said to *dominate* all the southwest bundles (e.g. B_2) and to *be dominated by* all the northeast bundles (e.g. B_6): its rank in the ordering is superior to those of the former and inferior to those of the latter. And since this same partitioning of Red's option set is performable with respect to every other bundle as well, purely quantitative differences determine the relative ranks of many of them in the single unified ordering implied by the completeness axiom.

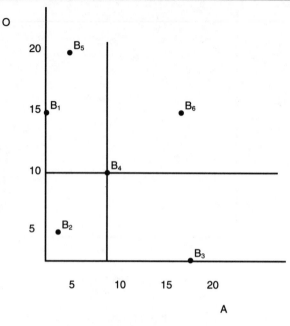

Figure 5.2.

But clearly not all of them. For none of the bundles in both the northwest and the southeast quadrants can be either inferior or superior to B_4 on purely quantitative grounds. Northwest bundles (e.g. B_1, B_5) contain less A than B_4 but also more O, while the converse is true of southeast bundles (e.g. B_3). No relation of dominance exists between B_4 and any of these options. Whether a bundle containing seven O and five A is superior or inferior to a bundle containing thirteen O and two A is evidently not something that Red can determine by ascertaining which one of them is bigger, since neither of them is bigger. Accordingly, their relative ranks in the ordering must be assigned on the basis of other sorts of consideration.

Upon what sort of grounds can Red determine the relative positions of B_1, B_3, B_4 and B_5 in his ordering? If he has to choose one of them, what would his reason be? Since these bundles are collections of means to his ends, the considerations bearing on this assignment of ranks are instrumental ones. Specifically, Red must determine whether B_4 is superior or inferior to B_5 on the basis of whether the ends to which B_4 is the means are themselves superior or inferior to the ends subserved by B_5. The ordering of his ends is, of course, not itself an object of economic reasoning which, as Robbins insists, presupposes it. But once it is established, Red can assess the relative superiority and inferiority of B_4 and all the bundles in its northwest and southeast quadrants on the basis of their respective instrumentally associated ends, and thereby identify which one of them is his best option.

As Red proceeds laboriously to do so, however, Archimedes intervenes to introduce his favourite choice axiom, one of the remaining two needed to complete the construction of the indifference curve map. The axiom of *continuity*, he explains, states that not all of the bundles in these two quadrants are either superior or inferior to B_4. So far as their instrumental value is concerned, a good many of them are as efficacious as – are *indifferent* to – B_4 in bringing about Red's ends.

"But how do you know that?" exclaims a somewhat perplexed Red. "I haven't told you what my various ends are nor how they are ranked. The northwest and southeast bundles contain amounts of O and A that differ – in some cases, considerably – from B_4's, let alone one another's. How can they all be means to the same ends? I thought you were here to help me identify uniquely best options. Instead, what do you do? You simply brush aside my discriminating attempts to rank the instrumental differences between these various bundles and tell me that there are none. Are you trying to entrap me in a violation of the completeness axiom?"

"Cool it, old sport," counsels Archimedes. "You've slightly exaggerated what I said. The continuity axiom doesn't state that *all* the bundles in these two quadrants are indifferent to B_4 and to one another. Only some of them are. Surely if you reflect on your ends and what's needed to attain them, you'll find this to be true. Consider some bundle in the southeast quadrant that is very close to B_4. Admittedly, it has more A and less O than B_4. But you're not seriously going to tell me that these minute differences are sufficient to annex these bundles instrumentally to different ends. Or if you do insist on this, I'll nominate another southeast bundle with slightly different proportional contents that's even closer to B_4. It simply must be the case that there is some southeast bundle whose greater amount of A is perfectly *substitutable* for B_4's greater amount of O, so far as attaining the same ends is concerned. Its increment of A exactly counterbalances – or as I like to say, compensates for – its decrement of O. So you should rationally regard it as exchangeable with B_4."

"Well," Red warily replies, "I'm going to reserve judgement on that suggestion for the moment. In any case and even if there is a southeast bundle instrumentally equivalent to B_4, I don't see that this gets us any nearer to narrowing down the range of eligible options, much less, singling one out as uniquely optimal. Rather the opposite, I should think. And I'm still worried about a completeness violation."

"Patience my boy," twinkles the wise cartographer. "All in good time. For as with so many intellectual exercises, things have to get a bit worse before they start getting better. Now, if there's a southeast bundle equivalent to B_4, it stands to reason that there's a similarly equivalent northwest one, doesn't it? And if those two bundles are equivalent to B_4 then, recalling transitivity, they must be equivalent to each other as well. But that's not all. For if some southeast bundle adjacent to B_4 is equivalent to it then, by parity of reasoning, there's some *further* southeast bundle suitably adjacent to that southeast bundle and hence equivalent to it. And needless to say, exactly the same thing is going on in the northwest. So by generalizing this line of thought and taking a ride on the transitivity axiom, we can travel along an unbroken northwest–southeast route populated only by mutually equivalent bundles. *Voilà*, an indifference curve! What's more, we can generalize this still further to bundles other than B_4 and its instrumental equivalents. Let me show you what I have in mind, in figure 5.3 (opposite). Here I've picked out six of the bundles that we'll suppose are equivalent to B_4 and are thus on the same indifference curve (B_7–B_{12}). But there's also another bundle, B_{13}, which we can infer is *not* on B_4's indifference curve. How do we know this? It's certainly true that, since B_{13} is in B_4's southeast quadrant, it neither dominates nor is dominated by B_4. Hence it can't be ranked relative to B_4 on quantitative grounds. But it *is* dominated by B_{12} which, being directly north of it, contains more O and no less A than it and is consequently bigger than it. And we know that B_{12} is equivalent, indifferent, to B_4. Hence B_{13} and its equivalents constitute an indifference curve other than that of B_4 and its equivalents. So you can see that, through the joint co-

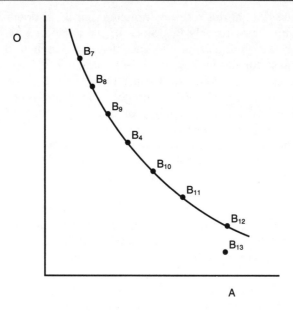

Figure 5.3.

operation of the axioms of transitivity, dominance, and continuity, all the bundles in your set of options can be partitioned into several equivalence sets and these can be represented as a series of discrete, non-intersecting indifference curves."

"Well *eureka* and all that!" retorts Red resentfully. "Now we're really in a fix. I had begun carefully to assemble a pair-wise ordering of every bundle and now you've replaced it – indeed, wiped it out – with an epidemic of indifference. In my search for my best option, you've cast me adrift on a sea of indeterminacy to be battered by wave upon wave of indifference curves."

Archimedes winces at this outburst. "You do me an injustice," he complains. "Far from consigning your option set to chaotic disarray, I've equipped you with a powerful instrument for ordering it. Again your impatience has blinded you to the import of what I'm saying. It's true that the continuity axiom rules out any *strong ordering* of your bundles. They can't all be pair-wise ranked as superior or inferior one to another since each is, on this axiom, equivalent to some others. But what it doesn't rule out is a strong ordering of these *sets* of equivalent bundles. Indeed, in conjunction with the transitivity and dominance axioms, it requires such an ordering. Remember how we established that B_{13} and its equivalents are on an indifference curve other than B_4 and its equivalents? We got this result by noticing that B_{13} is dominated by one of B_4's equivalents, namely B_{12}. Since B_{13} is dominated by B_{12}, it must be inferior to it. And it readily follows that any bundle in B_{13}'s equivalence set must equally be inferior to any bundle in B_4's. So once we've enrolled each bundle in an equivalence set, i.e. placed it on an indifference curve, what we have is admittedly a weak ordering of individual bundles but also a strong ordering of equivalence sets. Which, I trust you'll agree, is hardly a chaos."

Red concedes that he might have been a bit hasty in his accusation. "Nonetheless, the fact that equivalence sets or indifference curves are strongly ordered doesn't eliminate indeterminacy. All it does is to contain it a little. And, I should add, a lot less so than a strong ordering of individual bundles. The bundles equivalent to B_4 could lie along any old tortuous path meandering through the northwest and southeast quadrants. Recall that you're only supposing that bundles B_7–B_{12} may be inferior or superior to it. So quite a bit is still left up in the air, isn't it?"

"Up to a point, you're undoubtedly right," Archimedes allows. "Just which bundles are instrumentally equivalent to which must, of course, be regarded as a question of fact, the answer to which depends upon what your ends actually are and how you've ordered them. But there is one restriction, on respective bundles' eligibility for mutual equivalence, that you'll find helpful in tracking your indifference curves. The axiom of *strict convexity* states that the path of an indifference curve – the location or identity of a set of equivalent bundles – isn't to be discovered just anywhere in the northwest and southeast quadrants. It's not quite as tortuous an affair as you fear. In figure 5.4 (opposite), I've transected the northwest and southeast quadrants into four sectors by drawing a continuous diagonal straight line through B_4. This line could have been drawn at any angle. No matter which angle it's drawn at, one thing that's implied by the convexity axiom is that there are no equivalents to B_4 in *both* the second *and* the third sectors: they may be in either of them (or in neither) but not in both. Moreover, whichever of these two sectors contains no bundles equivalent to B_4 contains only bundles which are inferior to B_4. A further implication of strict convexity is that, if you draw a straight line between any two bundles in B_4's equivalence set, all the bundles located on that line are *not* members of that set and are in fact superior to it. That is, any average of two equivalent bundles is a bundle which outranks them."

"Goodness!" exclaims Red, considerably impressed. "I can see that this convexity restriction on the shape of the indifference curve goes a fair distance towards reducing the indeterminacy threatened by the continuity axiom. But it is a rather bold assumption, don't you think?

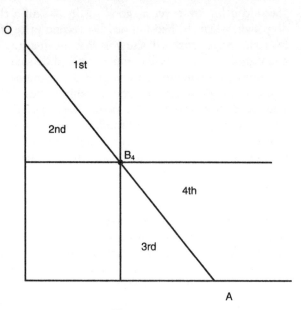

Figure 5.4.

You still don't know the first thing about my ends. And yet here you are assuring me that (only) options laid out in this particular way are equally efficacious in securing them. Why is any bundle which is simply the average of two mutually equivalent bundles not itself equivalent but, rather, superior to them? That strikes me as a bit counter-intuitive. Its superiority can't be based on quantitative grounds: it doesn't dominate them. So what possible reason can there be for this presumption?"

"A very sensible question," Archimedes replies. "Let me give you ten formulations of the answer to it – some of them, I fear, rather less fashionable these days than others, but all making pretty much the same point.

1   Increase of means then, affording proportionately increased repetition of the conditions of pleasure, does not afford proportionately increased pleasure.[8]
2   The more one possesses of a given good the less of another is necessary in order to compensate for giving up a small quantity, always the same, of the first.[9]

[8] Edgeworth, *Mathematical Psychics*, 62.
[9] Pareto, *Manual of Political Economy*, 196.

3   "Second helps are never as good as first," said a child, with a deep sigh, when she had finished her second plate of jam-roll.[10]

4   Everyday experience will show us that the quantity of X which a marginal unit of Y will compensate will be smaller the more of Y and consequently the less of X are contained in the current chosen combination of both commodities.[11]

5   The more champagne I have available per year, the less I will pay in sacrifice of clothes, or food, or cars, or any other goods, to get one more bottle of champagne per year.[12]

6   One's desire for a commodity generally becomes less "urgent" the more one has of it.[13]

7   Even if man can live by bread alone, he will prefer a balanced diet.[14]

8   If he is indifferent between three slices of bread and an ounce of cheese, and one slice of bread and three ounces of cheese, the [convexity axiom] says that he prefers to either of them two slices of bread and two ounces of cheese (or 1.5 slices of bread and 2.5 ounces of cheese, or . . . . .).[15]

9   The more you have of something the more of it you will be willing to give up to get something else you want.[16]

10   Variety is the spice of life.[17]

Now as you say, Red, I have no idea whether your ends are ones requiring pleasures, jam-rolls, champagne, bread, cheese, spicy lives or, for that matter, the prayers and good works of Robbins's previously mentioned saint. What all these chaps are suggesting is merely this: that when it comes to your forgoing one A, it's going to take more O to lure you off B_4 into the northwest than it is to lure you from the southeast on to B_4; that the converse is equally true when it comes to your forgoing a unit of O; and that the same holds for all combination bundles other than B_4 as well."[18]

"Well," Red allows, "I must admit that, all things being equal, I am a bit partial to spicy lives. Though I'm not sure that convexity actually delivers variety in quite the catholic sense you're suggesting. But even if

---

[10] Wicksteed, The Common Sense of Political Economy, 40.

[11] von Stackelberg, The Theory of the Market Economy, 100.

[12] Alchian and Allen, University Economics, 15.

[13] Newman, The Theory of Exchange, 32.

[14] Chipman, "The Nature and Meaning of Equilibrium in Economic Theory," 442.

[15] Gravelle and Rees, Microeconomics, 61.

[16] Dyke, Philosophy of Economics, 51.

[17] Simmons, Choice and Demand, 10.

[18] That is, that Red's valuation of bundles exhibits a diminishing marginal rate of substitutability.

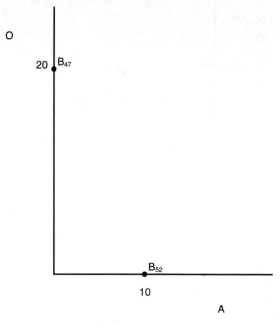

Figure 5.5.

convexity is true – even if instrumental equivalence or substitutability does have this particular shape – I still don't see how we've entirely escaped the problem of choice indeterminacy. A problem, may I remind you, which didn't arise before you introduced your continuity axiom. What I seem to have now, with your convex indifference curves, is an indefinitely large number of equivalence sets each containing an indefinitely large number of bundles or options. How are you ever going to pull a uniquely optimal bundle out of that expansive hat?"

"Having got this far, I can assure you that that's the last and least of our difficulties," Archimedes responds confidently. "In the first place, I need hardly remind you that the basic reason we're going through this whole exercise is that we're not in Disneyland: the total supply of means available to you is insufficient for all your ends. That's why we're talking about *choosing* rather than *wishing*. The amounts of O and/or A you can secure are limited. And those limits depend on the extent of what I'll call your *endowment*: the resources, including services, you have at your disposal and can exchange for O and A. Now, we've done a quick audit of your resources: had a word with your attorney, bank manager, stockbroker, book-maker, parole officer, astrologer and sundry other persons in a position to identify and assess your resource holdings, which seem to consist entirely of five R. So if you consult figure 5.5, you'll see

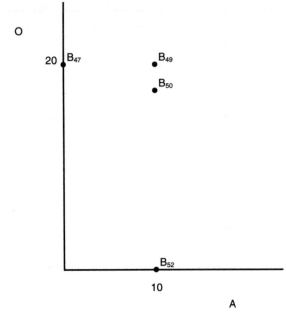

Figure 5.6.

that we reckon you can secure a maximum of twenty O (B_{47}) or alternatively a maximum of ten A (B_{52}). There's no point in your contemplating the choice of any bundle containing more than twenty O or more than ten A because, so to speak, it's beyond your means. It's not part of your set of attainable options."

"Frankly," replies Red, "I don't find that very helpful. Knowing that Ordinate won't give me more than B_{47}, nor Abscissa more than B_{52}, doesn't cut much ice since, according to your convexity axiom, I wouldn't choose either of those non-combination bundles anyway. Nor any other bundle containing only O or only A. What I need to know is which combination bundles I can have within those limits. For instance, how about bundles B_{49} or B_{50} in figure 5.6? B_{49} contains twenty O and ten A, while B_{50} has one less O. I'm not greedy, you understand. I just want to do the best I can for my ends."

"An eminently sensible attitude, Red, but quite out of the question in the case of these two bundles, I fear. Recall that I said your limit is twenty O *or* ten A, not *and*. So B_{49} is beyond your reach and so too, regrettably, is B_{50}. In fact, we can identify your set of attainable combination bundles by drawing a straight line, in figure 5.7 (opposite),

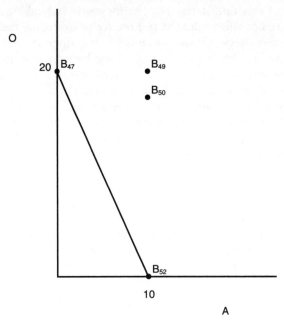

Figure 5.7.

between your two limiting bundles. Let's call it your *budget line*. All bundles to the left of (and on) the budget line are in your attainable set while all those to the right of it, like B_{49} and B_{50}, are sadly not available to you. You see, what the slope of this budget line is telling you is that, since B_{47} and B_{52} can each be purchased for the same amount of resources, they each have the same value. And that means one A is worth two O. Furthermore, since in your case that same amount of resources comes to your endowment of five R, you can readily deduce that one R is worth two A or four O. So the value of R, in conjunction with the fact that you have five of them (and nothing else to speak of), determines the amounts of O and/or A you can acquire."

Red is annoyed and unconvinced. "I'm just not sure that you've put my budget line in the right place," he retorts. "I can see how its slope represents the price ratio of O and A. And I can also see that its height – its distance along both axes, so to speak – is meant to reflect not only how much R there is in my endowment but also what each of them is worth. Your auditors are right to say that I have only five R. But I'm sure that they're worth more than you claim and, consequently, that my budget line should be higher. However, I'm willing to postpone discussion of this until later. For the moment, and taking that budget line as given, I'm still unclear as to how we've overcome the problem of choice indeterminacy. Obviously, quite a few options have been ruled out by the budget line's partitioning all the bundles into attainable and unattainable sets. And I can see that, since I want to optimize, I'm going to be choosing one of the bundles on the budget line as they're the only ones undominated by any others in my attainable set. Convexity tells me that it's not going to be either B_{47} or B_{52}. But that still leaves a virtually infinite number of bundles between them. How do you propose to determine which one is uniquely optimal?"

"Elementary, my dear Watson," Archimedes beams. "We simply lay out your map of convex indifference curves (*ICs*) and superimpose your budget line on it, as I've done in figure 5.8. Of course the complete map includes many more indifference curves than the three I've drawn, but these will suffice for our present purposes. Your aim is evidently to secure a bundle on your *most superior attainable curve*. IC_3 is the most superior curve here but, alas, it's entirely to the right of your budget line. Hence all its bundles are unattainable. On the other hand, quite a few of IC_1's bundles are within your means. Though as you can see,

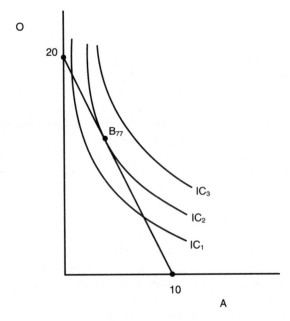

Figure 5.8.

they're all inferior to those on IC_2. But the good news is that one (and only one) of IC_2's bundles, namely B_{77}, is in your attainable set because it's the one point where IC_2 and your budget line are tangent to one another. All the other bundles on your budget line, though available to you, are inferior to B_{77} because they lie on curves inferior to IC_2. So B_{77} is your uniquely optimal option. It's the highest attainable point at which your personal rate of exchangeability coincides with the prevailing social rate of exchangeability. Put slightly differently, B_{77} is the most northeasterly attainable bundle at which your own rate of substitution between O and A is equal to the prevailing prices of O and A."

"Okay Archimedes, it's a good story and I may well buy it. But before I do, we've got to have a closer look at the two items we put aside in our journey to B_{77}: continuity and endowments."

John Chipman has rightly emphasized the singular importance of the convexity axiom in economic reasoning: "It is amazing how many economic laws stand or fall with this principle ... There does not seem to be anything corresponding to this law in other social sciences."[19] The strict convexity of a person's sets of equivalent bundles is what ensures his well-adjusted price-sensitivity, uniquely determines his optimal option in each choice situation and renders his rational conduct obedient to the Law of Demand. Moreover, by restricting the membership of any equivalence set to only those mutually undominant pairs of bundles that successively display a particular relation between the rates of substitution of O for A, convexity renders those sets representable by a mathematical function. In thereby metricating rational choices, it enables the economic theorems generated by the choice axioms to take the form of scientific laws, as Chipman suggests.

Trivially, however, convexity presupposes equivalence. If B_4 has no equivalents, it *a fortiori* has no equivalents forming a convex indifference curve. Convexity is the shape of economic equivalence and has no existence independent of it. So if we want to understand why it's rational for persons with given endowments to substitute convexly when prices (the slopes of their budget lines) change, we have first to consider the reasons for substituting at all. We have to consider the grounds for the continuity axiom.

In his classic account of the discipline, Robbins details four conditions which are said to be necessary and jointly sufficient for a person to be in a situation of economic choice:

1   He has a multiplicity of ends.
2   The means available to him are insufficient for their complete achievement.
3   These scarce means have alternative applications, i.e. any particular kind of means can be applied to more than one of the multiple ends.
4   The multiple ends are ranked in order of importance.[20]

[19] Chipman, "The Nature and Meaning of Equilibrium in Economic Theory," 442.
[20] Robbins, *The Nature and Significance of Economic Science*, 12–13.

Now although the set of ends comprehended here is not confined to moral ones, one thing that will be apparent is that we've already encountered at least three of these conditions in the previous discussion of moral reasoning. Blue's polynomic code contains a multiplicity of ends (primary rules or values) which are ordered (by priority rules) and the available means to which can be both aggregately insufficient and capable of alternative applications (hence the possibility of moral conflict).

Another fairly obvious point is that these conditions are not entirely logically independent of one another. Arguably, it's an implication of the very idea of having an end that the means for achieving it are at least temporarily insufficient. (This is not a counsel of despair: it simply implies that having an end is not identical with its realization – if, by "end," we mean something to do with action. In Disneyland there are, so to speak, no actors.) Second, if one has multiple ends, it's the alternative applicability of these scarce means – at the very least, of one's time and attention – that necessitates an ordering of the ends.[21]

It might thus appear that all four of Robbins's conditions are satisfied in complex situations of (polynomic) moral choice and, therefore, that the latter entirely correspond to the conditions of economic choice. Yet in investigating the nature of moral reasoning and especially of moral ordering, we came across nothing that remotely resembles the requirements of continuity and convexity. Was this due to a failure to pursue that investigation to its logical conclusion? In the last but one paragraph, I rather guardedly remarked that we've encountered "at least three" of Robbins's conditions in the prior discussion of moral reasoning. This scruple was motivated by the fact that, as we'll presently see, Robbins's condition (3) – alternative applicability – requires a narrower interpretation in any account of economic choice than in an account of moral choice. And this narrower interpretation has implications for our understanding of his fourth condition about ordering. To grasp why this is so, we need briefly to consider how the absence of any one of his conditions precludes the presence of a specifically *economic* choice situation.

Consider Robbins's condition (1). Near the start of this chapter, we noted his widely shared insistence that economics makes no assumptions about the content and relative importance of persons' multiple ends which it treats simply as data: determined exogenously to the economic choice model by such factors as ethics, aesthetics, wants and needs. But

---

[21] This necessity is certainly present in the case of moral ends since actions in pursuit of them are reason-implicating which, in the present context, means priority-rule-implicating. Whether non-moral ends must be ordered depends upon whether non-moral action must be reason-implicating: a question I shall sidestep.

what if one's ends are *not* multiple? What if one has only a single end? Is the mononomist, in making his moral choices, not also having to make economic ones?

There is a certain irony in the negative answer to this question. For the historically infamous *homo economicus*, discarded earlier, is usually conceived as an archetypal mononomist insofar as he engages in moral thinking at all. Yet it seems clear that the choice problem confronting someone, for whom only one and the same natural dimension of any act determines whether and to what extent it's valuable, can never be anything other than what Robbins regards as a problem of *technology*.[22]

Let's take the standard case. If desire-satisfaction or pleasure is construed as a single natural dimension (e.g. a brain-state) – something of which there can be measurably more or less – and if there are alternative means for its realization, then it is the physiologist and the engineer who can be relied upon to select one's best option in pursuing this sole end. Questions of optimal instrumental choice, when nothing else of value is instrumentally at stake, are questions of applied natural science and not of economics. This indeed seems to capture much of what was characteristic in at least the aspiration of the Benthamite enterprise. Of course, if "desire-satisfaction" or "pleasure" covers more than one natural dimension – if there are said to be different *types*, as distinct from different *sources*, of pleasure – then a person professing such pleasure as his sole moral end is merely using the word as a convenient umbrella term to denote what is actually a polynomic commitment which, as such, satisfies Robbins's multiplicity condition.

What about his condition (2)? Enough, perhaps, has already been said about the regrettable absence of Disneyland worlds to make any further chat about the connection between scarcity of means and economic choice tedious. Indeed, scarcity is simply the circumstantial counterpart of purposive conduct. If all the means to all our ends were available on the same terms as clean air is (or used to be), there wouldn't be an awful lot left to do.[23]

Because there are things to do and because, whatever they are, their doing demands some effort and attention, the alternative applicability of at least some means to our multiple ends looks to be an equally entrenched feature of purposive conduct. This is not necessarily true of all means. If Robinson Crusoe has several ends and only one of them requires the use of his supply of wood, his decisions about how to deploy

<hr/>

[22] Robbins, *The Nature and Significance of Economic Science*, 32–5.
[23] Robbins, *The Nature and Significance of Economic Science*, 13–15.

its components are of a purely technical kind.[24]   Still, until we can be said to have ends which are self-achieving, Robbins's condition (3) must be at least partly satisfied inasmuch as alternative applicability must inform some of the means at our disposal. And this in turn suggests the satisfaction of condition (4) since, as was previously remarked, the absence of an ordering among multiple ends (at least *moral* ends) rules out anything recognizable as a rational choice between options instrumental to their achievement.[25]

That said, however, just how much alternative applicability is implied by the axioms of economic choice? The short answer is "quite a lot." Indifference curves represent any two kinds of means as mutual substitutes at varying rates of substitution. It's this interpretation of Robbins's alternative applicability condition – as *ubiquitous substitutability* (hereafter *US*) – that is necessary for the existence of equivalence sets and, thus, for the northwest–southeast peripateticism of NI choosers.

The matter at issue is not simply one of degree. It's widely recognized in the literature on this subject that US is predicated on levels of physical divisibility (of means) and of perceptual discernment (by choosers) that are, in many cases, unrealistically high. Obviously enough, the minimally-sized unit of some less divisible items or, conversely, the minimally perceivable amount of some highly divisible items – is still too gross to permit the rather fine-grained quantitative distinctions and substitutions implicit in indifference curves. Few would now share Alfred Marshall's confident embrace of continuity, inscribed in the motto of his influential *Principles*: "*Natura non facit saltum.*"[26] And to that extent, US is conceived by such writers as an unrealistic idealization in the economic choice model.[27]

But nature's intractabilities are not our present concern. Echoing a generally shared view in the philosophy of science, Joan Robinson persuasively contends that "A model which took account of all the variegation of reality would be of no more use than a map at the scale of

[24] Robbins, *The Nature and Significance of Economic Science*, 35.

[25] Robbins, *The Nature and Significance of Economic Science*, 13–14.

[26] Marshall, *Principles of Economics*, frontispiece; cf. his Prefaces, vi, xii, where he suggests that "If the book has any special character of its own, that may perhaps be said to lie in the prominence which it gives to ... applications of the Principle of Continuity." Boland, *The Principles of Economics: Some Lies My Teachers Told Me*, ch. 3, describes the motivation for Marshall's preoccupation with continuity and his importation of it from contemporary biology.

[27] Some writers propose the integration of probability indices into preference rankings as a method for establishing continuity as an axiomatic feature of rational choice. For criticism of this move, see Davidson, McKinsey, and Suppes, "Outlines of a Formal Theory of Value," 158–9.

one to one."[28] What we want to know is not whether the model's discernment and divisibility requirements are realistic but rather, if they
were realistic, what else would have to be true.[29] *What is the ideal of
the US idealization?*

Recall the arguments of Archimedes in introducing the continuity
axiom to a sceptical Red. It couldn't seriously be denied, he insisted, that
for any particular O–A combination there are other O–A combinations
(southeast and northwest of it) which, though necessarily different, are
nonetheless all equally valuable. Regardless of what ends O and A are
means to, these various combinations are all capable of achieving equally
valuable results. Why would this be so?

Consider an apparent counter-example offered by Vivian Walsh.[30] In
prescribing drugs for the treatment of illness, physicians often specify an
exact dose: lesser quantities may be useless and greater ones fatal. Let's
suppose that recovery from his illness is one of Red's ends, that O is the
relevant drug and that B_4 contains exactly the prescribed amount. On
the face of it, there seem to be three sorts of reason for thinking that a
southeast bundle B_5, containing less O and more A, is nonetheless equally valuable to B_4:

1   Perhaps the physician is mistaken, and B_5's less O will secure
      the same recovery effect.

2   Perhaps B_5's increment of A is causally capable of securing
      the same recovery effect as its decrement (B_4's increment) of
      O.

3:a   Perhaps B_5's increment of A, though incapable of that recov-
      ery effect, is causally capable of securing an increment of
      another end that is as valuable to Red as that recovery effect
      and that could not be secured with B_4's lesser amount of A.

3:b   Perhaps B_5's less O, though incapable of securing the recov-
      ery effect of B_4's greater O, can secure some lesser recovery
      effect; *and* its increment of A is capable of securing another
      effect which, as an increment of another end, is as valuable
      to Red as the forgone degree of recovery and could not be
      secured by B_4.

[28] Robinson, *Essays on the Theory of Economic Growth*, 33.

[29] Realism aside, there seems to be some tension between the model's discrimination
requirements: cf. Hicks, *Value and Capital*, 11–12, where it's suggested that units are
presumed to be not too small to be separately chosen but too small to warrant different
marginal valuations of any two successive units; also Wicksteed, *The Common Sense of
Political Economy*, 47–57.

[30] Walsh, *Introduction to Contemporary Microeconomics*, 27, 142 (a text which
remains as entertaining as it is instructive).

And the same sorts of reason, stated in suitably converse form, would be the grounds for regarding a northwest bundle B_3, containing more O and less A, as nonetheless equivalent to B_4.[31]

These alternative reasons, for regarding B_4 and B_5 as equivalents, warrant close attention. A moment's reflection indicates that (1) counts against, rather than for, that equivalence. For if B_5's less O can secure the same recovery effect as B_4's greater O, then the former bundle must be superior and not equivalent to the latter, since B_4's increment of O is thus wasted and B_5's greater A is capable of some additional valued effect which B_4's less A cannot secure. So if we are to attribute equivalence to B_4 and B_5 (and B_3), it will be for reasons (2) or (3).

Two quite different kinds of equivalence are respectively implied by these two reasons. Both, of course, assert the valuational equivalence of these different O–A combinations. But (2) does so on the grounds of their common capacity to secure one and the same result: namely, the same recovery effect. Whereas (3) does so because, although they lack this common capacity and each secures a different result, those two results are equally valuable. The former valuational equivalence is implied by the inherent equality of identical causal properties, properties which secure the same (qualitative and quantitative) effects; the latter is implied by the supervenient valuational equality of different effects. In the former, these two O–A bundles are mutually substitutable because they each do the *same* job. In the latter, they are mutually substitutable because although they each do a different job, those two jobs are *just as good* as one another.

Let's call these two types of equivalence, respectively, *causal equivalence* (CE) and *effect equivalence* (EE).[32] So our question about the aforementioned idealization can now be formulated more precisely thus: Is it CE or EE that is presupposed by US, the ubiquitous substitutability implied by convex indifference curves?

The literature itself offers no unambiguous answer. In his lucid presentation of the choice axioms, Peter Newman suggests that the idea implicit in postulating the existence of equivalence sets is "that there is, as it were, more than one path to Rome, more than one bundle . . . to attain a given level of satisfaction."[33] Is Rome where we necessarily want to go? Evidently what we need to know here is the meaning of "satisfaction." Is it to be understood, like some conceptions of pleasure, as a

---

[31] We could suppose that B_3's extra dose of O makes a contribution to the valued (by Red) recovery of someone else.

[32] Causal-equivalent bundles are thus a strict subset of effect-equivalent bundles. So "EE bundles" refers to only those effect-equivalent bundles which are *not* causal-equivalent.

[33] Newman, *The Theory of Exchange*, 29.

single dimension such as a particular brain-state? Or is it a compendious term, comprehending a set of heterogeneous dimensions? If it's the first, then a "given level of satisfaction" is to be interpreted as a given magnitude of that single dimension and the equivalence of B_4's increment of O and B_5's increment of A is of the CE type. They both possess a causal property that yields the same amount of that brain-state, or whatever. Persons' economic choices, on this view, are reducible to what Robbins previously characterized as technological problems – problems best handled by the bio-engineering firm of Bentham & Co.[34]

On the other hand, if a given level of satisfaction is a set of heterogeneous dimensions and if B_4's increment of O contributes a different element of that set than B_5's increment of A, then these alternative increments are of the EE type. And the qualitative difference between their respective contributions implies that the given level consists of varying proportions of these diverse dimensions. In other words, one and the same level of value is alternatively constituted by different proportional "mixes" of different ends. Unlike the case of CE bundles, there's no implication that "level of satisfaction," thus interpreted, can be measured as distinct from ranked. The superiority (or inferiority) of B_4 and its equivalents to bundles on other levels of satisfaction, can be meaningfully asserted but its magnitude cannot.

Veterans of the controversies surrounding this subject will have grown impatient with the by now rather strained effort to avoid the use of the term *utility*. For what the "CE versus EE question" is ultimately about is whether the instrumental value – the utility – of various choice options is directly representable by a *cardinal* number or by (only) an *ordinal* ranking.[35] And this has rightly been seen to depend upon whether what those options are useful for is to be understood as a single end or a plurality of ends. If pushpin is as good as poetry, is this because certain amounts of either of them deliver the same amount of pleasure? Or is it because what they respectively deliver are certain amounts of amusement and insight, both of which inhabit the same level of value but are not reducible to amounts of pleasure or any other single thing?

Historically, the conception of utility in economic theory has evolved away from its initial uni-dimensional character – typically, though not

[34] Cf. Schabas, *A World Ruled by Number*, 34–9.

[35] Cardinal scaling of utility (like that of length) measures absolute amounts of it and permits comparisons such as "Red gets twice as much utility from B_4 as Blue" or "Red gets twice as much utility from B_4 as from B_9." *Some* ordinal rankings of utility allow the construction of interval scales (like those for temperature) or ratio scales, whose measurements preclude such comparisons. On measurability, see Cohen and Nagel, *Introduction to Logic and Scientific Method*, 293–301.

necessarily, of a hedonistic sort – in the direction of greater generality which allows for the possibility that rational choosers' sets of ends may be irreducibly pluralistic or multi-dimensional. It's not unfair to describe this evolution as a protracted one, with successive writers at once repudiating uni-dimensionality while still retaining presuppositional vestiges of it in their analytical and mathematical apparatus.[36] For this development, undertaken to detach economic science from contestable psychological and ethical premises, created new conceptual problems for quantifying the utility of different options and, hence, for demonstrating that their mutual substitutability takes the form required by NI choice. Under uni-dimensionality, the amount of the single end produced by a certain quantity of O is cardinally expressible and directly determines the amount of utility attributable to that O.[37] So if O and A are indeed alternatively applicable means, there must be some quantity of A which produces the same amount of that sole end, possesses the same utility, thereby allowing one to infer the unique amount of substitution – the change in optimal bundles – consequent upon any change in O and A prices.[38] The equivalence of the two quantities is of the CE type and their utility is thus guaranteed cardinal representability.

The position is quite otherwise if what varying O–A combinations produce are certain amounts of two (or more) ends, E_1 and E_2. Here too Robbins's "alternative applicability" assumption does imply that, for the production of any given amount of E_1, there's a set of several CE combinations of O and A; and the same holds for any given amount of E_2. But what is *not* thereby implied is that these two equivalence sets are *identical*. If E_1 and E_2 are irreducibly different ends, the CE combinations of O and A can be different for given amounts of each of them. That is, "alternative applicability" does not imply the existence of any one set of different O–A combinations that each produce unvarying amounts of both E_1 and E_2. Yet a person's relative valuations of O and A – his judgements as to what increments of each of them are mutually substitutable – are held, by the theory, to be representable by a single

---

[36] Cf. Stigler, "The Development of Utility Theory"; Kirzner, *The Economic Point of View*; Kauder, *A History of Marginal Utility Theory*; Hicks, *Value and Capital*, ch. 1.

[37] Early neoclassical economic theorists did not purport to have discovered the Benthamite holy grail: namely, a method of measuring pleasure directly. Rather, they assumed that money could serve as an adequate cardinal surrogate for such a metric. That is, they (unwarrantedly) assumed the constancy of money's marginal utility. For cardinal measurability, "what counts is that some operation exists by which subsumption is carried out"; Georgescu-Roegen, "Measure, Quality and Optimum Scale," 235.

[38] Hence the frequently encountered comparison of the utility function, $u = u(x_i \ldots x_n)$, with the production function, $q = q(x_i \ldots x_n)$

set of indifference curves and not to require two such sets, one for E_1 and one for E_2. The utility of various O–A combinations is representable on a single scale.

The upshot of all this is the conclusion that what is implied by the continuity axiom in the case of multiple ends is that the equivalence of mutually substitutable bundles is of the EE type. It is varying increments of different *ends*, as well as of different means, that are mutually substitutable. Robbins's "alternatively applicable means" condition is matched by the condition that each level of value consists of alternative compositions of ends. Illustrating this mutual substitutability of diverse ends, Wicksteed argues that "the same law holds in intellectual, moral or spiritual as in material matters":

> In a story of South America, after the war, we are told of a planter who, when warned by his wife in the middle of his prayers that the enemy was at the gate, concluded his devotions with a few brief and earnest petitions, and then set about defending himself.[39]

So the ideal of the US idealization is (a person with) a set of ends which are so structured that, under changing attainability conditions (changing prices), increments of any end are eligible to be traded off against – can be compensated by – increments of others. An increment of physical survival is worth a decrement of spiritual communion. Adapting a term from decision theory, I'll call a set of ends ordered in this way a *compensatory set*.[40]

We've encountered compensatory sets before, when discussing the problem of little patriotisms versus big promise-keepings in the previous chapter. There we found that it was perfectly consistent with Blue's polynomism for her to impose an exogenous commensurability on her primary values or ends, by numerically weighting them. Her code would thereby mandate trade-offs between different ends according to which one, of several jointly unattainable instances of them, promised the greatest amount of moral value (act size multiplied by moral weighting) in a particular choice situation. This way of structuring moral priorities, though it reduces the distance between polynomic and mononomic codes, was nonetheless seen to leave the distinction between them intact. Correspondingly, *homo compensatio* is not the identical twin of his oft-maligned, single-minded sibling, *homo economicus*. Commensurating

---

[39] Wicksteed, *The Common Sense of Political Economy*, 79.

[40] Cf. Anderson, Deane, Hammond, McClelland, and Shanteau, *Concepts in Judgement and Decision Research*, 45.

ends, and trading off increments of some of them for increments of others, are not the same – in either theoretical description or practical application – as reductively homogenizing them.

But it will also be recalled that this isn't the *only* way in which polynomic codes can be structured. (Hence Red's previously expressed doubt about the catholicity of the variety promised by the convexity axiom.) For there's no reason why such a code cannot eschew numerical weightings for some or all of its plural ends. It can immunize ends against mutual substitutability so that no increment of a superior one is to be forgone in favour of a lower ranked alternative, regardless of how small the former is. This sort of code requires the realization of all attainable instances (i.e. the highest attainable magnitude) of a superior end before permitting any realization of an end inferior to it. Codes affording this protection to any of their superior ends contain *lexical* orderings and, to that extent, are *non-compensatory* ones. Accordingly, the utility of items instrumentally associated with any set of such ends can be expressed only in an ordinal ranking and cannot be represented on an interval (much less a cardinal) scale. Put simply, it cannot be measured.

This has important consequences for the generality of the economic choice model. Since economic choice is the selection of means to given ends, and since the continuity axiom implies a compensatory set of ends, rational instrumental choices in pursuit of lexically ranked ends are not covered by that model. Its generality, though unquestionably greater than that of the utilitarian models deployed by earlier neoclassical economics, does not extend to choices informed by non-compensatory values.[41] Increases in the relative prices of means to a lexically superior end do *not* occasion an NI shift in the direction of greater amounts of (means to) inferior ends, for these are not equivalents. Instead, "belts are tightened" in order to continue to secure as much as possible of that now more expensive superior end. A polynomic code, as we saw in the previous chapter, can contain both compensatory and non-compensatory elements: that is, both commensurated and lexically ranked ends. To the extent that it contains the latter, indifference curve maps offer no guidance in the quest for an optimal bundle.

This limitation on the scope of economic reasoning, consequent upon its anti-lexical continuity axiom, has been duly noted (and variously

[41] The continuity axiom, unlike the other axioms, does *not* express a condition of rational choice, but rather a condition of numerically measurable rational choice. Axioms like transitivity and dominance, we might say, articulate aspects of the *concept* of comparative rationality. Continuity asserts the *existence* of comparative equivalents. Some texts, e.g. Walsh, *Introduction to Contemporary Microeconomics*, 142–3, display greater sensitivity to this distinction than others.

appraised) in many discussions of the choice model.[42] Karl Borch observes that

> A basic assumption . . . is that some kind of "trade-off" will always be possible. Formally we can express this by assuming the so-called *Axiom of Archimedes* . . . This means that a loss of some units of one commodity can always be compensated by a gain of some units of another commodity or, to put it another way, *everything has its price*. It may be tempting to define economics as the science of things which have a price, in a very general sense. Questions of life and death and ethical principles like an absolute aversion to gambling would then be considered as belonging to the more general social sciences.[43]

It can hardly be doubted that many, indeed nearly all, things *must* have their prices. Even questions of life and death often – and, with advancing medical technology, increasingly – require answers which can rationally be reached only by substitutional calculation.[44]

As to absolute ethical principles, these were discussed near the end of the previous chapter where it was seen, unsurprisingly, that much depends on the meaning of "absolute." If an absolute principle is understood in what I take to be its colloquial sense, viz. that no instance of complying with it is to be forgone (traded off) for any other purpose or combination of purposes, then a person can have only one absolute principle in non-Disneyland worlds. (In Disneyland, you can have as many as you like.) It will be lexically ranked and, although any larger instance of it necessarily dominates and presumably has priority over any con-

---

[42] Cf. von Neumann and Morgenstern, *Theory of Games and Economic Behavior*, 630–2; Arrow, "Alternative Approaches to the Theory of Choice in Risk-taking Situations," 425; Debreu, "Representation of a Preference Ordering by a Numerical Function," 159–65, and *Theory of Value*, 72–3; Georgescu-Roegen, *Analytical Economics*, 40–1, 188–90; Davidson, McKinsey, and Suppes, "Outlines of a Formal Theory of Value," 155; Chipman, "The Foundations of Utility," and "On the Lexicographic Representation of Preference Orderings"; Newman and Read, "Representation Problems for Preference Orderings"; Skala, *Non-Archimedean Utility Theory*, 26; Bacharach, *Economics and the Theory of Games*, 141; Elster, *Ulysses and the Sirens*, 124–27; Strasnick, "Neo-Utilitarian Ethics and the Ordinal Representation Assumption."

[43] Borch, *The Economics of Uncertainty*, 22. A sweeping gloss of a great deal of intellectual history might thus nominate Archimedes as the godfather of economics, inasmuch as it becomes separable from its origins in moral philosophy at the point where – to the extent that – moral values form a compensatory set.

[44] Such advances, in enlarging our repertoire of actions, turn every healthy kidney into an "alternatively applicable means."

flicting smaller instance of it, no instance of it gives way to the pursuit of any other principle. If it's appropriate to speak of "weighting" at all in this sort of case, we should describe (undominated) instances of such a principle as infinitely weighty.

It's also true that the impossibility of having more than one absolute principle doesn't imply that all others are compensatorily structured. They too can be lexically ranked in descending succession. Nonetheless and as a matter of purely empirical conjecture, Archimedes would probably be correct to imagine that we structure at least a large proportion of our ends in a compensatory manner and might well share Blue's reluctance to judge a little promise-keeping superior to a big act of familial devotion.

Nor does the fact that economic reasoning applies only to compensatory sets imply (as some utopian writers apparently believe) that other structurings of our ends would exempt us from the general exigencies systematized by economic laws. Departure from continuity doesn't amount to arrival in Disneyland. It's not even a first step on that journey. We remain in a condition of scarcity, of aggregately insufficient means, regardless of how our ends are structured. All that's being claimed here is that, if persons pursue ends which are not compensatorily structured, the impact of scarcity on their rational choosing cannot be patterned or determined along the lines indicated by economic laws. Not all constrained rational choices need be NI choices. It's in this sense that there *can* be morally desirable courses of action which, though economically impossible – in that they are contrary to the Law of Demand – are nonetheless not impossible.

Indeed, a somewhat stronger claim is warranted. On the conventional interpretation of the theory, not all instrumental choices *can* be NI choices. For although some of the literature displays a clear appreciation of the continuity axiom's restriction on the generality of the economic choice model, it commonly fails to attend to the presence of a presupposed non-compensatory factor. Correctly noting both the possibility and exceptionality of lexical ordering,[45] many writers on this subject have neglected the fact that one of the model's parameters, at least as standardly interpreted, is itself an object of choice – and one which therefore cannot consistently be viewed as standing in a compensatory relation to other ends. The reasons for this claim will be developed in the next section.

---

[45] Cf. Hicks, *A Revision of Demand Theory*, 193; Banerjee, "Choice and Order: Or First Things First," 166.

Red's other qualm, left over from his encounter with the axioms, has to do with endowments. Recall that it's his endowment (as represented by his budget line) and his highest attainable indifference curve that are the co-ordinates of – jointly and uniquely determine – that point on his indifference curve map that represents his best attainable bundle, his optimal option. Red's complaint was that his budget line should be higher: that Archimedes's auditors have underestimated his endowment. And this complaint implies that B_{77} is not his best choice.[46]

An important feature of this complaint is its ambiguity, for it's open to four alternative interpretations. That Red's endowment is greater than the auditors have estimated can mean any one of the following:

1   that his endowment contains more than the five R claimed;
2   that it does indeed contain only five R, but that these are worth more than twenty O and more than ten A;
3   that it does indeed contain only five R and that, although these are worth twenty O, they are worth more than ten A;
4   that it does indeed contain only five R and that, although these are worth ten A, they are worth more than twenty O.

These four alternative complaints fall into two distinct categories. The first (1) registers a claim about the content of his stock of resources: namely, that it hasn't been exhaustively identified. The remaining three (2), (3), and (4) are complaints that his identified resources have been undervalued.

Now we already know that Red does not intend (1), since he's conceded that the auditors have counted correctly and that five R is all he has.[47] A shared characteristic of (2), (3), and (4) is that they each directly or implicitly challenge two exchange ratios but do not dispute a third. If Red intends (2), he's not challenging the O:A exchange ratio of 2:1. What he is challenging are the R:O and R:A exchange ratios of 1:4 and 1:2 respectively. He's implicitly alleging that, in any exchange with Ordinate and Abscissa, he's being underpaid for his wares. In (3) this

---

[46] See above, pp. 162–3.
[47] See above, p. 163.

charge is confined to Abscissa, as only the R:A ratio is directly challenged. And conversely in (4), the charge is directed at Ordinate and the
R:O ratio. Furthermore, via transitivity, (3) and (4) contain an implicit
challenge to the O:A ratio; if Abscissa (Ordinate) alone is underpaying
Red, then he's also underpaying Ordinate (Abscissa). Were these ratios
different and this underpayment not occurring, Red's budget line would
swing in some northeasterly direction, thereby enlarging his set of attainable bundles and allowing him to reach a higher indifference curve and
a better bundle.

In fairly common parlance, a person who is underpaid in a voluntary
exchange – whose goods or services command less than they are worth –
is said to be *exploited*. He is receiving less than he otherwise would in
return for them. But just which counterfactual circumstances should
count as the "otherwise"? And indeed, some have doubted that any
sense at all can be made of the idea that a voluntary exchange could be
one of unequally (economically) valuable things. To see whether sense
can be made of this idea and whether Red has a case, we need first to
look briefly at the standard account of how the exchange ratios confronting him are formed.

Consider the O:A ratio. We've seen that, by taking Red's budget line –
whose slope reflects the O:A ratio – in conjunction with his indifference
curves, we can identify his optimal bundle. If we alter this ratio (alter
the slope), a different bundle is rendered optimal. For each alternative
exchange ratio, Red has a different optimal bundle. On this basis, we
can construct his effective demand functions for O and A: functions
which associate the varying quantities of O and A he would choose with
the different O:A exchange ratios at which he would choose them. And
the same can be done for everyone else. By summing these individual
demand functions, we get the aggregate or social demand functions for
O and A. In a simple two-good world, the aggregate demand function
for O is the aggregate supply function for A, and *vice versa*. The ratio
of the O and A quantities at which these functions coincide constitutes
the *equilibrium prices* of O and A. Different aggregate functions imply
different coincident ratios and, hence, different equilibrium prices. And
different aggregate functions may in turn be implied by differences in
the variables determining individual functions. Thus as Newman notes,
"prices are not given exogenously in the exchange situation, from the
outside so to say, but are intrinsic to the problem, embedded in the
individuals' (axiomatized) preferences and initial endowments of
goods."[48] Although Red and each other person are price-takers – treat

---

[48] Newman, *The Theory of Exchange*, 50.

prices as *parameters* of their choice situation – these prices are themselves variables which are parametrically determined by the preference orderings (relative valuations) of individuals as weighted by their respective endowments. Prices determine each person's post-exchange income or allocation of O and A, but are in turn derived from the interplay of all persons' endowment-weighted orderings.[49] And the same is true in a world of more than two goods – a world of R as well as O and A – where, however, the complexity of computing equilibrium prices is exponentially greater.

In the light of this, how are we to understand Red's complaint that his five-R endowment is undervalued, that the price of R is too low? Evidently, since prices are determined endogenously in the exchange process, his complaint must lie against one of the exogenous or parametric features of that process. It must lie either against individuals' preference orderings or against their endowments.

Now it's not inconceivable that it lies against preference orderings. Perhaps Red really does think that the Ordinates and/or Abscissas of this world have failed fully to appreciate the usefulness of R. Perhaps they simply haven't realized just how many of their ends R can help to achieve. Alternatively and even if they are aware of this, maybe they don't have the right ends or, at least, don't have them properly ranked or weighted. Maybe they don't "see" that R-produced ends are more important than many that can be secured by O and/or A.[50] And that's why they're undervaluing R. No doubt a great deal of what are commonly regarded as exploitative relationships are due to these two sorts of failing which are then reflected in preference orderings. Suppliers of household labour, for instance, are often said to be exploited either because the full extent of its contribution to the family's other goals tends to go unperceived or because the intrinsic worth of its own product is unappreciated.

Let's suppose, however, that Red's complaint is not based on any such claim of non-recognition and that the desirability of R is as well understood by Ordinate and Abscissa as by Red himself. That is, Red is taking everyone's preference ordering as given. In which case, his complaint must lie against endowments.

What could be relevantly wrong with endowments? It's a crucial fea-

---

[49] Analogies abound for the parametric determination of equilibrium prices. One might be the process determining the final location of the middle of the rope in a game of tug-of-war. That location is jointly determined by each player's endowment (of weight, strength, energy) and each player's preference ordering (of victory and repose).

[50] Though not so much more important as to make Red's willingness to trade R for O and A inexplicable.

ture of the theory of economic exchange that "by varying the distribution of endowments we change the equilibrium allocation (and
prices)."[51] How is the distribution of endowments determined? And how
is it varied? What exactly are endowments? As a first approximation,
Archimedes previously suggested that a person's endowment is the stock
of resources (goods and services) he has at his disposal and can exchange
for others' resources. Let's proceed with this purely *descriptive* definition
a bit further in exploring Red's complaint. For by so doing, we can
illuminate an important connection between economic and non-economic choice.

If Red's complaint is about the distribution of endowments, it's not
about his own endowment: his complaint is not that of interpretation
(1). Accepting that his endowment is five R, what he's challenging is
their price. He's saying that, in selling an R for O and/or A, he receives
less than that R is worth. And this underselling is due to something
pertaining to the size of others' endowments. Why? How?

Take the archetypal setting in which the price of something is determined: an auction. We'll suppose that Red has just sold an R for some
O. Thus his complaint, under interpretations (2) and (4), is that Ordinate's winning bid of four O is less than his R would have fetched from
a rival O-bidder whom we'll call Grey. Grey's preference ordering is
such that an R is worth as much as five O to her. Why then didn't she
outbid Ordinate?

What we're going to do is consider a series of alternatively counterfactual answers to this question, each beginning "Grey would have outbid
Ordinate if...," in order to see how they supply grounds for a claim
that R was undersold.

1   Grey would have outbid Ordinate if she hadn't been forcibly
    deprived of (some or all of) her supply of O.
2   Grey would have outbid Ordinate if there hadn't been a ceiling
    forcibly imposed on the bidding.
3   Grey would have outbid Ordinate if there hadn't been a sur-
    charge forcibly imposed (and appropriated by someone other
    than Red) on the selling price of R.
4   Grey would have outbid Ordinate if someone hadn't clamped
    a hand over her mouth as she was about to respond to Ordi-
    nate's last bid.
5   Grey would have outbid Ordinate if someone, who would have

---

[51] Hahn, "General Equilibrium Theory," 125; see also Walsh and Gram, *Classical and
Neoclassical Theories of General Equilibrium*, chs 7–10.

supplied Grey with the requisite O (or would have supplied someone who would have supplied Grey, or would have ... etc.), had not been deprived of it through one of the sorts of circumstance detailed in (1)–(4).[52]

Each of these cases is one in which Grey's failure to outbid Ordinate is attributed to a *diminution of her endowment*: to the stock of O at her disposal being permanently or temporarily or wholly or partially reduced. This is clearest in case (1). But it's also true of the remaining cases. In (2), Grey is prevented from disposing as she wishes of that part of her stock of O that exceeds the ceiling price of four O. In (3), the compulsory surcharge prevents her from conjunctively disposing of the five O required to outbid Ordinate and whatever the surcharge levy amounts to. Thus if we suppose a surcharge of one O, Ordinate's winning bid of four O entails that the gross cost to him of R is five O. For Grey to have outbid him, she would have had to part with a total of six O, which is more than an R is worth to her. Case (4) is an instance of Grey's having the whole of her endowment temporarily reduced to zero. And case (5) is, in effect, an epicyclical version of case (1).[53]

---

[52] This last case schematically represents how endowment reductions can compound and transmit exploitations historically through an indefinitely long series of transactions.

[53] A further apparent reason why Grey failed to outbid Ordinate might be that she wasn't at the auction, i.e. Ordinate was a monopoly buyer. But a monopoly price is not necessarily an exploitative one. For this reason lacks any independent status inasmuch as Grey's absence, and Ordinate's consequent monopoly position, are due either to reasons like those already listed or to Grey's preference ordering being other than the one we're taking as given. See Steiner, "Exploitation: A Liberal Theory Amended, Defended and Extended," 136–41, for a more extensive listing of purported grounds for a claim that R was undersold, and an argument to show that some of these grounds are reducible to those mentioned above and that the remaining ones do not support that claim. Amongst the latter may be one proposed by D. Miller, *Market, State and Community*, 180–1, whereby Red sells to Ordinate for less than he would have obtained from Grey, because Ordinate persuades potentially rival bidder Grey that Red's R aren't what they appear to be (e.g. that they're not genuine Old Masters). Was Red thereby exploited? In approaching an answer to this question, one thing that's irrelevant here is Ordinate's own interest in persuading Grey. For presumably we'd want to say that, *if* the lower price at which Red's R were sold was exploitative, he would equally have been exploited had it been someone other than Ordinate who, due to Grey's withdrawal, managed to purchase those R at that price. Whether Red *was* exploited depends on whether Ordinate's forgery charge is true and whether Grey has some right not to be misinformed by Ordinate. This gives us four possibilities: (i) if there *is* this right and if the forgery charge is *false*, Red has indeed been exploited and this, as my account suggests, is due to Ordinate's diminution of Grey's endowment (that is, his depriving her of something, true information, to which she's entitled); (ii) if there *isn't* this right and if the charge is *false*, Grey, having no guaranteed

So Red's claim that his R was undersold is based on the fact that Grey's endowment was not as large as it would have been if none of these forcible interventions had occurred. But how can the *fact* that it wasn't larger, and consequently didn't yield a higher winning bid, give rise to complaint? It can do so only if Red believes that it *should* have been larger and therefore that the intervention which diminished it *should not* have occurred. That complaint, in short, is predicated on a *normative* conception of endowments and not a purely descriptive one.

Now, we do usually conceive persons' endowments normatively. That is, we would normally identify persons' stocks of disposable resources by reference to what they *own* rather than by reference to what they *possess* (i.e. can in fact exercise exclusive control over). Of course, there's no reason why these two can't coincide. On the other hand, there's no reason why they need do so. Thus I may own five O and my neighbour may own three A. But due to my superior strength and intelligence, it may be true as a matter of empirical fact that what I possess are not only my five O but also two of his A, while my hapless neighbour possesses only one A. So the relative vulnerability of my neighbour's property rights implies a different set of endowments than is normatively the case. Generalizing, we might call this purely descriptive conception the *natural* or *Hobbesian* endowment set: the distribution of endowments based on might, as distinguished from the normative endowment set which is the distribution of endowments based on rights.

When we derive individuals' effective demand functions (in order to compile the social demand function and derive a set of prices), in whose function should those two A figure? Mine or my neighbour's? Clearly, neither they nor any other endowment items can figure in more than one person's function without double-counting. So on which of these types of endowment set is the four-O price of Red's R parametrically based?

Economic theory itself mandates no answer to these questions. And as far as I can see, there is no conceptual reason for disqualifying the Hobbesian endowment set, even if a normative set is the type customarily assumed. Thus the *Dictionary of Modern Economics* defines

---

reason to believe Ordinate and nevertheless doing so, is simply acting on a risk-aversion preference in declining to bid for Red's R, so Red is not exploited (just as he wouldn't be if Grey had reached this erroneous conclusion from her own inadequate research); (iii) if there *is* this right, and if the forgery charge is *true*, the case is the same as (ii); and finally (iv) if there *isn't* this right and if the forgery charge is *true*, the case is again the same as (ii). We can readily test these judgements by asking ourselves in which of these four cases might Grey be successful in claiming damages from Ordinate. Answer: only (i).

"wealth," which is synonymous with "endowment," without any restriction to ownership or property rights:

> Anything which has a market value and can be exchanged for money or goods can be regarded as wealth. It can include physical goods and assets, financial assets and personal skills which can generate an income. These are considered to be wealth when they can be traded in a market for goods or money. Wealth can be subdivided into two main types; tangible, which is referred to as capital or non-human wealth; and intangible which is human capital. All wealth has the basic property of being able to generate income which is the return on wealth. Thus, whereas wealth is a stock, income is a flow concept. The *present value* of this flow constitutes the *value* of the stock of wealth.[54]

There are, to be sure, strong Hobbesian reasons for doubting that any very extensive exchange system can subsist where the endowments deployed by exchangers are Hobbesian ones. But such considerations are insufficient to rule out the possibility of equilibrium price formation in those circumstances.[55] There's nothing incoherent about markets in stolen goods nor, for that matter, labour markets in larcenous skills. They exist.

If the exchange value of things is taken to be based on the purely descriptive or Hobbesian conception of endowments, then Red's R must be worth only four O and his complaint can be summarily dismissed. What Grey's undiminished endowment *would have been*, what higher price Red's R *would have* consequently commanded, are simply irrelevant. All that's relevant are the endowments that people actually possess and the bids they actually make. The prices formed by parametric Hobbesian endowment sets cannot fail to reflect the relative values of exchanged objects if all that counts are the possessory facts.[56]

This is not to suggest, however, that Red does have a proven case under the normative conception of endowments. For it's still an open question – of a kind to be addressed in the next three chapters – whether Grey had a right to her undiminished endowment: the one that would have yielded a five-O price for R. Perhaps she had no right against the

[54] Pearce (ed.), *Dictionary of Modern Economics*, 470–1.

[55] Cf. Bush, "Individual Welfare in Anarchy"; Buchanan, *The Limits of Liberty*, 23–5.

[56] Ryan, "Exploitation, Justice and the Rational Man," 33, correctly remarks that "rational man theories have to call in a theory of justice to decide when rational man's treatment of his fellows is *exploitative*."

forcible intervention that diminished it. Perhaps the intervenors were perfectly at liberty, or even mandated, to do what they did. Hence the most that can be said so far is that, for Red to have a case – for it to be possible that he has been exploited – it's necessary (though not sufficient) to assume, as the literature standardly does, that the relevant endowment set is a normative one. The big question, of course, is "Which normative one?"

I think this analysis supports what many writers have come to recognize about the longstanding controversy over whether it's an ethical or an empirical claim that's being registered by statements like "This class of persons is exploited." The modulating answer appears to be "both." Such statements are empirical insofar as it's a matter of (complex mathematical) *fact* as to what set of prices would be formed under a particular set of endowments. But they're also ethical inasmuch as it's a matter of *choice* as to which endowment set is to be taken as the relevant point of reference. And one thing that's certain in this respect is that, whatever happens to be the prevailing *legal* endowment set, it enjoys no *ipso facto* privileged status in the field of candidates for selection. Although possession may well be nine-tenths of the law, the institution of legal slavery is a sufficient reminder that *rightful* possession can be a good deal less than that.

Which brings us to what was earlier described as an important connection between economic and non-economic choice. *If* the relevant endowment set is a normative (legal, moral) rather than a natural precipitate, it is an object of choice. Yet evidently its parametric status with respect to economic choices implies that it itself is not one of them. In non-Disneyland worlds, my endowment determines the effective weight of my preferences and not the other way round. *A normative endowment set is a set of chosen constraints on economic choices.*

Chosen by whom? Clearly not by anyone for whom it stands in a compensatory relation to other ends. It can't consistently be regarded as subject to incremental trade-offs with the ends represented on indifference curves, since it is a presumed constraint on such trade-offs. Kenneth Arrow has observed that

> The price system, in order to work at all, must involve the concept of property . . . Property systems are in general not completely self-enforcing. They depend for their definition upon a constellation of legal procedures, both civil and criminal. The course of the law itself cannot be regarded as subject to the price system. The judges and the police may indeed be paid, but the system itself would disappear if on each occasion they were to sell their services and

decisions ... The price system is not, and perhaps in some basic sense cannot be, universal.[57]

Even if property systems required no enforcement – because persons chose not to violate others' rights – Arrow's central point, that the price system cannot be universal, would still hold. So long as endowment sets are understood as consisting of rights rather than Hobbesian possessions, the price system cannot extend to embracing respect for others' property rights as merely one amongst various mutually substitutable ends.[58]

To say this is not to say several things. Specifically, it's not to say that all rights-respecting rational conduct is informed by value structures in which such conduct figures as a non-compensatable end. Conduct can be rights-respecting for other reasons as well. Most obviously, my neighbour's non-violation of my right to my five O may be due to his *inability*: I or rights-enforcing agencies may prevent him from violating my right and thereby exclude rights-violating actions even from membership in his set of possible choices. On the other hand, and even where such actions are members of his possible choice set, they may be non-optimal options due to my own or those enforcing agencies' capacity to deliver a subsequent penalty of a magnitude sufficient to make those options unprofitable.[59]

In either case, the upshot is this: except in worlds where persons are each able to enforce their own rights, the absence of rights-violating conduct – and consequently, the integrity of any particular normative endowment set – can only be due to respect for its rights being present as a non-compensatory element in at least some persons' value structures. And as Arrow's remarks suggest, this group must consist of all those who ultimately control the legal system including, one might add, legislators themselves. For the competitive purchasability of their decisions and services would, indeed, imply a Hobbesian endowment set rather than a rights-based one.

We could, it's true, do worse than to heed Edgeworth's admonition that "To treat *variables* as *constants* is the characteristic vice of the

---

[57] Arrow, "Gifts and Exchanges," 357.

[58] This does not imply that *any* rights-based endowment set (notably, an unjust one) is superior to a Hobbesian one.

[59] Cf. Becker, "Crime and Punishment: An Economic Approach"; Rottenberg (ed.), *The Economics of Crime and Punishment*; Ehrlich, "Participation in Illegitimate Activities: A Theoretical and Empirical Investigation."

unmathematical economist."[60] But it's also true that where its rules as well as its prizes are biddable, the game is not the same. Nor, therefore, are its optimal strategies. Just what those rules might be is the subject of the remaining three chapters.

---

[60] Edgeworth, *Mathematical Psychics*, 127.

6
Justice

It's almost time to start deploying some of the chips I hope we've won in the preceding chapters. These analyses – of rights, of their relation to liberty and of the structures of moral and economic thinking into which they can be embedded – are capable of delivering a general description of persons' basic moral rights and the rights compatible with them. And if, like myself, you regard such a description as amounting to a principle of justice, then that delivery would suffice to achieve the aspiration of this chapter. But a healthy respect for the work of others on the subject of justice suggests the advisability of a less linear approach to this target.

For it's by no means the case that most attempts to discover what justice is have pursued what was referred to, in the introduction, as the "elementary particle strategy." They have not sought to derive the nature of justice from its microfoundations in the formal characteristics of moral rights. Rather, their approach has been to elicit it from careful explorations of various moral ideals whose relation to justice is widely presumed to be one of inclusion or near-synonymy: ideals such as impartiality, fairness, neutrality, and perhaps even things akin to Edgeworth's notion of an arbitration principle that diminishes groaning.

The association of these concepts with that of justice is an undeniable feature of our ordinary thinking. And a rather spare microfoundational derivation of basic rights therefore runs the risk of failing to exhibit these pre-theoretical connections. So there seems to be some point in trying to cast a wider net by integrating the relevant parts of the analyses already in hand into a discussion focused on some of these associated ideas.

Presumably the most promising place to track down these ideas is in their native habitat: namely, *adversarial circumstances*. People disagreeing supply a necessary element of situations occasioning the exercise of impartiality, arbitration and the rest, as well as the invocation of rights. Necessary, but not sufficient. Only some disagreements provide such occasions. To find out which ones, we need to look at several sorts of disagreement. And since disagreement is a type of conflict, what better place to begin our search than back in the little shop where we first encountered MJM (Moral Judgement Machine)?

(A) DISAGREEMENT AND DEADLOCK

Not a perspicuous move, you may think. After all, the MJM story was about only one person, Blue, working out her own moral priorities in a series of increasingly complex situations. It was the oft-told tale of the mononomic blandishments which can be put in the way of someone who is struggling with a plurality of primary rules or values in an effort to reach a judgement about what to do. Personal moral conflicts – dilemmas – whatever else they occasion, do not call for impartiality, fairness or arbitration except, perhaps, in a metaphoric sense. Since we are not taking a Platonic view of justice, since we regard it as but one value amongst others, MJM would seem to be a quite inappropriate instrument for fashioning an account of justice. Moreover, not all conflicts occasioning arbitration or appeals to rights are conflicts between moral values or rules.

There is much truth in these complaints. But not enough. Take the second complaint first. It's certainly true that our actions, and the actions we wish others to perform, are not always ones pursuant of moral values. We and they also have wants, preferences and interests which strongly inform many practical choices. So conflicts between two or more persons – conflicts occasioning arbitration and rights-appeals – may be conflicts between their respective preferences or between one's preferences and the other's moral values.

Sometimes, of course, it may be a conflict of moral values that underlies a conflict of two persons' preferences. Thus, if we assume that our preferences reign over those options which are left open by our moral rules – options occupying the space of moral *indifference*[1] – some interpersonal preference conflicts can be partly traced to opposed views of where that space is. In which case, any argument between such persons as to whose preference should prevail may eventually become a conflict between moral values. But it must be acknowledged that not all conflicts between opposed preferences (wants, interests) are built on moral differences. Your preference that we go out for a big meal on Thursday evening, and my desire to spend that time at the movies, may be partly traceable to differing views about what is morally obligatory, prohibited

---

[1] An option is morally indifferent if it's morally permissible to secure it *and* morally permissible to forbear from securing it.

or indifferent. (You may regard fasting on Friday as obligatory.) But they need not be. So the most that can be said at this point is that, although an MJM exercise may seem to have no bearing on such conflicts, I hope to show that the principle of justice that emerges from it does set a limit on the permissible pursuit of an opposed preference.

Where MJM really comes into its own is in what is, by all accounts, the most intractable form of interpersonal conflict: conflicts between different persons' moral values. "Most intractable" because, in this case, a particular act which one person denounces as impermissible the other defends as permissible and even obligatory. No clearer form of opposition exists. And the scepticism of the first complaint above notwithstanding, MJM is admirably suited to give us some purchase on the several ways in which two persons who morally disagree may nevertheless, and *consistently*, arrive at the same judgement as to what may and what must not be done on that particular occasion.

So let's set it up this way. We're back in the shop where Operator is putting Blue through her moral paces on MJM under the ever watchful eye of Evaluator who waits to pounce on any inconsistent judgement. In walks White who has been here before. Having been here before, he knows that players' first-level orderings – their rankings of their several primary rules or values – are represented by the spectral colour sequence: red>orange>yellow>etc. About to settle back in a chair and watch Blue cope with few easy rounds of play – not more than one ball of each colour, all of uniform size – White casually enquires of Operator what Blue's primary rules are and how they're ordered. And he is utterly shocked to learn that, for her, these are Patriotism>Promise-keeping>Familial Devotion. Indeed, before he's had time to recover his equanimity, the situation device ejects a red ball and an orange one, the constraint mechanism flashes "1," and Blue goes to remove the red ball.

"Stop!" screams White, leaping to his feet. "You can't be serious! Do you realize what you're about to do? If you pull out the red ball and leave the orange one, you'll be defaulting on a promise merely for the sake of some imagined patriotic duty."

Blue, taken aback, hesitates. "I'm pretty sure," she ventures anxiously, "that red balls really do represent patriotic acts and that there's nothing imaginary about this one." Operator gives her a confirming nod.

"Yes, yes," retorts White impatiently, "no one is disputing the *facts* of the case. What I'm questioning is whether the doing of that patriotic act is a duty or, at least, whether it's a duty of greater importance than your duty to keep promises. Surely you can't believe that?"

However, any creeping doubts that Blue might have about her judgement here are quickly dispelled by an ominous rumbling noise emanating from Evaluator's direction. "Yes," she says firmly, "I'm afraid that is precisely what I do believe. Keeping promises is undoubtedly very important and I should be remiss, indeed wicked, to break one for any other reason, any reason other than patriotism." (Evaluator subsides.)

Shaking his head in disbelief, White slumps into his chair. "All I can say is that you have a very strange set of moral priorities. As far as I'm concerned, patriotism comes way down the list if it's on the list at all." But then a more troubled expression crosses his face. "Wait just a moment," he says, rising slowly. "My moral code commits me to assigning much greater value to promise-keepings than to patriotisms. A world in which promises are kept and patriotism is absent is far better than one where the reverse is true. If that's what I believe, and it is, am I not morally bound to take such actions as are available to me to bring that better world about? And if so, doesn't that mean that I must here and now do everything in my power to ensure that it's the orange ball, and not the red one, that gets removed by you?"

Blue is alarmed. She glances at Evaluator, hoping for some sign of support. But none is forthcoming because, of course, nothing that White has said or hinted at doing is at all inconsistent with *his* registered moral code. So being basically a peaceable sort of person, Blue begins to consider withdrawing from this prospective battle: either by removing the orange ball after all or by simply removing neither ball. But Evaluator is having none of this. His telepathic circuits, activated by Blue's contemplated dereliction, initiate that same rumbling noise as a prelude to the full-scale "This does not compute" din that will inevitably ensue upon any failure to undertake her duty.

Nor is it irrelevant to note that White, too, is a peaceable person and equally disinclined to engage in the threatened struggle. But what (consistent, principled, etc.) alternative does he have? If he retreats, Evaluator will administer the same censorious treatment to him. Nor is the fact entirely lost, on either Blue or White, that one very possible outcome of the prospective battle to which their respective moral codes apparently commit them is that *neither* of the two balls will be removed. So long as each is still able to do her/his morally requisite action, the duty to do so does not lapse: only "cannot" implies "not ought" in this situation. Hence the fact that the nuclear-tipped brass knuckles, with which they are even now grimly girding themselves, promise to promote at least one – if not both – of them to "cannot" status, is insufficient to relieve either of them of this duty.

Operator nervously intervenes in a last-ditch effort to avert the imminent destruction of his shop. Affecting a not unstrained air of geniality, he volunteers: "Come on, you two. You can't be serious. There must be some room for a reasonable reconciliation here. I'm absolutely confident that if you both take a closer look at the particular acts actually involved, you'll soon agree on which one of them is better than the other. What you need to do is examine this particular promise-keeping and this particular patriotism and ask yourselves, impartially, which one of them looks like achieving more good. Which one of them, all things considered, is going to produce more happiness (or preference-satisfaction or regret-minimization or self-development or organic unity)?"

"Nice try, Operator," respond Blue and White in sarcastic unison, "but if that's your best suggestion, this shop is definitely doomed. We all took your mononomics lesson back in chapter 4. Remember? Because if you do, you'll surely also recall that you failed to convince us that morally valuable acts are commensurable by virtue of some single dimension present in all of them. To be sure (and as was said there) we could impose an *exogenous* commensurability on them by assigning numerical weightings to the types of act they are. And this would still allow us to reach principled judgements about which one, of two valuable acts of different types, is the better one. But even if we did, there's no reason for those weightings to be the same for each of us. So your proposal holds out no prospect of eliminating our disagreement about which of these two is the better act and, hence, no reason for either of us to stand down. We're well and truly *deadlocked*."

"All right, all right," Operator wearily concedes. "I can see that you're both indissolubly wedded to your polynomic pieties. Come to that, it wouldn't make much difference even if you could be converted to mononomism unless you both then hit on the same single commensurating dimension. What I'm about to do really goes against all my principles (sorry – principle), but I suppose there's nothing else for it. This is very unsound, mononomically speaking, but there's this strange lady just down the road who seems somehow able to cope with these situations when we get stuck with obstinately adversarial customers such as yourselves." And so saying, Operator reaches under the counter to push a rusty old button labelled *"Justice: press only in cases of deadlock."*

A few minutes later, a familiar harassed-looking figure shuffles into the shop, dragging an overstuffed plastic shopping-bag behind her. It is, of course, our old friend Adjudicator who then proceeds to empty the bag of its contents which include a black robe, a sword, a set of scales and a blindfold. "Just hang on a moment," she says, "while I get all this gear on. Then we'll get down to business."

Having decked herself out, she continues: "Right. Now before I listen to anything that either of you has to say, you're going to listen to my standard opening speech. It's short and it's pithy. I'm here because you two are in a deadlock. That's the only reason I'm here. And you might as well know straight off that when I leave this shop, *you're still going to be in disagreement*. You'll still disagree about which is the better act. All I can do is get rid of the deadlock. So if what you're hoping for is some sudden outbreak of complete moral rapport, you've called in the wrong functionary."

"With all due respect, your honour," interjects White, "and without wishing in any way to suggest that we wouldn't welcome the elimination of this deadlock, I really don't see how you can accomplish that without also getting rid of the disagreement. The two are surely inseparable. I trust that what you have in mind isn't some shoddy little *ad hoc* compromise requiring one of us (at the point of your sword?) to reverse his/her priorities. Because we're perfectly capable of accomplishing that unremarkable feat ourselves. And besides, we've got Evaluator over there who's just waiting for one or the other of us to commit an expedient dereliction."

"Look, Sunshine," retorts Adjudicator brusquely, "I work for Evaluator too. So I don't need you to tell me that the required resolution has to be a principled one that involves no priority-reversals for either of you. Would I be standing around here blindfolded in this itchy robe and struggling with these blasted scales if my job was simply to lean on one of you until you did a priority-reversal? The sword would suffice for that. What I'm here for is to supply one or the other of you with an impartial reason for standing down on this particular occasion: a reason you can accept without setting Evaluator off on one of his tantrums. Which one of you should do the standing down, on the basis of that reason, is what we've got to work out. So let's get on with it, shall we?"

Now it's Blue's turn to intervene. Affecting a less confrontational tone, she says: "Please don't misunderstand us, Adjudicator. We really do appreciate the trouble you're going to on our behalf. It's just that we don't want to waste your time. We've each reflected quite thoroughly on the structure of our respective moral codes and we've done an exhaustive survey of the facts. So we're in absolutely no doubt that the action each of us regards as obligatory must be judged impermissible by the other. You say you have this magic reason for one of us to stand down from the threatened battle. I can't see how any reason can be a reason for standing down unless it implies the impermissibility of an action which one of us deems obligatory. And if it does imply that, I can't see how its acceptance by that person could fail to amount to a priority-reversal."

"A very reasonable suspicion, Blue, but ultimately mistaken," replies Adjudicator. "Perhaps we can better approach this arbitration process, not by my simply telling you what my magic reason is, but rather by our discussing what features a standing-down reason has to have in order to get rid of this deadlock satisfactorily. One thing we're agreed on is that it mustn't be such as to require a priority-reversal from either of you. That's crucial. So you've got to be able to leave the shop satisfied that you haven't reneged on your commitment to the priority of patriotism over promise-keeping. And White has to be left with his contrary view similarly intact. Now in my neck of the woods, we sometimes call that relation one of *toleration*. That is, whichever of you winds up doing the standing down gets a round of applause for being tolerant."

"Well," says Blue, "I don't want to be a chronic wet blanket, but I think we've already got a problem here. Because in *my* neck of the woods, toleration is generally regarded as an excuse for fudging one's duties. It is a pretty woolly concept, I think you'll have to admit. I mean it's not exactly like letting others get on with conduct of which one approves or to which one is quite indifferent. There's no strain in that. Toleration is letting them get on with items of which one disapproves, sometimes quite strongly. And as such, it looks like a congenial label for what really amounts to nothing less than hypocritical dereliction. Even apart from that, even if you think toleration's not so bad, you've still got the classic problem of how to avoid tolerating the intolerant. So I don't see that we're going to get much mileage out of toleration."

"Again, you're partly right, Blue. When I described standing down as practising tolerance, I was only trying to convey the possible temperament of the person doing it. But it's certainly true that, unless that temperament is informed by my magic reason – unless it's a discriminating sort of tolerance that draws a line between some impermissible acts and others – it does indeed amount to precisely the kind of moral mushiness you mention. And it also generates that 'tolerating intolerance paradox.' So I'm not saying that everyone who is tolerantly disposed is just. And in any case, I'm not recommending toleration *per se*, i.e. as a primary rule or value. That would be absurd. For imagine what would happen if both you and White were to adopt it. You'd both wander out of the shop with neither ball removed from the machine. No, the aim of anyone seriously engaged in deadlock resolution is to get only one of the adversaries to stand down, letting the other get on with his or her action."

"I find this whole thing utterly mysterious," interrupts White. "You say we're not to do any indiscriminate standing down and that your magic reason will tell us when we should stand down. I take it that, even if tolerance isn't going to be a primary rule, your reason is. But I already know what all my primary rules are. And so does Blue. And none of them provides either of us with grounds for standing down on this occasion. Furthermore, if you're thinking that you're now going to add some new primary rule to our moral codes, how can you be confident that it doesn't contradict one we already have? If you agree that no-priority-reversal is a constraint on any resolution, you can't very well turn around and insist on either of us simply dropping one of our primary rules."

"I fully accept what you say, White," Adjudicator responds patiently. "It's true that, for my magic reason to work, you have to adopt it as one of your primary rules. But I'm proud to tell you that my company, *Deadlock Resolution Unlimited*, issues a lifetime guarantee that this magic reason cannot contradict any primary rule you happen to have and, so, will not require you to drop any of them. In fact, the folks down at our factory consider this reason to be so effective in removing all kinds of deadlock from the social fabric that they like to call it the 'universal solvent.' No matter what primary rules are at stake in a deadlock and regardless of how their protagonists have prioritized them, this magic reason can do the job."

And visibly warming to her subject, Adjudicator continues: "You see, what happens when we apply the magic reason to a deadlock is that it crystallizes into these wonderfully handy little gadgets, called *rights*, which go to work instantly to supply one of the adversaries with the grounds for standing down in that situation. He or she can walk away clean from that deadlock, with all primary rules intact and no priority-reversals to mar the occasion. Oops, sorry! I'm getting a bit ahead of myself here. We'll come to rights in due course."

"No, wait a moment," says White. "I find what you say fascinating. But haven't you already given a hostage to fortune? It's true that I don't yet know exactly what these rights gadgets are, much less the content of the reason that produces them. But by the same token, you don't know all my primary rules, let alone which ones I might yet come to adopt. So going purely on the basis of what you've said thus far, how would you respond if I were to tell you that one of my primary rules specifically enjoins me to violate moral rights? Wouldn't the adoption of your magic reason as one of my primary rules then entrap me in a contradiction and require me, your guarantee notwithstanding, to drop my rights-violation rule?"

"Come on, White," Adjudicator chides. "That's a bit below the belt. Or to put it more philosophically, your objection is question-begging. If your code contains a rights-violation rule, it's already self-contradictory. You can't regard an act as rights-violating unless you already acknowledge that its victim has that right. So your code would already have to contain a rights-producing reason as one of its rules. 'Where there are no property rights, there is no theft,' as Locke once nearly said.[2] Of course, it would be an entirely different matter if my reason were a rule enjoining happiness production or charity. Then you would be entitled to doubt the company's non-contradiction guarantee since, however misanthropically, your code could contain primary rules enjoining misery production or uncharitableness. But my reason has nothing to do with such things."

"If I've understood you correctly," White cautiously replies after long reflection, "you're claiming something quite extraordinary for your reason. You're saying that this reason amounts to a primary rule that, unlike any other primary rule I know of, is one which we are *logically compelled* to adopt. You're saying that a rule enjoining the opposite of what yours enjoins is self-contradictory."

"Almost but not quite wholly correct," beams Adjudicator. "I am indeed making the claim about self-contradictoriness. But I'm *not* saying that this rule's adoption is logically compulsory.[3] There was a time, mind you, when my colleagues at the company were heavily under the influ-

---

[2] Locke, *An Essay Concerning Human Understanding*, 549.

[3] For an argument that a moral code's inclusion of a rights rule, though not logically compulsory, is necessary for the avoidance of strongly absurd judgements, see Steiner, "The Natural Right to Equal Freedom," 194–200.

ence of Kant and did believe that its adoption is logically compulsory –
that an action's being a violation of rights is a sufficient condition of
its moral impermissibility. I'll explain why they held this belief a little
later on when I come to reveal the reason itself. Nowadays however,
we take a slightly less exalted view of it and insist only that a rights-
violating action cannot be justified as such but only as an incidental
feature of a duty implied by some other primary rule. Whereas, as I said
before, a misanthrope could justify an uncharitable act as such, i.e. by
invoking a primary rule enjoining uncharitableness. The impartiality or
neutrality of our reason consists in its not being contradictory of any
other primary rule. And that is due to the fact that any putative primary
rule contradicting it is self-contradictory: that is, not a possible primary rule."

"Okay," White acquiesces, "I'll take your guarantee at its word for
the moment, pending the revelation of this magic reason. But I still think
your argument is in trouble. Even if I can't have a primary rule enjoining
rights-violation, who's to say where or how I'll rank your magic reason
among the primary rules I do have? What if I were to put your reason
way down there below even patriotism? Or what if I were to assign it a
numerical weighting so that some instances of complying with it – perhaps the present one? – are morally outweighed by some promise-keepings? Maybe my moral code would tell me that defaulting on some particular promise is worse than violating whatever right is involved: either
because any promise-keeping is more important than any right or
because that particular promise-keeping is more important than that
particular right. So how can you claim that your magic reason is
inherently capable of solving our deadlock, let alone all others?"

"A thoroughly excellent point, White," affirms Adjudicator. "I
couldn't have put it better myself. So you can see, on your own testimony, just what would have to be the rank and weight of a primary rule
for resolving all deadlocks. If your code is to incorporate such a rule
(remember, it needn't), it must be given *lexically prime* status, like the
word 'a' in the dictionary. It must outrank every other primary rule in
your code. Any act enjoined by it must be morally better than any act
that violates it, however good that latter act might be. Compared to the
finite moral weight of a duty pursuant to any other primary rule, any
duty not to violate rights is infinitely weighty and ineligible for trade-
offs with other duties, however weighty they might be. You'll probably
recall that it was precisely this same point – about the non-substitut-
ability of respect for rights – that was made at the end of the previous
chapter, on economic reasoning. One nice way of describing this idea is

to say that *'rights are trumps.'*[4] Another might be to see them as vetoes."

"I must say," interjects Blue, "I find this idea of giving your rights rule lexical primacy – making rights trumps – a bit disturbing. And for two reasons. What if the only way to avoid a catastrophe is to do something that violates rights? I'm not now talking about your everyday run-of-the-mill deadlock where what may be at stake is, say, defaulting on a promise or doing something unpatriotic. I mean some genuine 'catastrophic moral horror.'[5] And I take it that if we're bound to treat rights as trumps, we'd just have to stand down and countenance this catastrophe."

Adjudicator hesitates, but then bites the bullet. "The short answer is that you're right. But let's be absolutely clear about what we're saying here. In the first place, it's important to appreciate that your objection applies more generally than to the rights rule alone. And it also applies more generally than to only lexical *primacy*. It applies equally to any rule or value which is given any sort of lexical priority over others. There are conceivable situations where the non-compensatability of any lexically prior rule requires you to sacrifice a great deal of moral value in complying with its injunctions. So that aspect of your objection would tell against any moral code that immunizes any of its rules against trade-offs with lower-ranked rules.[6]

"Now, I'm not unsympathetic to your concerns on that score. You'll recall that, in the chapters on moral and economic reasoning, some doubt was expressed about both the reasonableness and the realism of orderings that are totally devoid of any compensatory elements. My hunch would be that most of us are profoundly ambivalent at this nearly meta-ethical level. On the one hand, we're loath to assign indefeasible status to *any* rule or value. That's precisely why many of us balk at

---

[4] Cf. Dworkin, "Is There a Right to Pornography?"; on the lexical primacy of justice, see Rawls, *A Theory of Justice*, 42ff.

[5] Cf. Nozick, *Anarchy, State and Utopia*, 30; see also Thomson, "Preferential Hiring," 378.

[6] Or that immunizes any minimum degree (or threshold) of compliance with a rule against such trade-offs. See Griffin, *Well-Being*, 83–9, who distinguishes this form of discontinuity which he regards as plausible, from lexical ordering which he suggests is "probably not seriously intended." But this is a distinction without a difference. Griffin's proposal is extensionally equivalent to (Operator's ch. 4 suggestion of) splitting one rule into two – one prescribing performances up to the minimum required threshold and the other prescribing performances above it – and assigning lexical priority to the former. Moreover lexical ordering *does* seem to be seriously intended by, for example, Rawls who thus immunizes *all* degrees of compliance with his principles of justice against any competing demands, however urgent, of lower ranked principles. Recall that, in the previous chapter, Archimedes' favorite axiom – the one excluding lexical orderings and thereby making utilitarian computation possible – is the Axiom of Continuity.

mononomic codes. On the other hand, we're pretty resistant to the idea that everything has its price. And I fear that, at this level of abstraction, these two possibilities are all there is.

"That said, however, we do need to be a bit more precise about the nature of situations where the options are, as you put it, either countenancing a catastrophic moral horror or violating rights. Presumably in describing the alternatives this way you mean that, whatever is morally bad about this catastrophe, it doesn't itself include rights-violations. And presumably it's also the case that, if countenancing the catastrophe is indeed an alternative in a choosing situation, your catastrophe can't be the sort of disaster that no one has the ability to avert.

"Now as far as I can see, what such a catastrophe must amount to is the expected result of an avoidable failure to satisfy the demands – in this case, weighty – of some primary rule (or several of them). That is, your proposed choice situation is one where this other rule and the rights rule are competitors. But if that's so, it must be the case that there are some persons *whose moral codes do not include* that other rule or, at least, the way it's prioritized: namely, those persons whose rights would have to be violated to satisfy its demands. For them, whatever would occur as a result of their rights not being violated simply does not amount to a moral catastrophe. Because if it did, *they would thereby have sufficient reason to stand down* and waive the correlative duties owed to them. They would themselves have sufficient reason to extinguish others' duties to respect their rights, in order to avert the catastrophe, and hence no violation of their rights would be necessary for that purpose.[7] On the other hand, if they won't waive, if they insist upon respect for their rights, chances are that it's in behalf of something they consider pretty important and certainly more important than averting the catastrophe. Remember, a moral catastrophe only *is* a moral catastrophe relative to some moral rule or value. There simply are no rule-independent or value-free conceptions of moral catastrophe.

"In short, any such situation in which what's at stake is said to be a moral catastrophe cannot *ex hypothesi* be regarded as such by all the

---

[7] To this, the type of counter-example sometimes offered is that the right-holder refusing to issue such a waiver, despite this impending catastrophe, might be a psychopath: more generally, that theories assigning "trump" status to rights render us hostage to psychopaths. This argument is surely self-defeating. Few moral theories ascribe moral agency to psychopaths: they don't standardly regard them as persons capable of having duties nor, therefore, as standardly liable for punishment in the event of dereliction. Hence they cannot be said to have rights, though we doubtless have (non-correlative) duties to care for them. For more on these grounds for denying rights to some persons, see the discussion of minors in ch. 7, section (b).

persons concerned. And if you think, as I do, that rights are very important, you may find it difficult – I don't say impossible – to persuade yourself that there can be situations where the options are as you've described."

"Okay," concedes Blue, "I take your point. But part of the way in which you developed it leads very nicely into my second worry about rights as trumps. You sought to clarify my counter-argument by presuming that the catastrophe I counterposed to the rights-violation didn't itself include any rights-violation. What if it *does*? I'm talking about cases where whatever act each party to a deadlock wishes to do also amounts to a violation of the other's rights. You've assumed that only one of our two proposed acts, White's and mine, can be rights-violating. Suppose it turns out that both White and I are within our respective rights in each trying to enact our opposed moral judgements. You've said that your rights rule doesn't contradict any of our primary rules or how they're prioritized. Doesn't that mean that we could both be within our rights in proceeding and that, in stopping one of us from doing so, you'd be violating that person's rights in order to uphold the other's? How then are we to understand the stopped person's rights as trumps? Or, to use a phrase of yours, how can the duties to respect opposed rights *both* be infinitely weighty?"

"Excellent question, Blue. Earlier I said that my magic reason, or rights rule, would supply one of you with a reason to stand down. Then I went on to enumerate the ways in which my rule is independent of, or neutral with respect to, the content of your respective rules and their relative priorities. Now you're asking me how I can be so confident that, if it has such independence, it won't confer rights on both of you in this deadlock situation. How can I guarantee that it doesn't imply that neither of you need stand down? How can rights be trumps if they can tie with each other?

"My short answer is that they *can't* tie with each other. Why not? Well on the face of it, one answer might seem to be that they can be strongly ordered. After all, each card in a trump suit is strongly ordered and cannot tie with another. But that can't be a satisfactory answer when it comes to rights. And the reason is obvious enough. If we try to rank *types* of rights, we immediately create the possibility of undecidable cases – ties – whenever the two parties to a deadlock are exercising rights of the same type. It would be like playing a card game, involving a trump suit, with *two* decks of cards!

"So the rights rule has to be such that, in any conceivable deadlock, only one of the parties is within his/her rights. And the way in which this is guaranteed is by having a rights rule that generates only rights which are *compossible*. Chapter 3, you'll recall, is a very long disquisition on the characteristics required by a set of rights for them all to be compossible. Any rights rule worthy of the name has to be one that generates such a set. If it does so, it ensures that one and only one party to any deadlock is holding a trump. Its rights don't need to be traded off against each other, they don't require commensuration, because they can't conflict with one another. The inviolability of each right doesn't rest precariously on some contestable weighting or ranking, nor therefore is it contingent upon the varying calculational outcomes of what has aptly been called a 'utilitarianism of rights.'[8] Happily, the company's rights rule satisfies these demanding requirements. In relieving us functionaries of what chapter 3 described as 'the sovereign prerogative of choice,' it effectively embodies the idea of the rule of law. That's why I can do my job blindfolded."

"Let me get this straight," interrupts White. "You're saying that all rights can be trumps, provided (i) that they're all compossible, and (ii) that the rights rule is lexically prime. I can see why both of these conditions are necessary for every right to be a trump and, thus, for your rights rule to supply only one right answer for every deadlock question. What I'm not entirely clear about is the status of the reason assigning lexical primacy to your rights rule. Let me try to spell out my worry on this score. If I correctly understood part of the argument on moral reasoning in chapter 4, it maintained that some priority rules are themselves objects of logically unconstrained choice (like primary rules) while the rest are logically inferable from those chosen priority rules.[9] However, what you seem to be suggesting here is that the lexically prime prioritization of your rights rule is derived in neither of these two ways but rather is some sort of conceptual truth. How can this be so?"

"I'm a bit surprised at your question, White," Adjudicator replies. "Surprised, because it was you yourself who more or less supplied the answer to it a few pages ago, when you pointed out the implications of *not* ranking the rights rule as lexically prime. You correctly observed that, if it were not so ranked, it might not get a grip on your current deadlock. And if it didn't, then, given your and Blue's respective commitments, there's no way that your deadlock could be resolved impartially. There is no way that it could be resolved without relying on one, and dismissing the other, of your respective opposed prioritizations. The lexically prime priority of the rights rule is indeed a conceptual truth: it's a conceptual truth about the implications of resolving deadlocks impar-

---

[8] Cf. Nozick, *Anarchy, State and Utopia*, 28–30.
[9] See above, pp. 119–25.

tially. That is, it's a conceptual truth about justice. Remember, I'm not telling you that you *must* accept impartial deadlock resolution, that you have to act justly. All I'm doing is describing what's involved *if* you do. If you consult chapter 4 again, you'll find that a caveat was entered on that claim about the two sources of priority rules, precisely with the present point in mind."[10]

"May I get a word in?" Blue interjects, slightly annoyed at White's interruption of her line of questioning. "You were saying, just before, that the compossibility of your set of rights makes it unnecessary to trade them off against one another: that they don't need to be commensurated by weighting or ranking them in relation to each other nor do they have to be subjected to a utilitarianism of rights. In short, duties to respect rights can't conflict with one another. But surely there can be instances where they do conflict. Suppose the only way to stop me committing a rights-violation against White is for you to do something that *inter alia* violates Red's rights.[11] Or suppose that the only way to get me to redress a rights-violation I've already committed against White is, again, for you to act in such a way as to violate Red's rights.[12] Surely this is conceivable. And just as surely, it involves a conflict of duties as between White's rights and Red's. Won't you then have to commensurate those duties to determine what to do?"[13]

"Nice, very nice," mutters Adjudicator. "This is a problem that has bedevilled theories of rights since they first saw the light of day. So we

[10] See ch. 4, n. 12.

[11] Cf. Nozick, *Anarchy, State and Utopia*, 28–35; Sen, "Rights and Agency," 7–19.

[12] Cf. Thomson, "Preferential Hiring," 379–84, and more generally, the literature on justice and reverse discrimination.

[13] George Sher, "Right Violations and Injustice," 222, offers epistemic (imperfect information) reasons for regarding rights as being, in many cases, unavoidably subject to mutual trade-offs. He argues "that a trade-off is unavoidable when anything the agent does or abstains from doing can be expected to violate someone's rights or treat someone unjustly, and that ignorance frequently places agents in just this position." Thus if my forcing you to make redress to Red is based upon imperfect evidence of (or imperfect procedures for ascertaining) your guilt, my enforcement action may violate your right while my inaction may violate Red's. Hence, Sher claims, my decision as to what to do here inevitably amounts to one which trades off one right against the other. This seems mistaken. My decision here need in no way be based upon any comparison of the two rights involved, much less any consideration as to which of them is the more valuable. It can be entirely based upon the balance of probabilities as to your guilt. For no clear sense can be made of the suggestion that an action, intended to uphold rights and based upon the ignorance inherent in imperfect or probabilistic information, "can be *expected*" to violate rights: improbable outcomes cannot be expected ones. If my action probably upholds Red's rights, then *ipso facto* it improbably violates yours, i.e. in a compossible set of rights.

need to take it slowly and in steps. The first step is to distinguish the sorts of duty that are allegedly in conflict here. Because when you describe one of them as a duty to stop (or to get you to make redress for) your violation of White's rights, what you're talking about is a duty to *enforce* White's rights. A duty to enforce rights is different from a duty to respect them. Enforcement duties can arise only when defaults on respect duties are impending or committed.

"Now my compossibility claim, as you stated it yourself, is that duties to *respect* rights can't conflict with one another. The demand for respect for (compossible) rights is always equal to our ability to supply it. Compossible rights, as was noted in chapter 3, are *funded* ones. That's why there's no call for commensurating and trading such duties off against one another. By way of contrast, it's worth remarking that the same cannot be claimed about the demands of other moral rules, say, on occasions for being benevolent. For, try as we might, it looks like the demand for benevolence *can* exceed our ability to supply it. And so we're often driven to weight and rank and trade off less urgent benevolence demands against more urgent ones, due to shortage of resources. Put it this way: if everyone always respected rights, no rights would go unrespected. Whereas if everyone was always benevolent, there could still be occasions where further benevolence would be appropriate.

"But what you're asking me now is whether, in certain circumstances where you withhold some of your available supply of respect for White's rights by violating them, you don't thereby create a conflict of duties for me. Note that you're assuming that I have a duty to enforce White's rights. Let's accept this assumption. Then your question is whether there isn't an incompossibility here by virtue of the fact that I can't fulfil both my enforcement duty to White and my respect duty to Red?

"The answer is 'no,' because you've misdescribed the situation. To see why, we need to take a second step. Where the first step was to distinguish the types of duty – respect and enforcement – involved in your examples, the second step is to identify and locate the bearers of these particular duties. What I want to argue is that, although it's true that your violation gives rise to two duties, they don't conflict because only one of them is mine.

"This can be seen by examining a series of three cases. In the first, suppose you pick up a pot of hot coffee and proceed to spill it on Red's lap. We'll further suppose that people have a right not to have coffee spilled on them. As you've suggested, a rights-violation occasions a duty in the violator to make redress. The person owing the redress is the bearer of the respect duty that was defaulted on. In this case, it's you. What happens in the second case is that I'm holding the pot of coffee and you come along and push my arm, forcing me to spill it on Red. I take it that you'd agree that the redress owed to Red is owed to him by you since it's your respect duty, not mine, that's been defaulted on.[14] In the third case, I'm again the one holding the coffee. But this time you push my arm in such a way as to force me to spill it on either Red or White. And what happens is that, pursuant to my enforcement duty to stop you violating White's rights, I spill it on Red. Presumably you wouldn't deny that, in this case too, it's you and not myself who owes the redress. Hence the defaulted duty to respect Red's rights is, as in the previous case, yours and not mine.

"Now this third case exactly instances the salient features of your examples. And as you can see, what's involved here is only one duty of mine, not two. Hence, no conflict of duties. Of course, if I also have a duty to enforce Red's rights, I'll have to get you to make redress for violating them. But as far as the terms of your example go, that duty doesn't conflict with any other duty I have. So there's no incompossibility here and no call to commensurate rights."

Blue ponders this argument for a while. "Okay, I see that because I'm going to be liable for the redress involved in these examples, it's incorrect to describe the defaulted respect duty as yours. But I do think that your third case is slightly rigged, so far as the compossibility-commensuration issue is concerned. Suppose you *do* have a duty to enforce Red's rights as well as White's. And suppose that what my pushing your arm forces you to do is to spill the coffee either on Red's lap or on White's table-cloth. And further suppose that people have rights against having coffee spilled, not only on themselves, but also on their table-cloths. It may be that I'm the one who would ultimately have to foot the bill for the damage done. But that doesn't alter the fact that you would be confronted with a conflict of enforcement duties and that, in deciding where to spill and thus which duty to default on, you'd probably want to weigh up rights to undamaged laps against rights to undamaged table-cloths."

"Another nice point," Adjudicator replies, "though it too labours under a misdescription. I think you're correct to suppose that I'd probably compare laps to table-cloths in deciding where to spill. But I wouldn't thereby be deliberating about which one of my two enforcement duties to default on. For I wouldn't have to default on either of them. All I'd be thereby deciding is which one to fulfil by stopping a rights-violation and which one to fulfil by getting you to make redress.

---

[14] Or if it *is* mine and I am therefore liable for redress to Red, your liability for redress to me (for violating your duty not to push my arm) will include the value of the damages I owe to Red.

Stopping violations and getting their perpetrators to make redress for them are, as you've indicated, both forms of enforcement. And there's no reason why I can't do both in the case you've described."

Blue's challenge is swift: "But what if, as a matter of fact, you simply can't do both?"

"Ah, now we are into much deeper waters," sighs Adjudicator. "I think that what you have to mean by 'can't do both' is that at least one of the violations is, in some sense, non-redressable. Because if they're both redressable, and even if I (can or do) stop neither of them, there's no reason why I can't fulfil both of my enforcement duties by getting both violations redressed. Moreover there's also no problem if only one of them is non-redressable, since that's obviously the one I'll choose to stop.

"Where your challenge gets some kind of grip is in a case where *both* violations are non-redressable and I can stop either one but not both of them. But here we have to pause and consider what it would mean to say that a violation is non-redressable. Does it mean that there is nothing that can appropriately be exacted from its perpetrator? I'm certainly not going to dispute the possibility of non-redressable violations. The historical fact, that reparations have been demanded for some of the most heinous violations imaginable, doesn't show that those violations could ever be fully redressed.

"What I'm not sure about, however, is the extent to which the difficulty posed by the present double duty case is essentially different from that posed by those hopeless cases involving only a *single* violation which is both non-stoppable and non-redressable. It's true that in the former case, but not the latter, I have to make a choice. And it may also be true that, to make that choice, I'd want to weigh up the two rights at stake. Though God alone knows how I'd do that if they're both such that their respective violations are literally beyond redress, let alone if they're both rights of the same type.[15] On the other hand, if there's any form of enforcement that's appropriate in response to a single non-stoppable, non-redressable violation, then my doing that might constitute fulfilling my second enforcement duty. But perhaps there isn't. So what can I say here? I think I'm going to have to concede that, if there isn't, then in this sort of double duty case – and only in this sort of case – it's correct to describe my choice as defaulting on one of my two enforcement duties. Can any theory of justice do better?"

"Thank you," says Blue, "We've come fairly far in exploring the for-

[15] Cf. Styron, *Sophie's Choice*, 642–3.

mal characteristics of your rights rule and I think it's about time to have a look at its content. What we've established so far is that an arbitration rule that supplies a neutral, impartial and principled resolution of any deadlock is going to have the following features: (i) acting in compliance with it, by standing down, doesn't imply any reversal of one's moral priorities; (ii) it doesn't contradict any other primary rule; i.e. (iii) its negation is implicitly self-contradictory; (iv) it has lexically prime status in any polynomic code that includes it; and (v) it directs its standing-down injunction at one of the two opposed parties in any deadlock. Sounds promising. So tell us what it is."

(C) LIBERTY AND EQUALITY

"'Everybody Has the Right to be Wrong'. Does anyone remember that song from a Broadway musical of a few years back?" asks Adjudicator. "Because that's basically what we're looking for here. A person standing down from a deadlock, out of respect for his adversary's rights, is often respecting a right to do wrong.[16] What sort of rule is it that generates such a counter-intuitive right? Well obviously it's not going to be the morally mushy rule of the undiscriminating tolerator: the rule that tells you to stand down whenever you're in the way of somebody doing something wrong. People don't have rights to do wrong *per se*. Indeed, strictly speaking and as we saw back in chapter 3, they don't have rights to *do* anything. To repeat: 'No one ever has a right to do something: he only has a right that some one else shall do (or refrain from doing) something. In other words, every right in the strict sense relates to the conduct of another.'[17] What a person does have are rights which are such that your respecting them will, in some circumstances, amount to your removing an impediment to their owner doing a wrong act. The right that its owner has is a right to your removal of that impediment and not a right to do that act as such."[18]

"Fine!" snaps White. "My situation here fits your analysis to a T. I'm

[16] On rights as rights to do wrong, see Dworkin, *Taking Rights Seriously*, 188–9; Raz, *The Authority of Law*, 266ff; Waldron, "A Right to Do Wrong," 21–39.

[17] Williams, "The Concept of Legal Liberty," 139.

[18] Waldron, "A Right to Do Wrong," 24, succinctly characterizes the view, of those who mistakenly deny the possibility of a moral right to do wrong, as returning an affirmative answer to the question "Do moral rights contain moral privileges?" i.e. in the Hohfeldian sense of privileges as liberties or permissions. What they overlook is that although a rights rule may not deem a certain act obligatory – may leave persons with a liberty to do it – some other moral rule may prohibit it. Hence their oversight partly consists in their neglect of the nature of polynomic moral codes. *Every* moral rule, considered in isolation from others, implies that some acts are morally indifferent (permissibly performable *and* forbearable), while another rule may deem them otherwise. My unkind act A may be one which a rights rule permits but which another moral rule forbids. The sole effect of the rights rule here is thus to forbid others to impede me from doing this unkind and wrong act. Doing it is a wrong exercise of my rights (strictly, my liberties) and I would do better not to exercise them in this manner. O'Neill, *Constructions of Reason*, 191–2, justifiably castigates those rights theories that imply that all non-rights-violating actions are morally indifferent.

not claiming a right to extract the orange promise-keeping ball from MJM. All I'm saying is that Blue, by attempting to extract the red ball, is impeding me from doing so. She ought to respect my rights by removing that impediment and thereby allowing me to get on with what she mistakenly considers to be my wrong act. Problem solved. End of deadlock. Mission accomplished, Adjudicator."

"Wait just a minute!" retorts Blue. "We're in symmetrical positions here and there's no reason why I can't make exactly the same claim about your impeding me. We're in a zero-sum situation, so far as our each securing impediment removal is concerned."

"Quite right, Blue," Adjudicator remarks. "Perhaps I didn't make myself as clear as I could have done. The service of deadlock resolution is listed in the *Yellow Pages* under 'Impediment *Distribution*,' not 'Impediment *Diminution*.' I frankly have no idea how one would bring about an overall decrease in impediments nor, for that matter, an overall increase either. So by 'impediment removal' I meant no more than the removal of a particular impeding by one person of another's acting. And of course, the latter's acting is an impediment to the former. No way round that, I'm afraid."

"I think there's something I'd like to have clarified," interjects White. "You say that rights are rights to impediment removals and that that's how we can make sense of the notion of a right to do wrong. But then you say that impediment removal is the removal of the impeding by one person of another's (i.e. the right-holder's) acting. Isn't it the case, however, that a right-holder can sometimes have a right to another person's *doing* an action: that the right-holder may not be attempting to act at all nor therefore be being impeded? For instance, maybe I could have a contractual right that Blue herself extract the orange promise-keeping ball. How then would her extracting the red patriotism ball, instead, count as an impediment? She wouldn't be impeding any action of mine?"

"A good question," replies Adjudicator. "My explication of impediment removal was indeed too narrow. What I should have said is that impediment removal is the removal of the impeding by one person of actions chosen by another, i.e. the right-holder. Often, of course, the chosen action is one to be performed by the right-holder himself. He may have a vested liberty to do it. But as your example suggests, not always. In your example, the chosen action is a performance of Blue's. And her extracting the red ball counts as an impediment to that chosen action because it stops it from happening. She cannot extract both the orange ball and the red one. So what your right to impediment removal is in such cases is a right that she do nothing to stop the chosen action from happening. In this particular case, it amounts more specifically to your right that she extract the orange ball.

"I guess the general description I'm looking for here is that rights are rights that certain action-events not be impeded by the correlative duty-holders. This covers cases where the impediment removal you have a right to is Blue's forbearance from doing any action precluding the one she owes you, as well as cases where it's her forbearance from doing an action which would impede your own acting. Any duty which she has to do A can equally be described as a duty to forbear not-A. And that owed action is describable as 'chosen by the right-holder' inasmuch as the duty to do it can be waived by him."

"Unless I've badly mistaken your drift," ventures Blue, "you appear to be leading us in the direction of understanding rights as claims to *freedom*. At least, that's what's strongly indicated by all your talk of standing down, impediment removal and not stopping actions from occurring. And this also fits with the chapter 3 idea of rights as distributing freedom by forming domains of vested liberties surrounded by enforceably protective perimeters. Further, you suggest that impediment removal is a constant-sum enterprise, that impediments can only be distributed and neither decreased nor increased overall. Am I right to suspect that this too points to freedom as the object of rights claims and represents the chapter 2 argument, that there can be no absolute losses or gains in freedom in society?"

"Correct on all counts," Adjudicator confirms. "In your present deadlock, we get the rights rule solution by asking 'Who should have the freedom here?' and *not* by asking 'Which one of your respective opposing actions is the morally better one?' We know that there's no agreed answer to that latter question. That's why, even if you both accept the rights rule solution, you're not going to leave the shop in perfect rapport with one another. But each of you can agree to the same answer to the former question despite, or consistently with, your disagreement on the latter. That's why embracing the rights rule solution involves no priority reversals nor primary rule negations.

"You see, the intensional descriptions of your respective actions – what your intentions or purposes in acting are – are of no relevance to the rights rule. All it's interested in is the impact your action has on the other's freedom. As Giorgio del Vecchio suggests,

> Each person's acting is not considered by the standard of justice except in so far as it actually encounters or interferes with the acting of others; wherefore, for example, the duty of 'doing good' or of 'doing one's own task' is not a precept of justice in the proper

sense, nor is any other similar principle which applies to a subject considered in himself alone.[19]

Kant makes this very clear by partitioning the realm of moral judgement into the aspect concerned with the virtue of an action (*Tugend*) and that which bears on whether it is just (*Recht*). Indulge me while I quote him in full:

> The concept of justice, insofar as it relates to an obligation corresponding to it (that is, the moral concept of justice) applies [only under the following three conditions]. First, it applies only to the external and – what is more – practical relationship of one person to another in which their actions can in fact exert an influence on each other (directly or indirectly). Second, the concept applies only to the relationship of a will to another person's will, not to his wishes or desires (or even just his needs), which are the concern of acts of benevolence and charity. Third, *the concept of justice does not take into consideration the matter [content] of the will, that is, the end that a person intends to accomplish by means of the object that he wills*; for example, we do not ask whether someone who buys wares from me for his own business will profit from the transaction. *Instead, in applying the concept of justice we take into consideration only the form of the relationship between the wills insofar as they are regarded as free, and whether the action of one of them can be conjoined with the freedom of the other in accordance with a universal law.*[20]

The virtue of an action depends, for Kant, on the intention with which it's done: that is, on whether it's done pursuant to your primary rules (and their prioritization). Whereas its justness has to do with whether and how far it restricts someone else's freedom. Any action can be appraised from both these standpoints."

"But I thought you said the rights rule, justice, has itself to be a primary rule," White protests. "Doesn't that erode the distinction you and Kant are insisting upon?"

"Not quite," replies Adjudicator, "though you've raised an interesting issue. I didn't say that the rights rule has to be adopted as a primary rule. There's no necessity for it to be in your moral code. Of course, if it *is* in your code, if you stand down *because* of your respect for

---

[19] del Vecchio, *Justice*, 83–4.
[20] Kant, *The Metaphysical Elements of Justice*, 34, emphasis added.

someone's rights, then you are indeed acting virtuously in Kantian terms. The point is, however, that you can also act justly without acting virtuously and, conversely (though here Kant mistakenly disagrees, as we'll presently see), you can act unjustly without acting viciously. That is, you can do actions that don't violate rights without justice being among your reasons for doing those actions or for not doing other actions that do violate rights. For instance, your reason might be to avoid the nasty end of my sword. I can coerce you to act justly: I can force you not to encroach on someone else's freedom or to make redress for having done so. Whereas, as Kant suggests, I can't force you to act benevolently. I can't do that because whether an act is a benevolent one partly depends on the intention with which it's done, on the consequences desired by the actor. And I can't force you to have certain intentions or to desire certain consequences. Force applied for that purpose is simply self-defeating: the only intention it produces in you is one to be relieved of that force.

"But whether an act is just doesn't depend on the intention with which it's done. It doesn't depend on its having a certain intensional description. It depends, rather, on its having a certain extensional description: that is, on whether it's compatible with a certain distribution of freedom, with a certain set of rights. Your stopping me from taking my seat in the theatre is unjust. It's unjust regardless of whether you do so because you want it for yourself or because you want to spare me from watching an utterly boring performance (virtuous) or because you want me to miss an enjoyable experience (vicious). Your *not* stopping me is just, regardless of whether you do so to avoid forcible ejection by me or because you want to respect my rights (virtuous) or because you want me to suffer three hours of unmitigated boredom (vicious) or because you want me not to miss an enjoyable experience (virtuous).

"In fact, it's on the basis of rights being claims to freedom – and not claims to the performance of irreducibly intensionally described acts – that Kant insists on the conceptual link (suggested in chapter 3) between a right and the entitlement or power to enforce it:

> Any opposition that counteracts the hindrance of an effect promotes that effect and is consistent with it. Now, everything that is unjust is a hindrance to freedom according to universal laws. Coercion, however, is a hindrance or opposition to freedom. Consequently, if a certain use of freedom is itself a hindrance to freedom according to universal laws (that is, is unjust), then the use of freedom to counteract it, inasmuch as it is the prevention of a hindrance to freedom, is consistent with freedom according to

universal laws; in other words, this use of coercion is just. It follows by the law of contradiction that justice [a moral right] is united with the authorization to use coercion against anyone who violates justice.[21]

I read Kant here to be saying that a set of rights is a prescribed interpersonal distribution of freedom; that a rights-violator, by engrossing some of his victim's allotted freedom and therefore (in a compossible set of rights) exceeding his own, alters that distribution; and that one is thus licensed by that same prescription to use force against the violator, i.e. to diminish his freedom, in order to restore that distribution.[22]

"Clearly, if all persons were invariably to act justly – either because their initially intended actions were mutually non-adverse or because, even if adverse, everyone complied with the rights rule – then I'd be out of a job. But as was mentioned at the end of the previous chapter, the integrity of a set of rights can be sustained even if only some subscribe to the rights rule: namely, those who control the dominant swords. The converse of this is the bad news that, if those who control the dominant swords are *not* keen supporters of the rights rule, it's pretty hard to see how that set of rights can remain intact even if everyone else wants it to."[23]

"Okay," says Blue, "where we've got to is this. You've shown us how the extensional character of compossible rights and compatible negative freedoms dovetail into the idea of justice as an impartial, lexically prime, freedom-distributing rule and how such a rule may vest someone with a right to do a wrong action. My accepting that White has a right (and I a correlative duty) that I extract the orange ball, wouldn't commit me to regarding my compliance in doing it as morally better than my not doing it, had White waived my duty. It doesn't commit me to a priority-

<hr/>

[21] Kant, *The Metaphysical Elements of Justice*, 35–6.

[22] Cf. Hart, "Are There Any Natural Rights?," 56: "And it is I think a very important feature of a moral right that the possessor of it is conceived as having a moral justification for limiting the freedom of another and that he has this justification not because the action he is entitled to require of another has some moral quality but simply because in the circumstances a certain distribution of human freedom will be maintained if he by his choice is allowed to determine how that other shall act."

[23] On the Kantian connections between justice, rights, enforcement powers, non-intensionally described actions and negative (or what Kant calls "external") freedom, see: Aune, *Kant's Theory of Morals*, ch. V; Gregor, *Laws of Freedom*, ch. III; Kant, *The Metaphysical Elements of Justice*, Ladd's introduction, ix–xxviii; Murphy, *Kant: The Philosophy of Right*, chs. 3–4; Nell, *Acting on Principle*, ch. 4; Shell, *The Rights of Reason*, 122–6; Williams, *Kant's Political Philosophy*, ch. 3; Sullivan, *Immanuel Kant's Moral Theory*, 242–3, 246–8; Kant, *The Metaphysics of Morals*, Gregor's introduction, 10–12.

reversal. All it commits me to is that violating his right would have been still worse. So my best world is one where White waives my contractual duty to extract the orange ball; my second-best is where he doesn't waive and I comply; and my third-best world is where he doesn't waive but I don't comply. That's clear enough, I suppose. What isn't clear is how all this is going to issue in a determinate answer to the question you posed: Who should have the freedom here? How does the rights rule get applied to our particular deadlock? If it's truly a rule, it has to be perfectly general in its formulation: no proper names, no definite descriptions, etc. How can such a formulation answer a question with 'who' in it?"

Adjudicator replies: "The 'who' is going to emerge from a rather extended bit of reasoning. What we're looking for here is whose allotted portion of freedom, whose right – yours or White's – is at stake in this deadlock. To find that out we first have to discover what sort of freedom-distribution justice mandates. And as you suggest, this distributive rule has to be perfectly general in its formulation, as well as being consistent with all the characteristics you listed at the end of the last section."

"Well, if you're looking for a distributive criterion," volunteers White, "you need look no further than my moral code. What's wrong with saying that, in any deadlock, the freedom/right belongs to whoever is engaged in a promise-keeping action? Or if it's not a promise-keeping that's at stake, to whoever is engaged in the morally next-most-important type of action? Why not, in short, allocate the freedom to do actions according to the moral importance of those actions? After all, freedom is action-space. So if you're looking for a morally sensible way to distribute it, you should surely take into account what actions it's going to be used for. And a rule distributing freedom in conformity to the priorities of a moral code does meet your requirement of generality, doesn't it? Moreover, armed with such a rule, you'd have a solid substantive basis for applying the traditional maxim of justice: 'Treat like cases alike and different cases commensurately differently.' As everyone knows, this maxim is merely an empty formalism – simply a way of stating the universalizability requirement – until supplemented by a criterion stipulating the respect in which cases are relevantly alike or different."[24]

"I'd like to second a lot of what White's just said," ventures Blue, "with the reservation, of course, that it should be *my* moral code and

---

[24] Cf. Perelman, *The Idea of Justice and the Problem of Argument*, chs I–III.

my priorities that go to form the distributive criterion. We surely can't ignore what actions this freedom is going to be used for, in deciding how to allocate it."

Adjudicator is incensed. "What is it with you two? Have I been talking to myself for these last few pages? How are you ever going to get a right to do wrong out of a rule that distributes freedom according to moral priorities? I won't even bother to ask '*Whose* priorities?' since we'll obviously get nowhere on that one.[25] Of course a distributive rule based on moral priorities satisfies the generality requirement. That's just about the only requirement it does satisfy! If you two could agree on one such rule, you wouldn't need it in the first place. You wouldn't even be in a deadlock. You wouldn't be concerned with the distribution of freedom between you. Justice and rights would be utterly superfluous. All you'd need to do is ascertain which one of your two opposed actions has the agreed moral priority and take it from there. No need to bother about who should have the freedom to act when you can both agree on which action it's better to do. But when I first appeared, both of you were insistent that you'd been down that road already, to no avail. Are you now going to tell me that I've been standing around here, in all this cumbersome gear, for nothing?"

"A thousand pardons," murmurs Blue contritely. "You're quite right. What we were suggesting does logically presuppose the opposite of the situation that brought you in here. But I frankly think we've now reached an impasse. We agree that justice, as the rights rule, is a freedom-distributing rule. White, however, is surely also correct about the pure formalism of the 'like cases' maxim of justice. It needs a substantive criterion to be operative. Yet the duties implied by any such criterion, insofar as it grades actions, are going to be instrumentally linked to some particular set of moral rules or values. And therefore, as you've suggested, it's going to be otiose and question-begging so far as a freedom-distributing rule is concerned.[26] Thus, if we say that two cases are relevantly different from each other, we necessarily have to specify their dimension and degree of difference in order to determine how to treat each of them. But that specification inevitably implicates some moral code which, if acceptable to the adversarial parties, would belie their adversarial situation. And a rights rule would thereby be superfluous.

---

[25] Nor will I bother to ask the unanswerable question of how you'd resolve deadlocks between two opposed actions of the same type, i.e. having the same moral priority/weight.

[26] Hume offers an essentially similar objection to the proposal that personal merit be used as the basis of just property distribution; cf. Miller, *Philosophy and Ideology in Hume's Political Thought*, 66.

So it looks like any substantive conception of justice is going to be incoherent inasmuch as it has mutually contradictory presuppositions: it presupposes that the persons between whom it impartially arbitrates both
are and are not in adversarial positions."

"Well put," replies Adjudicator, "but your pessimistic conclusion is a
shade too sweeping. I must confess that I've never had a high regard for
the 'like cases' maxim as a guide to *distributive* justice. It's useful, I
suppose, when we come to derivative issues of redressing violations of
rights and procedural justice: that is, those aspects of justice that presuppose an already given distribution of rights/freedom. But even if we take
the problem as you've just formulated it, surely we're led to another
conclusion. It's simply a tautology to say that different cases are different. What we want is to know is whether they can be described as *relevantly* different. And if, as you agree, no criterion for relevantly differentiating cases can be eligible to serve as a standard of distributive
justice, the inference must be that no cases can be regarded as relevantly
different: that is, all cases are relevantly alike. In this context that means
that the freedom-distribution mandated by justice is an *equal* one, that
everyone is justly entitled to equal freedom.

"As we'll presently see, the matter is a bit more complicated than this.
But for the moment, let's provisionally say that justice is a rule vesting
each person with a right to equal freedom. This finding can be defended
as more than the merely residual conclusion we drew above. A rule that
distributes freedom equally is obviously untainted by tendentious instrumental considerations of what that freedom is going to be used for. It
maximizes nothing. Its freedom-allocations can be used for actions
which are good, bad or morally indifferent. So it can underwrite a right
to do wrong. Accepting it entails no priority-reversals in anyone's moral
code. Nor does it contradict any other primary rule, whereas a rule vesting persons with rights to *un*equal freedom necessarily requires the sort
of differentiating criterion that would render it otiose in the way you
just described. Furthermore and because these allocated portions of freedom can be used for any sort of action, including morally indifferent
ones, this rule can also be applied to adjudicate those deadlocks where
at least one of the opposed actions is informed not by someone's moral
values but rather by his preferences, wants or interests. In short, if you're
looking for something that's truly versatile and perfectly impartial, the
equal freedom rule is clearly your best buy. Indeed, it's probably your
only buy."[27]

[27] On the right to equal freedom as justice or a natural right, see: Locke, *Two Treatises
of Government*, 287–9; Kant, *The Metaphysical Elements of Justice*, 35–9; Spencer, *Social*

"Well I don't see that it's my only buy," objects White. "Why wouldn't distributing freedom by a purely random process be equally versatile and impartial? Why couldn't we distribute freedom by drawing straws?"

"Actually," ventures Blue, "my own preference would be for a lottery rather than drawing straws."

"Not another deadlock!" Adjudicator chides. "As I understand it, what you're proposing is a *procedural* rule for distribution as an alternative to my substantive one. I don't think this proposal is a genuine alternative, however, essentially because either it's distributively indeterminate or it presupposes the very rule I'm offering here.

"Suppose what's to be distributed is a bundle of apples. Apples are a lot like freedom, as will soon become evident. There is, first, the problem indicated by your preceding remarks: namely, the question of how to determine which of the many possible random procedures is the one to be used. Second, substantive equality may not be quite as dispensable, even under one of these procedures, as you seem to be suggesting. Presumably, equality would still govern the distribution of lottery tickets or straw-drawings. After all, you wouldn't be giving different people different numbers of straws or tickets. And substantive equality looks like being the only reason for not doing so. Third, there's the matter of how success in this random procedure is to be structured. Will one person get all the apples or will there be a graduated scale of apple prizes and, if so, which one of the many conceivable scales? A rule telling you to distribute according to a random process is distributively indeterminate without answers to these questions."

"No problem there," volunteers White. "I can readily supply a set of answers."

"I don't doubt it," Adjudicator responds. "So can Blue. So can I, for that matter. The problem, as far as impartiality is concerned, is how to get a set of answers which are untainted by any particular set of values or preferences: a set of answers that don't belie your adversarial situation. It's pretty obvious, for instance, that some structurings of the

---

Statics, ch. VI and appendix A; George, *Social Problems*, ch. IX; Hart, "Are There Any Natural Rights?"; Gewirth, *Reason and Morality*, ch. 3; Pollock, *The Freedom Principle*, ch. 1. Rawls, in *A Theory of Justice*, offers "equal basic liberty" as lexically prime among the *several* primary rules constitutive of his conception of justice. Steiner, "Capitalism, Justice and Equal Starts," 55–9, argues that an important premiss of Nozick's theory of just holdings, in *Anarchy, State and Utopia*, implicitly invokes something like the equal freedom rule. Sidgwick, *The Methods of Ethics*, 274–8, supplies a critical discussion of the claim that justice prescribes a right to equal freedom; some of his objections are of kinds addressed in the next two chapters.

prizes will be more congenial to some persons' attitudes to, say, risk or benevolence than to those of others."

"Okay," says White, "so we'll call a meeting and hammer out a set of answers together."

"Well that sounds more promising," Adjudicator acknowledges. "But I detect a slight shifting of ground here. What if the meeting decides to dispense with random processes altogether? I mean, if we prefer not to go down that procedural road, to whom could we conceivably owe a duty nonetheless to do so?"

"Yes, yes," replies White, a bit impatiently. "I guess if the meeting has the power to decide on prize structures, it must equally be empowered to distribute the apples in any other way it chooses. Your point, I take it, is that I'm presupposing that the meeting owns the apples."

"Correct," confirms Adjudicator. "You're saying that the apple distribution that emerges from the meeting's decision amounts to a set of apple rights and correlative duties because those titles and duties are created by an exercise of a power the meeting has – a power which it has by virtue of its being the antecedent title-holder of those apples. The meeting extinguishes its own title and creates various new titles to the apples, along with the correlative duties to respect them."

"Exactly right, Adjudicator. Any problem with that?"

"Well, I'm not sure," Adjudicator replies. "I mean, what if the majority at the meeting votes to assign all the apples severally to its own members and leaves the minority out in the cold? Would members of the minority really be describable as having created duties to respect that set of titles?"

"Who said anything about majorities?" queries White. "This is simply a standard chapter 3 title-transfer. The point is that, in making that joint decision, everyone at the meeting is extinguishing all the new title-holders' previous duties to forbear using those apples which are being severally assigned to them. And *everyone else*, by virtue of that same exercise of powers, is taking on the correlative forbearance duties owed to the new title-holders."

"Well I just can't see how a minority member, who votes against those title-transfers, can be said to be doing that," counters Adjudicator.

"You and your minorities!" retorts White. "Okay, what if I were to say that the transfer decisions have to be unanimous, that each person has a transfer power? Or if you prefer, that there has to be a unanimous prior decision to empower a majority to make transfer decisions? Wouldn't that allay your qualms about the validity of every person's duty to respect each new title?"

"It would indeed," replies Adjudicator. "But let's now examine some of the implications of this. We agree that the validity of these new titles implies the exercise of the meeting's transfer power and that it has that power by virtue of its being the antecedent title-holder to those apples. Surely it follows that if that power is constituted by every person's own transfer power (or is derived from an exercise of every person's power to empower a majority), then they each have that power by virtue of being still-more-antecedent title-holders to those apples. The meeting's corporate title can't be an original one. It must be derivative from each person's individual title. How could we otherwise account for each person's being an equal voting member of the meeting?" "That seems right," agrees White, "but I still can't see where all this is going."

"Where it's going," suggests Adjudicator, "is in the direction of discovering the rights ultimately underlying your counter-proposal to the equal freedom rule. What we have to do now is to identify the nature of these antecedent individual titles, from which the meeting's corporate title derives. Since each person is vested with the same power as everyone else, each person's antecedent title must be the same as everyone else's.

"Now unless I've missed something, there are only two possible interpretations of what those titles are titles to. One is that each person has a title to the whole bundle of apples. And the other is that each has a title to an equal share of the apples. And we know that the trouble with the first interpretation is the same trouble that besets Hobbes's so-called 'rights of nature': namely, that these are not really rights at all. Being different persons' titles to one and the same set of things, they entail no compossible set of correlative duties. Your prevention of my using some apples would be both *permissible*, as an exercise of the enforcement power implied by your apples title, and *impermissible*, as a violation of your forbearance duty correlative to my apples title. Hence only the second interpretation of these antecedent individual titles makes sense. Each person has an antecedent right to an equal share of the apples. And what's true of apples is also true of freedom."

"So what you're claiming," says White, "is that for my random process proposal to work – for it to generate determinate titles and valid duties – it has to include a joint decision procedure which itself implies the equal freedom rule. My proposal is not an alternative to your rule but, rather, only one possible application of it."

"Precisely. And if it's open to the meeting to dispense with the random process – if random distribution is only one of the various options the title-holding meeting may choose[28] – it's similarly and antecedently open

---

[28] That is, no one holds a right against the meeting that it shall/shall not distribute in any particular way.

to each person to dispense with the meeting. Pooling some or all of their
equal freedom with others', for distribution by joint decision, is only
one of the options each title-holder is empowered to choose.[29] One inference we might draw from this is that social contract theories of distributive justice are applications of natural right theories and not alternatives
to them."[30]

"Well that all sounds convincing, as far as it goes," says White. "But
I don't think we're out of the woods yet with regard to distributive
indeterminacy. You say that what's true of apples is also true of freedom. One thing that's true of apples is that they come in different kinds
and people have differentiated preferences and even moral valuations
with respect to them. I, for instance, am highly partial to Granny Smiths,
though not if they're ones supplied by firms who practise racial or sexual
discrimination. Surely the same is true of freedom. In which case, what
does 'equal freedom' amount to? How do you propose to commensurate
a multitude of heterogeneous freedoms – and to commensurate them
impartially – so as to divide and assign them equally?"

"A first-rate question," allows Adjudicator, "and one the answer to
which should emerge in the next chapter."

"I think there's still one more loose end that needs tying up," observes
Blue. "Much earlier on in this chapter you promised to explain why
your colleagues at the company, influenced by Kant, once believed that
an action's being a right-violation is a sufficient condition of its moral
impermissibility. In view of the singularity of the equal freedom rule as
a moral rule – particularly the necessity of its being ranked lexically
prime and the non-affirmability of any *un*equal freedom rule – why is
their belief mistaken?"

"It's mistaken," Adjudicator replies, "because there is no logical
necessity to adopt the equal freedom rule. It's true that, if you do adopt
it, it must be lexically prime. And it's also true that you can't consistently
affirm a rule entitling persons to unequal freedom. But these are not
sufficient reasons for holding that an act encroaching on someone else's
equal freedom, although it is necessarily unjust, is also necessarily
wrong. Why did they think otherwise? Well clearly, because they
believed that it *is* logically necessary to adopt the equal freedom rule.
And why did they believe that? Because they held a mistaken view of one
of Kant's formulations of the Categorical Imperative. Let me explain.

"Kant's formulation of the equal freedom rule, or what he calls the

[29] No one holds a right against any title-holders that they shall/shall not pool some or
all of their equal freedom.
[30] Cf. Dworkin, *Taking Rights Seriously*, ch. 6.

Universal Principle of Justice, runs as follows: "Every action is just that in itself or in its maxim is such that the freedom of will of each can coexist together with the freedom of everyone in accordance with a universal law."[31] As we've seen, it's the fact that an action can be appraised as just or unjust 'in itself', and without reference to its agent's maxim or purpose in doing it, that underpins Kant's claim that justice (unlike virtue) need not be concerned with the content of the will, with the intention informing that action. Kant scholars have plausibly viewed the Universal Principle of Justice as implied by the second major formulation of the Categorical Imperative (CI2): 'Act so that you treat humanity, whether in your own person or in that of another, always as an end and never as a means only.'[32] Certainly there's a strong connection, perhaps even extensional equivalence, between these two injunctions. CI2 is generally interpreted as requiring one to respect the agency of others by performing no action that subordinates their sets of purposes to one's own. Warner Wick argues that 'To treat someone as a mere means is to regard his purposes as if they did not count – as if he were just an object that entered one's calculations as an instrument to be used or an obstacle to be pushed aside.'[33] Since one's freedom is a necessary condition of one's pursuing any purposes at all, actions that diminish one's freedom to less than that enjoyed by their perpetrators are pretty strong candidates for being described as actions subordinating one's purposes to theirs. Equal freedom is thus a necessary condition, perhaps also sufficient, for the non-subordination of anyone's set of purposes to those of others. Moreover, CI2 shares an important logical property with the equal freedom rule: its negation is implicitly non-affirmable. Thus actions which treat one merely as a means, by subordinating one's purposes to those of their perpetrators, cannot be justified as such. For 'any maxim formulating such treatment entails, when it is universalized, that one be willing to be treated that way in return. But that is a contradiction, for it can be no one's purpose that his purpose count as nothing.'[34] Given this close affinity between the equal freedom rule and CI2, as well as the criterial role played by the Categorical Imperative in the Kantian account of moral judgement, it might seem quite correct to hold that an action's injustice is a sufficient condition of its moral impermissibility.

[31] Kant, *The Metaphysical Elements of Justice*, 35.
[32] Kant, *Foundations of the Metaphysics of Morals*, 47. On the connection between the Universal Principle of Justice and CI2, see: Gregor, *Laws of Freedom*, 39ff, and Aune, *Kant's Theory of Morals*, 137.
[33] Kant, *The Metaphysical Principles of Virtue*, Wick's introduction, xix.
[34] Kant, *The Metaphysical Principles of Virtue*, Wick's introduction, xix.

"But it's not correct. The view that it is correct is based on the mistaken belief that CI2 is an implication of the first formulation of the Categorical Imperative (CI1): 'Act only according to that maxim by which you can at the same time will that it should become a universal law.'[35] CI1 *is* criterial for moral judgement. It expresses the formal condition of universalizability and declares that an action's moral permissibility depends on one's willingness to accept that anyone may pursue maxims (intentions, purposes) of the sort informing that action. An action's CI1-permissibility depends on its not being prohibited by the set of rules in one's moral code. So CI1-permissibility and moral permissibility are identical. CI1 is, if you like, the definition of a morally permissible act and, as such, expresses a necessary truth.

"Now the test of whether CI2 is implied by CI1, and shares its necessary truth, consists in seeing if there are actions that conform to one of them but violate the other. And very clearly, there are. If I force you to work for a deserving charity or steal your money on its behalf or, indeed, force you to do something that's in your own interest, I may be perfectly happy to universalize my benevolent intention in doing so. I may include benevolence among my moral rules. But that willingness in no way implies that my action is not a reduction of your equal freedom and a subordination of your purposes to mine. Conversely, I may malevolently refuse to stake you in a poker game. But the fact that I'm unwilling to universalize this intention to inconvenience you – I might stake someone else – in no way implies that I reduce your otherwise equal freedom or subordinate your purposes to mine.

"The reason why an act can conform to one of the Categorical Imperative's formulations and not the other isn't hard to find. CI1-conformity depends on that intensionally-described action's relation to whatever moral rules we accept. But its conformity to CI2 and to Kant's Universal Principle of Justice doesn't require us to refer that action or its intention to those rules. CI2 directly prohibits any action in which other persons figure purely instrumentally. And the same is true of the equal freedom rule: 'For anyone can still be free, even though I am quite indifferent to his freedom or even though I might in my heart wish to infringe on his freedom, as long as I do not through an external action violate his freedom.'[36] Thus, as Jeffrie Murphy observes,

> Kant is not telling us merely to plan to leave others' freedom secure; he is telling us to leave it secure *in fact*. Whether or not an

[35] Kant, *Foundations of the Metaphysics of Morals*, 39.
[36] Kant, *The Metaphysical Elements of Justice*, 35.

act of mine would be compatible with a like liberty for others is something capable of an objective determination and is not a function solely of my intentions.[37]

Since actions can be morally permissible but unjust or morally impermissible but just, it's simply untrue that an action's being a rights-violation is a sufficient condition of its moral impermissibility. Its injustice is such a condition only *if* justice is one of our moral rules.[38] But it needn't be. Whereas CI1 expresses a necessary truth about moral permissibility in general, the equal freedom rule expresses a necessary truth only about moral rights. It expresses no necessary truth about the moral impermissibility of actions violating those rights. So Kant's own apparent belief that such actions are morally impermissible must be taken to reflect his moral commitments rather than any philosophically derived conclusion."[39]

[37] Murphy, *Kant: The Philosophy of Right*, 104.
[38] Because if it is one of our rules, it must be lexically prime and its implied duties therefore cannot permissibly be overridden by duties enjoined by other rules.
[39] Evidence for this reflection is to be found in Kant, *Lectures on Ethics*, 211.

Let's take a break from the dialogue and get back to apples. What we need to do in this section is to see how the equal freedom rule must be expressed in a set of compossible rights. I begin by recapitulating a point made near the end of chapter 3.

Suppose that you and I each have a right to the same number of apples. One way in which I can violate your rights is presumably by stealing one of your apples. And one way in which I can redress this violation is by returning that apple or giving you a similar one of mine.

But if the distributive rule implying our equal apple rights is an end-state or patterned one,[40] there is another way in which I can violate your rights: namely, by eating one of *my* apples. And the paradoxical, indeed contradictory, character of such rights is even more sharply revealed in the fact that one way I can apparently redress this latter violation is by committing another one: namely, by stealing half of one of your remaining apples. For this, too, would restore an equal distribution enjoined by such rules. Alternatively, my eating my apple might be construed as occasioning a duty in you to eat one of yours or in some other manner diminish your stock proportionally. Ascriptions of liability and culpability are evidently a tricky business under these sorts of distributive rule.

The silliness of these results is not terribly surprising. For it's the same silliness that's invoked in the ancient joke about the parenticide demanding more lenient punishment on grounds of his orphanhood. What these results implicitly corroborate is the earlier argument that, for our respective rights to be compossible, they have to be exhaustively reducible to the titles composing our respective domains. And what's wrong with the sets of rights implied by these sorts of distributive rule is that they aren't.

For as well as apple titles, such rules also invest us with rights to a *relation* (in this case, equality) between our apple domains. Or rather, they appear to do so. Your domain and mine appear to contain rights entailing in each of us a correlative duty, owed to the other, to forbear

---

[40] Cf. ch. 3, n. 62.

from using our apples in ways destructive of parity between our respective apple stocks. However, this appearance is deceptive.

It's deceptive because these parity-maintaining duties, if they are
indeed ones which we have, are not ones which we owe to each other.
For if they were, we could each waive them: you would be empowered to
allow me to eat one of my apples without either of us thereby incurring a
liability to eat any of yours. But under these sorts of distributive rule,
you can't do that. What such rules affect to do is to give each of us
unwaivable rights to parity-maintenance. But as we saw in the earlier
discussion of unwaivable rights,[41] our lack of powers to waive their correlative duties implies that those rights are not ones vested in *us*. They
are not components of *our* domains.

Compossible rights form compossible domains. Within their domains,
persons are at liberty (lack *correlative* duties not) to do as they choose.[42]
These domains assign them pure negative freedom inasmuch as those
doings are impermissibly obstructable. Those doings create histories.
That is, by exercising liberties and powers right-holders transform and
transfer objects and thereby extinguish and create titles and correlative
duties. Those titles and duties are the bearers of those histories. Extinguished ones stand in a relation of antecedence to created ones whose histories thus consist in causal and proprietorial pedigrees. Any created
title or duty lacking such a pedigree – lacking antecedents which were
extinguished by the exercise of a liberty or power – has been created by
a violation: by an exercise of might rather than right. In the absence of
redress for that violation, it cannot be a valid title or duty. Nor, therefore, can it figure in the pedigree of one.

That compossible created rights have such histories is the conceptual
truth which is captured by "historical entitlement" conceptions of distributive rules and which eludes end-state and patterned conceptions and
various complex mixtures of them. For it's only if created rights have
such histories that we can unequivocally ascribe culpabilities and liabilities in respect of their violation. There is a transparent affinity between
ordinary notions of personal responsibility and historical entitlement

---

[41] Cf. ch. 3, end of section (a).

[42] Again and because it cannot be over-emphasized, to say that they are at liberty to do
A (lack a correlative duty to forbear A) is not to say that they lack any moral duty to
forbear A. They may well have such a duty. The point here is simply that it's not being a
correlative duty implies that no one has a right that they forbear A and that compelling
them to do so would be a violation of their rights. It's in that sense alone that they are at
liberty to do A, which may well be the wrong thing for them to do.

conceptions. And that affinity lies in the pivotal role they both assign to persons' actions.

Thus what Nozick has identified as historical entitlement principles of transfer and rectification are not really independent prescriptive rules at all. They're simply implications of the conceptual fact that rights vest their owners with powers of waiver and redress. Such principles necessarily govern any arrangements in which persons take exclusive responsibility for their own actions, in the sense that general compliance with them is a necessary condition of the consequences (valuable or disvaluable) of anyone's actions not enforceably accruing to anyone else.[43]

Hence much of the moral criticism levelled against historical entitlement conceptions of justice is utterly misdirected, inasmuch as it simply neglects the conceptual characteristics of rights themselves. Such criticism is commonly informed by rules which, as I suggested in chapter 3, fail to take rights seriously. For although they purport to prescribe a set of rights, those rights are so structured as to render them incompossible. Loosely speaking, all that historical entitlement principles of transfer and rectification do, in ensuring that all rights are compossible and all duties thereby jointly performable, is simply to distribute personal responsibility to agents. They do this by attaching consequences exclusively to their causers.

But only loosely. Because for a person to bear exclusive responsibility for his actions, as Kant and others would have him do, something more is needed. An only approximate description of that something more is that others have not prevented him from doing otherwise, that he was free to do otherwise. But "otherwise" covers a lot of territory – too much territory, in a world where any one person's acting has necessarily prevented some conceivable actions of others. So a closer approximation of what's needed is that he has been no *more* prevented than others. In short, that all have been equally free. And that requirement unavoidably directs our attention to persons' antecedent conditions of acting.

Two balls roll down a hill and one reaches the bottom in less time than the other. Any scientific explanation of this difference will have to refer not only to the respective characteristics of the balls and the comparative obstructedness of their respective paths, but also to their

---

[43] These principles do not preclude the consequences of one's choices *non-enforceably* accruing to others. There are weighty moral reasons why some of these consequences should accrue to others, i.e. why one's exclusively self-incurred benefits should be non-forcibly transferred to needy others, including others whose needs are the consequences of self-incurred harms.

comparative starting points. Regardless of which ball arrived first, that explanation would be different if one ball started rolling from only half-way up the hill while the other started at the top – different than it would be if both balls started at the same level.

Similarly, ascriptions of responsibility to different persons for the comparative size of their respective current domains will need to refer to their comparative rights-assigned starting points. Am I *exclusively* responsible for my final score in a card game if I only started to play an hour later than the other players? The answer seems to be "no."[44] But what if my inferior starting-time was due to my dilatory arrival at the game's venue? On the other hand, what if that dilatory arrival was in turn due to my being caught in a traffic-jam en route to the game? But on the previous hand, what if it was my erratic driving that caused the traffic-jam? And so on.

These are all very old and familiar types of argument. Nevertheless what they suggest is quite important and fits rather closely with the point advanced towards the end of chapter 3. What they suggest is that whether persons are each exclusively responsible for the comparative consequences of their actions in adversarial circumstances – in the circumstances where justice has application[45] – depends on their antecedent conditions. More specifically, it depends on whether their antecedent conditions were equal. Given that adversarial circumstances are inherently ones in which each person's activity partly impedes the others', were my antecedent conditions such that I was subject to more obstruction than the other players?

Moreover and as these old arguments further indicate, it is not to a comparison of only *immediately* antecedent conditions that we must look in order to ascertain the exclusiveness of the responsibility each bears for the consequences he incurs. The inferiority of my starting-time does not imply that others share responsibility for my incurred consequences, if that inferiority is due to an action of mine or derives from a still more antecedent inferior condition, the inferiority of which was due to an action of mine. Hence my reduced responsibility can be inferred only if this series of inferior antecedent conditions originated in an inferior *ultimately antecedent* one.

In a set of compossible domains, the way in which their constituent created rights are determined is not by reference to some set of independent prescriptive rules. It is given by the conceptual characteristics of

---

[44] The same answer may be true of each of the other players' responsibility for their scores.

[45] A card game is an adversarial circumstance.

rights themselves: these created rights are determined by exercises of their owners' liberties and powers. It is to such rights that we sometimes attach the label *conventional*. They are conventional, not in the sense of being non-moral, but rather because they are the consequences of persons' doings, their impermissibly obstructable transferring and transforming activities.

What evidently cannot be determined in these ways are each person's non-created, initial rights. Being non-conventional, being presupposed by conventional rights, these non-created rights are not inappropriately termed *natural* rights. This is where an independent prescriptive rule does have purchase. This is the job of a conception of justice that takes rights seriously.

The equal freedom rule is expressed in a set of compossible domains to the extent that it informs the contents of persons' ultimately antecedent or natural or *original* rights – their initial assigned conditions. Persons are assigned equal freedom when they are assigned equal original rights, with all exercises of the powers and liberties attached to those rights, and to the rights successively derived from those exercises, being impermissibly obstructable. What therefore remains to be done in our search for the meaning of justice is to discover the contents of these equal original rights.

7
Original Rights

Justice is a moral rule assigning equal freedom to each of us through a structure of rights. How we use this freedom, whether for good or ill, is up to us so far as justice is concerned but *not* so far as other moral rules and values are concerned. Chapters 3 and 6 argued for two things: first, that these assignments of freedom come in the form of property rights; and second, that those property rights are equal original ones and their created derivatives. Original property rights constitute our initial domains – our initial allotted action-spaces – which are successively modified by our transforming and transferring choices through exercises of liberties and powers.

The job of this chapter (and the next one) is actually threefold. Principally what we want is an identification of the contents of our original property rights: we want to know what sorts of thing we have original property rights to. And therefore we also want to know how to distinguish these from the sorts of thing to which we have non-original property rights, since justice requires only the former but not the latter to be equal. Finally, we need to find out who counts as being one of "us."

Perhaps not surprisingly, the answers to these three questions are very intricately interconnected. For although the world of justice (though not of other values) is exhaustively partitioned into owners and what can be owned; although everything is, so to speak, either a subject or an object of assigned freedom; and although we all have pretty clear and well-justified beliefs about what items constitute the core membership of each of these categories; it requires little argument to show that much perennial moral and political controversy is traceable to the uncertain classification of items inhabiting these categories' interfacing peripheries. Prominent among such controversies are those about whether and, if so, what rights are held by (and what correlative duties are owed to) foetuses, minors, the talented, the destitute, the disabled, the deceased, members of future generations and members of other societies.

By keeping a reasonably firm grip on the formal characteristics of rights and on the conditions of their compossibility, we can make some progress towards locating these partitions, both between owners and ownables and between original and non-original ownables. But this advance will be a somewhat gradual one, proceeding initially with the aid of several casual assumptions, through stages at which these will be subjected to less relaxed assessment. And I suppose we could do worse than to begin this journey by following Kant and provisionally adopting his classification of all items as either *persons* or *things*.

(A) Persons and Things

Evidently persons who are owned by other persons possess no assigned freedom whatsoever. It's not that slaves have few rights: they have none. Of course, they usually do have some freedom. How else could they perform tasks? But that freedom doesn't *belong* to them. It lies, as they do, entirely within their owners' domains. And their being deprived of any or all of it, by their owners, is always permissible within that set of rights. A slave is a thing: a piece of domestic livestock, an energy resource, even a body tissue bank. Hence slavery is often seen as paradigmatically unjust. For while we might be uncertain about whether two persons' original bundles are equal, there is little room for doubt in the case where one of them simply has no such bundle and is indeed part of the contents of the other's bundle. To have any rights at all, he has to be out of that bundle.

It follows fairly readily from this that our respective bundles of original property rights must include at least ourselves. We must each be self-owners.[1] Writing from Newgate Prison in 1646, Richard Overton famously proclaimed:

> To every Individuall in nature, is given an individuall property by nature, not to be invaded or usurped by any: for every one as he is himselfe, so he hath a selfe propriety, else could he not be himselfe, and on this no second may presume to deprive any of, without manifest violation and affront to the very principles of nature,

[1] The view that persons must be owned, either by themselves or by others, has sometimes been challenged. Its critics contend that the (justice-based) impermissibility of assaulting other persons, murdering them or confiscating their transplantable body parts can be alternatively grounded in the various protective prohibitions implied by civil liberties and suchlike. See for example, Williams, "Cohen on Locke, Land and Labour," 64–5. This contention, however, either is false or poses no genuine alternative to self-ownership. It's false if those prohibitions are insufficient to create the dense network of impenetrable perimeters needed to render each of those liberties "vested" rather than leave any of them "naked" and exposed to "numbing." Conversely and if they *are* sufficient to create that network, then (as we've seen above, ch. 3, sections (b), (c)) such a set of perimeters itself implies a set of compossible rights and correlative duties that are fully equivalent to civil liberty-holders having property rights in their own bodies, as extensional components of actions exercising those liberties. The duties implied by a fully vested set of civil liberties are correlatively constitutive of a right of self-ownership.

and of the Rules of equity and justice between man and man; mine
and thine cannot be, except this be.[2]

G. A. Cohen provides an apt description of this right:

> Each person is the morally rightful owner of himself. He possesses
> over himself, as a matter of moral right, all those rights that a
> slaveholder has over a complete chattel slave as a matter of legal
> right, and he is entitled, morally speaking, to dispose over himself
> in the way such a slaveholder is entitled, morally speaking, to dis-
> pose over his slave.[3]

In short, our bodies must be owner-occupied. Self-ownership gives us
what was referred to in chapter 3 as "full liberal ownership" of our
bodies. Being the holders of all the incidents of their ownership, we have
unencumbered titles to them.

At least originally. For to say that we must also be self-owners *non*-
originally, that we lack the powers to abandon[4] some or all of the incidents of our original self-ownership, is self-contradictorily to ground
these self-ownership rights in an end-state principle. It is to say that our
rights to our selves are unwaivable by us. And we've already seen that
there can be no such rights. Or, more precisely, that in whomever those
rights may be vested, they cannot be vested in us. They are not rights of
self-ownership.[5] On the contrary, they are rights of ownership to our
selves held by others.[6]

---

[2] Overton, "An Arrow against all Tyrants," 68.

[3] Cohen, "Self-Ownership, World-Ownership and Equality," 109; cf. Scott, *The Body
as Property* for a discussion of the moral and legal issues raised by medical advances in
the use of human body parts.

[4] Presumably *abandonment* of this right is the only possible mode of incurring self-
enslavement (by creating a necessary though insufficient condition of it). That is, it cannot
be incurred by a self-owner's *transferring* (selling or donating) that right, since such transfers entail that transferrors thereby acquire duties to their transferees, whereas slaves, as
things wholly owned by others, must lack duties as well as rights. Debates about the
permissibility of self-enslavement tend to neglect this fact.

[5] Ingram, *A Political Theory of Rights*, ch. 2, claims that, in thus permitting self-enslavement, the right of self-ownership loses much of its ideological appeal and diminishes the
moral authority it enjoys as a bulwark against permissible slavery. For what makes slavery
wrong is "surely the fact that a person needs liberty in order to pursue the ends or interests
which she inevitably has as a human being no less than the next person." Where this
argument errs, I think, is in its implicit assumption that what liberty a person needs to
secure her particular ends or interests is somehow not an empirical question. Whether my
ends are best served by relinquishing any or all of the incidents of my self-ownership –
most persons' ends usually do, as in donated services and labour contracts, require the
relinquishment of some of them – must surely depend upon what my ends happen to be

If our bodies are at least originally self-owned, then our original domains contain vested (impermissibly obstructable) liberties to dispose of them and their parts as we choose. So long as we retain these property rights, it's impermissible for anyone (non-contractually) to prevent our suicides or our keeping our body tissues or our donating them or our selling them. Our doing some of these things, in some circumstances, may be morally wrong on other grounds and deserving of strong condemnation. But it's not unjust. And preventing it is.

How do we get from the unencumbered ownership of our bodies to the unencumbered ownership of things external to them? The path of this argument is well trodden so let's take the easy part first. Our bodies are factories. They produce things like blood, skin, hair, etc. Self-ownership gives us the titles to these and protects our liberty to dispose of them, just as it does in the case of our non-renewable types of tissue. Not that I have a protected liberty to bleed on your carpet. But that's because it's *your* carpet. If it were mine, I'd have a right (which I might be more than happy to waive!) to your non-interference.

Similarly, our bodies produce energy. They convert body tissue into energy, some of which gets expended in our acting. A good deal of this expended energy is simply abandoned by us in the course of this acting. It's absorbed into parts of the external environment that we make no consequent claim to. Other portions of our expended energy are infused into parts of the external environment, transforming their features in various ways. Sometimes we claim these things for ourselves as the fruits of our labour. And sometimes, where such a transformation violates another's rights, it forms the basis of a claim against us.[7]

---

and what alternative means, if any, are available for securing them. Presumably few persons relinquish their full complement of self-ownership incidents frivolously. Hence the right of self-ownership *is* a bulwark against involuntary enslavement and against paternalistic preventions of voluntary self-enslavement, as well as against abrogations of freedom of contract.

[6] Thus Locke, *Two Treatises of Government*, 289, 302, apparently infers that we lack the powers to enslave ourselves from the premiss that we are owned not by ourselves but by God.

[7] The idea of labour-mixing has long had its critics. Hume's objection was that "We cannot be said to join our labour in any thing but in a figurative sense. Properly speaking, we only make an alteration on it by our labour"; *A Treatise of Human Nature*, 505–6. Since Hume's distinction here, between "in" and "on," is unclear, unexplained and arguably unavailable to his empiricism, and since the energy-infusion construal of labour-mixing suggests that he was in any case mistaken, recent critics have offered the following amended objections. Thus Waldron, *The Right to Private Property*, 187: "Although matter and energy are physically interconvertible and therefore in principle talk of a mixture of matter and energy makes sense, it is not true that every act of labouring ... will involve the *addition* of energy to the thing [laboured on]. Sometimes as in the killing or capturing

If the carpet I'm about to bleed on is mine, then it seems unexceptionable to claim that the blood-stained carpet is also mine. I have an unencumbered title to it. If the lumber and tools to which I'm about to transfer some of my body's energy are mine (and if I've not transferred my title to that energy), then claiming the wooden bench I thereby make as mine seems to be equally unproblematic. My labouring activity occurs, in this case, entirely within my domain and is an exercise of a vested liberty.[8] To regard that manufactured bench as *not* belonging to me – to say that others are at liberty to dispose of it without my consent – is to deny my unencumbered antecedent titles to its production factors and/or my vested liberty to perform that labouring act. And these denials are *ex hypothesi* untrue.

Conversely, if the carpet I'm about to bleed on is yours, I don't acquire title to the blood-stained carpet. Similarly, if I contractually mix labour with your antiquarian copy of Locke's *Two Treatises*, restoring its mildewed pages and scarred leather binding, I don't thereby become its owner. It's not the fruit of my labour, because the title to that labour has been contractually transferred to you.[9]

What if the thing I'm about to bleed on or mix my (uncontracted) labour with is a piece of land which belongs to neither you nor me nor anyone else? What if, that is, everyone is at liberty to use it? If I cultivate it and if others could then permissibly use it without my consent, they would thereby have an unagreed (by me) liberty to dispose of something containing a product of my body. Wouldn't their having this liberty be

---

of a wild beast, it involves the application of energy to oppose or negate the energy that was already there. In this case, labour and energy have been expended on a resource, but on no plausible physical analysis does the tamed resource now *contain* the energy that has been expended." Similarly, Geras, "Private Property and Moral Equality," 70: "If you pursue a hare, the energy you expend is not, or is hardly at all, *in* the hare." While it's true that the hunter's expended energy cannot be fully located in his captured quarry – much of it having dispersed into other parts of the external environment – it's plainly true (i) that this environment, including his quarry, has been transformed *by* his energy expenditure and (ii) that, as the First Law of Thermodynamics tells us, the total amount of energy present has not diminished even though some of it has changed form in the course of its being transferred. The causal explanation of a shot quarry is not more mysterious than that of a driven nail, even if the energy transfers are slightly more complex in the former case than in the latter.

[8] See the story of the van, ch. 3, section (d), above.

[9] There seems to be some tension in the conjunction of Locke's views that: (i) we own our labour because we own our bodies; (ii) we can sell or donate our labour to others; but (iii) we lack the powers to enslave ourselves (see n. 4, above). Would he prohibit or permit our sale or donation of body parts?

a denial to me of the fruits of my labour? Wouldn't it transgress my self-ownership?

The answer, as we know only too well, is uncertain. For any claim, to the effect that its being infused with my labour makes this land mine, can be met with the counter-claim that, in so infusing the land, I was relinquishing my title to that labour, just as I did in undertaking the repair of your book. To which the inconclusive rejoinder is that in the book-repair case there's a duty on my part to relinquish, whereas in the present case – as in the bench case – there's no such duty, and the bench is uncontroversially mine. To which the counter-arguments are: (i) that even had the book-repair *not* been contracted, my nonetheless repairing it would still have constituted a relinquishment of my labour since the book wasn't mine; and (ii) that the bench, unlike the cultivated land, is a product all the factors of which (being already owned by me) were ones which everyone else already had a duty to forbear from using, so my labour-mixing makes no difference in this case.

The familiar lesson here is that while self-ownership is a sufficient basis for creating unencumbered titles to things produced solely from self-owned things,[10] it cannot do a similar job for products whose factors include unowned things. Nothing can be produced by labour alone. Nothing can be made *ex nihilo*. All labouring, simply by virtue of being action, requires extensional (material, spatial) factors which are either already owned or as yet unowned. Yet as the earlier discussion of rights-compossibility – and more specifically, of its historical dimension in title and duty pedigrees – indicates, any current set of domains, to be valid, must derive from a set of original rights and duties concerning things which were *ipso facto* antecedently unowned. Initially unowned things must be justly ownable. But how?

The evident answer is that our equal original property rights entitle us to equal bundles of these things. That is, we each have a vested liberty to mix our self-owned labour with only as many of these things as would, in Locke's famous phrase, leave "enough and as good" for others.[11] And the correlative original duties vesting that liberty are ones

---

[10] And, *via* contractual understandings, from other-owned things.

[11] Does this mean that raw natural resources are not, after all, describable as "unowned"? The answer, I suppose, is "yes and no." They're owned in the weak sense that a specified *proportion* of them belongs to each person. But they're unowned in the strong sense that none of them is specifically ascribed to any particular person as an item in a property title. Epstein, "Possession as the Root of Title," 1227–8, groundlessly assumes that things unowned in the strong sense by individuals must be owned in the strong sense by the "collectivity at large." See ch. 6, section (c), above, for an argument that collective ownership must be a derivative and *not* an original right.

not to appropriate more than this amount. We are each entitled to an equal share of (at least) raw natural resources.[12] Mixing our labour with more than this share constitutes a relinquishment of our titles to that labour.

Self-ownership is, then, a sufficient basis for creating unencumbered titles both to things produced solely from self-owned things *and* to things produced from this equal portion of unowned things. We each own the fruits of our labour inasmuch as all the factors entering into their production are either things already owned by us or initially unowned things amounting to no more than an equal portion of them.

These titles generate a set of continuously compossible domains with each title, as a right *in rem*, having its correlative counterpart in the duty of each person (other than that title's holder) to respect that title, as well as all titles successively derived from it through exercises of the powers and liberties attached to them. In short, this set of mutually consistent right-and-duty pedigrees flows out of all persons' two original rights which are ones to self-ownership and to an equal share of initially unowned things.[13]

---

[12] At least raw natural resources, since these are things which *ex hypothesi* embody no one's labour. In section (c), below, I argue that the class of unowned things includes more than raw natural resources.

[13] Nozick, *Anarchy, State and Utopia*, 174–82, while embracing self-ownership as one of these two original rights, alternatively interprets the other (along Benefit Theory lines) as one to whatever level of wellbeing we would have enjoyed in the absence of a resource's having been appropriated. This right appears to be derived from some unspecified prohibition against harming others. For criticism of this derivation, see Steiner, "Capitalism, Justice and Equal Starts," 55–9. Advocacy of the claim that all persons have original rights to an equal share of natural resources has a long and distinguished and, these days, unduly neglected history. Among the more noteworthy contributions to follow in the footsteps of Locke's "enough and as good" formula are: Spence, "The Real Rights of Man"; Ogilvie, "An Essay on the Right of Property in Land"; Paine, "Agrarian Justice"; Dove, *The Theory of Human Progression and Natural Probability of a Reign of Justice: The Science of Politics*, Part I, and *The Elements of Politics: The Science of Politics*, Part II; Spencer, *Social Statics*; George, *Progress and Poverty*, and George's many other works; Wallace, *Land Nationalisation*; Walras, *Etudes D'Economie Sociale*, 214, 218, 266. See also Geiger, *The Philosophy of Henry George*; Andelson (ed.), *Critics of Henry George*; and the bibliographical entries by Cunliffe.

Unencumbered self-ownership is one of our two original rights. As we've just seen, it's from this right that our rights to the fruits of our labour (partly) derive. Indeed our being deprived of the fruits of our labour, whether by theft or exploitation, is commonly held to be an encroachment on our self-ownership. Much political rhetoric right across the ideological spectrum, as well as much of our own pre-theoretical reflection, implicitly identify the injustice of such deprivations with the injustice of violating that original right.

Yet there is a striking problem besetting this common identification, a problem that afflicts the very idea of a right of self-ownership. For each of *us* is the fruit of other persons' labour. How can we each own what we produce if we ourselves are others' products? How can we each own ourselves? Many past and present theories of justice, including historical entitlement theories, have notably failed to address this problem and it's time to put this right.

A useful way to begin, I think, is by exploring the concept of *begetting*. "Begetting" is an archaic term. But the relation for which it stands is evidently not. That relation is interesting because it oscillates intriguingly between its broad meaning, to produce or bring about, and its narrower one, to procreate. Indeed, a central theme of this section is the significance of that oscillation. And we can bring it into clearer focus by first examining the begetting relation from the perspective of the logician's classification of relational properties.

One thing we know for sure is that the relation "is a begetter of" is *irreflexive*: nothing is a begetter of itself. It's also asymmetrical. Unlike the symmetrical relation "is a cousin of," if A is a begetter of B then B is not a begetter of A. Examples of other asymmetrical relations are "is taller than" and "is preferred to": if A is taller than or preferred to B, then B is not taller than or preferred to A.

Now the question I want to pose is whether this begetting relation is a *transitive* or an *intransitive* one. If A is taller than B and B is taller than C, then A is taller than C: the relation "is taller than" is a transitive one. On the other hand, if A is divorced from B and B is divorced from C, it doesn't follow – and, indeed, it's extremely unlikely in most homophobic societies – that A is divorced from C: the relation "is divorced from" is intransitive. So what do we say in this regard about the relation "is a begetter of"? Transitive or intransitive?

Suppose you are A and you produce B which is a machine programmed in such a way that it then proceeds to produce bricks, of which C is one. What I think we'd normally say in such cases is that you are a producer, a begetter, of C.

But for some reason, things look very different when we shift to the narrower or procreative meaning of the begetting relation. Let's suppose that A is a member of a male–female couple that produces an offspring, B, who, in conjunction with another, produces an offspring, C. Here we're usually unwilling to say that A is a begetter of C, even though A is a begetter of B and B is a begetter of C. Here, unlike the previous case of production, we treat the begetting relation as *intransitive*. Why is this?

Consider now what my linguistic intuition tells me is an intermediate case. Again, you are A and you plant an acorn which becomes B, an oak tree, which drops an acorn which becomes C, another oak tree. If you produced B, did you produce C? Here, I think, we tend to hesitate – vacillating between transitivity and intransitivity. And this vacillation is the mirror image of the oscillation I mentioned previously, between the broad and narrow meanings of begetting.

Why the vacillation? Cultivation is, after all, a perfectly common form of production. People mostly do it for exactly the same general reasons that other people make bricks. So why are we uncertain whether A is a begetter of the second oak tree when we're sure that A is a begetter of the brick? It can't, I think, be anything to do with some difference in intentionality. In programming your machine to produce bricks, you certainly intend to bring about the brick, C. But it's equally true that people engaged in extensive re-forestation projects plant seeds or saplings for some trees with a view to thereby generating other trees. That is, it's simply untrue that every tree can claim to have grown *directly* from its own specifically planted seed or sapling. In planting Bs, those re-foresters intend to bring about Cs.

Nor can we attribute the difference between the brick case and the tree case to the fact that the latter requires many inputs, in addition to B's operations, for C to be brought about. It's true that a seed needs moisture, chemically conducive soil, appropriate light and so forth if it's to become a tree. But then a programmed brick-making machine also has additional needs which include ones for electricity, clay, water and so forth.

So, for the moment anyway, let's stop this vacillating and just accept that there is no relevant difference here between a brick-maker and a re-forester. In both cases, A is a producer of C and the begetting relation is therefore transitive.

Where does this take us when we turn back to the case of the male–female couples? Here, recall, we were fairly sure that the begetting involved was intransitive. Shouldn't we now begin at least to vacillate a little on this judgement, and perhaps even completely reverse it? Is there really any fundamental conceptual difference between the way plants are produced and the way animals are produced? Don't some people breed livestock for much the same reasons as others cultivate plants? And in doing so, aren't they basically doing much the same thing in both cases?

Molecular biology tells us quite unequivocally that they are. The first step in the production of *any* organism – plant and animal alike – occurs by virtue of the replicative and recombinant operations of the DNA strands within and between the nuclei of the germ cells or gametes supplied by other organisms. Obviously, the circumstances needed to occasion these operations vary widely from species to species. And so one of the main tasks of livestock-breeders and re-foresters essentially consists in supplying those circumstances as best they can.

Now, the issue I want to wrestle with arises like this. We've previously established that you own whatever is begotten by what you own. You own the fruits of your labour because you own your labour. My acquiring those fruits without your consent is theft. And my acquiring them in exchange for something of inferior value is exploitation.[14] Both are classic forms of injustice. Because persons are the owners of their own labour, they are also entitled to sell or give it to others. And preventing them from doing so is yet another form of injustice: preventers thereby act as if they, and not those prevented, are the owners of that labour. So if you own the contracted labour of the brick-machine-maker, the re-forester and the livestock-breeder, along with all the other ingredients necessary to produce their respective Bs and Cs, then you own those Bs and Cs. Your ownership is as transitive as their begetting because it superveniently rides "piggy-back" on it.

So far, so good. What I want to do now is to say a bit more about livestock breeding. As we all know, this can take many forms, depending on the types of animals being produced. Trout-farming is very different from cattle-ranching which, in turn, differs greatly from raising chickens. But the kind of livestock breeding to which I particularly want to draw attention, if only briefly, is the breeding of human slaves.

---

[14] Exploitations occur against the background of rights violations; cf. ch. 5, section (d), above.

In one of the foremost studies of American slavery, Kenneth Stampp
has convincingly documented the presence and profitability of this form
of agriculture, citing plantation books, court records, trade periodicals
as well as the reports of contemporary observers. A few quotations
will suffice:

> Many masters counted the fecundity of Negro women as an econ-
> omic asset and encouraged them to bear children as rapidly as
> possible ... a Virginia planter boasted to Olmsted that his slave
> women were "uncommonly good breeders; he did not suppose that
> there was a lot of women anywhere that bred faster than his."
> Every infant, he exulted, was worth two hundred dollars at current
> prices, the moment it was born.

> In 1844, a South Carolinian tried to sell two female slaves because
> they were afflicted with a malady which he thought "rendered
> them unprofitable as breeding women."

> "Your negroes will breed much faster when well clothed, fed and
> housed," advised a Virginia planter in an agricultural periodical.

> An Alabama planter felt cheated when a female he purchased as a
> "breeding woman" proved to be "incapable of bearing children"
> and he sued the vendor for fraud. The Alabama Supreme Court
> agreed that any jury "would place a higher value on a female
> promising issue than on one of a contrary description."

> The printed instructions in Thomas Affleck's plantation record
> book warned overseers to "bear in mind that a *fine crop* consists,
> first, in an increase in the number, and a marked improvement in
> the condition and value of the negroes."

> A Georgia overseer assured his employer that he used "every
> means" to promote an increase of the slave force. "I consider every
> child raised as part of the crop ..."

> In an essay on plantation management one master recommended
> his policy to others: "No inconsiderable part of a farmer's profits
> being in little negroes he succeeds in raising; the breeding women,
> when lusty, are allowed a great many privileges and required to
> work pretty much as they please."[15]

---

[15] Stampp, *The Peculiar Institution*, 237–42.

Drawing on interviews conducted with ex-slaves during the 1930s under the auspices of the WPA Federal Writers' Project Slave Narratives, Paul Escott records:

> "Durin' slavery there were stockmen," explained Maggie Stenhouse. "They was weighed and tested. A man would rent the stockman and put him in a room with some young women he wanted to raise children from." Detailing the financial arrangements involved, another slave said that the owners of the male slave "charged a fee of one out of every four offspring for his services."[16]

Doubtless, this same kind of agricultural production has had its place in the economies of many other slave-holding societies as well.

Returning now to the matter of ownership, we can begin to discern the vague outlines of an emergent paradox. You justly own whatever your labour produces (provided, of course, that the other factors entering into that production process are all things owned by you). What counts as *your labour* is whatever labour your body generates that you haven't already contracted to someone else, *plus* whatever labour of other persons' bodies they've contracted to you. You own these two lots of labour because both you and your employees are all *self-owners*. That is, your body and theirs are all owner-occupied and, being so, the disposition of the parts and labour of these bodies is at the sole discretion of those owners.

So it looks like what is unjust about involuntary slavery is that it paradigmatically contravenes the original right of self-ownership. The slave-owner bases his or her claim to the fruits of the slave's labour on a claim to own that labour – a claim which is, in turn, based not on any claim to have contracted that labour but rather on a far more inclusive claim to own the very body which generates that labour. It thus appears that what we need to do to get rid of this injustice is to abolish that latter claim. We fight an exceptionally bloody civil war and issue an emancipation proclamation to make each slave the original owner of his or her own body and thereby ensure that he or she alone is the

---

[16] Escott, *Slavery Remembered*, 45. In their controversial cliometric study of American slavery, Fogel and Engerman challenged the view that slave-breeding accounted for a major share of slaveholders' profits; *Time on the Cross*, 78–86. Their claims have in turn been challenged by Gutman and Sutch in David, Gutman, Sutch, Temin and Wright, *Reckoning with Slavery*, 154–61. More recently, Fogel has suggested that breeding policies cannot fully account for the higher fertility rates among American than among West Indian slaves; *Without Consent or Contract*, 151–3.

rightful claimant to the fruits of that body's labour. Will this do the trick?

Not for long. Some of these emancipated slaves, no doubt, will become contractually- or self-employed brick-machine-makers. Others will engage in re-forestation and other forms of agriculture. What's very likely, however, is that most of them – brick-makers and re-foresters included – will also be doing another type of begetting: namely, procreating. They, as self-owning As, will be producing Bs who produce Cs.

Are they, after all that struggle and sacrifice, once again to be denied the fruits of their labour? Are we to say that they don't own their offspring and, transitively, their offspring's offspring? If we make all the Bs original self-owners too, won't we be denying the self-ownership of the As? And if we also make the Cs original self-owners, won't we be denying the self-ownership of the Bs as well as the As? In making everyone an original self-owner, wouldn't we be denying everyone's original self-ownership, just as Hobbes denies any one a natural right to anything by giving everyone a natural right to everything? Or to put the matter in a somewhat Kantian fashion: *How is universal original self-ownership possible?*

I'm going to call this conundrum "the paradox of universal self-ownership." To the best of my knowledge, credit for what amounts to its discovery must go to Locke's great seventeenth-century opponent, Sir Robert Filmer.[17] Filmer's way with the paradox is short and swift. He simply accepts its force and denies that universal self-ownership is possible. Upon this denial, he erects a moral and political theory vindicating undiluted royal absolutism. And the cornerstone of this theory is none other than our cherished principle that persons are entitled to the fruits of their labour.

The broad outline of his argument runs like this. Sharing his contemporaries' endorsement of the Old Testament as literal historical truth, Filmer notes that God created the Earth and all that dwelt therein, including Adam to whom God gave sole dominion over this creation. God similarly created Eve from a part of Adam's body, and she too was placed under Adam's dominion. Being the owner of Eve, Adam becomes the owner of their offspring and their offspring's offspring and, upon his demise, his ownership passes to his eldest son. And so it goes on from there, with this rather comprehensive sovereign title descending primogenitally through the ages to only one person at a time who is, therefore,

---

[17] Filmer, *Patriarcha and Other Writings*. Nozick alludes to it in *Anarchy, State and Utopia*, 288–9.

the sole existing person who can be a self-owner. Everyone else is owned by that current successor.

Now evidently there are a lot of problems with this kind of story and Locke picked up many of them in the course of the ponderous counter-argument he mounted in his *First Treatise*. We can ask why Adam should have had only one designated successor. Or why subsequent designated successors should have had only one designated successor. Or why singular succession need be primogenital. Or we can wonder about Noah and the Great Flood and ask how this might have interrupted the line of descent from Adam's successor. Or we can worry about why the Old Testament reports God as apparently countenancing a plurality of kings and nations at various subsequent times. And so on. All of these, as well as his own numerous inconsistencies, can fatally embarrass some of the particular political conclusions Filmer drew from his argument. But I don't think they come anywhere near to damaging its core structure insofar as that rules out universal self-ownership.

Nor do we get much closer to damaging it by simply shedding any commitment to the sexism and the creationism of the Old Testament and embracing evolutionism.[18] Why? Because although the evidence supporting species' evolutionary origins is overwhelming and although it's possible that our own primordial human ancestors might have been more numerous than just the two persons of the Book of Genesis, such considerations offer no hope of expanding the class of originally self-owning persons to the extent of universal incidence.

For even if some of these primordial ancestors or their designated successors might have chosen to relinquish their ownership of some or all of their offspring – and might have emancipatorily conferred self-ownership upon them – there is no reason to suppose that all of them (to say nothing of all their self-owning descendants) would have chosen likewise. Whether any of us and if so, who, would be self-owners would thus depend upon the preferences of whoever owns our parents. Maybe they own themselves. Maybe not. If they or whoever else may own them were suddenly seized by a liberal impulse, then we and our siblings would stand a pretty good chance of being self-owners. Otherwise we are, as the core of Filmer's argument suggests, simply slaves.

Or are we? Is there a way out of this conundrum – a way that doesn't merely evade the paradox by substituting for Filmer's preposterous historical claims an historical claim which is equally preposterous: namely, that all our begetters have invariably been good liberals? What we

[18] "Evolutionism," at *this* stage of the argument, is intended to be non-committal as between Lamarckian and Darwinian–Weismannian theories.

obviously want is some solution that vests us all with the ownership of ourselves and the fruits of our labour, and that doesn't rely on a fortuitously wide incidence of liberal impulses amongst our ancestors. We want a solution that guarantees our offspring's self-ownership as well as our own, regardless of whether we or our parents are liberals.

I think that such a solution *can* be constructed and I'll try to describe it in a moment. Before doing so, however, we need to be clear about what solutions to paradoxes amount to. What is involved in many paradoxes is that the conjunction of several well-affirmed (descriptive or prescriptive) propositions leads to a contradiction. The paradox of universal self-ownership amply displays this property, as the following statement of it indicates:

1   It's logically possible that all persons (originally) are self-owners.
2   All self-owners (originally) own the fruits of their labour.
3   All persons (originally) *are* the fruits of other persons' labour.
4   Therefore it's logically impossible that all persons (originally) are self-owners.[19]

Historically, as we know, some paradoxes have proved simply insoluble. Others have lent themselves to solutions reached through operations of clarifying or modifying their constituent propositions.[20] Naturally, the plausibility of any such strategy entirely depends upon whether the reasons for those operations are themselves independently plausible.

---

[19] Or to give creationism and evolutionism their due, the third proposition should read:

3 *Almost* all persons (originally) are the fruits of other persons' labour.

Strictly speaking, the paradox of universal self-ownership itself *derives* from one which is logically anterior to it (concerning persons' ownership of the fruits of their labour) and which can be loosely stated thus:

(i)   All persons (originally) own the fruits of their labour.
(ii) All persons (originally) *are* the fruits of other persons' labour.
(iii) Therefore no persons (originally) own the fruits of their labour.

[20] For an example in political philosophy, see the strategies employed by Richard Wollheim and his commentators to solve his "paradox of democracy" which can be stated thus:

(i)   Policy A should be enacted.
(ii) The policy chosen by the majority should be enacted.
(iii) The policy chosen by the majority is not-A.
(iv) Therefore policy not-A should be enacted.

Cf. Wollheim, "A Paradox in the Theory of Democracy". For a useful summary of some commentators' strategies, see Graham, "Democracy, Paradox and the Real World."

What would count as a solution here is getting rid of (4), while still sustaining (1) and (2).[21] We need to find a way in which the affirmation of (1) doesn't imply the denial of (2). And I propose to do this by clarifying (1) and (2) and modifying (3) in ways which, I hope, possess the requisite degree of independent plausibility.

Let's consider the first of these operations. It seems reasonably certain that there's one thing that *no* account of universal self-ownership can do or be. All moral theories encumber us with duties and liabilities. But when I say "us" I don't intend to include – nor do such theories – persons who haven't yet attained their majority. Just when persons do attain their majority is a matter of perennial debate and, in most legal systems, one that tends to get decided on a largely piecemeal and pragmatic basis. Probably many of us believe as I do that, broadly speaking, it should be earlier in a person's life than it legally tends to be. But whether you believe this or not, we would all agree that there is some age or developmental stage prior to which the harms and damage which such young persons may inflict on others are ones for which they should not be legally punished; ones which their parents and other adults should have legal duties to try to prevent; and ones for which their parents and/or other adults should be the persons legally liable to pay redress and, in some cases, even suffer punishment.

It is our very reasons for believing this about minors that are equally reasons why, strictly speaking, they cannot have *rights*. That is, their presumed incapacity to make responsible decisions – the characteristic that makes them inappropriate subjects of duties and liabilities – makes them equally inappropriate subjects of powers and liberties whose possession is precisely what having rights amounts to. And this, not least, because one of the standard exercises of such powers and liberties is the incurring of duties and liabilities.

Of course, for political and rhetorical purposes we do sometimes want to speak of minors as having rights. But a moment's reflection on any such claim is usually all it takes to appreciate that what is thereby being proposed is that some presumed interest of minors (including foetuses) would be better protected by transferring a certain bundle of legal powers and liberties from one set of adults to another set of adults. So in some arguments for privatizing schools or decompulsorizing vaccination, the proposed transfer is from state officials to parents, while many arguments concerning child abuse, adoption, surrogacy and

---

[21] Filmer, in rejecting (1), thereby implicitly denies the paradox's solubility. The same is true of Becker, *Property Rights*, 37–9, who construes the paradox as a reason for rejecting (2); a similar view is presented in Okin, *Justice, Gender and the Family*, ch. 4.

abortion standardly propose a transfer in the opposite direction, or from one set of state officials to another. In all such advocacy, and there are many other types as well, much of what is proposed is advanced in the name of children's rights. But what is actually the case, as it must inevitably be, is that the measures advocated would empower and extend the discretion of adults, not children.[22] In short, because children cannot have rights, they cannot be included amongst those to whom *any* account of universal self-ownership extends.

So how can we put together such an account? Recall that what we want is something that gives our parents self-ownership *plus* the ownership of the fruits of their labour but *not* the ownership of us. Somehow, we have to be construable as not being the fruits of our parents' labour. Now you don't need to have undergone pregnancy or raised a child to appreciate that this is a tall order. For it would seem that virtually everything that goes into the production of *us* up to adulthood is supplied by the labour of our parents and of persons they elect or employ for that purpose. Even in cases where eggs are harvested from some persons, fertilized, and then implanted in other persons (or for that matter, in test-tubes) – or in societies where non-contractual child-rearing duties are also vested in persons other than biological parents – how can the resultant offspring claim not to have been produced by parental labour? Their parents may be more numerous than the conventional duo, but these offspring are just as much those persons' products. How can something which is so evidently the result of others' labour expenditures *not* be the fruit of that labour and hence, following our principle, *not* belong to those who expended that labour?

I'm going to try to answer these questions by deploying a sequence of examples, each of which involves some type of labour-mixing. The aim of this exercise is to provide reasons for modifying proposition (3) in my statement of the paradox, in order to clarify proposition (2).

Suppose I steal some lumber from you, sand it down, carve it carefully and fashion it into a table. Does the fact that I've poured so much of my labour and resources into this production process give me a clear unencumbered title to the table? Presumably few would disagree that the answer must be "no."

Suppose that instead of stealing your lumber, I steal a drawing you've

---

[22] The idea that children's interests may be better protected through such divisions of custodial powers is presumably based on the same thought that underlies constitutional doctrines of "checks and balances." And as in those latter cases, consensus amongst all the several parties vested with these powers leaves their charges with no residual *rights-based* grounds for any grievance.

made of Boadicea revolting against the Romans and, before returning it, I replicate it with my photocopier. Would we say that the fact that the photocopier, copy-paper and labour used are all mine gives me an unencumbered title to that photocopy? Again, I think the answer must be "no."

Our third example simply recalls the earlier discussion of the just ownership of natural resources. Suppose I appropriate an unowned raw acre of land by cultivating it and transforming it into a fertile field. So I'm not guilty of stealing in the sense that I was in the previous two cases. Does my cultivation of that acre therefore give me an unencumbered title to that field? Again, "no."

In the fourth example, we return to the previous case of the photocopied drawing. Here I am with the photocopy of the Boadicea drawing which I stole from you and copied with the use of my labour and materials. Suppose that Mrs Thatcher comes along, takes that photocopy and, before returning it, she photocopies it with her photocopier on to a sketched self-portrait, thereby superimposing the one image on the other. Does she have an unencumbered title to this new photocopy? Once again, "no."

The fifth example is the one which finally brings us back to the problem of universal self-ownership. Consider a representative pair of primordial persons whom we'll uninventively call Adam and Eve. One thing we know from Darwin about Adam and Eve is that their parents were not persons. Nor, *ex hypothesi*, were they the products of persons' labour. So these parents (and their predecessors) were natural resources.

Now consider how Adam and Eve were produced. According to molecular biology, the critical initial step in that production process consisted in the replication and recombination of DNA strands within and between the gametes of their respective parents. The DNA strands within their parents' germ cells were, so to speak, separately photocopied and two of these copies were then superimposed on two others to yield two zygotes, each of which then got very busy generating an extended sequence of DNA-strand replications and recombinations which, with the concomitant cell divisions and differentiations, resulted in two sizeable clusters of somatic and germ cells whom we call Adam and Eve. And that same photocopying process was again at work in *their* germ cells, preparatory to the conception of their offspring, Cain.[23]

---

[23] Long before the isolation of the mechanism for this reiterative and transitive continuity of germ-line genetic information, Samuel Butler aptly observed that "a hen is merely an egg's way of making another egg." It's this fact – that the information in each generation's germ cells is a composite replicate of the information in the germ cells of its predecessor – that ultimately tells against Lamarckian evolutionism. For the "central dogma" of molecular biology – that genetic information flows in only one direction, from DNA to

So is Cain the product of Adam's and Eve's labour? Is Mrs Thatcher's photocopy the product of her labour? We can hardly deny that Adam and Eve poured a great deal of their labour and other belongings into Cain's production, just as we cannot deny that Mrs Thatcher made a significant corresponding contribution to the production of her photocopy. But what we can deny is that *all* the factors entering into either of these two processes were the products of those producers, or of other persons who voluntarily supplied them. In the case of the photocopy, one of these factors was involuntarily supplied by you. In the case of Cain, some of these factors were supplied by nature.

The conjunction of these examples, along with the earlier discussion of children's rights, furnish us with the desired independently plausible reasons for altering the terms of our paradox in a way that allows its solution. Universal self-ownership is non-paradoxically possible if Cain's self-ownership is permissible. What the example sequence shows is that, contrary to proposition (3), Cain is not fully the fruit of his parents' labour. For his production required them to mix their labour with natural resources in the form of *germ-line genetic information transmitted from his grandparents*. Hence denying his parents full liberal ownership of him doesn't amount to a denial of proposition (2). That is, encumbering their ownership is permissible. And what the children's rights discussion does is to mobilize that permissibility to sustain proposition (1), by implying that this encumbrance consists in the liability of their ownership to expiry on the occasion of Cain's attaining his majority.[24] Prior to the onset of majority – during his zygotic, foetal and minority phases – he is at their disposal.[25] After that, he is a self-owner. And so are we.[26,27]

RNA to protein – implies that it's germ cell information that controls the development of somatic cells or bodily characteristics, and not *vice versa*. Hence, and contrary to Lamarck, characteristics acquired during an organism's lifetime are not inherited by its offspring. Cf. Arthur, *Theories of Life*, esp. chs 5–8, and Rosenberg, *The Structure of Biological Science*, chs 4, 5.

[24] Deploying Honoré's terminology, we can thereby describe Adam's and Eve's ownership of Cain as a "determinable interest" – one which lacks the full liberal ownership incident of "absence of term"; cf. Honoré, "Ownership," 121–2.

[25] Or perhaps we should say (following the previous discussion of divided powers over minors) that he's at the disposal of two sets of persons: his parents on the one hand and everyone else on the other, inasmuch as everyone has an equal claim to natural resources. Just what this division of claims or powers might be, as between these two sets of owners (beyond what is indicated in the next chapter), is a question I'll not attempt to answer.

[26] Can our germ-line genetic information really be construed as unappropriated and hence unowned until we use it? The foregoing discussion shows that it's a natural resource.

The holders of rights are adult persons. But *which* adult persons? For these come in many assorted shapes and sizes. More pertinently, they also come in many different temporal locations. Some are dead and some are living and some are yet to exist. Many views of the rights which are morally ascribable to adult persons implicitly or explicitly assign rights

---

So to ask this question is to ask how this resource can be contained by self-owned bodies without itself thereby being owned. For if it isn't owned, doesn't this endanger our self-ownership by licensing (as with other natural resources) its appropriation by anyone else? I think not. Thus suppose I appropriate a site adjacent to an unappropriated one. And suppose that, over a period of years, a series of other persons appropriate similarly adjacent sites – beside, above and below it – such that the unappropriated site is eventually completely surrounded by our sites. Although others lack permissible access to it, none of it can be described as appropriated (unless one of us mixes labour with part of it). If it could, when did this happen and who did it? Nor, therefore, would it count as appropriated if I were to become the sole owner of all the surrounding sites, say, by purchasing them. (On the other hand, and disanalogously to the natural resources surrounded by self-owned bodies, some of the *value* of those surrounding sites would be due to their each being a means of access to the unappropriated one; see the next chapter's discussion of redistributive claims on the value of appropriated natural resources.)

[27] Can normative principles rest on facts of biology? Surely not. Nor is that what's happening in this argument. For we need to distinguish between contingent facts of *biology* and non-contingent truths about *living things*. Biology is the science of living things. And a defining feature of living things is that they're produced from other living things, that one factor in the production of any cell is another cell. Thus it's not a fact of biology but an analytic truth that "Life is born of life, and of life alone ... Every organism, therefore, originates from a unit taken from the preceding generation"; Jacob, *The Logic of Life*, 126. Cf. Maynard Smith, *The Problems of Biology*, ch. 1; Arthur, *Theories of Life*, chs 1–2. A very general non-analytic truth is that "the theory of the genetic code constitutes the fundamental basis of biology"; Monod, *Chance and Necessity*, 12. But even if the actual mechanism of transitive begetting proved to be something other than germ-line genetic information – as, say, in the theory of Lamarck or those of the seventeenth-century "preformationists" (cf. Magner, *A History of the Life Sciences*, chs 8, 12) – that transitivity would remain an analytic feature of the concept of a "living thing." (None of this touches the difficult question of whether non-living things, such as well-programmed robots, can be persons and hence self-owners.) I'm grateful to Jerry Cohen for prompting me to address this issue.

to the dead and to members of future generations.[28] That is, they are rights entailing correlative duties in living persons, duties which we owe to dead or future persons.

I want to argue that these views are mistaken. For although we undoubtedly do have serious moral duties with regard to dead and future persons, these are not correlative ones. Dead and future persons have no rights. Why not? Let's deal first with the dead. And let's do so by examining the paradigm case of dead persons' rights – the right of bequest.[29]

It's an unforgivable pun, but also true, to say that the significance of the "graveyard vote" in Chicago politics lies within living memory. Humorists have sometimes remarked that in that deeply divided electorate, beset by racial, ethnic, and class antagonism along with its attendant transient political alliances, only the resolute loyalty of the stalwart dead contributed a measure of stability and continuity to the electoral vicissitudes of Cook County. Does it make a difference that it was against Edmund Burke's theory, and not Chicago politicians' practice, that Tom Paine declaimed? "When man ceases to be, his power and his wants cease with him; and having no longer any participation in the concerns of this world, he has no longer any authority in directing who shall be its governors, or how its government shall be organized, or how administered."[30] Does this statement reveal a flaw in Paine's otherwise impeccably radical credentials – a failure, that is, of the imaginative vision to embrace Burke's ancestrophilia and deploy it in behalf of that most progressive of causes, the extension of the suffrage?

Any reservations we might entertain about enfranchising the dead – or perhaps more precisely, about not *dis*enfranchising them – should not, of course, be occasioned by those politicians' cynical manipulation of this constituency's ballots. The practice of casting votes by *proxy* in

---

[28] In using phrases like "members of future generations" or simply "future persons," I refer to persons whose lives share no element of contemporaneity – no temporal overlap – with those of existing persons.

[29] Of the two other types of right commonly ascribed to dead persons, the right against (posthumous) defamation is one that evidently relies upon the Benefit or Interest Theory of rights which was criticized in ch. 3, while the right to determine the disposal of their bodily remains (to the extent that it's not similarly reliant) is vulnerable to some of the same criticisms as bequest.

[30] Paine, "The Rights of Man," 251. Foner, *The Life and Major Writings of Thomas Paine*, 251-2, quotes a letter from Thomas Jefferson, stating: "Each generation is independent of the preceding, as that was of all which had gone before. It has then, like them, a right to choose for itself the form of government it believes most promotive of its own happiness . . . The dead have no rights. They are nothing, and nothing cannot own something . . ."

many decision-making groups is sufficiently familiar to ensure that the conditions for authentic posthumous deputation could be applied in elections for public office.

And why, indeed, should the dead be denied this voice? After all, their numbers include many persons of outstanding experience in public affairs and still more whose commitment to the future wellbeing of their society engaged them in considerable personal sacrifice and even the supreme sacrifice in times of war. Is it transparently fair that others, whose interest in weighty civic issues verges on the inert, should nonetheless enjoy enfranchisement simply because they are alive, while those who evinced a lifelong concern for such matters are altogether silenced?

Many arguments offered in defence of a right of bequest can, it seems to me, be brought with equal force in support of enfranchising the dead. Chief among these, historically, has been the contention that allowing persons a power of posthumous property disposition increases their incentive to develop and conserve resources which are productive of wellbeing for contemporaries and successors alike.[31] By the same token, we might expect that extending the electorate's temporal horizon – giving persons the assurance that their political preferences will exert a more enduring influence – would induce a less self-seeking, more public-spirited approach to collective decisions. Conversely, some philosophers have suggested that it makes sense to ascribe to persons interests which outlive them and which can deserve legal protection. If this is true, it must also be true that there are posthumous interests pertaining to the conduct of the agencies charged with such protection and that these interests, too, should be accompanied by whatever political authorizing powers thereby attach to such interest-holders when alive.

Hence in arguing against the notion of a right to bequeath, I don't commit myself to the view that there cannot be utilitarian or interest-based accounts of the practice of bequest. There clearly can be. And insofar as there are, these will go some way to justifying enfranchisement of the dead. My argument is simply that the power of bequest cannot be included in the bundle of incidents that constitute just property rights as described in previous sections.

Why not? According to that account of rights, there are only four ways for a person to acquire titles to things: (i) by his appropriating (not more than an equal portion of) unowned things; (ii) by his transforming other self-owned things into those things; (iii) by his having the titles to those things voluntarily transferred to him by their owners; and (iv) by

---

[31] Some doubts as to the truth of this contention are presented in Haslett, "Is Inheritance Justified?" 142ff.

his having the titles to those things transferred to him from their owners in redress for their having violated his rights. Ownership acquired through bequest is held to fall under the third mode of acquisition, voluntary interpersonal transfer, which itself is broadly of two types: purchase and gift-receiving. Bequest is said to be simply an extension of gift-giving. The question is: Is it?

Many discussions of the *legal* right of bequest begin by citing the remarks of Sir William Harcourt, offered on the occasion of his introducing the first bill for graduated death duties in Parliament in 1894:

> Nature gives a man no power over his earthly goods beyond the term of his life; what power he possesses to prolong his will beyond his life – the right of a dead man to dispose of property – is a pure creation of the law, and the State has the right to prescribe the conditions and limitations under which that power shall be exercised.[32]

Similar prominence has been given to the opinion of Mr Justice McKenna speaking for the American Supreme Court in the historic case of *Magoun v. Illinois Trust and Savings Bank* (1897): "An inheritance tax is not one on property, but one on succession. The right to take property by devise or descent is the creature of the law and not a natural right – a privilege and therefore the authority which confers it may impose conditions upon it."[33] These statements do indeed express a view which has been held by a long line of natural right thinkers including Pufendorf, Burlamaqui and Blackstone. Sir Henry Maine scathingly dismissed the idea that there is a natural right of bequest, recording that in most ancient and classical legal systems – and even where the institution of private property was sacrosanct and highly developed – the emergence of testamentary succession either did not occur or was so structured as to constitute the right involved as one of inheritance rather than bequest.[34]

On the other hand, we have such writers as Grotius, Locke and (more ambiguously) Kant and Fichte affirming the power to bequeath as an

---

[32] Quoted in Ely, *Property and Contract*, 416.

[33] Ely, *Property and Contract*, 416.

[34] Maine, *Ancient Law*, chs VI, VII. An independent right of inheritance (one not derived from an exercise of bequest and thus a possible constraint upon it) is, of course, *not* compatible with the account of just rights advanced here, since this mode of title acquisition is not one of the four listed above. Bequeathers do not *owe* their heirs what they bequeath to them.

incident inherent in the natural right to private property. Even here, however, one still finds that incident defended in terms of the needs of the deceased's dependants and his or her presumed overriding concern for their welfare; the possibility of non-dependants being heirs is rarely considered.[35] Nevertheless many natural right thinkers, Herbert Spencer and Robert Nozick among them, treat the power of unfettered bequest as presenting no more conceptual difficulties than the power to make gifts *inter vivos*, which they correctly regard as being an unimpeachable incident of natural property rights.[36]

Why then the disagreement, even among those subscribing to the natural right of private property? If a living person (Blue) accepts a gift from another living person (Red), Blue clearly has a right to it and others are correlatively obligated not to interfere with her possession of it. How could what some describe as "the intercession of Red's death," in the process of gifting, be thought to affect in any way the location of the rights and duties in question?

To see why it *does* affect them, we need to recall some of the features of Hohfeldian jural relations and positions. Rights and powers are respectively correlative to duties and liabilities. If your duty not to kill me is one owed to me then, trivially, I have a right against being killed by you. But if your duty isn't waivable by me – if, say, despite my being painfully and terminally ill and requesting your assistance in ending my life, your duty still stands – then, although there may be a correlative right that I not be killed by you, that right does not vest in *me*. Someone else, often the state, is invested with that right in relation to which I am (at best) a third party beneficiary. Possessed of that right, it is the state who is possessed of the power to waive your duty or to forgive its breach or to punish you for its breach.

Transfers of ownership, whether by sale or *inter vivos* donation, involve an exchange of correlatives. When Red transfers the title of an object O to Blue, he thereby transfers to her (with her agreement) the rights and powers he held against Blue with respect to O. His right that Blue not interfere with his possession of O is replaced by her right that Red not interfere. Correlatively, Blue's duty not to interfere is transferred to Red. Blue is released from a previous restriction on her conduct and Red, as vendor or donor, acquires a corresponding restriction.

Now, quite clearly, transfers of ownership by bequest are not at all

[35] See also Kant's rather strained attempt to construe bequest as a transfer based on a *contract* between testator and heir; *The Metaphysics of Morals*, 110–11, 171–2.

[36] More recently, Nozick, *The Examined Life*, ch. 3, has modified his earlier endorsement of unfettered bequest.

like this. Red, as testator, incurs no restriction whatsoever in assigning ownership of O to Blue only posthumously. It's grossly misleading to describe what is going on here as "the intercession of Red's death in the process of gifting Blue." And the simple reason why that description is misleading is that this process *cannot begin until after Red's demise.* Up to the moment of his death, there is no certified heir since, until that moment, Red is empowered to alter his will as he chooses.[37] In short, the transfer of ownership by bequest can be performed only by a living person.

Bequeathing therefore lacks a quite central jural feature of *inter vivos* gift-making, a feature which can – and apparently does – make a very substantial difference in practice. Testators, unlike donors, incur no duty not to interfere with the recipient's possession of the object whose ownership is transferred. Presumably it's precisely in order to avoid incurring such a duty that persons choose to transfer things by bequest rather than by gift.[38] For what bequest does, at the least, is supply a form of *insurance* for the bequeather: it ensures him against the fate of King Lear, against the ingratitude and cupidity of prospective heirs upon whom the bequeather is unwilling to rely up to the moment of his death. At most, it's a lever by which the bequeather can, during his lifetime, strongly influence the current behaviour of aspiring heirs.

But, of course, it's not the fact that the bequeather's generosity is rather less selfless and more calculated than the gift-giver's that warrants denying him the power to bequeath. Nor do we need to linger over the question of whether rights to such insurance and influence can really be natural ones. Just rights, as I've repeatedly urged, indiscriminately afford protection to conduct which varies all the way from saintly through prudent to downright sleazy. What makes bequest *not* an incident of just rights is the impossibility of locating all its implied Hohfeldian jural positions in the holders of those rights. Why?

If the act of transferring ownership of a dead person's property can

[37] What if, counterfactually, Red lacks this power to alter the clause in his will leaving O to Blue? Wouldn't this make Blue the certified inheritor of O? The answer is that it could do so, but only at the cost of this transfer losing the distinctive characteristics of a bequest. For if Red is thus disempowered, he holds a Hohfeldian disability to which Blue holds the correlative immunity. She is thereby empowered to prevent Red from disposing of O – from transforming it into something else or transferring its ownership to someone else – during the remainder of his lifetime. Hence under this hypothesized condition, his inclusion of that clause would amount to an *immediate*, rather than posthumous, relinquishment of these major incidents of his ownership of O.

[38] This motivational conjecture is strongly corroborated by the fact that bequests commonly attract a greater liability to taxation than do gifts in most Western societies.

be performed only by a living person, we need to identify its jural status. Is it an exercise of a power or a compliance with a duty? Or both? If it's a duty, it evidently cannot be one owed to the designated heir since she can acquire no right to the bequeathed object until and unless this act has been performed. Is it, perhaps, a duty owed to the bequeathing Red? At first glance, this seems plausible. Red has appointed this living person, White, as his executor and authorized him to perform the transfer. But here we encounter the problem of how White's duty, if he has it, can be understood as a correlative one: a duty owed to another person. For a correlative duty, it will be recalled, is one which another person holds powers to waive or demand (and enforce) compliance. Who has these powers in respect of White's duty? Obviously not Red, since *ex hypothesi* White's duty cannot be performed until Red dies and is not merely contingently, but rather necessarily, incapable of waiving or demanding anything. Can these powers vest in Blue as the designated heir? Again no, since if it were possible for Red posthumously to transfer these powers directly to Blue, it would be possible for him so to transfer the ownership itself, and the executor's duty would be superfluous.

Is what the executor has, then, not a duty but a power? If it's a power, how did he acquire it? Before the moment of Red's death, White lacks any power to dispose of Red's property and is, like everyone else, under a duty not to interfere with Red's dispositions. So White can acquire this power only after that moment. But again, if it were thus possible for the testator posthumously to transfer the power of disposal to the executor, the executor would be superfluous inasmuch as it would equally be possible for Red posthumously to transfer the property directly to Blue. Moreover the executor's having the power of disposal after the testator's death does not, in itself, imply that the disposition need be in favour of the designated heir. We might try saying that White's power is conjoined with a duty to dispose in favour of Blue. But this simply brings us back to the problem of how such a duty can be construed as a correlative one, as one owed to another person. In whom does the power to demand compliance with it vest? And how did it get there?[39]

In practice, the answer to the first of these questions is "the state."

---

[39] Perhaps we could counterfactualize that, *prior* to his death, the testator empowers some fourth person, Black, to demand (enforce) the executor's compliance with his duty. But adding this epicycle merely displaces the problem; it doesn't solve it. Is Black disabled from waiving the executor's duty? If not, then there's no necessity for disposal in favour of Blue. If so, then we need a fifth person who holds the immunity correlative to Black's disability. And so on. A similar problem besets the counterfactual proposal that the executor is empowered by the testator prior to his death.

What is more significant is that it is the state *in theory* as well. For the rights, duties, and powers involved in testamentary succession are, as most texts in jurisprudence confirm, necessarily founded upon a fiction. J. W. Salmond explains:

> The rights which a dead man thus leaves behind him vest in his *representative*. They pass to some person whom the dead man, or the law on his behalf, has appointed to represent him in the world of the living. This representative bears the person of the deceased ... Inheritance is in some sort a legal and fictitious continuation of the personality of the dead man, for the representative is in some sort identified by the law with him whom he represents ... To this extent, and in this fashion, it may be said that the legal personality of a man survives his natural personality ... Although a dead man has no rights, a man while yet alive has the right, or speaking more exactly, the power, to determine the disposition after he is dead of the property which he leaves behind him ... This power of the dead hand (*mortua manus*) is so familiar a feature in the law that we accept it as a matter of course, and have some difficulty in realising what a singular phenomenon it in reality is.[40]

Similarly, Oliver Wendell Holmes:

> The theory of succession to persons deceased ... is easily shown to be founded upon a fictitious identification between the deceased and his successor ... Thus the Roman heir came to be treated as identified with his ancestor for the purposes of the law ... Rights to which B as B could show no title, he could readily maintain under the fiction that he was the same person as A, whose title was not denied ... The modern executor derives his characteristics from the Roman heir ... The executor "represents the person of his testator." The meaning of this feigned identity has been found in history, but the aid which it furnished in overcoming a technical difficulty must also be appreciated.[41]

Several comments seem in order. First, and as will be argued presently, what this feigned identity actually aids in overcoming is no mere techni-

---

[40] Williams, *Salmond on Jurisprudence*, 482–4.

[41] Holmes, *The Common Law*, 266–9. The Roman fictional identification of heir with testator was evidently greatly facilitated by singular succession. A plurality of heirs would pose some difficulty in this respect.

cal difficulty. But second, the identification of the executor with the testator, even if accepted, still does not account for the presence of any duty in the former to dispose of the property in accordance with the wishes of the latter. Indeed, if Red and White are considered to be one and the same person, it becomes even more difficult to understand how the executor can owe any correlative duty to the testator, since a person's (i.e. White's) present wishes would supersede "his own" (i.e. Red's) earlier ones. One cannot have rights against oneself. Hence it would appear that if the executor *does* have a duty, and moreover one which is correlative to a right, this duty is one correlative to a right held by the state which is the only possible author of the requisite fiction.

For as Holmes says, under the practice of testamentary succession, those rights to which B could show no title, he could readily maintain under the fiction that he was A. One distinctly non-technical consequence of this is that restrictions which would otherwise be impermissibly imposable on the conduct of other persons, become permissibly imposable on the basis of this fiction. A property right, being a right *in rem*, entails duties in all persons other than the owner not to interfere with his possession. In the absence of this fiction, such persons would – with regard to the deceased A's property – possess whatever rights, powers and liberties persons possess with regard to *unowned* things, just as they would with regard to any property which A might have abandoned during his lifetime. So the principal effect of the fiction is to imply that the deceased A's property remains in uninterrupted ownership and does not become *res nullius*. In the absence of this fiction, acquiring titles to the property of deceased persons would fall under the description of appropriating unowned things and not under that of receiving transferred owned things.

There now follows a series of rhetorical questions. Why should the property of deceased persons *not* be regarded as abandoned? Upon what grounds can all other persons be said to lack appropriative entitlements to it? Are all persons other than B similarly entitled to the promulgation of a fiction that they are A? That is, can this power of promulgating fictions be derived from a set of just rights? Can my just duty to repay a loan be voided by my creation of a fiction that I never undertook to do so when, in fact, I did?

Regrettably, we cannot here pursue in any depth the fascinating subject of legal fictions. Bentham offers the characteristically trenchant observation that

> In English law, fiction is a syphilis, which runs in every vein, and carries into every part of the system the principle of rottenness

... Fiction of use to justice? Exactly as swindling is to trade ... It affords presumptive and conclusive evidence of moral turpitude in those by whom it was invented and first employed.[42]

Lon Fuller, in his book specifically on this subject, remarks more circumspectly that

> Generally a fiction is intended to escape the consequences of an existing, specific rule of law ... But occasionally the matter is more obscure. In some cases a fiction seems to be intended to avoid the implications, not of any specific and recognised rule of law, but of some unexpressed and rather general and vague principle of jurisprudence or morals.[43]

Doubtless some legal fictions are more innocent, more purely "aids to overcoming technical difficulties," than others. But what does seem reasonably clear is, at the very least, that persons cannot be said to be under a just duty to accept a legal fiction. There are no legal fictions in the state of nature.

Hence the practice of bequest cannot be explicated in the terms standardly employed to describe the transferring exercise of property rights: an exercise constituted by a set of binary jural relations between private persons, whether they be testator and heir or testator, executor and heir. The rights, powers and duties constitutive of bequest are, in Harcourt's phrase, "a pure creation of the law." They ineluctably rely upon a universally binding fiction, a fiction which belies the fact that the duty of title transfer can be owed neither to the testator nor to the heir and can, therefore, be owed (if at all) only to the state. No person's just rights can empower him to promulgate such a fiction, much less derive permissibly enforceable claims against others from it.

In short, there can be no *moral* counterpart to the *legal* power of bequest. So the justification of bequest, if there is one, cannot lie in the demands of justice. And the property of the dead thereby joins raw natural resources in the category of initially unowned things: things to an equal portion of which, as we've seen, each person has an original right.[44]

---

[42] Quoted in Fuller, *Legal Fictions*, 2–3. See also Ogden, *Bentham's Theory of Fictions*, esp. 148.

[43] Fuller, *Legal Fictions*, 53.

[44] Except under that precise description, dead persons' belongings (like abandoned ones) aren't, of course, literally describable as *initially* unowned things.

If dead persons therefore lack rights, what about future persons? A common view, particularly in these days of mounting ecological concern, is that present persons are morally encumbered with duties to those who will start to exist only after we have passed away. This concern is not misplaced. You don't need to be an expert in statistical extrapolation to perceive the broad outlines of the threat many current activities pose to the eventual inhabitability of this planet. Nor, therefore, is it unwarranted to claim that present persons have moral duties to conserve the environment for their more remote descendants and to restrict their own standards of living accordingly.[45] So I agree with the following argument offered by Derek Parfit:

> Suppose that I leave some broken glass in the undergrowth of a wood. A hundred years later this glass wounds a child. My act harms this child. If I had safely buried the glass, this child would have walked through the wood unharmed. Does it make a moral difference that the child whom I harm does not now exist? On one view, moral principles cover only people who can *reciprocate*, or harm and benefit each other. If I cannot be harmed or benefited by this child, as we can plausibly suppose, the harm that I cause this child has no moral importance. I assume that we should reject this view . . . Remoteness in time has, in itself, no more significance than remoteness in space.[46]

We do have moral duties with respect to our own and our contemporaries' remote descendants. However the question we again need to ask is, as in the case of dead persons, whether these duties to future persons can be *correlative* ones. Are they requirements of *justice*? Do future persons have *rights* that we conserve, rights which thus entail the permissibility of enforcing conservation upon us?[47]

In *A Theory of Justice*, John Rawls advances a "just savings principle"

[45] Though the precise object of these duties is rendered somewhat opaque by the fact that the size of each generation (and hence the extent of its environmental needs) – far from being preordained – is determined by the procreative choices of members of the preceding generation. The latter, in making these choices, presumably take into account not only their own consumption preferences but also how these would affect the prospective living (including environmental) conditions of their offspring. On some of the moral complexities thereby engendered, see Steiner, "Markets and Law: The Case of Environmental Conservation," 52–7.

[46] Parfit, *Reasons and Persons*, 356–7.

[47] That present persons can have rights that other present persons conserve is not disputed.

and thereby implies that there are indeed such rights.[48] It's true that his account of the material legacy we are justly obligated to leave behind us diverges from the problem I've posed in two respects. First, Rawls's discussion of the issue is formulated in terms of what each generation owes to its immediate successor rather than to future (i.e. temporally remote) persons. Second, he focuses on *produced* factors of production – capital accumulation – rather than environmental resources. Nevertheless, these differences don't controvert the claim that a premiss of future persons' rights underlies his proposal. For Rawls's inclusion of representatives of "family lines" in the "original position" is intended to ensure that future persons' interests play a controlling role in determining the minimum permissible level of present persons' savings. And I think we can safely assume that the just savings principle is also intended to be responsive to current ecological anxieties and thus to mandate the intergenerational transmission of some package of conserved environment and accumulated capital. Both, after all, are forms of saving entailing restrictions on present persons' levels of consumption. In Rawls's view and that of many others, these restrictions are imposable as demands of justice and, as such, entail that future persons have moral rights against present ones.[49]

Now one rather peremptory way of showing that there can be no such rights is simply to point out that what they amount to are rights of *inheritance* which, as was previously remarked, do not figure among the four modes of acquiring just titles.[50] Less peremptorily, the idea of future persons having rights of any kind against present persons encounters the same general problem as confronts bequest. And this is the impossibility of locating all the Hohfeldian jural positions it implies.

To have a right is to be in possession of the powers to waive or demand and enforce compliance with its correlative duty. Having a right to such compliance certainly doesn't imply that the right-holder is actually able to exercise such powers, say, by personally wielding the requisite force: he can confer them on others (such as the state) and thereby authorize them to do so. But it does imply that there's nothing logically absurd or inconceivable about his exercising them or about his authorizing others to do so. And in this regard, it's perhaps worth emphasizing that such powers can be conferred – their exercise by others can be authorized – only by the right-holder himself. For White's waiving or

[48] Rawls, *A Theory of Justice*, 284ff; cf. Barry, *Theories of Justice*, 189–203.
[49] See some of the essays in Laslett and Fishkin (eds), *Justice Between Age Groups and Generations*. For a contrary view, see Sagoff, *The Economy of the Earth*, esp. 63–4.
[50] See above, pp. 251–2 and n. 34.

enforcing Red's duty to do A to count as an exercise of the powers entailed by Blue's right that Red do A, it must be the case that Blue has conferred those powers upon White. If White's possession of those powers did *not* presuppose Blue's authorization, there would be no reason why anybody else might not equally claim to be possessed of those powers and hence authorized to decide whether to enforce or waive Red's compliance with his duty to do A. In short, to be possessed of the power to uphold a right is either to be, or to be authorized by, that right's holder.

It follows fairly readily from these formal considerations that the moral duties present persons have to future persons are not correlative ones. Future persons are able neither to waive nor to demand nor to enforce present persons' compliance with those duties. And this inability isn't merely a physical incapacity, an empirical impossibility.[51] A future person is necessarily incapable of either waiving or demanding a present person's compliance or preventing a present person's non-compliance or penalizing him for it, because *ex hypothesi* two such persons lack any element of contemporaneity.[52] And this necessary lack of contemporaneity also implies the logical impossibility of future persons authorizing some present persons to exercise those powers. Hence such demands and enforcement cannot be regarded as an exercise of powers attached to future persons' rights. They have no rights against present persons nor, therefore, any rights that present persons save or conserve anything for them.

[51] As it *is* in the case of right-holders who are ill, asleep, or geographically remote from persons who owe them duties.

[52] An anonymous reviewer of an earlier paper where this argument was advanced objected that the impossibility of future persons exercising these powers is merely contingent rather than necessary, on the grounds that *time-travel* is a technological rather than logical impossibility. The idea of time-travel has, of course, been widely canvassed in many popular books and films, and I don't wish to prejudge it here. The *conceptual* problems besetting it are also well known, not the least of them being its implication that all persons who will ever have existed are, in some literal sense, contemporaries who could therefore interact with one another. Indeed, it implies that my earlier and later selves are such contemporaries. So I suppose that what my claim amounts to is that, *if* any two persons can be non-contemporaries, future persons cannot exercise these powers against present ones. Nor, for that matter, can dead persons.

Here's a simple rights violation. Blue is sitting in her garden and Red, whose garden adjoins hers, points his gun across the fence at her and fires, wounding her. There's no contractual understanding between them, nor any previous violation of Red's rights by Blue, that could make this shooting permissible. So Red's action is a clear encroachment on Blue's self-ownership.

Suppose, instead, that the person Red aims at and hits is White, whose garden is adjacent to the other side of Blue's garden. And suppose that a contractual understanding or previous violation which might license this action is similarly lacking. Isn't Red's action an encroachment on White's self-ownership? Does it make any relevant difference that the fence separating White's garden from Blue's, unlike the one between Red's and Blue's, is an *international boundary*? Clearly not. Red's shooting outsider White is as much a violation of original rights as his shooting insider Blue. Our moral duties to respect other persons' original rights and the rights derived from them don't suddenly evaporate at international boundaries.[53] More generally, they don't end at the borders of whatever local, regional or national jurisdiction we happen to be in. These duties are *global* in scope.

Not all our moral duties are global ones, of course. Many types of non-correlative duty – ones enjoined by values or rules other than justice – are plausibly regarded as more localized in their scope. This is obviously true of duties to ourselves and of duties associated with intimate relationships or friendship or communal solidarity or patriotism. It's less true in the case of benevolence where strong arguments can be adduced for treating the needs of strangers and outsiders on a par with those of others.[54] And it's barely if at all true in the case of utility-maximization.[55] In all of these cases, whether localized or not, morality

---

[53] That these duties pertain to *all* derived rights, *in personam* as well as *in rem* rights, was argued in the earlier discussion (ch. 3, section (c)) of "paucital" and "multital" rights.

[54] Cf. Singer, "Famine, Affluence and Morality."

[55] Though there may be empirical reasons for believing that duties of utility-maximization and benevolence are more effectively performed locally, at least insofar as all localities are equally capable of performing them (which, typically, they aren't). Such reasons, when conjoined with these principles, thereby yield what Sidgwick called "middle axioms" – derivative principles or rules of thumb – enjoining the priority of localized

frequently demands that we waive some of the correlative duties we are
justly owed by other persons: that we render them goods and services
which we rightfully own, or excuse them from rendering goods and services which they rightfully owe us. The lexical primacy of justice and
the global scope of its correlative duties certainly don't prohibit any such
waiver. What they prohibit is anyone's defaulting on those duties in its
absence. Red's shooting outsider White may well be an act of patriotism
or communal solidarity. But it's nevertheless unjust.

Suppose Blue purchases a car from White or invites him round for a
cup of tea or employs him to do a spot of work in her garden or even
allows him to camp out there indefinitely. How can the original rights
of Red, her compatriot, possibly empower him to prevent any of these
transactions or even to impose a surcharge on them? Wouldn't his doing
so, in the absence of any prior agreement by Blue licensing such interference, be as much a violation of her rights as it clearly would be had
her offers been extended instead to an insider? Alternatively, suppose
it's White who invites Blue to come round for tea, gardening or camping
out: actions which no previous undertaking commits her to forbear. Is
Red originally empowered to detain her within their national boundaries? Evidently not.[56]

What if Blue decides to remove not only herself but also her garden
from within those national boundaries? What if, that is, she decides to
secede? Is Red empowered to prevent this? Locke apparently thought
so. Notwithstanding his account of the formation of legitimate political
jurisdictions by individual consent, whereby a nation state's territory is
co-extensive with that of the several landowners who wish jointly to
constitute it, Locke seems to endorse the practice of "Commonwealths
not permitting any part of their Dominions to be dismembered."[57]

---

performances. For arguments that important types of benevolence are "public goods," see
A. Buchanan, *Ethics, Efficiency and the Market*, 71–4, and Hahn, "Benevolence."

[56] Walzer, *Spheres of Justice*, 39, agrees that Red is disempowered from detaining Blue
but insists that he *is* empowered to prevent White's entry. The argument for this moral
asymmetry between emigration and immigration runs thus: "This right to control immigration does not include or entail the right to control emigration . . . The restraint of entry
serves to defend the liberty and welfare, the politics and culture of a group of people
committed to one another and to their common life. But the restraint of exit replaces
commitment with coercion." It's difficult to see, however, why Red is not replacing commitment with coercion in preventing Blue from lodging White.

[57] Locke, *Two Treatises of Government*, 364. Here, as in several passages in his extensive discussion of property rights (ch. V), there's a rather unexpected shift from prescriptive
to descriptive language at the point where Locke reports some pertinent prevailing practice
which violates his previously propounded principles but which he nonetheless appears
unwilling to condemn.

In thereby denying that landowners' rights can include the power to secede, Locke succumbs (as have so many others) to the mysterious charms of what has been called the "theory of magic dates."[58] The theory goes like this. Prior to a magic date, landowners, like any other rights-holders, are empowered to enter into longer- or shorter-term agreements for the joint protection of their rights by an agency whom they authorize. But after a magic date, these powers are inexplicably truncated and all such arrangements *must* be ones which are binding in perpetuity, i.e. which are irrevocable by all landowners and their successors. Hence the sole permissible form of exit thenceforth available to landowners is the removal of only themselves and their *movable* belongings, but not "their" landed property, from that legal jurisdiction. There is, on this theory, a fundamental moral asymmetry between the conditions for conjoining a piece of territory with others into a legal jurisdiction and the conditions for disjoining it from them.

The "theory of magic dates" is notoriously incomplete. It offers neither an explanation of why there should be any such date nor one of why there can be a plurality of them in human history nor any formula for locating them. But even if these deficiencies could somehow be made good, it's clear that no such categorical prohibition of secession can be derived from individuals' rights. Of course, any set of landowners can, if they wish, choose to bind themselves with contractual duties to one another not to secede. And they can similarly choose to bind their assignees (those to whom they sell or give their land titles) with such a duty.[59] It's also a further and fascinating question – one which considerably exercised classical liberal writers – as to whether rights-holders, in general, are morally empowered contractually to bind their assignees to bind their assignees in turn.[60] Perhaps so. But even if such entailed duties are permissible terms of contracts, they're still not the mandatory ones prescribed by the "theory of magic dates." So Blue *can* be unencumbered by any such duty. And if she is, Red lacks the power to prevent her taking her garden with her.[61]

---

[58] I owe this apt phrase to Nicolaus Tideman.

[59] One presumable cost of doing so, as with any restriction on the ownership of a thing, being a diminution in the value of the title to it.

[60] Indeed, to preserve the territorial integrity of a state over time, founding landowners would also need to bind *one another* to bind their successive assignees to assume the (presumably joint) ownership of any of their land for which there was no assignee.

[61] Buchanan, *Secession*, derives the power to secede from *group*, rather than individual, rights: rights which are non-reducible to collections of individual rights. Doubts about the possibility of such non-reducible group rights were expressed in ch. 5, section (c), above.

In short, the moral asymmetries of the "theory of magic dates" and of what we might correspondingly call the "theory of magic gates" – the theory that others may exercise control over who enters through our gates but not over who exits through them – have nothing to do with justice. Our original rights and rights derivable from them empower us to secede and to contract with outsiders to import them and/or their belongings as well as to export ourselves and/or our belongings. To be sure, the demands of communal solidarity, patriotism, and intimate relationships might well be such as to prohibit some or all of these actions.[62] Perhaps Blue, were she to engage in them, would be exercising her rights exceedingly wrongly. But she would be acting within her rights. And preventing her from doing so would therefore be unjust.

What applies to self-ownership and to rights derived from it evidently also applies to our other original right, the right to an equal portion of initially unowned things, from which right those derived rights also partly derive.[63] Like the incidence of self-ownership rights, the equality mandated by this right is global, not local. Red owes duties correlative to this right to White as well as to Blue. It's not sufficient that he allow an equal portion of these things to only Blue and each of their compatriots: he must also respect White's and everyone else's similar entitlement, regardless of where on the globe they are. The fact that where they are is on the far side of some international boundary no more licenses him to deprive them of these entitlements than it does to shoot them.

As much of Buchanan's thorough discussion itself reveals, such group rights are highly likely to generate claims incompossible with the rights of other groups, to say nothing of individuals' rights. Nor is this surprising since, although these claims (as ones to territory) are extensionally specifiable, the criteria for identifying their subjects – groups – contain irreducibly intensional elements, described as interests in "cultural membership." Buchanan attempts to allay liberal doubts as to the tenability of such "mixed" (group plus individual) rights theories by claiming that "classical liberal democratic theory contains at least one fundamental group right: the right of *the* people to form a political association," (p. 77, emphasis added). But this claim's use of the definite article renders that argument circular. Powers to form political associations are ones which classical liberal democratic theory standardly ascribes simply to *people*, not *the* people – except, of course, where "the people" is already (and trivially) identified territorially, and even here it's doubtful that the theory restricts them to forming only one inclusive political association. No standard construal of classical liberalism vests persons with powers to conscript others into political (or any other) associations.

[62] This is suggested by O'Neill, "Magic Associations and Imperfect People," 118–19.

[63] Pre-eminent among such initially unowned things are, of course, plots of land. It's important, however, to distinguish the issue (discussed in the next chapter) of how this original right affects land ownership from that of who is vested with powers to determine the jurisdictional location of landed property.

8
Epilogue: Just Redistributions

Rights and their compossibility conditions being what they are, there can be only four ways of acquiring just titles to things: appropriation, production, voluntary transfer, and redress. Of these, only the latter two are straightforwardly describable as *redistributive*: as involving changes of the persons named in titles to things. Voluntary transfers, typically gifts and exchanges, are non-mandatory redistributions. They're not mandatory in the sense that, without their having agreed to it, the title-holders are under no correlative duty to transfer title to the recipients. So in the absence of such agreement, no one is empowered to secure those transfers. And in its presence, securing those transfers is just.

Redress transfers, on the other hand, are mandatory redistributions and the just empowerment of someone to secure them presupposes no prior agreement on the part of the title-holders. In effect, they have no *valid* titles to the things involved, whereas the recipients do. Redress transfers are redistributions which, very broadly, *undo* the unjust redistributions imposed by encroachments on rights: they restore just distributions.[1] Persons have correlative duties to make such transfers when they take or use or, still more generally, assume possession of things – things to which other persons are entitled – without the latter's permission.

The preceding account of those entitlements implies that redress transfers are of two types. Acts occasioning the first type are ones which impose unjust redistributions by encroaching on specific titles: that is, on specific persons' rights of self-ownership, rights to the fruits of their

---

[1] But only "very broadly," for the sufficiently familiar reason (canvassed in ch. 6, section (b)) that an encroachment may be such that (i) its sufferer no longer exists and the recipients of redress can consequently be only those surviving persons who would have been his assignees had he not died, and/or (ii) its gravity is so great as to make full compensation impossible.

labour or rights that have – or *would have* – been derived from these, through acts of production or voluntary transfer.[2] The particular perpetrator of any such encroachment owes redress to the specific person suffering that encroachment, the amount of that redress being equal to the magnitude of the encroachment suffered. And this further implies that some current successors of past victims of (unredressed) injustices are owed redress by some current successors of the perpetrators of those injustices.[3]

---

[2] To describe an act as encroaching on rights that *would have* been derived from exercises of other rights is to describe an *exploitation*; see above, ch. 5, section (d). Exploited persons are ones who would have struck more favourable (to themselves) bargains, had others – who would have offered them more – not suffered prior rights encroachments which critically reduced the amount they could offer. Accordingly, a portion of exploiters' gains from the bargains actually struck is imputable to those unjust encroachments, is consequently unjust and thereby occasions a duty of redress. How the burden of that duty should be shared between the encroachers and the exploiters (if they are different persons), is an important question which I don't attempt to answer.

[3] The relevant current successors of past victims of injustice are subjunctively described as any current persons who would have been better off, via a succession of transfers originating in the victims, in the absence of the unredressed injustices that deprived their victims of the value that would have been transferred. Some literature on this subject has tended to suggest that the redress owed to such successors is bound to be *less* than the redress owed, but never paid, to the victims themselves. The motivation for this suggestion lies in some personal identity problems inherent in the "paradox of future individuals." It purports to rest on the indisputable fact that, in the absence of the past circumstances created by these injustices, many of their victims' current successors would never have come to exist at all and, hence, cannot claim that they would have been better off had the injustices not occurred. The conclusion that currently owed redress is therefore less than what was owed but never paid to the original victims depends, however, on an additional and entirely unwarranted premiss: namely, that the possible set of those victims' current successors is confined to those victims' *descendants*. Thus, for example, James Fishkin, *Justice, Equal Opportunity and the Family*, 101, plausibly argues that "while my grandmother may have suffered from sex discrimination and while certain disadvantages to her descendants may have causally followed, she would clearly have had different descendants had it not been for the sex discrimination. If we imagine her pursuing a professional career rather than that of a full-time housewife, she would surely have had fewer than the five children she did have; she might not have had any at all . . ." While this may show that Fishkin is not entitled to redress for any injustice suffered by his grandmother, it doesn't show that there can be *no* current claimant to that redress. The sex discrimination deprived his grandmother of something valuable. Had she not suffered that loss, that value would have found its way into the hands of various persons whose goods and services she would have purchased with her professional income, or into the hands of her various (related or unrelated) heirs and beneficiaries, or both – and eventually into the hands of some set of current persons *different* from the set of current persons in whose hands it has actually wound up. That former set may be empirically difficult to identify. But that is no reason to doubt its existence nor, therefore, to deny the debt owed to it by the latter set. Injustices redistribute value; they don't destroy it.

I'll occasionally refer to that first type of redress as "bilateral," in order to distinguish it from the type of redress transfers which I want to explore in this final chapter and which we might think of as "multilateral." For in addition to the various kinds of specific title listed above, we've seen that all persons are justly possessed of original rights to *initially unowned things*: that is, those things which are originally unowned (natural resources) and those things which have come to be unowned (through abandonment and death). It's true, *ex hypothesi*, that no specific person originally holds a title to any specific such thing. Nevertheless, each is entitled to an equal portion of them. Hence persons who appropriate a greater than equal portion ("over-appropriators") are thereby engaging in a redistribution. They are imposing an unjust distribution on some or all of those who have appropriated a less than equal portion ("under-appropriators").[4] And they consequently owe them redress.

Unlike encroachments occasioning bilateral redress, no particular over-appropriation encroaches on the rights of a specific under-appropriator.[5] This does not, however, preclude us from inferring that each particular over-appropriator owes redress equal to the amount of his over-appropriation. And hence the total amount of redress owed by over-appropriators is equal to the total amount of over-appropriation they've perpetrated. We can usefully construe this owed total as a *fund*, on which under-appropriators have just claims.

Precisely which under-appropriators have what claims may or may not be inferable. Consider, first, a five-person world where all initially unowned things are represented by 30 units and they have all been appropriated (i.e. none of them has been appropriated by "No one"); where an equal portion of those unowned things is therefore six units; and where Red and White are over-appropriators, Black and Pink are under-appropriators and Blue is neither (table 8.1). Here we know how much each of the two under-appropriators may claim from the fund.

But now consider a world like this one, except that Red has over-appropriated slightly less and some unowned things have *not* been appropriated (table 8.2). In this second world, we know that 1 unit is the maximum that under-appropriating Black can claim from the redress

---

[4] Whether over-appropriators have imposed unjustly on all, or only some, under-appropriators depends on the relative amount of unowned things still left to appropriate. If there are none, then *all* under-appropriators have suffered an encroachment.

[5] Except in the limiting case of there being only one over-appropriator and only one under-appropriator.

Table 8.1

	Unowned things appropriated	Owes to the fund	Is owed from the fund
Red	10	4	0
White	7	1	0
Blue	6	0	0
Black	5	0	1
Pink	2	0	4
No one	0	–	–
Total	30	5	5

Table 8.2

	Unowned things appropriated	Owes to the fund	Is owed from the fund
Red	9	3	0
White	7	1	0
Blue	6	0	0
Black	5	0	?
Pink	2	0	?
No one	1	–	–
Total	30	4	4

fund, leaving the 3 units remaining in the fund, along with the unappropriated unit, for Pink. Alternatively, Pink could claim the entire fund of 4, leaving the unappropriated unit for Black. The demands of justice are satisfied by either of these dispositions. In general, what these rather elementary illustrations tell us is that the total amount of under-appropriators' entitlements is equal to the sum of whatever is owed to the fund plus whatever remains unappropriated.

A further point of considerable redistributive significance is this. Recent decades have witnessed belated philosophical attention being brought to bear on the *international* dimension of the demands of distributive justice. Some of these demands concern issues discussed in the last section of the previous chapter: namely, international migrations of persons and capital, and secession.[6] Others focus on the wealth transfers which some nations are said to owe to others.[7]

In regard to these latter types of demand and with reference to the present argument, it's salient to recall that each person's original right to an equal portion of initially unowned things is correlative to a duty in *all* other persons. That is, and as was argued at the end of the previous chapter, the equality mandated by these rights is global in scope. We might call them rights to the "global average." They are individuals' rights to an equal portion of *all* such unowned things. There's no reason why Red, White, Black and Pink might not be members of respectively different societies, citizens of different countries. Hence the redress fund, as a mechanism for sustaining those rights, is a *global fund*.

Another point. Those charged with keeping the accounts of the global fund must also consider the following. Among the items falling into the class of initially unowned things may be ones which count as *public* or *nationalized* property within the countries containing them. That is, powers to regulate their disposition are vested in state officials who, accordingly, are the holders of the rights to them.[8] Red, White, Black and Pink might be not only citizens of different countries, but also the relevant state officials within them. Global fund accountants will thus need to incorporate this fact into their computations of under- and over-appropriation.[9]

Levies for that fund derive, as we've seen, from our duties correlative to everyone's original right to the global average. But the precise content of those rights and, hence, the content and incidence of those levies are not always perfectly transparent. The major sources of this opacity are reasonably obvious. We can approach them in this way.

Imagine a world where no natural resources have as yet had labour mixed with them, where these natural resources consist entirely of twelve

---

[6] In addition to the previously cited works of Walzer and Buchanan, see: Tagil, Gerner, Henrikson, Johansson, Oldberg and Salomon, *Studying Boundary Conflicts*; Brown and Shue (eds), *Boundaries*; Barry and Goodin (eds), *Free Movement*.

[7] Some of the important work in this area includes: Aiken and La Follette (eds), *World Hunger and Moral Obligation*; Schachter, *Sharing the World's Resources*; Beitz, *Political Theory and International Relations*; Shue, *Basic Rights*; Sen, *Poverty and Famine*; O'Neill, *Faces of Hunger*; Pogge, *Realizing Rawls*; Brown, *International Relations Theory*; and the essays by Barry, Nielsen, Franck, and Richards, in Pennock and Chapman (eds), *Nomos XXIV: Ethics, Economics and the Law*.

[8] See ch. 3, section (a).

[9] Broadly put, *states must pay rates*. Cf. Tideman, "Commons and Commonwealths," for an interesting account of how a mechanism like the global fund creates various benign incentive structures, including one for the peaceful resolution of international territorial disputes.

homogeneous acres and which contains only two persons, Red and Blue. Their original rights to the global average thus entitle each of them to six acres.

What if, before either of them has mixed any labour, White were to turn up as a blamelessly late third person? What are Red's and Blue's duties in respect of White's right to unowned things? A simple solution, and so the one we'll opt for, is that they each owe him two acres, leaving all of them with the new global average of four acres apiece. And if Black arrives a moment later, his original right to the global average (now three acres) is dutifully respected by each of his three predecessors giving him one acre.

But what if Black's arrival is slightly later than that? What if several pertinent things have transpired in the interval since White's appearance? One of these could be that Red has transferred not merely two, but all six, of his initial acres to White who therefore owns a total of eight. In these circumstances, Black's three-acre entitlement implies the aforesaid one-acre transfer from Blue and a *two*-acre transfer from White. Of course, if Red's voluntary transfer of the extra four acres to White was a sale, White might well be entitled to recover one quarter of what he paid for them from Red;[10] alternatively, Red might pay that amount to Black, leaving White to transfer only one acre.

Another possible development during that interval is that Blue has mixed her labour with all of her four acres, transforming them into fertile fields. In these circumstances, although what the others owe Black would still be resolvable in terms of acre-transfers, Blue's duty would not. What she owes is something *equivalent* to the one raw acre which she would have been able to transfer to Black, had she not mixed her labour so extensively. This something might be a section of one of those cultivated acres or some other labour-embodying object or some labour or some money or something else. Whatever it is, its value must not be less than that of one raw acre.

One generalization of these findings is simply that, in a fully appropriated world, each person's original right to an equal portion of initially unowned things amounts to a right to an equal share of their total *value*.[11] Correlatively, any person's possession of a just title to any such

[10] Just as a purchaser of stolen goods (i) has a duty to return them to their rightful owner, and (ii) might have a claim to reimbursement by his vendor.

[11] By "value" I mean *economic value*, i.e. price. Some earlier versions of this argument rejected this value-based interpretation of this original right, on the assumption that the distribution-relative character of prices (see ch. 5, section (d) biases them against later arrivals and, hence, disqualifies them as a just metric of their entitlements; cf. Steiner,

thing encumbers him with a duty to pay every person an equal share of its value. This interpretation of that original right is readily motivated by two real world circumstances inherently attendant on determining both the divisor and the dividend required to compute the quotient of unowned things owed to each person.[12]

The divisor must be informed by the fact that not all persons are exact contemporaries nor is their number knowable. Rather, they are respectively members of a series of indefinitely numerous and partially concurrent generations: holders of original rights arrive and depart at different times. Since persons have correlative duties to, and rights against, only those whose (adult) lives temporally overlap their own, earlier persons can acquire titles to initially unowned things, to some of which overlapping later persons have original rights against the former. Perhaps if the number of all such persons was knowable, it would in principle be possible for persons to limit their appropriations accordingly, leaving literally "enough and as good" natural resources for others. As it's not, the dominant form of those original rights increasingly becomes, with the passage of historical time, a redress claim to their equivalent value.

Correspondingly, the dividend is shaped by the fact that what count as initially unowned things are highly variable in several important respects. Natural resources, for example, are neither so nicely uniform nor so readily divisible as our twelve homogeneous raw acres. Nor, for that matter, do their respective values remain constant. Our world contains deserts and oceans, tropics and tundra, oilfields and geological faults, ozone-shaded areas and monsoon-swept regions. Acres in some of these sites are less valuable than acres in others. And these values vary with changes in the most valuable uses to which these sites can be put: uses which themselves vary with changes in technology and persons' preference functions. What doesn't change is each current person's right to an equal share of their value.

Nor is membership in the class of initially unowned things fixed and unchanging. For although sites – as spatial locations upon, above or below the earth's surface – are indestructible and therefore permanent members, other things are not. Titles to sites thus amount to leaseholds: each such owner owes to the global fund a sum equal to the site's rental value, that is, equal to the rental value of the site alone, exclusive of the

---

"Liberty and Equality," 563, and to some extent "Capitalism, Justice and Equal Starts," 65–8. I now think this assumption is groundless.

[12] "Inherently attendant" in our world, not in all logically possible worlds.

value of any alterations in it wrought by labour.[13] A very considerable literature now exists, some of it strongly influenced by the writings of Henry George, on the variety of property rights in sites, the methods for assessing their values and the forms which such payments can take.[14]

Non-permanent members of the class of initially unowned things include, as we've seen, the estates of dead persons. These comprise not only what are conventionally regarded as their belongings but also their cadavers, since their having been self-owners entails that their bodies counted among the things they owned.[15] Each of these things has an assessable value due, not least, to high levels of medical and scientific demand for human body tissue. And anyone wishing to acquire title to any of them owes that amount to the global fund.[16]

We come, finally, to an ostensibly other kind of item which our earlier discussion assigns to the class of initially unowned things, but about

[13] Is compensation for, or exemption from, this encumbrance thereby due to current owners of sites, who may have purchased them – including rights to their rental income – with the hard-earned fruits of their labour? Advocates of land nationalization or rent taxation (among them the early Herbert Spencer) were frequently pressed with this challenge by their opponents (among them the later Herbert Spencer). The response to it comes in two parts. First, this is a type of challenge facing any justice theory that underwrites labour entitlement and whose rights are at variance with those currently in force. And second, current owners may well be entitled to compensation – but, if so, it's owed by their vendors and *not* the global fund, since it's those vendors who have sold what wasn't justly theirs to sell (see n. 10, above, as well as the vindication story in ch. 3, section (d)).

[14] Cf. Gaffney (ed.), *Extractive Resources and Taxation*; Holland (ed.), *The Assessment of Land Value*; Prest, *The Taxation of Urban Land*; Lindholm and Lynn (eds), *Land Value Taxation*; Conrad and Gillis, "Progress and Poverty in Developing Countries: Rents and Resource Taxation." On legal rights to less familiar types of site, see: De Vany, Eckert, Meyers, O'Hara, and Scott, *A Property System Approach to the Electromagnetic Spectrum*; Cheng, *The Law of International Air Transport*; Garcia-Amador, *The Exploitation and Conservation of the Resources of the Sea*; Reijnen, *Utilization of Outer Space and International Law*. It should be said that very little literature on this subject – Tideman, "Commons and Commonwealths," is a notable exception – construes the fund created by these payments as a *global* one.

[15] Meyers, *The Human Body and the Law*, 101ff, notes that in English law before the nineteenth century "it was accepted that no property rights existed in a dead body, the corpse was *res nullius*"; cf. Scott, *The Body as Property*, 6–8. More recently, Harris, *The Value of Life*, 118–19, and (with Erin) "A Monopsonistic Market," has argued for the appropriability (though by nationalization) of cadavers.

[16] Nozick, *The Examined Life*, 30–3, has plausibly argued that your bequeathing things you earned can give morally valuable expression to the bonds of caring between you and your heirs – bonds which, being less salient between you and your heirs' successors, don't iteratively justify those things' further transmission by bequest. While it's difficult to see how the demands of justice can permit those of other moral values to warrant such divestments of (the claims on) the global fund, they presumably can allow a right of first refusal to such successors.

which one might expect more to have been written directly along these lines than is in fact the case.[17] My approach to it is accordingly determined but diffident. The reasons for this will presently become plain.

Germ-line genetic information, it was suggested in the previous chapter, is a natural resource. Its being so, I argued, is the reason why universal self-ownership is non-paradoxical. Of course, such information isn't confined to our own species. And especially in the case of uncultivated plant life, its value, like that of extractable mineral resources, is standardly amalgamated in the valuation of the sites where it's located.[18] Naturally verdant acres are going to be differently levied from naturally non-verdant but otherwise similar ones. And among the former, the same will be true as between acres whose vegetation would (absenting labour) reproduce itself for three hundred generations and ones whose otherwise similar vegetation would do so for only three.

The germ-line genetic information of species whose members are less closely tied to particular sites obviously doesn't lend itself to assessment in this way. Animals whose production involves no element of husbandry present no new problem in this regard since they are entirely natural resources – not products of labour – and all their attributes can be assessed conjunctively. Suppose we return Red and Blue to their initial two-person world and further populate it with two pairs of oppositely-sexed sheep.[19] If Red appropriates that pair which (unlike the pair appropriated by Blue) spontaneously produces an offspring, then he owes her some redress payment.

What if Blue does manage to augment her flock? That is, by skilful husbandry she brings about the production of a lamb which would not have been produced had her sheep been left to their own devices. Does this imply the requisite parity between Red's and Blue's natural resource holdings and thereby cancel his redress duty? No. For Blue, like everyone else, is entitled to the fruits of her labour. Red's lamb, unlike hers, is entirely a natural resource: of their six sheep, only five count as natural resources. And as Red owns three of these, he owes her redress.

But Blue's lamb is not *entirely* a labour product. Her husbanding has

---

[17] In the literature I've read, Ackerman, *Social Justice in the Liberal State*, 115–20, 129–38, comes closest. More work than could be listed here has addressed it tangentially.

[18] That is, its ownership is often included in the ownership of the site and its value is therefore represented in that owner's owed payment to the global fund. No payment to the global fund is owed by owners of things *manufactured* with the use of that germ-line genetic information, such as apple-sauce, just as nothing is owed to the global fund for the ownership of a marble sculpture.

[19] We'll assume that the sheep are valuable and not disvaluable, as various plants and animals can be in some circumstances.

consisted in using her labour and her sheep's germ-line genetic information to produce another sheep. If her sheep lacked such information, were thus barren, no amount of labouring on her part would produce this result. And her sheep would consequently be worth less – Red would owe her more – than is actually the case: in those circumstances, he would presumably owe her (the equivalent of) half a sheep. As it is, however, he owes her less than that. It is that difference, between the value of half a sheep and what Red owes Blue, that represents the value of the germ-line genetic information she used. It represents the value of that natural resource. And it will therefore need to be counted in computing the levy on Blue by the global fund which would come into operation with the subsequent arrival of White and other latecomers.

A further consideration is this. Germ-line genetic information varies between members of the same species, not only in the ease with which it can be used but also in its quality. If Blue's lamb spontaneously produces one harvestable coat of wool a year, while Red's produces two, then he owes her more redress. The germ-line genetic information borne by her sheep is less valuable because it produces less valuable somatic products.

What about us? Adult human beings, unlike sheep, are self-owned. But as we've seen, our non-paradoxically being so implies that our parents' germ-line genetic information is a natural resource, one which they use to produce us. Like Blue's lamb and unlike Red's, Cain is partly a product of human labour. And thus Adam and Eve partly own him. But not fully. Like Blue's ownership of her lamb, their ownership of Cain is an encumbered title and not an instance of full liberal ownership. In their case, that encumbrance – the thing that rids us of the paradox – consists in their ownership being temporary and expiring upon Cain's attainment of majority.

There is, however, an additional encumbrance on their ownership of Cain suggested by the foregoing discussion. Like sheep's germ-line genetic information, that employed in Cain's conception has a certain value: an amount which Adam and Eve owe to the global fund.[20] What that value is entirely depends, as with any other capital asset, upon the value

---

[20] Why should their ownership of Cain carry this second encumbrance? Doesn't this smack of double-billing? I think the answer can plausibly be "no." The amount they owe is equal to the value of this resource. As with any asset, that value varies directly with certain other variables, not least the duration of their title to Cain (and inversely with the extent, if any, to which powers to restrict their dispositions of him are vested in everyone else; see ch. 7, n. 25. Accordingly, the amount they owe is less than it would be if their ownership of him were of a longer duration (or if their powers of disposition were greater).

of what can be done with it. And what can be done with it is, these days, quite a lot of diverse things. It can be used to produce cells for experimental purposes or for innumerable kinds of gene replacement therapy.[21] Or it can be used, more conventionally, to build that entire cluster of differentiated somatic cells that will constitute Cain's body. Computation of the value of these uses evidently requires an algorithm incorporating the various production functions associated with their alternative outputs. But I think we can safely suppose that, mediately or immediately, this genetic information will be an input – a factor of production – in some body-building process.

What is the value of a body? All bodies are collections of abilities and disabilities, talents and incompetences. These vary from the highly valuable to the highly disvaluable. And parental germ-line genetic information contributes, along with many other factors, to their production. Unlike sheep, we're not genetically predisposed to grow coats of wool. But whether and to what degree we're predisposed to sing like Pavarotti, or set Olympic records, or cope with steep learning-curves, or react allergically to pollen, or contract cancer, or develop certain forms of schizophrenia, or undergo racist or sexist treatment at the hands of others, *are* at least partly determined by the parental genetic information controlling the construction of our bodies.[22]

Though not, of course, fully determined. For which set of abilities and disabilities actually gets produced depends, as in any production process, not on the characteristics of that production factor alone but also on the numerous other ones – gestational and postnatal – with which it interacts. Factoring out the contribution made to this process by any of these ingredients is a task which we all do impressionistically and which countless researchers in myriad fields do professionally. The most that needs to be said for present purposes is that such genetic information constrains the set of abilities that can be produced with it, just as the kind of steel used to build a bridge constrains its load-bearing capacity. And presumably the valuation of these abilities and disabilities is some function of what people would pay to acquire or be rid of them, or of the redress for which persons would be liable if they injured others so as to cause them losses of abilities or incurrences of disabilities.

Each person may thus be said to possess a certain level of ability-value, to the production of which his parents' germ-line genetic information has made some factorial contribution by determining the charac-

---

[21] For an extensive philosophical discussion of the moral issues raised by these possibilities, see Harris, *Wonderwoman and Superman*.

[22] Cf. Kevles and Hood (eds), *The Code of Codes*.

teristics of his genetic endowment. The value of Cain's genetic endowment is inferior to another person's, Abel's, if the cost of using it to produce a given level of ability-value is greater than the cost of using Abel's. Accordingly and if Cain's endowment is indeed inferior to Abel's, the ownership of Abel is encumbered with a heavier global fund levy than is the ownership of Cain. And the aggregate consequence of this is therefore to redistribute wealth, via the global fund, from those adults who own children with superior genetic endowments to those who don't.

What the global fund does not do is redistribute from adults who own children with superior levels of *ability*. The global fund is not a mechanism for "talent pooling."[23] Certainly not for pooling adults' talents nor even for pooling their children's. All that the global fund pools is (the value of) parents' germ-line genetic information. For children's abilities, and their somatic characteristics in general, are labour products: products whose factors are, so to speak, entirely bought and paid for by their parents once they've paid what they owe to the global fund.

As my rather laboured foregoing argument has tried to show, everything here turns on the isolation of what counts as "natural." In this regard, much that's been written on redistributive justice in this general area strikes me as insufficiently attentive to the importance of distinguishing not only between the ability levels of children and those of adults, but also between those factors of children's ability levels that are imputable to nature and those which aren't. A good deal of this literature brings the problem of differential abilities under the apparently wider issue of the just distribution of (the consequences of) *luck*. Are one's abilities a matter of luck? Is luck deserved? And whether or not deserved, does justice require that its consequences accrue to those who incur it (as Nozick would have it), or that they be pooled and thereby equalized (or, as Rawls would have it, equalized up to the threshold where equality is overridden by the demands of the "difference principle")?

Some of these arguments begin, promisingly enough, by hypothesizing an equal division of natural resources. But their subsequent reasoning about luck-distribution is often impaired by an insufficient appreciation of what (how much) that hypothesis implies. For the things that happen to people are standardly factorable into their own doings, the doings of others and the doings of nature. Of these, adverse factors of the first

---

[23] This apt phrase is due to Kronman, "Talent Pooling," 59, who describes it as "the idea that a person's natural abilities and disabilities should be treated as part of a common fund in which all share equally."

sort cannot (logically) occasion bilateral redress, since persons cannot have rights against themselves. Nor, for the same reason, can such factors occasion multilateral redress since that too presupposes that persons have rights against themselves: rights that (paternalistically) mandate compelling them to insure themselves against their own doings. Adverse factors of the second sort, the doings of others, *do* warrant redress. But that redress is justly bilateral – owed by those others – and not multilateral, for similar anti-paternalistic reasons.[24]

Which brings us to the third factor. The adverse (and benign) things that happen to people due to the doings of nature mostly happen to them by virtue of where they are. And an equal division of nature takes account of this. Thus a site on the Bangladeshi coast, being one acre in size, is not thereby equal to an acre in the Iowa cornbelt, the Arctic tundra, the Saudi Arabian desert or the heart of Tokyo. People looking to invest their money in the purchase of sites plainly know this. It's true that neither the full inventory of things (mineral deposits, mosquitoes, viruses, geological faults, long-range climatic conditions) they're thereby acquiring, nor how the value of those sites will also be affected by future scientific discoveries and varying patterns of social interaction, may or can be known at that time. Hence these may indeed be matters of luck. But provided they continue to pay the global fund levy on the current value of those sites, there seems no just reason why those owners should be further required to pool any gains and losses which such luck makes possible.

Neither children nor their ability levels are principally deliverances of luck. Eric Rakowski is surely correct to insist that

babies are not brought by storks whose whims are beyond our control. Specific individuals are responsible for their existence. It is therefore unjust to declare ... that because two people decide to have a child, or through carelessness find themselves with one, *everyone* is required to share their resources with the new arrival, and to the same extent as its parents. With what right can two people force all the rest, through deliberate behavior rather than

---

[24] The paternalistic reason for compulsory insurance against the adverse doings of others is, presumably, the risk of those others being unable to redress their victims. *Voluntary* insurance against self- and other-inflicted adversities is, of course, another matter.

bad brute luck, to settle for less than their fair shares after
resources have been divided justly?[25]

Children are labour products who are produced from *inter alia* natural
objects: objects to which their parents are in uniquely close proximity!
The differentials between persons' owned portions of nature, including
the natural factors appropriated for the production of their offspring,
are pooled by the global fund in the form of its differential levies on,
among others, parents of differentially genetically endowed children.
They are the ones who, duly equalized in this respect, go on to build
their children's abilities. So their abilities, like their birthday parties,
though not *deserved* by those children, are nevertheless deserved, i.e. by
their parents.

In general, the global fund levy on the ownership of natural resources
simply *is* a pooling of what Ronald Dworkin calls "brute luck" and
which he distinguishes from "option luck" (the luck of gamblers and
others who choose risky activities), the incurred consequences of which,
most agree, are not items which justice requires us to pool.[26] Failure to
take this on board in theories that purport to pool natural resources,
tends to result in their generating incompossible rights: ones which are
incompossible not only with persons' rights to self-ownership and the
fruits of their labour – rights which anyway enjoy, at most, a residual
and much truncated existence in such theories – but also with their rights
to equal natural resources.

All of that said, however, it should also be said that in a world of
generally redressed injustices – one where persons' current holdings are
no longer tainted by past or present bilateral rights-violations and
exploitations, as well as detentions of what is owed to the global fund –
there would be strong grounds for predicting that the operation of the
global fund would *superveniently* effect a pooling of children's talents.
That is, we might expect a much closer correlation between their genetic
differentials and their ability level differentials.

Why? Because as a matter of empirical conjecture, it would be surprising if the redistributive effects of such redress, particularly when secured
on a global scale, did not include an extensive dispersal of currently
concentrated holdings, a considerable reduction in inequalities of

[25] Rakowski, *Equal Justice*, 153. See also his remarks (154) on pregnancies due to rape
or failed contraceptive devices: remarks with which I largely agree, save for their suggestion
that children have rights – a suggestion ultimately sustained by the assumption that moral
rights can be incompossible (cf. 97, 336, 359).
[26] Dworkin, "What is Equality? Part 2: Equality of Resources," 293.

ownership. And it would thus be reasonable to suppose that the impact of this dispersal on opportunity costs, including those of producing a given level of ability in their children, would be downward for many more (largely poorer) persons than those (largely wealthier) for whom it would be upward. Having command over more/better production factors to combine with their children's genetic endowments, more people would have to sacrifice less to raise children who were healthier, more skilled and better informed.

In general, children's ability level differentials would be narrowed. And a result of both this and the broader economic redistribution engendering it would be that their positions at the starting-gate of adult life – the realm of choice-making – would be significantly less unequal. A world thus redressed, we might speculate, promises some not insubstantial expression of the maxim "From each as they choose, to each as they are chosen."[27] Nature's impact on persons' destinies having been equalized for all choosers, their choices would be left to determine the rest.

Over the years of writing this book, I've sometimes wondered whether that redressed world is better described as "capitalist" or "socialist." More recently this has perhaps become a less engaging question than it once seemed to be. In what he and others have taken to be a justification of fairly unalloyed capitalism, Nozick writes:

> One traditional socialist view is that workers are entitled to the product and full fruits of their labor; they have earned it; a distribution is unjust if it does not give the workers what they are entitled to. Such entitlements are based upon some past history ... This socialist rightly, in my view, holds onto the notions of earning, producing, entitlement, desert, and so forth.[28]

What, we might well ask, ever became of that socialist?

This is hardly the place, nor am I competent, to begin unravelling the tangled histories of political ideals enmeshed, as they invariably are, in both the exigencies (real or imagined) of contemporaneous events and the claims of theories (true or false) concerning the scope for moral action, to say nothing of the sometimes horrific operations of sheer power and political opportunism. Nevertheless it's worth noting that,

[27] The maxim is from Nozick, *Anarchy, State and Utopia*, 160.
[28] Nozick, *Anarchy, State and Utopia*, 154–5.

almost a century ago in his introduction to the English translation of
Anton Menger's *The Right to the Whole Produce of Labour*, H. S.
Foxwell observed that this historical survey of socialist doctrines "leaves
us with the conception of two great principles which dispute for primacy, the right to subsistence and the right to the whole produce of
labour. These two claims he clearly shows to be inconsistent both in
theory and in practice, in spirit and in effect."[29] Nearly half a century
earlier, the (then) radically individualist Herbert Spencer had declared
that

> we must not overlook the fact that, erroneous as are these poor-
> law and communist theories – these assertions of a man's right to
> a maintenance, and of his right to have work provided for him –
> they are, nevertheless, nearly related to a truth. They are unsuccess-
> ful efforts to express the fact, that whoso is born on this planet of
> ours thereby obtains some interest in it – may not be summarily
> dismissed again – may not have his existence ignored by those in
> possession. In other words, they are attempts to embody that
> thought which finds its legitimate utterance in the law – all men
> have equal rights to the use of the Earth.[30]

Nor is the distinct sense engendered by these reflections – of a road not
taken – less sharpened by even a passing acquaintance with the career
of Henry George and the vicissitudinary reception of his ideas. That
their current location on the conventional "left–right" spectrum is so
indeterminate, is only one of the more eloquent testimonies to its inad-
equacy.[31]

So I'm driven to conclude that the only doctrinal label to which the
theory of justice advanced here comfortably answers (if it answers to

[29] Menger, *The Right to the Whole Produce of Labour*, xx; cf. Trowbridge, *Bisocialism*.

[30] Spencer, *Social Statics*, 315. On Spencer's later renunciation of this position and, more
generally, on the late nineteenth-century transmogrification of radical individualism, see
Taylor, *Men Versus the State*, ch. 7.

[31] Of the several biographies of George, Barker's *Henry George* remains the most comprehensive. Some anticipators of his theory, as well as some proponents of his or similar
views, are indicated above in ch. 7, n. 13. George himself twice ran for the mayoralty of
New York City as the candidate of labour-backed parties and exerted a formative influence
on turn-of-the-century British socialists. His proposals numbered among their active advocates John Dewey on the one hand and, on the other, such arch-opponents of the welfare
state as the essayists Albert Jay Nock and Frank Chodorov (the latter's chief contribution
to political thought being his hyperbolically entitled work, *The Income Tax: Root of All
Evil*). Cf. Hellman, *Henry George Reconsidered*, for a good recent account of the changing
fortunes of the Georgist movement.

any of these porosities) is that of *liberalism* and, amongst liberalisms, that of classical *laisser faire* liberalism of the natural rights-based kind. True, it mandates a far more extensive redistribution, and one more globally directed, than anything contemplated by recent, much less earlier, classical liberals. But it is led to do so by deploying the same conceptual apparatus – the same (Choice Theory) model of rights, the same historical entitlement structuring of those rights, and virtually the same foundational rights – as is to be found in their writings. Its principal difference from them lies in its more inclusive interpretation of what counts as "nature," as well as its unequivocal (Choice Theory-based) denial that moral rights can be ascribed to the dead.

Like classical liberalism, it's not derived from any particular conception of what constitutes "a good life" – that is, from any theory of how people should exercise their moral rights – though it's not thereby unreceptive to these. For similar reasons and because it is an exploration of justice alone, none of its derivation relies upon premises about the diverse incentive structures which such a set of rights might be expected to put in place and how these might affect different types and levels of social activity and personal wellbeing. Many of these are extensively discussed in various economics literatures.

What I've tried to do in this book is to give reasons why that set of rights is just. I've offered no reasons as to why we should *be* just. Nor do I think that any can be found.

Bibliography

Ackerman, Bruce. *Social Justice in the Liberal State* (New Haven: Yale University Press, 1980).

Aiken, William and La Follette, Hugh (eds). *World Hunger and Moral Obligation* (Englewood Cliffs: Prentice Hall, 1977).

Alchian, Armen and Allen, William. *University Economics* (Belmont: Wadsworth, 1964).

Andelson, Robert (ed.). *Critics of Henry George* (London: Associated University Presses, 1979).

—— (ed.). *Commons Without Tragedy* (London: Shepheard-Walwyn, 1991).

Anderson, B., Deane, D., Hammond, K., McClelland, G., and Shanteau, J. *Concepts in Judgement and Decision Research* (New York: Praeger, 1981).

Aristotle. *Nicomachean Ethics*, transl. Sir David Ross (Oxford: Oxford University Press, 1954).

Arneson, Richard. "Freedom and Desire," *Canadian Journal of Philosophy*, 15 (1985), 425–48.

—— "Property Rights in Persons," *Social Philosophy and Policy*, 9 (1992), 201–30.

Arrow, Kenneth. "Alternative Approaches to the Theory of Choice in Risk-Taking Situations," *Econometrica*, 19 (1951), 404–37.

—— "Gifts and Exchanges," *Philosophy and Public Affairs*, 1 (1972), 343–62.

Arthur, Wallace. *Theories of Life* (Harmondsworth: Penguin, 1987).

Ashworth, Andrew. *Principles of Criminal Law* (Oxford: Oxford University Press, 1991).

Atiyah, P. S. *Promises, Morals and Law* (Oxford: Oxford University Press, 1981).

Aune, Bruce. *Kant's Theory of Morals* (Princeton: Princeton University Press, 1979).

Aylmer, G. E. (ed.). *The Levellers in the English Revolution* (London: Thames and Hudson, 1975).

Bacharach, Michael. *Economics and the Theory of Games* (London: Macmillan, 1976).

——— and Hurley, Susan (eds). *Foundations of Decision Theory* (Oxford: Blackwell, 1991).

Banerjee, D. "Choice and Order: Or First Things First," *Economica*, 31 (1964), 158–67.

Barker, Charles. *Henry George* (New York: Oxford University Press, 1955).

Barker, Stephen. *Philosophy of Mathematics* (Englewood Cliffs: Prentice Hall, 1964).

Barry, Brian. *Theories of Justice* (Hemel Hempstead: Harvester Wheatsheaf, 1989).

——— and Goodin, Robert (eds). *Free Movement* (Hemel Hempstead: Harvester Wheatsheaf, 1992).

Becker, Gary. "Crime and Punishment: An Economic Approach," *Journal of Political Economy*, 76 (1968), 169–217.

Becker, Lawrence. *Property Rights* (London: Routledge & Kegan Paul, 1977).

——— and Kipnis, Kenneth (eds). *Property: Cases, Concepts, Critiques* (Englewood Cliffs: Prentice Hall, 1984).

Beer, Max (ed.). *The Pioneers of Land Reform* (London: G. Bell & Sons, 1920).

Beitz, Charles. *Political Theory and International Relations* (Princeton: Princeton University Press, 1979).

Benn, S. I. and Weinstein, W. L. "Being Free to Act and Being a Free Man," *Mind*, lxxx (1971), 194–211.

Bentham, Jeremy. "Anarchical Fallacies," in *The Works of Jeremy Bentham*, vol. II, ed. John Bowring (Edinburgh: William Tait, 1843).

——— *An Introduction to the Principles of Morals and Legislation*, eds. J. H. Burns and H. L. A. Hart (London: Athlone Press, 1970).

Berlin, Isaiah. *Two Concepts of Liberty* (Oxford: Oxford University Press, 1958).

——— *Four Essays on Liberty* (Oxford: Oxford University Press, 1969).

Boland, Lawrence. *The Principles of Economics: Some Lies My Teachers Told Me* (London: Routledge, 1992).

Borch, Karl. *The Economics of Uncertainty* (Princeton: Princeton University Press, 1968).

Brown, Christopher. *International Relations Theory* (Hemel Hempstead: Harvester Wheatsheaf, 1992).

Brown, Harold. "Incommensurability," *Inquiry*, 26 (1983), 3–29.

Brown, Peter and Shue, Henry (eds). *Boundaries* (Totowa: Rowman & Littlefield, 1981).

Buchanan, Allen. *Ethics, Efficiency and the Market* (Oxford: Oxford University Press, 1985).

——— *Secession* (Boulder: Westview, 1991).

Buchanan, James. *The Limits of Liberty* (Chicago: University of Chicago Press, 1975).

Bush, Winston. "Individual Welfare in Anarchy," in Tullock (ed.).

Castaneda, Hector-Neri. "'Ought' and 'Better,'" *Analysis*, 34 (1973), 50–5.

——— *The Structure of Morality* (Springfield: Charles Thomas, 1974).

Cheng, Bin. *The Law of International Air Transport* (London: Stevens & Sons, 1962).

Chipman, John. "The Foundations of Utility," *Econometrica*, 28 (1960), 193–224.

—— "The Nature and Meaning of Equilibrium in Economic Theory," in Townsend (ed.).

—— "On the Lexicographic Representation of Preference Orderings," in Chipman, Hurwicz, Richter and Sonnenschein (eds).

——, Hurwicz, L., Richter, M., and Sonnenschein, H. (eds). *Preferences, Utility and Demand* (New York: Harcourt Brace Jovanovich, 1971).

Chisholm, Roderick. "Practical Reasoning and the Logic of Requirement," in Korner (ed.).

Cohen, G. A. "Self-Ownership, World-Ownership and Equality," in Lucash (ed.).

—— *History, Labour and Freedom* (Oxford: Oxford University Press, 1988).

Cohen, Joshua. "The Economic Basis of Deliberative Democracy," *Social Philosophy and Policy*, 6 (1989), 25–50.

Cohen, Morris. *Reason and Law* (New York: Collier, 1961).

—— and Nagel, Ernest. *Introduction to Logic and Scientific Method* (London: Routledge & Kegan Paul, 1966).

Conrad, Robert and Gillis, Malcolm. "Progress and Poverty in Developing Countries: Rents and Resource Taxation," in Lewis (ed.).

Cunliffe, John. "A Mutualist Theory of Exploitation," in Reeve (ed.).

—— "The Liberal Rationale of Rational Socialism," *Political Studies*, xxxvi (1988), 653–62.

—— "Intergenerational Justice and Productive Resources," *History of European Ideas*, 12 (1990), 227–38.

—— "The Neglected Background of Radical Liberalism: P. E. Dove's Theory of Property," *History of Political Thought*, xi (1990), 467–90.

David, P., Gutman, H., Sutch, R., Temin, P., and Wright, G. *Reckoning with Slavery* (New York: Oxford University Press, 1976).

Davidson, D., McKinsey, J., and Suppes, P. "Outlines of a Formal Theory of Value," *Philosophy of Science*, 22 (1955), 140–60.

Day, J. P. "On Liberty and the Real Will," *Philosophy*, xlv (1970), 177–92.

—— "Threats, Offers, Law, Opinion and Liberty," *American Philosophical Quarterly*, 14 (1977), 257–72.

Chodorov, Frank. *The Income Tax: Root of All Evil* (New York: Devin Adair, 1954).

De Vany, A., Eckert, R., Meyers, C., O'Hara, D., and Scott, R. *A Property System Approach to the Electromagnetic Spectrum* (San Francisco: Cato Institute, 1980).

Debreu, Gerard. "Representation of a Preference Ordering by a Numerical Function," in Thrall, Coombs and Davies (eds).

—— *Theory of Value*, Cowles Foundation Monograph 17 (New York: John Wiley, 1959).

del Vecchio, Giorgio. *Justice*, ed. A. H. Campbell (Edinburgh: Edinburgh University Press, 1952).

Dove, Patrick. *The Theory of Human Progression and Natural Probability of a Reign of Justice: The Science of Politics, Part I* (London: Johnstone & Hunter, 1850).

—— *The Elements of Politics: The Science of Politics*, Part II (Edinburgh: Johnstone & Hunter, 1854).

Dworkin, Ronald. *Taking Rights Seriously* (London: Duckworth, 1977).

—— "What is Equality? Part 2: Equality of Resources," *Philosophy and Public Affairs*, 10 (1981), 283–345.

—— "Is There a Right to Pornography?," *Oxford Journal of Legal Studies*, 1 (1981), 177–212.

Dyke, C. *Philosophy of Economics* (Englewood Cliffs: Prentice Hall, 1981).

Edgeworth, Francis. *Mathematical Psychics* (London: C. Kegan Paul, 1881).

Edwards, Ward. "The Theory of Decision Making," in Edwards and Tversky (eds).

—— and Tversky, Amos (eds). *Decision Making* (Harmondsworth: Penguin, 1967).

Eells, Ellery. *Rational Decision and Causality* (Cambridge: Cambridge University Press, 1982).

Ehrlich, Isaac. "Participation in Illegitimate Activities: A Theoretical and Empirical Investigation," *Journal of Political Economy*, 81 (1973), 521–65.

Elster, Jon. *Ulysses and the Sirens* (Cambridge: Cambridge University Press, 1979).

Ely, Richard. *Property and Contract* (1914) vol. 1 (London: Kennikat, 1971).

Epstein, Richard. "Possession as the Root of Title," *Georgia Law Review*, 13 (1979), 1221–43.

—— *Takings* (Cambridge, Mass.: Harvard University Press, 1985).

Escott, Paul. *Slavery Remembered* (Chapel Hill: University of North Carolina Press, 1979).

Feinberg, Joel. *Social Philosophy* (Englewood Cliffs: Prentice Hall, 1978).

Filmer, Robert. *Patriarcha and Other Writings*, ed. Johann Sommerville (Cambridge: Cambridge University Press, 1991).

Fishkin, James. *Justice, Equal Opportunity and the Family* (New Haven: Yale University Press, 1983).

Fitzgerald, P. J. *Criminal Law and Punishment* (Oxford: Oxford University Press, 1962).

Flathman, Richard. *The Practice of Rights* (Cambridge: Cambridge University Press, 1976).

—— *The Philosophy and Politics of Freedom* (Chicago: University of Chicago Press, 1987).

Fogel, Robert. *Without Consent or Contract* (New York: W. W. Norton, 1989).

—— and Engerman, Stanley. *Time on the Cross* (Boston: Little, Brown & Co., 1974).

Foner, Philip (ed.). *The Life and Major Writings of Thomas Paine* (Secaucus: Citadel, 1974).

Frankena, William. *Ethics* (Englewood Cliffs: Prentice Hall, 1973).

Fuller, Lon. *Legal Fictions* (Stanford: Stanford University Press, 1967).

Fung, Yuan-Cheng. *Biomechanics: Motion, Flow, Stress and Growth* (New York: Springer Verlag, 1981).

Gaffney, Mason (ed.). *Extractive Resources and Taxation* (Madison: University of Wisconsin Press, 1967).

Garcia-Amador, Francisco. *The Exploitation and Conservation of the Resources of the Sea* (Leyden: Sythoff, 1963).

Geiger, George. *The Philosophy of Henry George* (New York: Macmillan, 1933).

George, Henry. *Progress and Poverty*, 1879 (London: William Reeves, 1884).

—— *Social Problems* (London: Henry George Foundation, 1931).

Georgescu-Roegen, Nicholas. *Analytical Economics* (Cambridge, Mass.: Harvard University Press, 1967).

—— "Measure, Quality and Optimum Scale," in Rao (ed.).

Geras, Norman. "Private Property and Moral Equality," in Moran and Wright (eds).

Gewirth, Alan. *Reason and Morality* (Chicago: University of Chicago Press, 1978).

Gibbard, Alan. "Natural Property Rights," *Nous*, 10 (1976), 77–86.

Goebel, Julius. *Felony and Misdemeanor: A Study in the History of Criminal Law* (Philadelphia: University of Pennsylvania Press, 1976).

Goldman, Alvin and Kim, Jaegwon (eds). *Values and Morals* (Dordrecht: D. Reidel, 1978).

Gorr, Michael. *Coercion, Freedom and Exploitation* (New York: Peter Lang, 1989).

Gowans, Christopher (ed.). *Moral Dilemmas* (Oxford: Oxford University Press, 1987).

Graham, Keith. "Democracy, Paradox and the Real World," *Aristotelian Society Proceedings*, lxxvi (1976), 227–45.

Gravelle, H. and Rees, R. *Microeconomics* (London: Longman, 1981).

Gray, John. "On Negative and Positive Liberty," *Political Studies*, 28 (1980), 507–26.

Gray, John Chipman. *The Nature and Sources of the Law* (New York: Macmillan, 1921).

Green, T. H. *The Works of Thomas Hill Green*, vol. III, ed. R. L. Nettleship (London: Longmans Green, 1906).

Gregor, Mary. *Laws of Freedom* (Oxford: Blackwell, 1963).

Griffin, James. *Well-Being* (Oxford: Oxford University Press, 1987).

Guest, A.G. (ed.). *Oxford Essays in Jurisprudence*, First Series (Oxford: Oxford University Press, 1961).

Hacker, P. M. S. and Raz, J. (eds). *Law, Morality and Society* (Oxford: Oxford University Press, 1977).

Hahn, Frank. "General Equilibrium Theory" *The Public Interest*, special issue on "The Crisis in Economic Theory" (1980), 123–39.

—— "Benevolence," in Meeks (ed.).

Hare, R. M. *The Language of Morals* (Oxford: Oxford University Press, 1952).
—— *Freedom and Reason* (Oxford: Oxford University Press, 1963).
—— *Essays on the Moral Concepts* (London: Macmillan, 1972).
—— "Relevance," in Goldman and Kim (eds).
—— *Moral Thinking* (Oxford: Oxford University Press, 1981).
Hargreaves Heap, S., Hollis, M., Lyons, B., Sugden, R., and Weale, A. *The Theory of Choice* (Oxford: Blackwell, 1992).
Harris, John. *The Value of Life* (London: Routledge & Kegan Paul, 1985).
—— *Wonderwoman and Superman* (Oxford: Oxford University Press, 1992).
—— and Erin, Charles. "A Monopsonistic Market," in I. Robinson (ed.).
Hart, H. L. A. "Are There Any Natural Rights?" *Philosophical Review*, lxiv (1955), 175–91.
—— "Bentham on Legal Rights," reprinted in his *Essays on Bentham* (Oxford: Oxford University Press, 1982).
—— *Essays in Jurisprudence and Philosophy* (Oxford: Oxford Universty Press, 1985).
Haslett, D. W. "Is Inheritance Justified?" *Philosophy and Public Affairs*, 15 (1986), 122–55.
Hellman, Rhoda. *Henry George Reconsidered* (New York: Carlton Press, 1987).
Hicks, John. *Value and Capital* (Oxford: Oxford University Press, 1946).
—— *A Revision of Demand Theory* (Oxford: Oxford University Press, 1959).
Hobbes, Thomas. *Leviathan*, ed. Michael Oakeshott (Oxford: Blackwell, 1946).
Hohfeld, Wesley. *Fundamental Legal Conceptions*, ed. W. W. Cook (New Haven: Yale University Press, 1919).
Holland, Daniel (ed.). *The Assessment of Land Value* (Madison: University of Wisconsin Press, 1970).
Holland, T. E. *The Elements of Jurisprudence*, 10th edn (Oxford: Oxford University Press, 1906).
Hollis, Martin and Nell, Edward. *Rational Economic Man* (Cambridge: Cambridge University Press, 1975).
Holmes, Oliver Wendell. *The Common Law*, ed. M. D. Howe (London: Macmillan, 1968).
Honoré, A.M. "Ownership," in Guest (ed.).
Hume, David. *A Treatise of Human Nature*, ed. L. A. Selby-Bigge (Oxford: Oxford University Press, 1988).
Ingram, Attracta. *A Political Theory of Rights* (Oxford: Oxford University Press, forthcoming).
Jacob, François. *The Logic of Life* (New York: Vintage Books, 1973).
Jeffrey, Richard. *The Logic of Decision*, 2nd edn (Chicago: University of Chicago Press, 1983).
Kagan, Shelly. *The Limits of Morality* (Oxford: Oxford University Press, 1989).
Kant, Immanuel. *The Philosophy of Law*, ed. W. Hastie (Edinburgh: T. & T. Clark, 1887).
—— *Foundations of the Metaphysics of Morals*, transl. and ed. Lewis White Beck (Indianapolis: Bobbs-Merrill, 1959).
—— *Lectures on Ethics*, transl. Louis Infield (New York: Harper & Row, 1963).

—— *The Metaphysical Principles of Virtue*, ed. Warner Wick (Indianapolis: Bobbs-Merrill, 1964).

—— *The Metaphysical Elements of Justice*, transl. and ed. John Ladd (Indianapolis: Bobbs-Merrill, 1965).

—— *The Metaphysics of Morals*, transl. and ed. Mary Gregor (Cambridge: Cambridge University Press, 1991).

Kauder, Emil. *A History of Marginal Utility Theory* (Princeton: Princeton University Press, 1965).

Kearns, Thomas. "Rights, Benefits and Normative Systems," *Archiv für Rechts- und Sozialphilosophie*, lxi (1975), 465–84.

Kelsen, Hans. *General Theory of Law and State* (New York: Russell & Russell, 1961).

Kevles, Daniel and Hood, Leroy (eds). *The Code of Codes* (Cambridge, Mass.: Harvard University Press, 1992).

Kirzner, Israel. *The Economic Point of View* (Princeton: Van Nostrand, 1960).

Kocourek, Albert. *Jural Relations*, 2nd edn (Indianapolis: Bobbs-Merrill, 1928).

Korner, Stephan (ed.). *Practical Reason* (Oxford: Blackwell, 1974).

Kronman, Anthony. "Talent Pooling," in Pennock and Chapman (eds), *Nomos XXIII: Human Rights*.

Laslett, Peter and Fishkin, James (eds). *Justice Between Age Groups and Generations* (New Haven: Yale University Press, 1992).

—— and Runciman, W. G. (eds). *Philosophy, Politics and Society*, Second Series (Oxford: Blackwell, 1967).

Lawson, F. H. *Introduction to the Law of Property* (Oxford: Oxford University Press, 1958).

Lewis, David. "Causal Decision Theory," *Australasian Journal of Philosophy*, 58 (1981), 5–30.

Lewis, Stephen (ed.). *Henry George and Contemporary Economic Development* (Williamstown: Williams College monograph, 1985).

Lindahl, Lars. *Position and Change* (Dordrecht: D. Reidel, 1977).

Lindholm, Richard and Lynn, Arthur (eds). *Land Value Taxation* (Madison: University of Wisconsin Press, 1982).

Locke, John. *Two Treatises of Government*, ed. Peter Laslett (Cambridge: Cambridge University Press, 1967).

—— *An Essay Concerning Human Understanding*, ed. Peter Nidditch (Oxford: Oxford University Press, 1975).

Lucash, Frank (ed.). *Justice and Equality Here and Now* (Ithaca: Cornell University Press, 1986).

Lukes, Steven and Galnoor, Itzhak. *No Laughing Matter: A Collection of Political Jokes* (Harmondsworth: Penguin, 1987).

Lyons, David. "Rights, Claimants and Beneficiaries," *American Philosophical Quarterly*, 6 (1969), 173–85.

MacCormick, D. N. "Rights in Legislation," in Hacker and Raz (eds).

Machan, Tibor (ed.). *The Libertarian Reader* (Totowa: Rowman & Littlefield, 1982).

MacIntyre, Alasdair. *After Virtue* (Notre Dame: University of Notre Dame Press, 1981).

Magner, Lois. *A History of the Life Sciences* (New York: Marcel Dekker, 1979).

Maine, Henry. *Ancient Law*, 10th edn (London: John Murray, 1907).

Marey, E. J. *Movement* (London: Heinemann, 1895).

Marshall, Alfred. *Principles of Economics*, 8th edn (London: Macmillan, 1966).

Marshall, Geoffrey. "Rights, Options and Entitlements," in Simpson (ed.).

Marx, Karl. "Debates on Freedom of the Press, 1842," in *Karl Marx/Friedrich Engels Collected Works*, vol. 1 (London: Lawrence & Wishart, 1975).

Mates, Benson. *The Philosophy of Leibniz: Metaphysics and Language* (Oxford: Oxford University Press, 1986).

May, Kenneth. "Transitivity, Utility and Aggregation in Preference Theory," *Econometrica*, 22 (1954), 1–13.

Maynard Smith, John. *The Problems of Biology* (Oxford: Oxford University Press, 1986).

Meeks, Gay (ed.). *Thoughtful Economic Man* (Cambridge: Cambridge University Press, 1991).

Menger, Anton. *The Right to the Whole Produce of Labour*, Intro. H. S. Foxwell (London: Macmillan, 1899).

Meyers, David. *The Human Body and the Law* (Edinburgh: Edinburgh University Press, 1970).

Michalos, Alex. *Foundations of Decision-Making* (Ottawa: Canadian Library of Philosophy, 1978).

Mill, John Stuart. *A System of Logic*, vol. II (London: Parker, Son, and Bourn, 1862).

—— *Autobiography* (New York: New American Library, 1964).

Miller, David. *Social Justice* (Oxford: Oxford University Press, 1976).

—— *Philosophy and Ideology in Hume's Political Thought* (Oxford: Oxford University Press, 1981).

—— "Constraints on Freedom," *Ethics*, 94 (1983), 66–86.

—— *Market, State and Community* (Oxford: Oxford University Press, 1989).

—— (ed.). *Liberty* (Oxford: Oxford University Press, 1991).

Miller, Fred. "The Natural Right to Private Property," in Machan (ed.).

Monod, Jacques. *Chance and Necessity* (London: Collins, 1972).

Moran, Michael and Wright, Maurice (eds). *The Market and the State* (London: Macmillan, 1991).

Murphy, Jeffrie. *Kant: The Philosophy of Right* (London: Macmillan, 1970).

Narveson, Jan. *The Libertarian Idea* (Philadelphia: Temple University Press, 1988).

Nell, Onora (O'Neill). *Acting on Principle* (New York: Columbia University Press, 1975).

Nelson, Leonard. *Critique of Practical Reason* (Scarsdale: Leonard Nelson Foundation, 1970).

Newman, Peter. *The Theory of Exchange* (Englewood Cliffs: Prentice Hall, 1965).

—— and Read, Ronald. "Representation Problems for Preference Orderings," *Journal of Economic Behaviour*, 1 (1961), 149–69.

Nozick, Robert. *Anarchy, State and Utopia* (Oxford: Blackwell, 1974).
—— *The Examined Life* (New York: Simon & Schuster, 1989).
Ogden, C. K. *Bentham's Theory of Fictions* (London: Kegan Paul, 1932).
Ogilvie, William. "An Essay on the Right of Property in Land" (1781), in Beer (ed.).
Okin, Susan Moller. *Justice, Gender and the Family* (New York: Basic Books, 1989).
O'Neill, Onora. "The Most Extensive Liberty," *Aristotelian Society Proceedings*, lxxx (1980), 45–59.
—— *Faces of Hunger* (London: George Allen & Unwin, 1986).
—— *Constructions of Reason* (Cambridge: Cambridge University Press, 1989).
—— "Magic Associations and Imperfect People," in Barry and Goodin (eds).
Overton, Richard. "An Arrow Against All Tyrants" (1646), in Aylmer (ed.).
Paine, Thomas. "Agrarian Justice" (1796), in Beer (ed.).
—— "The Rights of Man," in Foner (ed.).
Pareto, Vilfredo. *Manual of Political Economy*, transl. A. S. Schwier (London: Macmillan, 1972).
Parfit, Derek. *Reasons and Persons* (Oxford: Oxford University Press, 1984).
Paton, G. W. *A Text-book of Jurisprudence* (Oxford: Oxford University Press, 1972).
Pearce, David (ed.). *Dictionary of Modern Economics* (London: Macmillan, 1983).
Pennock, Roland, and Chapman, John (eds). *Nomos XXIII: Human Rights* (New York: New York University Press, 1981).
—— *Nomos XXIV: Ethics, Economics and the Law* (New York: New York University Press, 1982).
Pennycuick, C. J. *Newton Rules Biology* (Oxford: Oxford University Press, 1992).
Perelman, Chaim. *The Idea of Justice and the Problem of Argument* (London: Routledge & Kegan Paul, 1963).
Pettit, Philip. "Decision Theory and Folk Psychology," in Bacharach and Hurley (eds).
Phillips Griffiths, A (ed.). *Of Liberty*, Royal Institute of Philosophy Lectures (Cambridge: Cambridge University Press, 1983).
Pilon, Roger. "Property and Constitutional Principles," *Wall Street Journal*, 28 February 1992.
Pitt, Joseph (ed.). *Philosophy in Economics* (Dordrecht: D. Reidel, 1981).
Plant, Raymond. *Modern Political Thought* (Oxford: Blackwell, 1991).
Pogge, Thomas. *Realizing Rawls* (Ithaca: Cornell University Press, 1989).
Pollock, Lansing. *The Freedom Principle* (Buffalo: Prometheus Books, 1981).
Prest, Alan. *The Taxation of Urban Land* (Manchester: Manchester University Press, 1981).
Quine, W. V. O. *Theories and Things* (Cambridge, Mass.: Harvard University Press, 1981).
Rakowski, Eric. *Equal Justice* (Oxford: Oxford University Press, 1991).

Rao, C. R. (ed.). *Essays on Econometrics and Planning* (Oxford: Oxford University Press, 1964).

Rawls, John. *A Theory of Justice* (Oxford: Oxford University Press, 1972).

Raz, Joseph. *The Authority of Law* (Oxford: Oxford University Press, 1979).

—— "On the Nature of Rights," *Mind*, xciii (1984), 194–214.

—— *The Morality of Freedom* (Oxford: Oxford University Press, 1986.

Reeve, Andrew (ed.). *Modern Theories of Exploitation* (Los Angeles: Sage, 1987).

Reichenbach, Hans. *The Philosophy of Space and Time* (New York: Dover, 1958).

Reijnen, Gijsbertha. *Utilization of Outer Space and International Law* (Amsterdam: Elsevier, 1981).

Rennie, M. K. "On Hare's 'Better,'" *Nous*, 2 (1968), 75–9.

Robbins, Lionel. *An Essay on the Nature and Significance of Economic Science* (London: Macmillan, 1935).

Robinson, Ian (ed.). *The Social Consequences of Life and Death under High Technology Medicine* (Manchester: Manchester University Press, in press).

Robinson, Joan. *Essays on the Theory of Economic Growth* (London: Macmillan, 1962).

Rosenberg, Alexander. *Microeconomic Laws* (Pittsburgh: University of Pittsburgh Press, 1976).

—— *The Structure of Biological Science* (Cambridge: Cambridge University Press, 1985).

Ross, Alf. *On Law and Justice* (London: Stevens & Sons, 1958).

—— *Directives and Norms* (London: Routledge & Kegan Paul, 1968).

Rottenberg, Simon (ed.). *The Economics of Crime and Punishment* (Washington D.C.: American Enterprise Institute, 1973).

Ryan, Alan. "Exploitation, Justice and the Rational Man," in Meeks (ed.).

—— (ed.). *The Idea of Freedom* (Oxford: Oxford University Press, 1979).

Ryle, Gilbert. *The Concept of Mind* (London: Hutchinson, 1949).

Sagoff, Mark. *The Economy of the Earth* (Cambridge: Cambridge University Press, 1988).

Sandel, Michael. *Liberalism and the Limits of Justice* (Cambridge: Cambridge University Press, 1982).

Sartre, Jean-Paul. *Existentialism and Humanism* (London: Methuen, 1948).

Scanlon, Thomas. "Nozick on Rights, Liberty and Property," *Philosophy and Public Affairs*, 6 (1976), 3–25.

Schabas, Margaret. *A World Ruled by Number* (Princeton: Princeton University Press, 1990).

Schachter, Oscar. *Sharing the World's Resources* (New York: Columbia University Press, 1977).

Scheffler, Samuel (ed.). *Consequentialism and its Critics* (Oxford: Oxford University Press, 1988).

Scott, Russell. *The Body as Property* (London: Allen Lane, 1981).

Sen, Amartya. *Poverty and Famine* (Oxford: Oxford University Press, 1981).

—— "Rights and Agency," *Philosophy and Public Affairs*, 11 (1982), 3–39.

—— "Welfare, Freedom and Social Choice: A Reply," *Recherches Economiques de Louvain*, 56 (1990), 451–85.

—— *Inequality Reexamined* (Oxford: Oxford University Press, 1992).

—— and Williams, Bernard (eds). *Utilitarianism and Beyond* (Cambridge: Cambridge University Press, 1982).

Shaw, Anne. *The Purpose and Practice of Motion Study* (Buxton: Columbine Press, 1968).

Shell, Susan. *The Rights of Reason* (Toronto: University of Toronto Press, 1980).

Sher, George. "Right Violations and Injustice," *Ethics*, 94 (1984), 212–24.

Shue, Henry. *Basic Rights* (Princeton: Princeton University Press, 1980).

Sidgwick, Henry. *The Methods of Ethics*, 7th edn (London: Macmillan, 1963).

Silverstein, H. S. "A Correction to Smyth's 'Better,'" *Analysis*, 34 (1973), 55–6.

Simmonds, Nigel. "Epstein's Theory of Strict Tort Liability," *Cambridge Law Journal*, 51 (1992), 113–37.

Simmons, Peter. *Choice and Demand* (London: Macmillan, 1974).

Simpson, A. W. B. (ed.). *Oxford Essays in Jurisprudence*, Second Series (Oxford: Oxford University Press, 1973).

Singer, Peter. "Famine, Affluence and Morality," *Philosophy and Public Affairs*, 1 (1972), 229–43.

Sinnott-Armstrong, Walter. *Moral Dilemmas* (Oxford: Blackwell, 1988).

Skala, H. K. J. *Non-Archimedean Utility Theory* (Dordrecht: D. Reidel, 1975).

Smart, J. J. C. and Williams, Bernard. *Utilitarianism: For and Against* (Cambridge: Cambridge University Press, 1973).

Smyth, M. B. "The Prescriptivist Definition of 'Better,'" *Analysis*, 33 (1972), 4–9.

Spector, Horacio. *Autonomy and Rights* (Oxford: Oxford University Press, 1992).

Spence, Thomas. "The Real Rights of Man" (1793), in Beer (ed.).

Spencer, Herbert. *Social Statics*, 1st edn (London: John Chapman, 1851).

Stampp, Kenneth. *The Peculiar Institution* (London: Eyre & Spottiswoode, 1964).

Steiner, Hillel. "The Natural Right to Equal Freedom," *Mind*, lxxxiii (1974), 194–210.

—— "Individual Liberty," *Aristotelian Society Proceedings*, lxxv (1975), 35–50, reprinted in Miller (ed.).

—— "The Structure of a Set of Compossible Rights," *Journal of Philosophy*, lxxiv (1977), 767–75.

—— "Liberty and Equality," *Political Studies*, xxix (1981), 555–69.

—— "How Free? Computing Personal Liberty," in Phillips Griffiths (ed.).

—— "Exploitation: A Liberal Theory Amended, Defended and Extended," in Reeve (ed.).

—— "Capitalism, Justice and Equal Starts," *Social Philosophy and Policy*, 5 (1987), 49–71.

—— "Markets and Law: The Case of Environmental Conservation," in Moran and Wright (eds).

Stigler, George. "The Development of Utility Theory," *Journal of Political Economy*, lviii (1950), 307–27, 373–96.

Stocker, Michael. *Plural and Conflicting Values* (Oxford: Oxford University Press, 1990).

Strasnick, Steven. "Neo-Utilitarian Ethics and the Ordinal Representation Assumption," in Pitt (ed.).

Styron, William. *Sophie's Choice* (London: Corgi Books, 1980).

Sullivan, Roger. *Immanuel Kant's Moral Theory* (Cambridge: Cambridge University Press, 1989).

Summers, Robert (ed.). *Essays in Legal Philosophy* (Oxford: Blackwell, 1970).

Sumner, L. W. *The Moral Foundation of Rights* (Oxford: Oxford University Press, 1987).

Tagil, S., Gerner, K., Henrikson, G., Johansson, R., Oldberg, I., and Salomon, K. *Studying Boundary Conflicts* (Lund: Scandinavian University Books, 1977).

Tawney, R. H. *Equality* (London: George Allen & Unwin, 1931).

Taylor, Charles. "What's Wrong with Negative Liberty," in Ryan (ed.).

Taylor, Michael. *Community, Anarchy and Liberty* (Cambridge: Cambridge University Press, 1982).

Taylor, M. W. *Men Versus the State* (Oxford: Oxford University Press, 1992).

Thomson, Judith. "Preferential Hiring," *Philosophy and Public Affairs*, 2 (1973), 364–84.

Thrall, R., Coombs, C., and Davies, R. (eds). *Decision Processes* (New York: John Wiley, 1954).

Tideman, Nicolaus. "Commons and Commonwealths," in Andelson (ed.), 1991.

Townsend, Harry (ed.). *Price Theory* (Harmondsworth: Penguin, 1980).

Trowbridge, Oliver. *Bisocialism* (New York: Moody, 1903).

Tuck, Richard. *Natural Rights Theories* (Cambridge: Cambridge University Press, 1979).

Tullock, Gordon (ed.). *Explorations in the Theory of Anarchy* (Blacksburg: Center for the Study of Public Choice, 1972).

Turner, J. W. C. *Kenny's Outlines of Criminal Law*, 19th edn (Cambridge: Cambridge University Press. 1966).

Urmson, J. O. "A Defence of Intuitionism," *Aristotelian Society Proceedings*, lxxv (1975), 111–19.

von Neumann, John and Morgenstern, Oskar. *Theory of Games and Economic Behavior*, 3rd edn (Princeton: Princeton University Press, 1955).

von Stackelberg, Heinrich. *The Theory of the Market Economy*, transl. Alan Peacock (London: William Hodge, 1952).

von Wright, G. H. *Norm and Action* (London: Routledge & Kegan Paul, 1963).

—— *The Logic of Preference* (Edinburgh: Edinburgh University Press, 1963).

Waldron, Jeremy. "A Right to Do Wrong," *Ethics*, 92 (1981), 21–39.

—— *The Right to Private Property* (Oxford: Oxford University Press, 1988).

—— "Rights in Conflict," *Ethics*, 99 (1989), 503–19.

—— *The Law* (London: Routledge, 1990).

Walker, David. *The Law of Contracts and Related Obligations in Scotland* (London: Butterworth, 1985).

Wallace, Alfred. *Land Nationalisation* (London: Swan Sonnenschein, 1892).

Walras, Leon. *Etudes d'Economie Sociale* (Lausanne: F. Rouge, 1896).

Walsh, Vivian. *Introduction to Contemporary Microeconomics* (New York: McGraw-Hill, 1970).

—— and Gram, Harvey. *Classical and Neoclassical Theories of General Equilibrium* (Oxford: Oxford University Press, 1980).

Walzer, Michael. *Spheres of Justice* (Oxford: Martin Robertson, 1983).

Warnock, Geoffrey. *Contemporary Moral Philosophy* (London, 1967).

Wellman, Carl. *A Theory of Rights* (Totowa: Rowman & Allanheld, 1985).

Wertheimer, Alan. "Freedom, Morality, Plea-Bargaining and the Supreme Court," *Philosophy and Public Affairs*, 8 (1979), 203–34.

Wicksteed, Philip. *The Common Sense of Political Economy* (London: George Routledge & Sons, 1933).

Williams, Andrew. "Cohen on Locke, Land and Labour," *Political Studies*, xl (1992), 51–66.

Williams, Bernard. *Problems of the Self* (Cambridge: Cambridge University Press, 1973).

—— *Moral Luck* (Cambridge: Cambridge University Press, 1981).

—— *Ethics and the Limits of Philosophy* (London: Fontana, 1985).

—— "Consequentialism and Integrity," in Scheffler (ed.).

Williams, Glanville. *Salmond on Jurisprudence*, 11th edn (London: Sweet & Maxwell, 1957).

—— "The Concept of Legal Liberty," in Summers (ed.).

Williams, Howard. *Kant's Political Philosophy* (Oxford: Blackwell, 1983).

Wolfe, Tom. *The Bonfire of the Vanities* (London: Jonathan Cape, 1988).

Wollheim, Richard. "A Paradox in the Theory of Democracy," in Laslett and Runciman (eds).

Zander, Michael. "How Bargains are Struck," *The Guardian*, 21 November 1979.

Index

Sinnott-Armstrong, Walter 111n
situation device 127-8
Skala, H. K. J. 176n
slavery 53-4, 185, 231-2, 240-2
Smart, J. J. C. 142n
Smyth, M. B. 141n
socialism 280-1
societies, advanced and primitive 43
Spector, Horacio 29n
Spence, Thomas 236n
Spencer, Herbert 216n, 236n, 253, 273n, 281
Stampp, Kenneth 240
state: officials 66, 68, 69-73, 270; role in bequests 255-6
Steedman, Ian 147n
Steiner, Hillel 39-40, 42n, 45n, 48n, 52n, 53n, 54n, 182n, 197n, 217n, 236n, 259n, 271n
Stenhouse, Maggie 241
Stigler, George 173n
Stocker, Michael 111n
Strasnick, Steven 176n
Styron, William 206n
Sugden, R. 145n
Sullivan, Roger 213n
Sumner, L. W. 59
Suppes, P. 169n, 176n
Sutch, R. 241n

Tagil, S. 270n
talent pooling 277, 279
Tawney, R. H. 52n
taxation 12
Taylor, Charles 9, 14, 15n, 19, 46-7, 48n
Taylor, Michael 9, 39-41
Taylor, M. W. 281n
technology 168
teleological theories 140
Temin, P. 241n
theft 246-7
things and persons 231-6
third-party beneficiaries 61-6, 72-3

Thomson, Judith 199n, 203n
threats and offers 22-32
throffer 24, 26
Tideman, Nicolaus 264n, 270n, 273n
time-travel 261n
times and persons 249-61
title-based domains 91-2, 102
titles: antecedents 104, 107; created 103; creation of unencumbered 235-6; extinguished 103; modes of acquiring just 251-2, 266; pedigrees 104, 105; temporally differentiated 99; to sites 272; transfers 218-19; vindications and 101-8
toleration 195-6
transitivity 120, 151-2
Trowbridge, Oliver 281n
Tuck, Richard 57n
Turner, J. W. C. 67n

ubiquitous substitutability (US) 169-70
unfreedom 4, 8-9, 10-14, 16, 22, 38-9
unowned things 105, 258, 268-73; *see also* natural resources
unwaivability 64-5, 71-2
Urmson, J. O. 113-15, 118
utilitarianism 113, 131
utility, conception of 172-3

valuation integration 46-8
valuational magnitudes 45-9
value, equal shares of total 271
verdicts 21
victims of injustice, past 268n
vindications and titles 102-8
virtue 211-12
von Neumann John 176n
von Stackelberg, Heinrich 160n
von Wright, G. H. 8n, 121n

waivability of duties 64-5, 68-9, 77-8